Immunology

A SCOPE® PUBLICATION

Upjohn

ISBN 0-89501-086-0

UED4889.00

Authors:

Benjamin D. Schwartz, MD, PhD *Editor-in-Chief*
Howard Hughes Medical Institute and the
Departments of Medicine (Rheumatology),
Microbiology, and Immunology
Washington University School of Medicine
St. Louis, Missouri

Chapter 1

Stanley J. Korsmeyer, MD
Howard Hughes Medical Institute and the
Departments of Medicine and
Molecular Microbiology
Washington University School of Medicine
St. Louis, Missouri

Chapter 2

Benjamin D. Schwartz, MD, PhD
Howard Hughes Medical Institute and the
Departments of Medicine (Rheumatology),
Microbiology, and Immunology
Washington University School of Medicine
St. Louis, Missouri

Chapter 3

Mark M. Davis, PhD
Howard Hughes Medical Institute and the
Departments of Microbiology and Immunology
Stanford University School of Medicine
Stanford, California

Chapter 4

John B. Imboden, MD
Associate Professor of Medicine
Department of Medicine
University of California, San Francisco
and the San Francisco VA Medical Center
San Francisco, California

Chapter 5

Laurie H. Glimcher, MD
Professor of Immunology
Department of Cancer Biology
Harvard School of Public Health
Harvard University
Boston, Massachusetts

Chapter 6

Emil R. Unanue, MD
Department of Pathology
Washington University School of Medicine
St. Louis, Missouri

Chapter 7

Robert D. Schreiber, PhD
Department of Pathology
Washington University School of Medicine
St. Louis, Missouri

Chapter 8

V. Michael Holers, MD
Howard Hughes Medical Institute and the
Departments of Medicine and Pathology
Washington University School of Medicine
St. Louis, Missouri
Eric J. Brown, MD
Departments of Medicine, Cell Biology,
and Molecular Microbiology
Washington University School of Medicine
St. Louis, Missouri

Chapter 9

John P. Atkinson, MD
Howard Hughes Medical Institute and the
Department of Medicine
Division of Rheumatology
Washington University School of Medicine
St. Louis, Missouri
M. Kathryn Liszewski
Howard Hughes Medical Institute
Washington University School of Medicine
St. Louis, Missouri

Chapter 10

Anthony Kulczycki, Jr, MD
Division of Allergy and Immunology
Washington University School of Medicine
St. Louis, Missouri

Chapter 11

Benjamin D. Schwartz, MD, PhD
Howard Hughes Medical Institute and the
Departments of Medicine (Rheumatology),
Microbiology, and Immunology
Washington University School of Medicine
St. Louis, Missouri
John P. Atkinson, MD
Howard Hughes Medical Institute and the
Department of Medicine
Division of Rheumatology
Washington University School of Medicine
St. Louis, Missouri
Thomas Braciale, MD, PhD
Department of Pathology
Washington University School of Medicine
St. Louis, Missouri

Chapter 12

Robert S. Schwartz, MD
Division of Hematology-Oncology
Department of Medicine
New England Medical Center
Tufts University School of Medicine
Boston, Massachusetts

Chapter 13

Stephen H. Polmar, PhD, MD
Professor of Pediatrics and of
Molecular Microbiology
Washington University School of Medicine
Director, Division of Allergy and Immunology
Children's Hospital
St. Louis, Missouri

Chapter 14

Edgar G. Engleman, MD
Stanford Medical School Blood Center
Palo Alto, California
Jeffrey D. Lifson, MD
Genelabs Incorporated
Redwood City, California

Chapter 15

John H. Klippel, MD
Clinical Director
National Institute of Arthritis,
Musculoskeletal and Skin Diseases
Bethesda, Maryland

Chapter 16

Ronald Levy, MD
Professor of Medicine
American Cancer Society, Clinical Research
Professor
Division of Oncology
Stanford University School of Medicine
Stanford, California
Michael J. Campbell, PhD
Research Assistant Professor
Department of Surgery
Stanford University School of Medicine
Stanford, California
Sherri L. Brown, MD
Medical Director of Oncology Products
Amgen
Thousand Oaks, California

Contents

Preface

Since the last edition of the Immunology Scope Monograph, tremendous advances have been made in our understanding of the immune system. These advances include the elucidation of the mechanisms by which antibody diversity is generated; the discovery of two distinct T-lymphocyte antigen receptors and the cloning of their genes; the definition of the crystalline structure of the HLA class I molecule; the demonstration that major histocompatibility complex class II molecules can directly bind peptides derived from exogenous antigens; the cloning of the genes encoding the interleukin molecules by which immune cells communicate; and the production of interleukins in sufficient quantities to allow their biological effects to be readily studied.

Despite these incredible advances, manipulation of the immune system remains a major challenge. Several diseases are now directly attributed to an overly exuberant immune response, while others can be traced to the inability to mount an adequate immune response. The introduction of AIDS into our society has made commonplace the ravages of immunodeficiency previously seen only in rare congenital defects, underscoring the importance of the immune system in protecting us from our environment.

The Immunology Scope Monograph presents an overview summarizing our current knowledge of the elements of the immune system and their interactions at the molecular and cellular levels.

The monograph also illustrates in clinical terms the consequences of the disruption of these interactions. This book is designed to convey to the reader not only this knowledge but also the excitement so prevalent in contemporary immunology, as the pace of discovery and advances continues to accelerate. It is hoped that, by making the reader aware of the challenges remaining in immunology, this monograph will entice the interested reader to acquire the skills necessary to successfully manipulate the immune system. Only through the acquisition of these skills will future generations of physicians and scientists realize the full benefit of immune therapy on disease.

Benjamin D. Schwartz, MD, PhD
Editor-in-Chief

Immunoglobulin: Proteins and Genes

1

Introduction

The immunoglobulins are among the most intriguing genetic systems in all of biology. Their capacity to specifically bind a given antigen constitutes the basis of humoral immunity. Moreover, immunoglobulins have the ability to perform many different effector functions designed to activate B-cell growth, lyse foreign invaders, protect mucosal surfaces, or clear antigen-antibody complexes. The genes that encode the immunoglobulin protein chains are among the most instructive genes ever analyzed. While most proteins are designed to perform a single repetitive function, the major goal of immunoglobulin is to display diversity so that an individual can generate 10^6 to 10^8 different antibodies. The immunoglobulin genes utilize a fascinating gene-shuffling mechanism to guarantee this breadth of immunity.

Antibody Protein Structure

Immunoglobulin molecules constitute a substantial portion of the plasma proteins. When they display the capacity to bind to antigens, immunoglobulins are called *antibodies*. Immunoglobulins are complex, multichain proteins composed of two identical heavy (H) chains and two identical light (L) chains (Figure 1). Each heavy and light chain is also bipartite. The amino-terminal portion is the variable (V) region and differs markedly from one immunoglobulin molecule to the next, while the carboxy-terminal portion is the constant (C) region and is invariant. This pattern parallels the functions of these regions: the variable regions must interact with myriad antigens, and the constant regions perform invariant functions, such as generating stabilizing disulfide bonds, binding to cell-surface receptors, and fixing complement.

Elucidation of the immunoglobulin structure was advanced by the discovery that reducing agents would break the interconnecting disulfide bonds and release free H and L chains. Moreover, papain and pepsin, two enzymes that cleave the heavy chain protein, were subsequently discovered. Papain cleaves the molecule at the amino-terminal side of the disulfide bonds between the heavy chains. This cleavage generates three frag-

Figure 1
Schematic model of an IgG antibody molecule

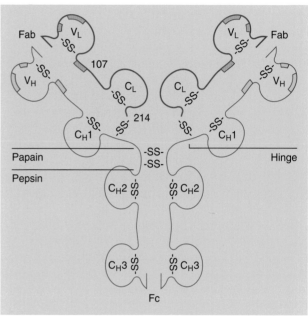

Two identical heavy (H) and light (L) chains have amino-terminal variable (V) and carboxy-terminal constant (C) regions. Within the V regions are three hypervariable or complementarity determining regions indicated by the broader lines.

ments: two Fab (*fragment antigen binding*) fragments and the Fc (so named because it readily crystallizes) fragment. Each Fab fragment contains an L chain and variable regions of the H chain. The Fc fragment contains the remainder of the H chain constant region (Figure 1). In contrast, pepsin cleaves the carboxy-terminal side of the interheavy chain disulfide bonds, producing the bivalent fragment $F(ab')_2$, which possesses both sets of H and L chain variable regions (Figure 1). The generation of these digestion fragments was a crucial step in determining the functional regions of the molecule.

Figure 1 also shows that the H chain constant region is divided into structural domains. The heavy chain is folded and can be divided into V_H, C_H1, hinge, C_H2, and C_H3 domains in an IgG molecule. The hinge is the flexible portion of the molecule and is susceptible to pepsin and papain digestion.

X-ray crystallographic studies of homogeneous immunoglobulins with antibody activity to a specific antigen confirmed that interaction with antigen occurs via the variable region of the molecule. The precise contact sites within the antigen are located within hypervariable regions of the V_H and V_L. The amino acid variation within V_H and V_L is clustered within three hypervariable regions, termed the *complementarity determining regions (CDRs)*, which are separated by relatively conserved framework regions (Figure 1). The framework regions provide supportive scaffolding that exposes the hypervariable regions to allow interaction with antigen.

The most distinctive portion of the antibody molecule is the CDR, the portion that interacts with antigen. The term *idiotype* is applied to the unique aspects within the variable portion of an individual antibody that distinguish it from other immunoglobulin molecules. Procedurally, the unique idiotypic determinants are themselves antigenic when injected into other members of the same genetic strain. The antibody that recognizes the idiotype is referred to as an *anti-idiotype*.

Immunoglobulin Classes

There are five different classes of immunoglobulins: IgG, IgA, IgM, IgD, and IgE (Table 1). A novel genetic mechanism allows all classes to share the same variable region repertoire. However, each class has an entirely different heavy chain constant region that is responsible for the different functions of the molecules. The H chain classes designated γ, α, μ, δ, and ε for IgG, IgA, IgM, IgD, and IgE, respectively, give a distinct conformation to the different molecules. Moreover, there are four IgG subclasses (γ1, γ2, γ3, and γ4) and two different IgA constant regions (α1 and α2). Light chains also come in two varieties; kappa (κ) light chains appear in 60% and lambda (λ) light chains in 40% of human immunoglobulin molecules.

The different heavy and light chain class molecules are also referred to as *isotypes*. Because humans are an outbred population, several different allelic forms of the genes encode these isotypes. The allelic variations are often detected as antigenic differences in the proteins and are referred to as *allotypes*. In humans the allotypes associated with γ chains are called *Gm markers*, those associated with α chains are called *Am markers*, and the κ chain differences are denoted as *Inv*.

Somatic Recombination of Separated Gene Subsegments

The structure of the immunoglobulin protein posed a dilemma for molecular geneticists. An immunoglobulin gene would be required to vary substantially at the amino-terminal region but remain unaltered at the carboxy-terminal constant region. Dreyer and Bennett solved this puzzle by proposing that two genes would encode a single immunoglobulin polypeptide chain. The subsequent molecular cloning of immunoglobulin genes by Tonegawa, Leder, and others documented the recombinational germline theory.

Immunoglobulin genes are discontinuous in their germline or embryonic form, being composed of separated variable and constant regions within their DNA (Figure 2). Moreover, two gene segments actually encode the variable portion of the protein. The variable region of the κ gene encodes only amino acids 1-95, and a joining (J_κ) segment contributes the remaining 13 amino acids (96-108). Each allele has only one C_κ region. The gene segments are separated by long stretches called *intervening sequences (IVS)*, or *introns*. While introns do not encode genes, they play important roles in the expression of genes and in maintaining their structural integrity.

Light Chain Recombination

During early B-cell development, a rearrangement of immunoglobulin DNA juxtaposes one of the many alternative variable regions with one of the alternative J segments. This VJ rearranged allele is then transcribed into RNA, and the remaining introns are removed by RNA splicing. The final mature κ messenger RNA (mRNA) has an associated leader or signal sequence encoding a highly

Table 1
Characteristics of the immunoglobulins

	IgG	IgA	IgM	IgD	IgE
Molecular formula	$\gamma_2 L_2$	$\alpha_2 L_2$ or $(\alpha_2 L_2)_2$	$\mu_2 L_2$ or $(\mu_2 L_2)_5$	$\delta_2 L_2$	$\varepsilon_2 L_2$
Molecular weight	150 000	160 000 (monomer)	950 000 (pentamer)	175 000	190 000
Associated chains	–	J chain, secretory piece	J chain	–	–
Subclasses (H chains)	$\gamma 1, \gamma 2, \gamma 3, \gamma 4$	$\alpha 1, \alpha 2$	–	–	–
Allotype marker (H chain)	Gm	Am	–	–	–
Serum level (mg/100 mL)* IgG1 IgG2 IgG3 IgG4	679-1537 470-1300 115-750 20-130 2-165	39-358	33-229	0-15	0-0.09
Half-life (days)†	23	5.8	5.1	2.8	2.5
Synthesis rate† (mg/kg/day)	33	24	6.7	0.4	0.016
Complement fixation	+	–	+	–	–
Placental transfer	+	–	–	–	–

*Adult levels. All normal ranges, including IgG subclasses, must be adjusted for age.
†Synthesis and catabolism data from Waldmann TA, Strober W, Blaese RM. Variations in the metabolism of immunoglobulins measured by turnover rates. In: Merler E, ed. *Immunoglobulins: Biologic Aspects and Clinical Uses.* Washington, DC: National Academy of Sciences; 1970:33-49.

hydrophobic signal peptide that enables transmembrane passage of the molecule and the V, J, and C regions. This κ mRNA is translated, and an enzyme, signal peptidase, removes the amino-terminal leader peptide from the secreted κ light chain protein (Figure 2).

Comparisons of germline V_κ and J_κ regions with $V_\kappa J_\kappa$ rearrangements reveal important details about this recombination process. Immediately flanking the 3' side of each germline V_κ region and the 5' side of each germline J_κ region is a heptanucleo-tide with the canonical sequence of CACTGTG. After this heptamer, flanking the V_κ is an 11-12 base-pair (bp) spacer and an AC-rich nona-nucleotide. Inversely, a 22-23 bp spacer and a GT-rich nonamer flank the heptamer of each J_κ segment (Figure 3). Models can be envisioned in which the homologous heptamer and nonamer sequences flanking the V and J region would pair, an arrangement that would almost certainly involve interaction with a putative immunoglobulin recombinase protein complex. The DNA-protein interactions would be responsible for the proper juxtaposition of V and J regions and the scission and religation of DNA strands. Recently, two molecules (RAG-1 and RAG-2) that activate

Figure 2
Schematic representation of the human κ gene locus and mechanism of recombination

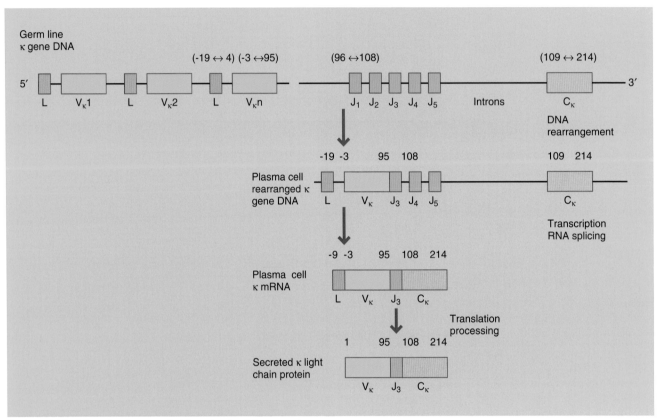

Each variable (V) region is preceded by a leader (L) segment. Each κ allele has several V regions and five alternative joining (J) segments, but only one constant (C) region. The remaining introns are removed at the RNA level.

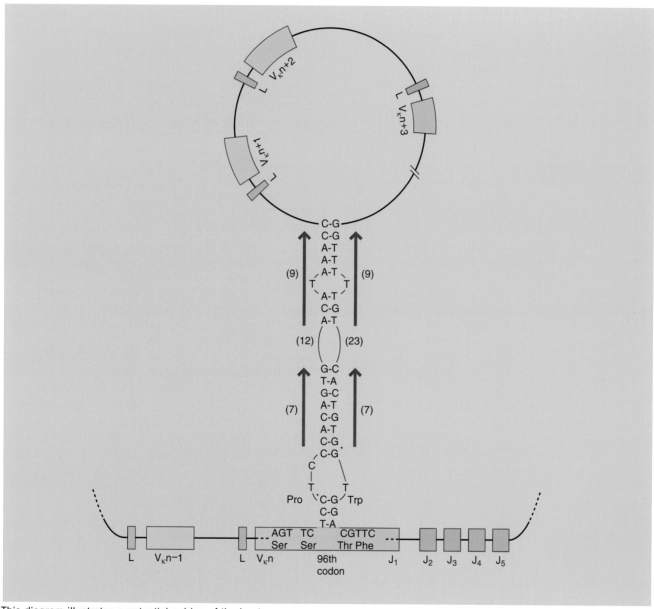

This diagram illustrates a potential pairing of the heptamers (CACTGTG) and homologous nonamers flanking variable (V) and joining (J) regions. The site of DNA scission and reunion is at the 96th codon.

immunoglobulin have been identified. Heptamers, spacers, and nonamers are also found flanking λ light chain and heavy chain gene segments. Moreover, recombinational units with 11-12 bp spacers are always rearranged with units with 22-23 bp spacers.

Allelic and Isotypic Exclusion

Humans express the two light chain classes in nearly equivalent proportions. The κ light chain gene resides on chromosome 2, and the λ light chain genes reside on chromosome 22 in humans. However, B cells that produce immunoglobulin display an unusual phenomenon when expressing these autosomal genes. An individual B cell that produces a κ chain expresses either its maternal or paternal allele but not both. The explanation for this phenomenon, which is termed *allelic exclusion*, lies at the DNA level and directly relates to the rearrangement process. The complex process that moves gene segments to generate antibody diversity is also prone to error. Any κ-producing B cell must possess one effective VJ recombination that produces the κ chain. However, the other κ allele is either in the germline form, aberrantly rearranged, or actually deleted from the genome. Thus, the excluded κ allele can be in one of three configurations, all of which prevent it from being expressed.

In addition, a single B cell makes either the κ or λ light chain isotype but not both. This phenomenon is termed *isotypic exclusion* and results from an ordered process of light chain rearrangement in which κ genes rearrange before λ genes. The first attempt at light chain rearrangement usually begins with the κ genes. If $V_κJ_κ$ rearrangement is effective, a κ-producing B cell results. Frequently, both κ alleles rearrange aberrantly. Such ineffective κ alleles are then eliminated by the rearrangement of a κ-deleting element that removes the $C_κ$ gene segment. This κ gene destruction sets the stage for λ gene rearrangement.

Heavy Chain Gene Organization

The format for heavy chain gene organization and recombination is conceptually similar to light chain rearrangement but is more complex. An additional family of genetic elements, the *diversity segments* (D_H), exists between the V_H and J_H regions (Figure 4). Thus, three segments must correctly recombine to create an effective VDJ rearrangement. Germline D_H segments are flanked on each side by a heptamer 11-12 bp spacer-nonamer that enables D_H segments to recombine with the 22-23 bp spacer bordering the V_H and J_H regions.

Antibody Diversity

Germline Contributions

Unmodified germline DNA contributes substantially to antibody diversity (Table 2). First, each heavy chain should be able to associate with any light chain and theoretically create a new antibody specificity. Second, many alternative germline V, D, and J segments are available to produce a multitude of rearrangements. Third, additional amino acid variation occurs at the sites of juncture because the exact site of recombination may vary within the codon. This contribution is termed *junctional diversity*. The site of VJ and VDJ recombination accounts for a substantial amount of diversity within the third complementarity determining region (CDR3). However, no further gene subsegments exist to account for the other two hypervariable regions, CDR1 and CDR2. This variation is inherited within the variable regions and may result from specialized mechanisms of gene cross-talking known as *gene conversion*, which maintains both the framework region and hypervariable regions.

Figure 4
Schematic representation of the human heavy chain gene locus

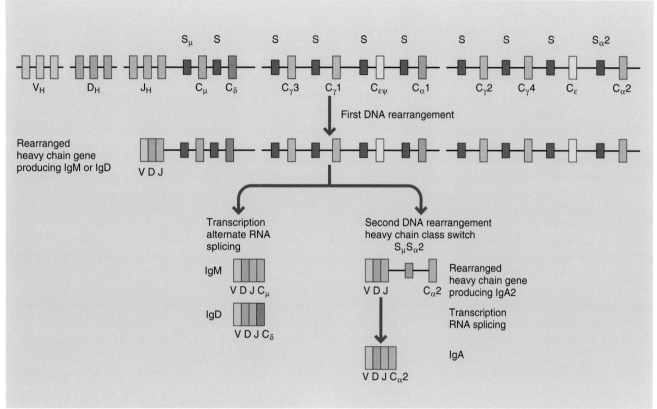

The first DNA rearrangement assembles the VDJ segments. This rearranged allele can display alternative splicing to simultaneously generate IgM and IgD. The heavy chain class switch is mediated by switch (S) regions that move distal constant regions so they can be expressed with the same VDJ.

Table 2
Mechanisms of antibody diversity

Contributions of germline information
Independent assortment of heavy and light chains
Recombinant assembly of many different V, D, and J regions
Flexible frame of recombination
Inherent variation in CDR1 and CDR2: gene conversion

Contributions of somatic changes
Extranucleotide (N segment) addition to CDR3
Somatic point mutation
Somatic gene conversion

Somatic Contributions

Modification of immunoglobulin genes also occurs during somatic development (Table 2). At the sites of $V_H D_H$ and $D_H J_H$ juncture, nucleotides may be lost, and extranucleotides called *N segments* are added. These bases appear to be inserted by terminal deoxynucleotidyl transferase, an enzyme that is present in the pre–B-cell stage. An additional somatic form of gene conversion in which germline variable region information is conveyed to assembled VJ rearrangements has been found in chicken immunoglobulin genes. Finally, a substantial amount of somatic point mutation has been noted within immunoglobulin genes. Rearranged VDJ and VJ segments display amino acid changes compared with their germline predecessors. Somatic mutation surrounds the assembled variable region but spares the constant regions. However, single base changes are not focused in CDR regions but occur throughout the variable region. Curiously, point mutation may occur more frequently in the higher affinity secondary response of IgG than it occurs in IgM. In addition, other mechanisms including clonal selection may play major roles in fine-tuning the affinities of any antibody response.

Heavy Chain Constant Region

Gene Structure

The heavy chain protein domains of the constant region are each encoded by distinct DNA gene segments. Like many other genes, the constant region is composed of multiple coding segments (exons) separated by noncoding introns (Figure 4). An intact coding region is assembled in RNA following removal of the intron by the process of RNA splicing.

The major immunoglobulin classes exist both as membrane-bound cell-surface receptors on B cells and as secreted humoral antibodies. Nature has devised a clever and conservative strategy to generate these two types of molecules with markedly different functions. Figure 5 details the creation of membrane (μm) versus secreted (μs) forms of RNA. In this process the same rearranged V, D, J, and constant region exons $C_\mu 1$, $C_\mu 2$, $C_\mu 3$, and $C_\mu 4$ are used by both RNA forms. However, at the 3' end of the $C_\mu 4$ domain is a contiguous μs gene segment encoding a hydrophilic secreted terminus. Conversely, the highly hydrophobic membrane terminus is encoded by two μm exons located downstream of $C_\mu 4$. As detailed in Figure 5, an alternative donor splice site exists at the $C_\mu 4$ and μs segment boundary. This permits an alternative RNA splice in which the $C_\mu 4$ segment is directly joined to the μm exons. The μm form of RNA predominates in early B cells bearing IgM surface receptors, but the secreted form is dominant in maturing secretory B cells and plasma cells. This remarkable process enables the cell to maximize the use of a correctly assembled variable region by placing this same antigen specificity with two markedly different effector functions.

Most IgM in serum exists as a pentameric molecule, and IgA in secretions appears as dimeric molecules. These dimers and pentamers are held together by a J chain, a 15 000 molecular weight protein. (The J chain should not be confused with the J segment.) The human J chain gene is a unique 4-exon gene located on chromosome 4 and does not rearrange during development. It is expressed in mature B cells secreting IgM and IgA.

Heavy Chain Class Switch

During lymphocyte development, an individual B cell expresses a single assembled VDJ first on surface IgM, then on IgM plus IgD, and finally may utilize VDJ with any γ, α, or ε constant region. Several genetic mechanisms enable the cell to express the same VDJ with different constant regions. Insights into this process were provided by determining the gene order of the constant regions (Figure 4).

The C_δ region is in close proximity to the C_μ region, an arrangement that permits the simultaneous production of IgM and IgD possessing the same variable information. This is accomplished by an alternative RNA splicing decision that places the VDJ with either C_μ or C_δ, accounting for the ability of lymphocytes to simultaneously produce IgM and IgD sharing the same idiotype. However, the C_γ, C_α, and C_ε regions lie a considerable distance downstream (Figure 4). IgA-

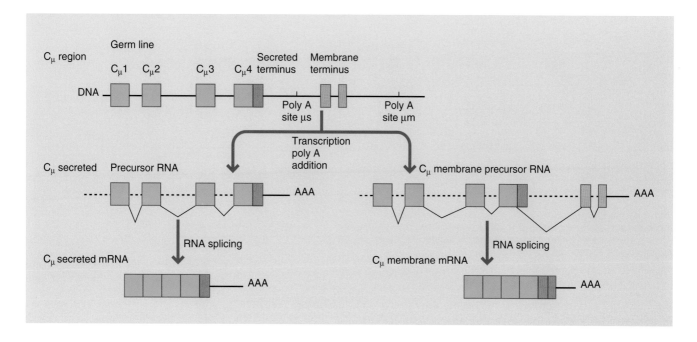

producing mature B cells lose all constant regions between the expressed C_α and the VDJ. This loss results from a second DNA rearrangement termed the *heavy chain class switch*, which moves a distal constant region into close proximity with the VDJ. Switch regions are found at the 5′ side of all constant regions and are the site of this recombination. Switch regions are composed of tandem repetitive units of short base-pair repeats, such as GAGCT and GGGGT. These regions are long (1000-3000 bp) and may promote recombinations that enable a different constant region to be expressed with an already assembled VDJ specificity.

Regulation of Immunoglobulin Gene Transcription

A plasma cell (the end stage of B-cell differentiation) serves as a remarkably efficient factory for immunoglobulin production. Although rearranged immunoglobulin genes are highly expressed within the B-cell series, these genes are not expressed when introduced into other tissues. This tissue specificity of immunoglobulin transcription suggests B cells possess additional proteins that interact with a portion of the immunoglobulin gene to increase RNA production.

Variable regions display the standard eukaryotic promoter element of a TATA box, but they also have a specialized regulator. Upstream of heavy and light chain variable regions within the gene promoter region (the region that regulates gene expression) is the octamer, a conserved 8–base-pair motif (ATGCAAAT or its opposite orientation,

Figure 6
Schematic model of immunoglobulin enhancer (E) regions

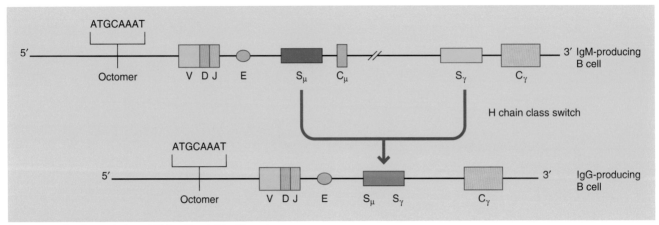

A conserved octamer is found 5′ to all variable (V) regions, while a downstream enhancer is strategically located between the joining (J) and switch (S) regions.

ATTTGCAT). This sequence functions as an enhancer element to increase the transcription rate of an associated gene (in this instance, immunoglobulin) in B cells but not in other cell types (Figure 6). Transcription is mediated by a protein product (Oct-2) that binds to this octamer sequence and is present only in B cells.

Cleverly, the immunoglobulin heavy chain locus has also positioned another enhancer element downstream between the J_H segment and the switch region (Figure 6). This location enables the same enhancer region to positively influence any introduced variable region and to be retained following any heavy chain class switch. The identification of enhancer elements and the characterization of their binding protein promise to provide insights into gene regulation at specific stages of development.

Clinical Aspects

IgG is the primary mediator of the humoral immune response and is the body's main defense against bacteria, viruses, and toxins. It is the most abundant of the immunoglobulins, composing about 80% of the total serum concentration in healthy individuals. The distribution of subclasses in the serum of normal adults is 50% to 65% IgG1, 25% to 35% IgG2, 5% to 10% IgG3, and 5% to 10% IgG4.

The immunologic roles of the IgG isotypes have been the subject of investigations since their discovery in the early 1960s. IgG1 and IgG3 are produced in T-cell–dependent responses to bacterial and viral proteins. IgG4 is increased after long exposure to hepatitis B virus and filaria infestation, and this isotype is produced in response to such common allergens as grass pollen, house dust, and bee venom. Abnormal serum concentrations of various subclasses (even when the total IgG level is within the normal range) are seen in several inflammatory disorders. For example, chronic pulmonary infections have been associated with IgG2 and IgG4 deficiencies.

IgM, whose large pentameric structure virtually confines it to the serum, appears earliest of all the antibodies in response to antigenic challenge. IgM is the primary antibody for gram-negative bacteria and polysaccharides. Because it does not cross the placenta, the finding of more than a minute amount of IgM in infants indicates the presence of infection.

IgA is found in the secretions of all mucous membranes exposed to the environment (eg, gastrointestinal and respiratory tract secretions, saliva, tears), providing the earliest defense against bacteria and viruses.

IgE is secreted mainly in the respiratory and gastrointestinal tracts. This immunoglobulin mediates type 1 hypersensitivity reactions (ie, atopic reactions, allergic rhinitis, asthma) and is elevated in parasitic infestations. Although the exact function of IgE has not been established, it may have a protective role in the lungs (see chapter 10).

Only trace amounts of IgD are found in the serum. IgD is important in T-cell–dependent B-cell responses and in generating memory B cells.

Conclusion

This chapter provides a molecular genetic description of immunoglobulin gene organization, rearrangement, and expression. These events provide the basis for generating antibody diversity and provide the humoral immune system with the capacity to perform a variety of physiologic functions. The basic principles of gene structure and regulation are also at the heart of understanding immunopathology, providing insights into the transforming events in B-cell malignancies and the basis of humoral immunodeficiency disease.

Selected Readings

Dreyer WJ, Bennett JC. The molecular basis of antibody formation: a paradox. **Proc Natl Acad Sci USA**. 1965;54:864-869.

Leder P. The genetics of antibody diversity. **Sci Am**. 1982;246(5):102-115.

Tonegawa S. Somatic generation of antibody diversity. **Nature**. 1983;302:575-581.

Waldmann TA, Strober W, Blaese RM. Variations in the metabolism of immunoglobulins measured by turnover rates. In: Merler E, ed. **Immunoglobulins: Biologic Aspects and Clinical Uses**. Washington, DC: National Academy of Sciences; 1970:33-49.

The HLA Complex and Disease Susceptibility

2

Introduction

Each of us lives in a potentially hostile environment. We survive in this environment because of the protection afforded us by the immune system. To render this protection, the immune system must be able to discriminate between an antigen against which an immune response would be harmful and an antigen against which an immune response would be beneficial; thus, the immune response must be able to distinguish "self" from "nonself." This critical distinction is realized via the molecules of the major histocompatibility complex (MHC), which in humans is called the *human leukocyte antigen (HLA) complex.*

Every antigen, both foreign and self, is recognized by the T lymphocytes of the immune system only in conjunction with HLA molecules. Thus, CD8 (generally cytotoxic) T cells recognize antigens that bind to HLA class I molecules, while CD4 (generally helper) T cells recognize antigens that bind to HLA class II molecules. This recognition of antigen only in the context of HLA molecules is responsible for the immunologic properties observed for HLA molecules. HLA molecules are the major determinant of the success of organ transplants, are defined as regulators of the human immune response, and are associated with predisposition to disease.

HLA molecules belong to the immunoglobulin "supergene" family and appear to have evolved from the same primordial molecule as did immunoglobulin and T-cell receptor molecules. Repeated gene duplications and mutations of the primordial HLA gene during evolution have resulted in a cluster of HLA genes in a relatively short chromosomal region. The cluster of genes that encodes the HLA molecules and displays the most polymorphism of any known gene in the human genome comprises the HLA complex. This chapter describes the biology of this remarkable complex.

Structure, Function, and Tissue Distribution of HLA Molecules

The HLA complex encodes several different types of molecules. Some of these molecules are membrane-bound cell-surface molecules that, based on their structure, function, and tissue distribution, have been categorized as either class I or class II molecules. Because of their importance in T-cell recognition of foreign antigens, the HLA class I and class II molecules are described in detail in the following paragraphs. Other molecules determined by genes in the HLA complex are soluble and are classified under the umbrella of class III molecules. The class III molecules are discussed briefly in this chapter. Chapters 7 and 9 discuss in further detail class III molecules of particular immunologic interest (TNF-α, TNF-β, C4A, and C4B).

Class I Molecules

An HLA class I molecule consists of an HLA-encoded polymorphic glycoprotein of 44 000 daltons (d), designated the heavy chain, in a noncovalent association with a non–HLA-encoded nonpolymorphic protein of 12 000 d, the β_2-microglobulin (Figure 7). The heavy chain serves to anchor the entire molecule in the cell membrane. This chain contains 338 amino acids and can be divided into the following three regions (beginning at the amino-terminal end): an extracellular hydrophilic region (amino acids 1 through 281), a transmembrane hydrophobic region (amino acids 282 through 306), and an intracytoplasmic hydrophilic region (amino acids 307 through 338). The extracellular hydrophilic region can in turn be divided into three domains that are denoted α_1, α_2, and α_3. These three domains plus β_2-microglobulin result in a class I molecule containing four extracellular domains of roughly 90 amino acids each. The α_3 domain and β_2-microglobulin are structurally homologous to the constant region of immunoglobulin, identifying the class I molecule

Figure 7
A schematic representation of an HLA class I molecule

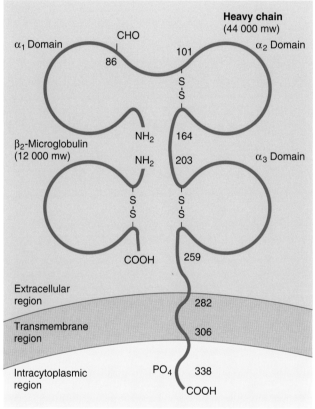

The molecule consists of a heavy chain, which anchors the molecule in the membrane, noncovalently associated with β_2-microglobulin. Numbers indicate amino acid residues where certain features are found. Abbreviations: NH$_2$, amino-terminus; COOH, carboxy-terminus; CHO, carbohydrate; PO$_4$, phosphate. The extracellular, transmembrane, and intracytoplasmic regions and the α_1, α_2, and α_3 domains are indicated.

as a member of the immunoglobulin supergene family. The α_1 and α_2 domains bear the majority of the polymorphism seen among class I molecules.

The physical structure of the HLA class I molecule has recently been elucidated by x-ray crystallography (Figure 8). The α_3 domain and the β_2-microglobulin form a base supporting the interactive portion of the molecule formed by the α_1 and α_2 domains. Structurally, each of the α_1 and α_2 domains consists of four β strands and an α-helix. (The β strand should not be confused with β_2-microglobulin, and the α-helix should not be confused with the α domains.) The α_1 and α_2 domains are juxtaposed so that the eight β strands form a flat β-pleated sheet upon which rest the two α-helices. The two α-helices form a cleft that serves as the antigen-binding site and can accept a foreign antigenic peptide fragment. The foreign antigenic peptide together with the two α-helices constitute the ligand that is recognized by the T-cell receptor. In addition, the majority of allo-antigenic determinants recognized both by antibodies and by T cells are located in or near the α-helices.

HLA class I molecules are found on virtually every human nucleated cell (Table 3). This widespread distribution fits the function of these molecules. When CD8-positive (in general, cyto-toxic) T cells recognize foreign antigenic (eg, viral) peptides, they do so in the context of a class I molecule. In other words, class I molecules and foreign antigenic peptides are recognized as a complex by the T-cell receptor on CD8$^+$ cytotoxic T lymphocytes (CTLs) (see chapter 3). When CTL precursors recognize the combination of a particular viral antigen and a particular class I molecule on a sensitizing cell, they proliferate and differentiate to become mature CTLs. The mature CTLs recognize and kill only those target cells that bear both the same class I molecule and the same viral antigen as were present on the sensitizing cells. That particular CTL will not lyse a target cell with a different class I molecule infected with the same virus, nor will it lyse a target cell with the same

Figure 8
Schematic representation of the crystallographic structure of
an HLA class I molecule

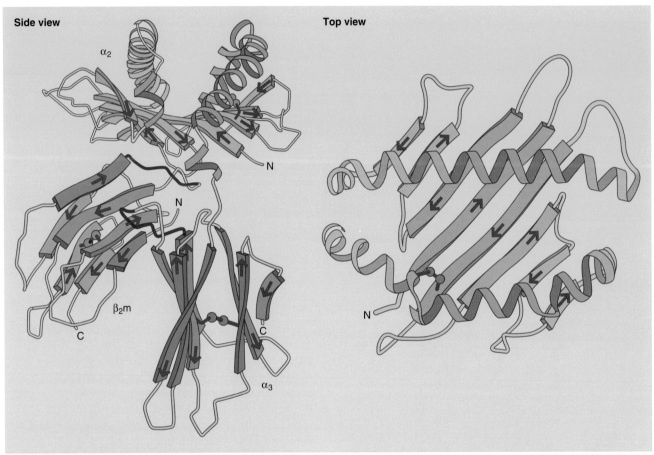

Side view

Top view

The β strands are depicted as thick arrows in the amino-to-carboxy direction, α-helices are represented as helical ribbons. Connecting loops are shown as thin lines. Disulfide bonds are shown as two connected spheres.
(**Side view**) The molecule is shown with the α_3 domain and β_2-microglobulin at the bottom, and the polymorphic α_1 and α_2

domains at the top. The platform created by the β-pleated strands is seen edge-on. The cleft formed by the α-helices into which foreign peptide fits is clearly seen.
(**Top view**) The α_1 and α_2 domains as seen from above. The platform of β-pleated sheets and the cleft formed by the α-helices are again visible.

Table 3
Comparison of HLA class I and class II molecules

	Class I	Class II
Molecules included	HLA-A, B, C	HLA-DR, DQ, DP
Structure	44 000 d heavy chain	~34 000 d α chain
	12 000 d β₂-microglobulin	~29 000 d β chain
Tissue distribution	On virtually every cell	Normally limited to immunocompetent cells, particularly B cells, macrophages, activated T cells
Function	Restrict cytotoxic T-cell killing of virus-infected cells	Restrict helper T-cell recognition of foreign antigen

class I molecule infected with a different virus (Figure 9). Thus, CTL killing is both antigen-specific and class I-restricted. In the "unnatural" context of a tissue or organ transplant, foreign class I antigens on the graft are recognized by the CTLs of the host during graft rejection. (Transplantation is considered unnatural because it does not normally occur in nature, except for pregnancy.)

Class II Molecules
Each class II molecule is composed of two HLA-encoded glycoprotein chains: an α chain of approximately 34 000 d and a β chain of about 29 000 d (Figure 10). Both chains span the membrane and serve to anchor the molecule. Like the class I heavy chain, each class II chain can be divided into the following three regions (beginning at the amino-terminal end): an extracellular hydrophilic region, a transmembrane hydrophobic region, and an intracytoplasmic hydrophilic tail. In contrast to the three domains within the extracellular region of the class I heavy chain, each class II extracellular region contains only two domains of approximately 90 amino acids each. The α chain domains are designated α_1 and α_2, and the β chain domains are β_1 and β_2. Thus, like the class I molecule, the class II molecule also has four external domains of approximately 90 amino acids each. The class II α_2 and β_2 domains, like the class I α_3 domain and β_2-microglobulin, show homology with immunoglobulin constant region domains, indicating that the class II molecules also belong to the immunoglobulin supergene family. The β_1 domains contain the majority of polymorphism of class II molecules.

The physical structure of the HLA class II molecule has not been elucidated as yet. However, based on parallels between class I and class II molecules, it is presumed that the class II α_1 and β_1 domains form a structure similar to that of the class I α_1 and α_2 domains, allowing a similar interaction with foreign antigenic peptide. A top view of the postulated class II crystal structure is shown in Figure 11.

Figure 9
Class I restriction of cytotoxic T cells

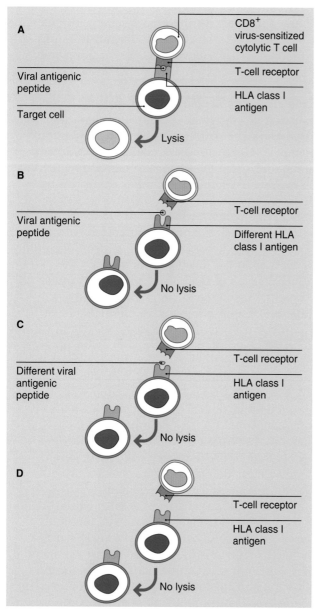

Once sensitized to a particular viral antigenic peptide in the context of a particular class I molecule, a given cytotoxic T cell can only recognize the same viral antigenic peptide in the context of the same class I molecule (**A**). It cannot recognize the same viral antigenic peptide in the context of a different class I molecule (**B**), nor a different viral antigenic peptide in conjunction with the same class I molecule (**C**), nor the same class I molecule in the absence of the viral peptide (**D**).

Figure 10
Schematic representation of an HLA-DR molecule

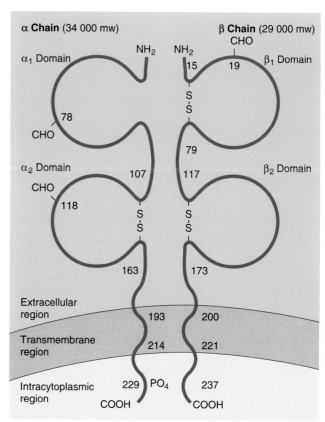

The molecule consists of an α chain transmembrane glycoprotein noncovalently associated with a β chain transmembrane glycoprotein. For explanation of symbols, see Figure 7.

Figure 11
Schematic representation of the hypothetical crystallographic structure of a class II molecule, as seen from above

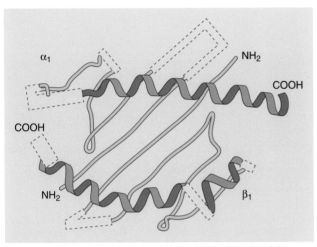

The antigen-binding cleft is formed by the α_1 domain of the α chain and the β_1 domain of the β chain. The β strands are depicted as flat thin lines, and the α-helices as helical ribbons. The cleft is very similar to that of the class I molecule. Abbreviations: NH_2, the amino-terminus; COOH, the carboxy-terminus; the dotted lines are portions of the molecule where the data do not allow a definitive structure to be proposed.

In contradistinction to the HLA class I molecules, class II molecules have a limited tissue distribution (Table 3). Class II molecules are present mainly on cells of the immune system, including B cells, monocytes, dendritic cells, and activated T cells. However, interferon gamma can induce expression of class II molecules on cells that do not normally express these molecules, including thyroid cells, epidermal cells, endothelial cells, and renal cells, and can stimulate increased expression of class II molecules on macrophages.

The function of class II molecules parallels that of the class I molecules. Just as CD8+ T cells recognize the complex of foreign antigenic peptide and a class I molecule, CD4+ (generally helper) T cells recognize the complex of foreign antigenic peptide and a class II molecule. In unnatural conditions such as graft transplantation, the foreign class II molecules present on the graft can elicit an immune response in the host by stimulating the host's CD4+ T cells.

Nomenclature and Genetic Organization of the HLA Complex

The HLA complex occupies approximately 3500 kilobases of DNA on the short arm of chromosome 6. As shown in the schematic representation of the HLA complex (Figure 12), the genetic loci are organized into three classes. Class I and class II genes determine the membrane-bound class I and class II molecules, whereas class III genes determine soluble molecules. Class I genes encode the HLA-A, -B, and -C classic histocompatibility molecules; class II genes within the HLA-D region encode the HLA-DR, -DQ, and -DP molecules; and class III genes determine the second and fourth components of complement (C2 and C4) and factor B (Bf) of the complement alternative pathway. A number of other genes have been found in the HLA complex, including: 21-hydroxylase, human tumor necrosis factor (TNF-α), lymphocytotoxin (TNF-β), heat shock protein 70, and the ATP-binding cassette peptide transporter. Additional genes whose functions are yet unknown have been mapped recently to the HLA complex.

Figure 12
The current concept of the HLA complex

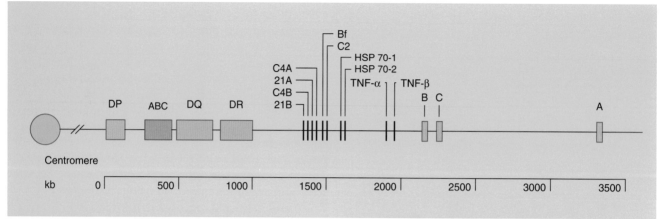

The class I loci, the class II subregions, and the class III loci are indicated. Distances are given in kilobases (kb). A, B, and C denote the HLA-A, HLA-B, and HLA-C loci; DP, DQ, and DR designate the HLA-DP, HLA-DQ, and HLA-DR subregions; C2, C4A, C4B, and Bf denote the loci encoding the second, fourth, and properdin factor B components of the complement system; 21A and 21B denote the loci encoding 21-hydroxylase A and B; HSP 70 indicates heat shock proteins; and ABC within the class II region indicates the ATP-binding cassette proteins, which act to transport cytoplasmic peptides into the endoplasmic reticulum.

Nomenclature

The HLA system is extremely polymorphic. At each locus, one of several alternative forms (alleles) of a gene may be present. Each functional allele determines a glycoprotein molecule that bears the HLA antigen. The International Histocompatibility Testing Workshops' list of the currently recognized HLA alleles and their respective HLA antigens is given in Tables 4 and 5, and indicates the polymorphism of the system. For instance, there are at least 26 distinct HLA-A alleles and at least 35 distinct HLA-B alleles.

Officially recognized alleles are denoted by the locus (or subregion) designation, an asterisk, and a four-digit notation. The first two digits refer to the most closely associated serologically determined antigen. The last two digits complete the allele number and allow designation of related alleles that encode the same serologically determined antigen (ie, HLA-A*0201 and A*0202).

Officially recognized antigens encoded by alleles at each locus (or within each subregion) are denoted by the locus (or subregion) letter and a number. For example, the number one antigen encoded at the HLA-A locus is designated HLA-A1. In some cases, several alleles (eg, HLA-

A*0201 through HLA-A*0210) encode distinct molecules, all of which bear the same serologically determined antigen (eg, HLA-A2).

The lowercase letter *w* (which stands for "workshop") placed before the number indicates that the antigen has been provisionally, but not officially, recognized. Upon official recognition, the *w* is removed so that HLA-DRw1 becomes HLA-DR1, for example.

A designation in which the HLA antigen is followed by a number in parentheses, such as HLA-A25(10) and HLA-A26(10), indicates that HLA-A25 and HLA-A26 are more recently defined, closely related antigens that were originally defined as the single antigen HLA-A10. HLA-A25 and HLA-A26 are termed *splits* of HLA-A10.

Genetic Organization

The HLA class I region has a relatively simple organization (Figure 12) compared with the HLA class II (HLA-D) region. Each HLA-A, -B, or -C gene determines a heavy gene on chromosome 15

Table 4
Designations of class I HLA-A, -B, -C alleles and antigens†

HLA-A alleles	HLA-A antigens	HLA-B alleles	HLA-B antigens	HLA-C alleles	HLA-C antigens
A*0101	A1	B*0701	B7	Cw*0101	Cw1
A*0201	A2	B*0702	B7	Cw*0201	Cw2
A*0202	A2	B*0801	B8	Cw*02021	Cw2
A*0203	A2	B*1301	B13	Cw*02022	Cw2
A*0204	A2	B*1302	B13	Cw*0301	Cw3
A*0205	A2	B*1401	B14	Cw*0501	Cw5
A*0206	A2	B*1402	Bw65(14)	Cw*0601	Cw6
A*0207	A2	B*1501	Bw62(15)	Cw*0701	Cw7
A*0208	A2	B*1801	B18	Cw*0702	Cw7
A*0209	A2	B*2701	B27	Cw*1101	Cw11
A*0210	A2	B*2702	B27	Cw*1201	–
A*0301	A3	B*2703	B27	Cw*1202	–
A*0302	A3	B*2704	B27	Cw*1301	–
A*1101	A11	B*2705	B27	Cw*1401	–
A*1102	A11	B*2706	B27		
A*2401	A24(9)	B*3501	B35		
A*2501	A25(10)	B*3502	B35		
A*2601	A26(10)	B*3701	B37		
A*2901	A29(w19)	B*3801	B38(16)		
A*3001	A30(w19)	B*3901	B39(16)		
A*3101	A31(w19)	B*4001	Bw60(40)		
A*3201	A32(w19)	B*4002	B40		
A*3301	Aw33(w19)	B*4101	Bw41		
A*6801	Aw68(28)	B*4201	Bw42		
A*6802	Aw68(28)	B*4401	B44(12)		
A*6901	Aw69(28)	B*4402	B44(12)		
		B*4601	Bw46		
		B*4701	Bw47		
		B*4901	B49(21)		
		B*5101	B51(5)		
		B*5201	Bw52(5)		
		B*5301	Bw53		
		B*5701	Bw57(17)		
		B*5801	Bw58(17)		
		B*7801	–		

†Committee Report. Nomenclature for factors of the HLA system, 1990.
Hum Immunol. 1991;31:186-194.

Table 5
Designations of class II alleles and antigens†

HLA-DR alleles	HLA-DR antigens	HLA-DR alleles	HLA-DR antigens
DRB1*0101	DR1	DRB1*1303	DRw13(w6)
DRB1*0102	DR1	DRB1*1304	DRw13(w6)
DRB1*0103	DR"BR"	DRB1*1305	DRw13(w6)
DRB1*1501	DRw15(2)	DRB1*1401	DRw14(w6)
DRB1*1502	DRw15(2)	DRB1*1402	DRw14(w6)
DRB1*1601	DRw16(2)	DRB1*1403	DRw14(w6)
DRB1*1602	DRw16(2)	DRB1*1404	–
DRB1*0301	DRw17(3)	DRB1*1405	DRw14(w6)
DRB1*0302	DRw18(3)	DRB1*0701	DR7
DRB1*0401	DR4	DRB1*0702	DR7
DRB1*0402	DR4	DRB1*0801	DRw8
DRB1*0403	DR4	DRB1*08021	DRw8
DRB1*0404	DR4	DRB1*08022	DRw8
DRB1*0405	DR4	DRB1*08031	DRw8
DRB1*0406	DR4	DRB1*08032	DRw8
DRB1*0407	DR4	DRB1*0804	DRw8
DRB1*0408	DR4	DRB1*09011	DR9
DRB1*0409	DR4	DRB1*09012	DR9
DRB1*0410	DR4	DRB1*1001	DRw10
DRB1*0411	DR4	DRB3*0101	DRw52a
DRB1*1101	DRw11(5)	DRB3*0201	DRw52b
DRB1*1102	DRw11(5)	DRB3*0202	DRw52b
DRB1*1103	DRw11(5)	DRB3*0301	DRw52c
DRB1*1104	DRw11(5)	DRB4*0101	DRw53
DRB1*1201	DRw12(5)	DRB5*0101	DRw15(2)
DRB1*1202	DRw12(5)	DRB5*0102	DRw15(2)
DRB1*1301	DRw13(w6)	DRB5*0201	DRw16(2)
DRB1*1302	DRw13(w6)	DRB5*0202	DRw16(2)

†Committee Report. Nomenclature for factors of the HLA system, 1990.
Hum Immunol. 1991;31:186-194.

Table 5
Designations of class II alleles and antigens† (continued)

HLA-DQ alleles	HLA-DQ antigens	HLA-DP alleles	HLA-DP antigens
DQA1*0101	–	DPA1*0101	–
DQA1*0102	–	DPA1*0102	–
DQA1*0103	–	DPA1*0103	–
DQA1*0201	–	DPA1*0201	–
DQA1*03011	–	DPB1*0101	DPw1
DQA1*03012	–	DPB1*0201	DPw2
DQA1*0302	–	DPB1*02011	DPw2
DQA1*0401	–	DPB1*02012	DPw2
DQA1*0501	–	DPB1*0202	DPw2
DQA1*05011	–	DPB1*0301	DPw3
DQA1*05012	–	DPB1*0401	DPw4
DQA1*05013	–	DPB1*0402	DPw4
DQA1*0601	–	DPB1*0501	DPw5
DQB1*0501	DQw5(w1)	DPB1*0601	DPw6
DQB1*0502	DQw5(w1)	DPB1*0801	–
DQB1*05031	DQw5(w1)	DPB1*0901	DP"Cp63"
DQB1*05032	DWw5(w1)	DPB1*1001	–
DQB1*0504	–	DPB1*1101	–
DQB1*0601	DQw6(w1)	DPB1*1301	–
DQB1*0602	DQw6(w1)	DPB1*1401	–
DQB1*0603	DQw6(w1)	DPB1*1501	–
DQB1*0604	DQw6(w1)	DPB1*1601	–
DQB1*0605	DQw6(w1)	DPB1*1701	–
DQB1*0201	DQw2	DPB1*1801	–
DQB1*0301	DQw7(w3)	DPB1*1901	–
DQB1*0302	DQw8(w3)		
DQB1*03031	DQw9(w3)		
DQB1*03032	DQw9(w3)		
DQB1*0401	DQw4		
DQB1*0402	DQw4		

†Committee Report. Nomenclature for factors of the HLA system, 1990.
Hum Immunol. 1991;31:186-194.

Figure 13
The HLA class I region and β₂-microglobulin

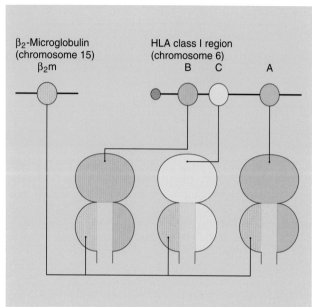

β₂-Microglobulin
(chromosome 15)
β₂m

HLA class I region
(chromosome 6)
B   C   A

Each class I gene determines a polymorphic heavy chain that associates with the nonpolymorphic β₂-microglobulin to form the class I molecule.

(Figure 13). For all class I molecules, all polymorphism resides in the heavy chain, and β₂-microglobulin is entirely nonpolymorphic.

The organization of the HLA-D region is shown in Figure 14. The region is divided into three subregions: DP, DQ, and DR. Each of these subregions includes one expressed α chain and at least one expressed β chain gene. The products of these expressed genes, the α and β chains, associate to form the class II αβ molecule. The HLA-DR region includes a single DR α chain, termed DRA, and in most DR types three β chain genes, termed DRB1, DRB2, and DRB3 (or DRB4). (A given HLA-DR subregion will express either the DRB3 gene or the DRB4 gene but not both. Some DR subregions express neither DRB3 nor DRB4, such as the DR1 subregion, which contains only DRB1; the DR8 subregion, which contains a DRB1/DRB3 fusion gene; and the DR2 subregion, which contains

DRB1 and DRB5.) In most DR types, one gene, usually the DRB2 gene, is a pseudogene and is not expressed. (A pseudogene, though similar to an active gene in its base sequence, has sustained a genetic mutation that prevents transcription and, therefore, expression.) However, the other two genes, usually the DRB1 and DRB3 (or DRB4 and DRB5) genes, are expressed. The DRα chain can associate with either the DRβ1 chain or the DRβ3 (or DRβ4 or DRβ5) chain to yield two distinct DR molecules: DRαβ1 and DRαβ3 (or DRαβ4 or DRαβ5).

On the basis of serologic reactions, certain HLA-DR antigens can be organized into "supertypic" groups. Thus, for example, DR3, DR5, DRw6, and DRw8 belong to the DRw52 supertypic group, and DR4, DR7, and DR9 belong to the DRw53 supertypic group (Table 6). It was initially thought that DRw52 was a common epitope on each of the molecules bearing the individual epitopes DR3, DR5, DRw6, and DRw8. However, it is now known that the DRαβ1 molecule bears the unique DR epitope (eg, DR3 or DR5), while the DRαβ3 molecule bears the supertypic antigen (eg, DRw52). Because of extremely tight linkage disequilibrium (see page 35), the DRB1 alleles encoding DR3, DR5, and DRw6 tend to be inherited in association with the DRB3 allele encoding DRw52. For example, an individual who is DR3 or DR5 is also DRw52. In the case of DR8, the DRB1/B3 fusion gene encodes a single β chain bearing both DRw8 and DRw52. Parallel comments apply to the DRw53 supertypic group in which the DRαβ4 molecule bears the DRw53 antigen (Table 6).

The DQ subregion includes two sets of αβ chain genes. One set contains the DQA2 and DQB2 pseudogenes, and the other set contains the DQA1 and DQB1 genes, which determine the DQα and DQβ chains. These two chains form the DQαβ molecule. Groups of DR antigens are associated with certain DQ antigens, most likely on the basis of linkage disequilibrium (Table 7).

Figure 14
The current concept of the HLA-D region, showing the organization of the three subregions, DP, DQ, and DR

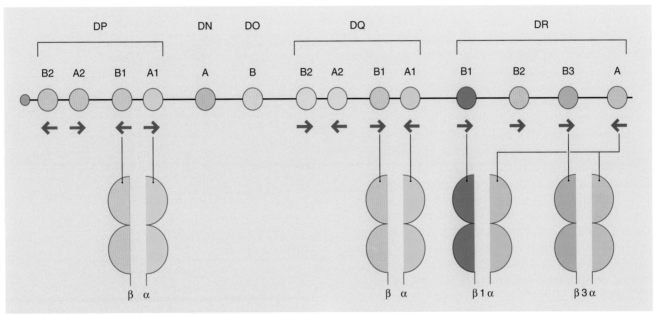

DPA2, DPB2, DQA2, DQB2, and DRB2 are pseudogenes and are not expressed. Pairs of expressed genes (DPA1 and DPB1; DQA1 and DQB1; DRA and DRB1; and DRA and DRB3) and the class II molecules they encode are indicated. DNA and DOB are not presently known to be transcribed in vivo. Arrows under genes give the direction of transcription (5' to 3').

Table 6
DRw52- and DRw53-associated DR antigens

DRw52	DRw53
DR3	DR4
DR5	DR7
DRw6	DR9
DRw8	
DRw11(5)	
DRw12(5)	
DRw13(w6)	
DRw14(w6)	
DRw17(3)	
DRw18(3)	

Table 7
DQ-associated HLA-DR antigens

HLA-DQ antigens	Associated HLA-DR antigens
DQw1	DR1, DRw10, DRw13(w6), DRw14(w6), DRw15(2), DRw16(2)
DQw2	DR3, DR7
DQw3	DR4, DR7, DR9, DRw11(5), DRw12(2)
DQw4	DRw8, DRw15
DQw5	DR1, DRw10, DRw14(w6), DRw16(2)
DQw6	DRw15(2), DRw13(w6)
DQw7	DRw11(5), DRw12(5), DR4
DQw8	DR4
DQw9	DR7, DR9

The DP subregion also includes two sets of αβ chain genes. One set contains the DPA2 and DPB2 pseudogenes. The other set contains the DPA1 and DPB1 genes, which encode the DPα and β chains that form the DPαβ molecule.

The polymorphism within each set of class II molecules differs depending on the set. For the DR molecules, the DRα chain is essentially nonpolymorphic among different DR types, while the DRβ chains are highly polymorphic. For the DQ molecules, the DQα and DQβ chains both possess a high degree of polymorphism. For the DP molecules, the DPα chains display limited polymorphism, and the DPβ chains are highly polymorphic.

Two other class II genes have been mapped within the HLA-D region between the DQ and DP subregions. These genes have been designated DNA and DOB, respectively (Figure 14). Although expression has been observed in in vitro systems, neither gene has yet been found to be expressed in vivo. At present, the function of these genes is unknown.

Although all HLA class II antigens are present on cell-surface molecules, different assays have been used to define and detect them (see the discussion of HLA typing on page 36). The DR and DQ class II antigens are defined and detected serologically. HLA-DP antigens were discovered and are still typed by a cellular reaction in the primed lymphocyte test (PLT). Now, however, DP antigens can also be detected with monoclonal antibodies. In contrast, HLA-D antigens are defined and detected solely by another cellular reaction, the mixed leukocyte reaction (MLR). There is no known HLA-D molecule or HLA-D locus per se. Responder cells in the MLR recognize an array of epitopes (antigenic determinants) present on the DR, DQ, and/or DP molecules. Analysis suggests that epitopes on HLA-DR molecules have a predominant role in stimulating the MLR. Therefore, as might be anticipated, HLA-D types are most highly correlated with HLA-DR types (Table 8).

The products of the C2, C4, and Bf class III loci are complement proteins that can be detected serologically and functionally and that also display polymorphism (Table 9). "Q0" designates a deficiency allele that does not express a function-

Table 8
HLA-DR and D associations

HLA-DR antigens	Associated HLA-D antigens
DR1	Dw1, Dw20
DRw15 (DR2)	Dw2, Dw12
DRw16 (DR2)	Dw21, Dw22
DR3	Dw3
DR4	Dw4, Dw10, Dw13, Dw14, Dw15
DRw11 (DR5)	Dw5
DRw13 (DRw6)	Dw6, Dw18, Dw19
DRw14 (DRw6)	Dw9, Dw16
DR7	Dw7, Dw11, Dw17
DRw8	Dw8
DR9	Dw23
DRw52	Dw24, Dw25, Dw26

Table 9
Well-defined alleles at the HLA-linked complement loci

C2	Bf	C4A	C4B
C2*C	Bf*F	C4A*2	C4B*1
C2*A	Bf*S	C4A*3	C4B*2
C2*Q0	Bf*F₁	C4A*4	C4B*3
	Bf*S0.7	C4A*6	C4B*Q0
		C4A*Q0	

al product. The C4 locus has been duplicated so that there are two distinct C4 loci, designated C4A and C4B. Their products differ in their affinities for amino and hydroxy groups (see also chapter 9).

The 21-hydroxylase locus appears to have been duplicated with the C4 locus. The product of the 21-hydroxylase locus is an enzyme in the adrenal steroid synthetic pathway. The C4A-linked 21-hydroxylase gene is a pseudogene. The C4B-linked 21-hydroxylase gene normally is functional.

The TNF-α and TNF-β loci are between the complement loci and the HLA-B locus (Figure 12). TNF-α and TNF-β molecules are 20 000 d, cause necrosis of several tumors, and share several other properties (see also chapter 7).

Haplotype

Haplotype is the combination of alleles at each locus on a single chromosome, for example, HLA-A1, B8, Cw2, DR3, DQw2, DPw4. Because HLA loci are tightly linked, this combination is usually inherited as a unit. Every individual inherits one set of chromosomes from each parent; thus, each individual has two HLA haplotypes. HLA genes are codominant; the alleles at a given HLA locus on both chromosomes are expressed, and thus two complete sets of HLA antigens will be present on cells. By simple mendelian genetics, there is a 25% chance that two siblings will share both haplotypes and be fully HLA compatible, a 50% chance that they will share one haplotype, and a 25% chance that they will share no haplotype and thus will be completely HLA incompatible (Figure 15).

Linkage Disequilibrium

Although haplotypes are usually inherited as a unit, recombination, though rare, does occur between HLA loci. Given the number of generations of the human species, one would expect recombination to have resulted in the random association of any two alleles at different HLA loci. If this were the case, the frequency of finding the combination of a given allele at one HLA locus and a given allele at a second HLA locus should be the product of the incidences of each allele in the population; in other words, frequency of haplotype = frequency of allele at locus 1 ×

Figure 15
Inheritance of HLA haplotypes

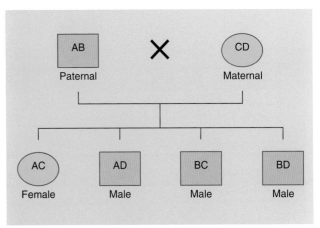

A haplotype is the combination of alleles at each locus on a single chromosome and is almost always inherited as a unit. Haplotype designations are given by A, B, C, and D. Paternal haplotypes are A and B, and maternal haplotypes are C and D. Offspring of this mating inherit one haplotype from each parent and will have one of four possible combinations of haplotypes: AC, AD, BC, and BD. Statistically, 25% of the offspring will be HLA identical (eg, AC and AC), 25% will be totally HLA nonidentical (eg, AC and BD), and 50% will be HLA haploidentical (eg, AC and AD).

frequency of allele at locus 2. However, particular combinations of alleles occur with a greater frequency than expected. This occurrence is termed *linkage disequilibrium* and is calculated as the difference (Δ) between the observed and expected frequencies.

For example, HLA-B*0801 is found in the white population with a frequency of 0.092, and HLA-DRB1*0301 is found with a frequency of 0.089. The *expected* frequency of HLA-B*0801/DRB1* 0301 in this population is the product of the two allelic frequencies, or 0.092 × 0.089 = 0.0082. However, the *observed* frequency is 0.0731. Thus the linkage disequilibrium or Δ is 0.0731 − 0.0082 = 0.0649. Linkage disequilibrium has been postulated to be attributed to two factors: (1) a selective advantage of a given haplotype, and/or (2) recent admixture of two inbred populations.

Figure 16
Serologic testing for HLA antigens by microcytotoxicity

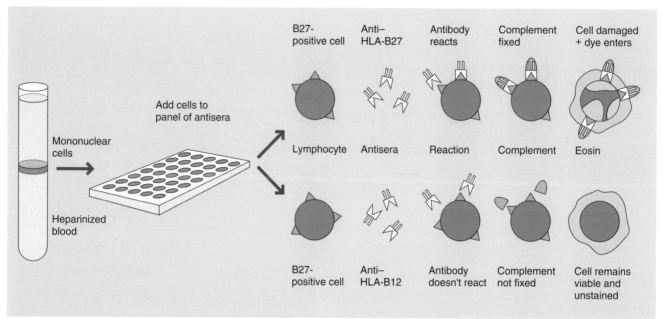

Mononuclear cells purified from the patients' heparinized blood are aliquoted into wells of a microtiter tray containing antisera to various HLA antigens. In this example, a B27-positive cell is shown in wells with anti-B27 antiserum (top) and with anti-B12 antiserum (bottom). (**Top**) The anti-B27 antibody binds to the B27 antigens of the cell, fixes complement, and causes lysis of the cell. Eosin, a vital dye, then enters the cell and the cell appears red. (**Bottom**) In contrast, the anti-B12 antibody cannot bind to the cell, complement is not fixed, the cell is not lysed, and the live cell excludes eosin and appears unstained. The cell is then typed as B27$^+$, B12$^-$. A modified microcytotoxicity test can be used to type DR and DQ antigens.

HLA Typing

Current Methods

HLA-A, -B, -C, -DR, and -DQ antigens are defined, detected, and typed with the microcytotoxicity assay, a serologic test. Although monoclonal antibodies recognizing a limited number of HLA antigens are available, the majority of typing is still done with sera obtained from multiparous women (Figure 16). HLA class I antigens are typed with purified populations of lymphocytes, while DR and DQ antigens are typed with purified populations of B lymphocytes. Alternatively, DR

and DQ antigens can be typed with the total lymphocyte population and a two-color dye procedure to determine B-cell cytotoxicity. As previously mentioned, HLA-DP antigens are typed by the primed lymphocyte test (Figure 17), and HLA-D antigens are typed by the mixed leukocyte reaction (Figure 18). HLA typing is used to determine HLA compatibility for organ and tissue transplantation and for platelet transfusion, to determine paternity, and to establish associations between HLA and disease.

The first widespread use of HLA typing was for organ transplantation. Organ donors and recipients were typed to identify HLA-compatible or partially compatible pairs. In general, the greater the compatibility, the more successful is the transplant. Experience over the years has indicated that the outcome with closely related living

Figure 17
HLA-DP antigen typing by the primed lymphocyte test (PLT)

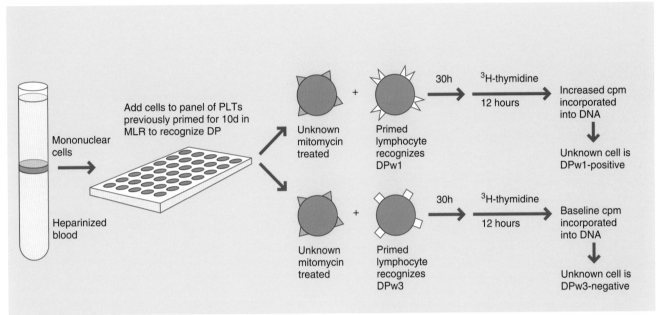

In the PLT, lymphocytes primed against specific DP antigens proliferate when exposed to the same DP antigen, but they will not proliferate if exposed to a different DP antigen. Mononuclear cells of unknown DP type are purified from heparinized blood and treated with mitomycin (or irradiation) to prevent their proliferation. The cells are then added to the wells of a microculture plate containing sets of lymphocytes previously primed to recognize the spectrum of DP antigens. The cells are incubated for 30 hours, after which ^{3}H-thymidine is added for an additional 12 hours to measure proliferation of the primed cells. In this example, the cell of unknown type is mixed with primed lymphocytes recognizing DPw1 or DPw3. The cell of unknown type stimulates the primed lymphocyte recognizing DPw1 to proliferate and incorporate ^{3}H-thymidine into DNA (top); thus, the unknown cell must be DPw1. In contrast, the cell of unknown type does not stimulate any proliferation of the primed lymphocyte recognizing DPw3 (bottom) and, therefore, is DPw3-negative.

donors matched with the recipient for one or both haplotypes is more favorable than that observed with unrelated cadaveric donors matched for the same number of HLA antigens. The explanation for this observation is that matching for known HLA antigens in a nuclear family almost always assures complete compatibility for the entire HLA complex, whereas complete compatibility is very rare with unrelated donors. Usually, the serologically determined class I and class II antigens are typed, and the lymphocytes of the donor and recipient are mixed in an MLR.

HLA typing has also been used in paternity testing. The relatively low frequency of a given HLA antigen, and the even lower frequency of a given HLA haplotype, have made HLA typing the next test if simple red blood cell typing does not exclude the putative father as the biologic father. If the child and putative father do not share an HLA haplotype, then the father is excluded as the biologic father. If the putative man and child share a haplotype, then there is a high probability, but not absolute proof, that the putative father is the biologic father. Comparison of the patterns of HLA restriction fragment length polymorphism (RFLP) between a putative father and child provides an even more exact way of establishing paternity, and identical patterns may eventually be accepted by the courts as proof of paternity.

Figure 18
HLA-D typing by one-way mixed leukocyte reaction (MLR)

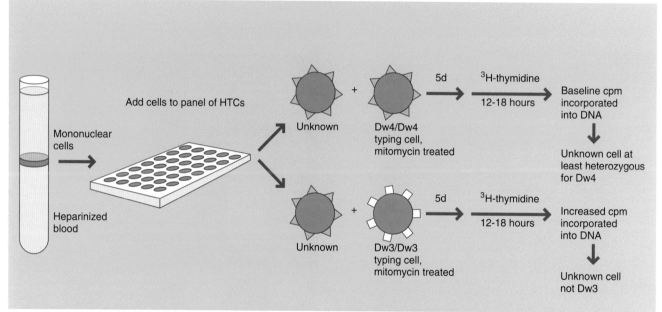

In an MLR, lymphocytes will proliferate in response to HLA-D antigens on another cell. Because the lymphocytes do not themselves possess the HLA-D antigen, they recognize it as foreign. Mononuclear cells of unknown HLA-D type are purified from heparinized blood and added to the wells of a microculture plate containing a panel of mitomycin-treated homozygous typing cells (HTCs) used as stimulator cells. The cells are incubated for 5 days, after which ^{3}H-thymidine is added for an additional 12-18 hours to measure proliferation of the cells of unknown HLA-D type. In this example, the unknown cell is tested for the ability to respond and proliferate to a Dw4/Dw4 HTC (top) or to a Dw3/Dw3 HTC (bottom). The unknown cell does not proliferate in response to the Dw4/Dw4 HTC and therefore must itself be at least heterozygous for Dw4. In contrast, the same unknown responder cell proliferates and incorporates ^{3}H-thymidine into DNA in response to the Dw3/Dw3 HTC. The unknown cell can then be typed as Dw4$^+$, Dw3$^-$.

Future Techniques

The application of molecular biology to the HLA complex has made possible new and more precise methods of HLA typing. Restriction endonuclease digestion of HLA genes produces patterns that are dependent on the restriction endonuclease, HLA gene, and probe used. Eventually, restriction fragment patterns may be correlated with particular HLA types, and HLA typing can be done by this method.

More recently, oligonucleotide typing has emerged as a prime candidate for HLA typing. Because each HLA allele has a unique nucleotide sequence that differentiates it from every other allele, it is possible to synthesize an oligonucleotide that will hybridize only to this unique sequence. A set of tagged oligonucleotides corresponding to various alleles at a given locus can then be tested for hybridization to an individual's DNA, identifying the allele he or she possesses. Eventually, oligonucleotide typing may be used to perform HLA typing at the DNA level.

Both RFLP typing and oligonucleotide typing are in their infancies, and the vast majority of HLA typing is done by conventional methods.

HLA-Associated Diseases

General Characteristics

In 1973, ankylosing spondylitis, a type of arthritis involving the spine, was found to be strongly associated with HLA-B27. This discovery initiated an exploration of other HLA-associated diseases. Over 100 diseases have now been associated with specific HLA antigens, albeit to different degrees. Table 10 lists some of the most common associations. (For a more complete listing, the reader is referred to the volume by Tiwari and Terasaki.)

Despite the broad range of disorders, HLA-associated diseases tend to share certain common characteristics. In general, these diseases have a hereditary tendency, but they do not follow simple mendelian genetics and they have weak penetrance. They lack both a known etiology and a known pathophysiology. These diseases are associated with immunologic abnormalities, and many of them are categorized as autoimmune disorders. They follow subacute or chronic courses and usually do not affect an individual's ability to produce offspring, thus allowing the HLA-associated diseases to persist in the species.

It is important to understand that no association between HLA and disease is absolute. The majority of individuals with a particular disease-associated HLA antigen do not contract the disease, and a particular HLA-associated disease can occur in individuals who do not possess the usual disease-associated HLA antigen. It is now appreciated that interaction of a particular HLA antigen, other genetic factors, and environmental agents must occur for the disease to manifest itself.

Quantitation of HLA-Associated Diseases

The magnitude of the association of a particular HLA antigen with a particular disease is quantitated by calculating the relative risk (RR). The relative risk is the chance of developing the HLA-associated disease for an individual who has the

Table 10
Selected HLA-associated diseases in white patients

Disease	Antigen	Approximate relative risk (where known)
Ankylosing spondylitis	B27	81.8
Reiter's syndrome	B27	40.4
Reactive arthritis (*Yersinia*)	B27	17.6
Rheumatoid arthritis	DR4	6.4
Juvenile rheumatoid arthritis		
Seropositive	DR4	7.2
	Dw4	25.8
	Dw14	47.0
	Dw4/Dw14	116.0
Pauciarticular	DR5	2.9
	DPw2	3.9
Systemic lupus erythematosus	DR3	2.7
Behçet's disease	B5	3.3
Sjögren's syndrome High-titer anti-SS-A (Ro) and anti-SS-B (La) antibody	DR3	5.6
	DQw1/DQw2	
Graves' disease	DR3	3.8
Insulin-dependent diabetes mellitus	DR3	3.0
	DR4	6.0
	DR3/DR4	33.0
	DQw8	31.8
	DQw2	
	DQw2/DQw8	
Celiac disease	DR3	13.3
	DQw2	
Psoriasis vulgaris	B13	4.5
	B17	3.1
	Cw6	7.2
Pemphigus vulgaris	DR4	21.4
Dermatitis herpetiformis	DR3	18.2
Idiopathic hemochromatosis	A3	6.6
	B14	3.7
Goodpasture's syndrome	DR2	19.8
Multiple sclerosis	DR2	2.8
Myasthenia gravis (without thymoma)	B8	3.3
Narcolepsy	DR2	129.0

disease-associated HLA antigen compared with an individual without that HLA antigen. Relative risk is determined by the formula:

$$RR = (P^+ \times C^-)/(P^- \times C^+)$$

where P^+ is the number of diseased patients possessing the disease-associated HLA antigen, C^- is the number of controls lacking that HLA antigen, P^- is the number of diseased patients lacking that HLA antigen, and C^+ is the number of controls possessing that HLA antigen. The greater the relative risk above 1, the greater the association between the HLA antigen and the disease.

The Role of Linkage Disequilibrium

Because of linkage disequilibrium and the chronologic order in which the HLA class I and class II antigens were discovered, some diseases that previously appeared to be associated with an HLA antigen at one locus are actually more strongly associated with another HLA antigen at a second locus. For example, the alleles encoding DQw2, DR3, and B8 are all in linkage disequilibrium. Before any HLA class II antigens were well defined, celiac disease was associated with HLA-B8, but delineation of the DR antigens allowed a stronger association to be made with HLA-DR3. Then the subsequent definition of the HLA-DQ antigens permitted an even stronger association between celiac disease and HLA-DQw2. The application of molecular biology techniques to the study of HLA and disease associations has now identified even more significant associations. Consequently, it has recently been reported that 90% of patients with celiac disease have a genomic DNA fragment corresponding to a portion of a DPβ chain gene.

Linkage disequilibrium is also responsible for the association of a number of diseases with what have been termed *extended haplotypes*. Two such examples are the association of systemic lupus erythematosus with the haplotype A*0101, B*0801, Bf*S, C2*C, C4A*Q0, C4B*1, DRB1*0301, and the association of C2 deficiency with the haplotype A*2501, B*1801, C2*Q0, BF*S, C4A*4, C4B*2, DRB1*1501.

A few diseases have been primarily associated with HLA class I antigens. The most notable associations are two types of arthritis, ankylosing

spondylitis and Reiter's syndrome, with HLA-B27. However, the majority of HLA-associated diseases involve the class II antigens.

Hypotheses to Explain Disease Associations

Several hypotheses have been presented to explain HLA-associated diseases. First, an HLA molecule may act as a receptor for an etiologic agent, much as CD4 is a receptor for human immunodeficiency virus (see chapter 14). If only a certain HLA antigen can act as receptor for agents that cause a particular disease, then the HLA-associated disease would result.

The second hypothesis suggests that the antigen-binding cleft of only a particular HLA molecule can accept a processed antigenic fragment that is ultimately responsible for causing the disease. Because this antigenic peptide fragment can be bound and presented only by this particular HLA molecule, only this HLA-antigenic peptide complex can be recognized by the T cell, and only this HLA molecule will be associated with the disease.

The third hypothesis suggests that the actual disease susceptibility genes are not the HLA genes themselves, but rather T-cell receptor α and β chain genes. This hypothesis holds that because a particular combination of T-cell receptor α and β chains that predisposes to disease can recognize an antigen only in the context of a particular HLA molecule, an *apparent* association with that HLA antigen is seen. The random process by which T-cell α and β receptor gene sequences are generated (see chapter 3) will result in genetically identical twins having nonidentical sets of T-cell receptors, which may partially explain why such twins are discordant for the development of a given HLA-associated disease.

The fourth hypothesis posits molecular mimicry as the basis for HLA-associated diseases. This hypothesis holds that the disease-associated HLA antigen is antigenically similar to the etiologic agent for the disease and then postulates one of two alternatives. The first alternative suggests that because of the similarity between the etiologic agent and the HLA antigen, no immune response is mounted against the etiologic agent and disease progresses unchallenged. The second alternative suggests that a vigorous immune response is mounted against the etiologic agent, and because of the antigenic similarity between the etiologic agent and the HLA antigen, the immune response is turned against the HLA antigen, and the resulting autoimmune response produces disease. Recent evidence supporting this hypothesis derives from observations on Reiter's syndrome. HLA-B27, the HLA antigen associated with Reiter's syndrome, and a protein found in strains of *Shigella*, which are etiologic for Reiter's syndrome, share an identical five amino acid sequence.

While any or all of the mechanisms postulated above can apply equally well to HLA class I- or class II-associated diseases, one potential mechanism applies only to class II-associated diseases. It suggests that the appearance of class II molecules on cells that do not normally express class II molecules may lead to disease. Tissue-specific cell-surface molecules undergo constant turnover and degradation. In a class II-negative cell, this degradation has no immunologic ramifications. However, if the cell is induced to express class II molecules, then the partially degraded tissue-specific molecules may enter an antigen-processing pathway (see chapter 6). A degraded peptide fragment may bind to the antigen-binding cleft of the induced class II molecule, forming an immunogenic complex that can be recognized by a helper T cell. This recognition can then result in an immunologic response against the tissue-specific molecule and the tissue, causing disease. This mechanism has been proposed for Graves' disease (hyperthyroidism) and insulin-dependent diabetes mellitus (IDDM), both of which are autoimmune diseases associated with class II antigens.

In addition, for certain diseases associated with class II antigens, the presence of "hybrid" molecules may increase predisposition to disease. Because both DQα and DQβ chains are polymorphic, the formation of hybrid molecules is possible when the DQα chain encoded by one haplotype pairs with the DQβ chain encoded by the second haplotype (Figure 19). It is thought that

Figure 19
Formation of HLA class II "hybrid" molecules

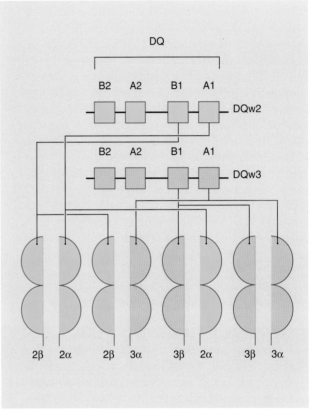

Because DQα and DQβ chains are both polymorphic, an individual who is a DQw2/DQw3 heterozygote has the potential for producing four distinct DQ molecules: two "parental-type" molecules, DQw2α/DQw2β and DQw3α/DQw3β, and two hybrid molecules, DQw2α/DQw3β and DQw3α/DQw2β. The hybrid molecules are unique to the heterozygote.

this hybrid molecule can present foreign antigen peptide to the appropriate helper T cell better than either "parental" molecule. For example, in Sjögren's syndrome the highest antibody response to the two antigens termed SS-A (Ro) and SS-B (La) occurs in patients who are DQw1/DQw2 heterozygotes. Presumably a DQw1α/DQw2β or a DQw1β/DQw2α molecule better presents the SS-A and SS-B antigens. A second example is that of insulin-dependent diabetes mellitus, which has been associated with both DR3 and DR4, but is most strongly associated with DR3/DR4 heterozygosity. Because DR3 is in linkage disequilibrium with DQw2, and DR4 is in linkage disequilibrium with DQw3, the majority of DR3/DR4 heterozygotes are also DQw2/DQw3 heterozygotes. IDDM is particularly associated with the DQw8 (formerly designated DQw3.2) subtype of DQw3. Thus, the presence of the DQw2/DQw8 heterozygous state, most likely because of a DQw2α/DQw8β hybrid molecule, predisposes to IDDM.

Recently, it was found that individuals who are predisposed to insulin-dependent diabetes mellitus lack an aspartic acid at position 57 of the DQβ chain (eg, the DQw8β chain), while individuals who are protected from IDDM possess this aspartic acid (eg, the DQw7β chain). Indeed, individuals who are DQw7 (formerly DQw3.1) homozygous (ie, DQw7/DQw7) and have two DQw7β chains with the protective aspartic acid residue are virtually totally protected from developing IDDM. Parallel findings have been observed in the murine system. Although these findings do not account for all IDDM-HLA associations, they appear to at least play some role. It seems likely that similar findings will be made with other diseases and other class II molecules.

Clinical Implications of HLA-Associated Diseases

The association of HLA antigens and disease has a number of theoretical clinical implications with respect to disease classification, diagnosis, prognosis, predictive risk of disease development, genetic counseling, and therapy. However, only a limited number of applications have been realized to date.

The finding that several diseases previously classified as variants of rheumatoid arthritis were associated with HLA-B27 allowed these diseases to be reclassified as the B27-associated spondyloarthropathies. The frequent associations of HLA-B27 with ankylosing spondylitis and Reiter's syndrome can aid in the diagnosis of these two diseases. However, because of the lack of absolute association, the absence of HLA-B27 in a patient with suspected disease should not exclude the diagnosis, nor should the presence of B27 be used to make the diagnosis in a patient who lacks a strong clinical picture for the disease.

In cases where an HLA-associated disease has been found in a family member and a particular disease susceptibility gene is known to map to the HLA complex, HLA typing of cells obtained during amniocentesis could be performed to determine whether the fetus will be at risk for the disease. Congenital adrenal hyperplasia attributed to 21-hydroxylase deficiency and idiopathic hemochromatosis caused by a deficient ferritin gene are examples of this potential application of HLA-associated diseases.

Further progress in elucidating the basis for HLA-associated diseases may allow additional theoretical implications to become reality.

Selected Readings

Bjorkman PJ, Saper MA, Samraoui B, Bennett WS, Strominger JL, Wiley DC. Structure of the human class I histocompatibility antigen, HLA-A2. **Nature**. 1987;329:506-512.

Braciale TJ, Braciale VL. Antigen presentation: structural themes and functional variations. **Immunol Today.** 1991;12:124-129.

Brown JH, Jardetzky T, Saper MA, Samraoui B, Bjorkman PJ, Wiley DC. A hypothetical model of the foreign antigen binding site of class II histocompatibility molecules. **Nature**. 1988;332: 845-847.

McDevitt HO. The HLA system and its relation to disease. **Hosp Pract**. 1985;20:57.

Moller G, ed. **HLA and Disease Susceptibility. Immunological Reviews**. Vol 70. Copenhagen, Denmark: Munksgaard; 1983.

Moller G, ed. **Molecular Genetics of Class I and II MHC Antigens.** Parts I and II. **Immunological Reviews**. Vols 84 and 85. Copenhagen, Denmark: Munksgaard; 1985.

Spies T, Bresnahan M, Bahram S, et al. A gene in the major histocompatibility complex class II region controlling the class I antigen presentation pathway. **Nature**. 1990;348:744-747.

Tiwari JL, Terasaki PI, eds. **HLA and Disease Associations.** New York, NY: Springer-Verlag; 1985.

T-Cell Receptors for Antigen

3

Introduction

T cells, like B lymphocytes, are able to recognize a large, seemingly infinite number of foreign entities. The cell-surface molecules responsible for this recognition are referred to as the T-cell antigen receptors (TcR). Unlike their B-cell counterparts (antibodies), T-cell receptors are not secreted and exist only on the cell surface complexed to at least four different species of CD3 polypeptides: γ, δ, ϵ, and ζ (Figure 20). In many cells, additional variations of the CD3 ζ homodimer are evident, such as ζ-η and ζ-Fc. This multipartite antigen recognition structure (TcR-CD3) is unique to T cells and may reflect more elaborate requirements for signal transduction in these cells (see chapter 4).

Recent work has established the nature of the T-cell receptor polypeptides and the rearranging gene families that encode them, as well as the way in which most or all T cells "see" antigen, as fragments embedded in molecules of the major histocompatibility complex (MHC) (see chapters 2 and 6).

Aberrations in TcR genetic loci have been correlated with some diseases, notably neoplasia, which probably results from oncogene translocations, and ataxia-telangiectasia. An intriguing byproduct of T-cell research has been the discovery of a category of T cells possessing a type of TcR, designated $\gamma\delta$, that is distinct from the $\alpha\beta$ receptor of the major T-cell populations (helper and cytotoxic T cells). The function of TcR $\gamma\delta$ is the object of intense study, which will further clarify T-cell contributions to immunity.

Types of T-Cell Receptor Heterodimers

It is now clear that at least two different types of antigen receptor heterodimers, $\alpha\beta$ and $\gamma\delta$ polypeptides, allow specific T cells to respond to different antigens. With the exception of certain $\gamma\delta$ pairings (Table 11), the different chains of each pair are covalently bound to each other by a single disulfide bond. Each polypeptide consists of a variable region and a single immunoglobulinlike constant region domain, followed by a connecting peptide or hingelike region that usually contains the extra cysteine residue thought to be involved in dimer formation, a membrane-spanning portion, and, in the case of β and γ, a short cytoplasmic tail (Figures 20 and 21). The variable (V) region is a composite of the different rearranging gene segments and includes contributions from V and joining (J) segments and, in the case of the β and δ chains, diversity (D) region gene segments. The number of gene segments involved is particularly large in the δ chain, where at least two and possibly three Dδ elements may contribute to amino acids between V and J. Both $\alpha\beta$ and $\gamma\delta$ TcRs are associated with CD3 polypeptides.

As summarized in Table 11, $\alpha\beta$ TcRs are the only antigen receptors that have been found on helper and cytotoxic T cells and seem solely responsible for the combined antigen-MHC specificities characteristic of those cells. T cells of this type make up 90% to 95% of the T cells in peripheral blood, as well as most of the T cells in the major lymphoid organs (spleen, thymus, and lymph nodes). The α chain ranges from 45 to 50 kd and the β chain from 37 to 40 kd. Mature $\alpha\beta$-bearing T cells are normally either CD4-positive (predominantly the helper T cells) or CD8-positive (largely cytotoxic T cells). Monoclonal antibodies specific for the TcR β chain have been derived and can be used to assay for $\alpha\beta$ TcRs in cell populations and tissue sections.

The second category of TcR, the heterodimer $\gamma\delta$, exists in various forms (Table 11). Much less is known about the function and targets of these cells, although preliminary indications suggest they may also recognize combinations of antigen-MHC–like molecules. A number of reports also link $\gamma\delta$ T cells to the recognition of proteins in the "heat shock" family of molecules, both of cellular and bacterial origin. It is known that $\gamma\delta$-bearing T cells are the first to appear in thymic ontogeny and constitute about 5% of the T cells in peripheral blood. In addition, dendritic epidermal cells

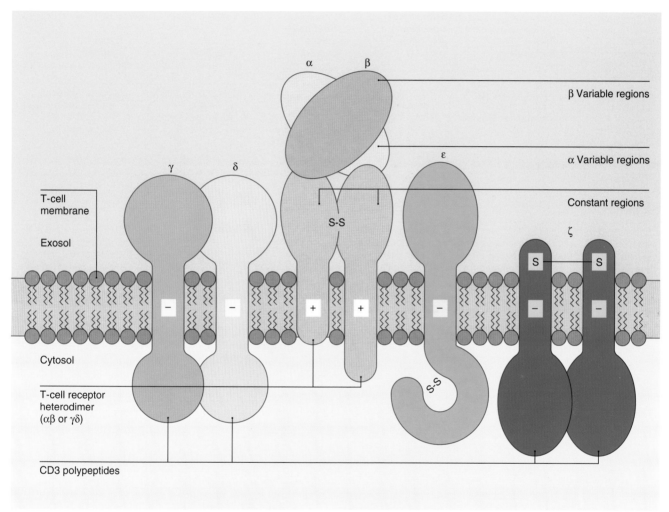

Schematic representation of a T-cell antigen receptor heterodimer (αβ or γδ) with the four distinct CD3 polypeptides
(γ, δ, ε, and ζ). CD3 ζ is found as a homodimer. (The γ and δ
polypeptides of CD3 should not be confused with the TcR γ
and δ chains.)

Adapted with permission from an illustration by Alan Iselin. In: Davis MM.
Molecular genetics of T-cell antigen receptors. *Hosp Pract.* May 15,
1988;157-170.

Table 11
Characteristics of T-cell receptors

Protein structure	Tissue distribution	Antireceptor monoclonal antibodies available	Other cell-surface markers	Function	Target ligand(s)
TcR αβ					
~90 kd (disulfide bonded) α = 45-50 kd β = 37-40 kd 2-3 N-glycosylation sites each chain	90%-95% of T cells of all major lymphoid organs and peripheral blood	Anti-β chain monoclonals (either V or C region-specific) Anti-α chain monoclonals (a very limited number of V region-specific)	CD4$^+$ or CD8$^+$ peripheral T cells In the thymus many are CD4$^+$ and CD8$^+$, and all are CD3$^+$	All known helper T cells All known cytotoxic T cells	Antigen fragments embedded in class I or class II MHC molecules
TcR γδ					

1. Disulfide bonded from ~90 kd (γ 1:δ):
  γ = 37 & 40 kd
  δ = 45 kd
2. Two allelic non-disulfide bonded forms:
  a. γ 2 = 60 kd
    δ = 45 kd
  b. γ 2 = 37 & 40 kd
    δ = 45 kd
Each form has several N-glycosylation sites
	5%-10% of peripheral blood cells
	Small fraction of major lymphoid organ T cells
		Anti-δ chain monoclonals (either V or C region-specific)
		Anti-γ chain monoclonals (some V region-specific)
			Mostly CD4$^-$ and CD8$^-$
			Some CD8$^+$
			All are CD3$^+$, CD2$^+$, CD5$^+$, CD7$^+$ in peripheral blood lymphocytes
				Unknown	MHC class I, class II, and related molecules have been identified as targets in a number of cases

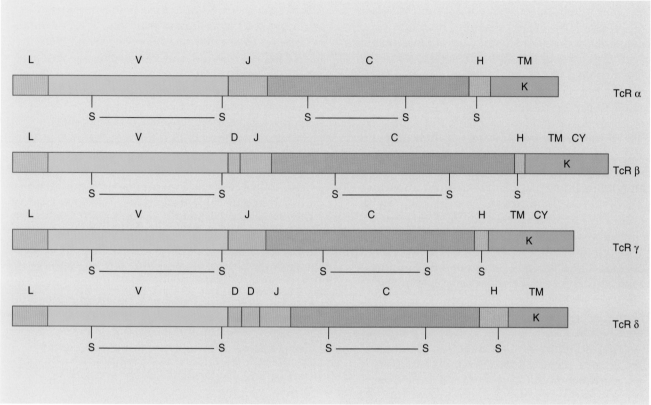

TcR α, β, γ, and δ polypeptides are shown with V, D, J, and C portions indicated. S denotes sulfhydryl residues capable of forming either intrachain or interchain SS bonds. Other abbreviations: L, leader; H, hinge; TM, transmembrane; CY, cytoplasm; K, lysine.

Adapted from Davis MM, Bjorkman PJ. T-cell antigen receptor genes and T-cell recognition. *Nature.* 1988;334:395-402, © 1988 Macmillan Magazines Ltd.

(DEC), a newly identified class of T cells that is almost exclusively γδ, have been discovered in the skin of mice. Preliminary reports also indicate that mice and chickens have γδ-bearing cells in the gut epithelium as well, but neither of these cell types seems to be present in humans. It seems likely that γδ cells play an important role in T-cell defenses, although the exact nature of this role (or roles) is not clear.

T-Cell Receptor Genes

The genes encoding the T-cell receptor polypeptides are composed of variable, diversity, joining, and constant region gene segments (following the nomenclature first established for immunoglobulins). The first three gene segments can recombine to a point adjacent to the C region to create a specific VJ (in the case of α, γ, or, rarely, β), VDJ (in β or some δ chains), or $VD_1D_2J/VD_1D_2D_3J$ (in some TcR δ chains). As in immunoglobulin genes, the different alternate segments of TcR genes are arrayed along the chromosomal DNA (Figure 22) and appear to randomly form different combinations. Also, the mechanism of recombination seems largely similar to that of immunoglobulins. Despite these similarities in organization and rearrangement, TcR genes lack three important features of immunoglobulin expression and diversity.

1. *Lack of a secretory form.* Thus far, no secretory form of TcR has been found. The absence of a secretory form is in contrast to immunoglobulins in which differential RNA splicing allows either a membrane or secretory form, depending on the stage of the response (see chapter 1). This difference probably relates to the fact that T cells are engaged solely in cell-cell interactions.

2. *Lack of somatic mutation.* In every study thus far, TcR variable regions express their germline sequences and do not exhibit the somatic hypermutation evident in immunoglobulins (see chapter 1). One possible explanation for this lack of somatic mutation is that T cells are stringently selected against self-reactivity in the thymus, and any further mutations could produce anti-self (autoimmune) reactions. Somatic

mutation is permissible with immunoglobulins because B-cell responses are strictly controlled by T cells, whereas only thymic selection apparently controls T-cell repertoire.

3. *No isotype (CH) switching.* No translocation of a given VJ or VDJ exon from one TcR constant region to another has been observed. Isotype switching may be unnecessary in the absence of secretory forms.

The TcR β and γ chain loci in the human genome are estimated to be 900 and 160 kb in length, respectively. The TcR δ locus seems contained entirely within the α locus and, in at least some cases, seems able to utilize V_α gene segments. In general, however, the two types of TcRs utilize distinct V elements, with the number of V_δ elements appearing to be quite low (approximately seven V_δ elements have been identified thus far in humans). Altogether, the TcR αβ locus extends over 1000 kb.

One interesting feature of T-cell receptors is the large amount of diversity between V and J and the relative lack of diversity in V region combinations. This is particularly striking in the case of the TcR δ chain with its multiple D region gene segments. Comparisons with immunoglobulin diversity (Table 12) indicate that the potential V-J junctional diversity is many orders of magnitude higher in TcRs than in immunoglobulin, and the V × V diversity is many orders of magnitude lower. This characteristic is particularly interesting because both helper and cytotoxic T cells recognize small (6- to 20-amino acid) fragments of degraded antigens embedded in molecules of the major histocompatibility complex. It has been suggested that the extreme V-J junctional diversity in TcRs may be directed largely at the antigenic fragment, and that the remainder of the variable portion of the TcR heterodimer may interact primarily with the MHC portion of the complex. This hypothesis

Figure 22
T-cell receptor gene loci

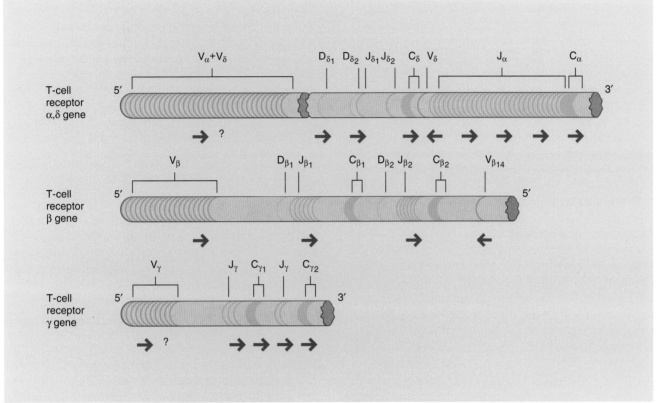

Approximate arrangement of V, D, J, and C element coding sequences for TcR α, δ, β, and γ. The direction of transcription is indicated by arrows. Arrows followed by question mark show probable orientation.

Adapted with permission from an illustration by Alan Iselin. In: Davis MM. Molecular genetics of T-cell antigen receptors. *Hosp Pract*. May 15, 1988;157-170.

Table 12
Sequence diversity in T-cell receptor and immunoglobulin genes

	Immunoglobulin		TcR αβ		TcR γδ	
	Heavy	κ	α	β	γ	δ
Variable segments	100-200	100	100	80	14	~7
Diversity segments	15	0	0	2	0	3
Ds read in all frames	Rarely	No	No	Often	No	Often
N segments	V/D, D/J	No	V/J	V/D, D/J	V/J	V/D_1, D_1/D_2 D_2/D_3, D_3/J
Joining segments	6	5	75	13	5	2
Variable region combinations	10 000-20 000		8000		50	
Junctional combinations	~10^{11}		~10^{15}		~10^{20}	

is illustrated in Figure 23, which shows the possible structural complementarity of a TcR (in this case, an immunoglobulin structure) and its probable ligand (antigen-MHC). The latter is represented by the membrane distal domains of the HLA-A2 molecule with a 12-amino acid peptide modeled into the antigen-binding site. In this juxtaposition, the V-J junctional residues of the immunoglobulin molecule (Figure 23) can be lined up squarely over the peptide, while the other portions of the two V regions can contact the HLA molecule. The even greater diversity in the junctional position of most γδ TcRs (Table 12) suggests that they also recognize small antigenic fragments embedded in MHC-like molecules.

TcR Gene Rearrangements

Expression in Ontogeny

As mentioned previously, TcR γδ-CD3–positive cells are the first to arise during fetal T-cell development, followed by TcR αβ-CD3–positive cells, which soon become the overwhelming majority in the thymus and in all other major lymphoid organs. This progression, together with the frequent rearrangement of TcR γ in αβ T cells and the placement of TcR δ between V_α and J_α gene segments of the α locus (Figure 22), suggests that all T cells initially pass through a γδ rearrangement stage (Figure 24A). In this model, the cells that are successful in producing γ and δ chains, which maintain the correct reading frame between V and JC, become γδ-positive and migrate to the periphery, whereas "unsuccessful" T cells proceed to rearrange β and α. An alternative model (Figure 24B), currently somewhat more in favor, suggests that the γδ and αβ cells occupy two distinct developmental compartments and are not linked to each other.

While differentiating in the thymus, T cells undergo at least two distinct forms of selection. In *negative selection*, self-antigen plus MHC-reactive cells are detected and induced to die. In *positive selection*, only those T cells with antigen receptors that can easily interact with one or more self-MHC molecules are allowed to advance to the most mature stage of thymic differentiation and migrate to the periphery. Negative selection seems designed to remove or inactivate potentially harmful cells, whereas positive selection seems important in "fine-tuning" the T-cell repertoire to the particular HLA haplotype of that individual. (Since no one person can express all possible TcRs, it seems more efficient to make a selection of those T cells with the best "fit.")

Diagnostic Use

Rearrangements of TcR loci have useful diagnostic implications. The first, well-documented use has been in demonstrating clonality. In cases in which a lymphoid infiltrate is seen but is not clearly malignant by histologic criteria, predominant rearrangements of TcR genes in T cells or immunoglobulin genes in B cells are strong evidence that a transformation event has occurred. T-cell leukemias and lymphomas can be subdivided into categories based in part on TcR gene rearrangements. For example, an uncommon form of early T-cell acute lymphoblastic leukemia (ALL) has no TcR rearrangements and may represent the transformation of a progenitor T cell (of the type indicated in Figure 24). Other T-cell tumors have TcR δ gene rearrangements alone or in combination with other TcRs. An additional category of T-cell tumors includes most TcR αβ-bearing T-cell lines and tumors in which TcR δ has been deleted from both chromosomes. Whether these subcategories of T cells will have prognostic or major diagnostic applications remains to be seen.

Chromosomal Location and Abnormalities Involving the TcR Loci

Figure 25 shows the chromosomal locations of the TcR αδ, β, and γ chain loci. The αδ locus is on chromosome 14 at position q11, and both β and γ are on chromosome 7 at q32-35 and p15, respectively. Translocations involving these loci have

Figure 23
Hypothetical TcR-antigen-MHC complex

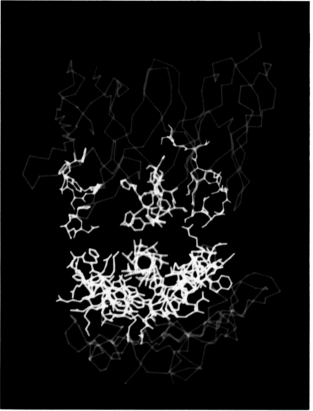

Modeling the TcR-ligand relationship. The protein structure of an antibody V$_H$V$_L$ (top, in blue, pink, and yellow) is juxtaposed over the topmost portion of the HLA-A2 structure in yellow and blue, with a 12-amino acid polyvaline helix (pink) in the presumptive antigen-binding groove of the A2 molecule. The two α-helices that form this site on the membrane distal side of the HLA-A2 molecule are seen edge-on and are yellow. The V-J junctional (CDR3) residues of the antibody molecules are shown in pink, lining up over the peptide, whereas the other contact residues of the Ig molecule (CDR1 and CDR2 of V$_H$ and V$_L$) line up over the α-helices of HLA-A2 and are also shown in yellow.

Reproduced with permission from Davis MM, Bjorkman PJ. T-cell antigen receptor genes and T-cell recognition. *Nature.* 1988;334:395-402, © 1988 Macmillan Magazines Ltd.

Figure 24
Possible T-cell lineages

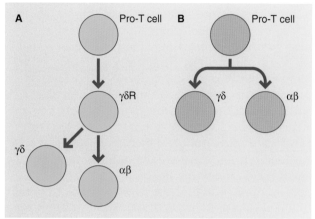

(**A**) An obligatory attempt to rearrange and express γ and δ chain genes prior to any rearrangement and expression of αβ chain genes.
(**B**) Two separate compartments of cells derived from a germline progenitor cell (a pro-T cell). R indicates attempted rearrangements.

Figure 25
Chromosomal location of T-cell receptor genes

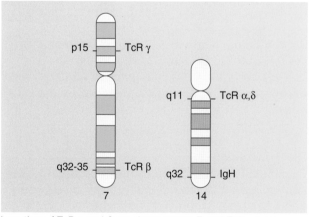

Location of TcR γ and β on chromosome 7 and TcR αδ on chromosome 14 in humans. Also shown is the immunoglobulin heavy chain locus at 14q32.

been categorized as potential oncogene translocations, $V_H \rightarrow J_\alpha$ inversions, and TcR rearrangements in ataxia-telangiectasia.

Potential Oncogene Translocations

Just as *c-myc* translocations to immunoglobulin gene loci have been strongly implicated in B-cell neoplasia, particularly Burkitt's lymphoma, it appears that oncogene translocations to TcR loci may occur in many T-cell tumors. In particular, cytogenic regions containing *c-myc*, *c-myb*, *L-myc*, *N-ras*, and *src-2* have been observed as having translocated into the q11 region of chromosome 14 in specific T-cell tumors. Although the chromosomal band containing the $\alpha\delta$ locus is by far the most common site of these translocations, several potential oncogene translocations into the TcR β region have also been reported. As with immunoglobulin-oncogene translocations, it is thought that translocating an oncogene into a T-cell receptor locus might activate a quiescent gene or disrupt regulation in a way that alters the normal growth control mechanism of a cell. This mechanism might also explain the apparent preference for the $\alpha\delta$ locus as a result of the larger target size presented by these gene segments, particularly the $J_\delta C_\delta J_\alpha C_\alpha$ coding segments extending over 100 kb. Another factor of potential importance is that TcR δ is rearranged and expressed early in T-cell differentiation, whereas TcR α appears to be the last TcR chain to be rearranged and expressed. The relatively larger "developmental window" for rearrangements at this whole region provides an increased opportunity for translocations and aberrant rearrangements.

$V_H \rightarrow J_\alpha$ Inversions

An unusual form of chromosomal abnormality has been observed in some T-cell tumors and is common in patients with ataxia-telangiectasia. In this form, a V_H gene segment in the immunoglobulin heavy chain locus at 14q32 (Figure 25) is rearranged by inversion to a J_α coding region in 14q11. In the several cases examined, these rearrangements are potentially productive (that is, capable of producing a $V_H J_\alpha C_\alpha$ polypeptide) and could have an effect on the physiology of the T cell. How this inversion might contribute to oncogenesis is unknown. The data on patients with ataxia-telangiectasia show that this chromosomal abnormality clearly is not the sole cause of neoplasia, and the inversion may only be an interesting consequence of the presence of these loci on the same chromosome.

TcR Rearrangements in Ataxia-Telangiectasia

Children with ataxia-telangiectasia have a high prevalence of neoplasia and an even higher prevalence of chromosomal abnormalities in peripheral blood lymphocytes. These abnormalities seem to center around 7p15, 7q32-35, and 14q11, precisely those regions that contain the T-cell receptor loci (Figure 25). As mentioned previously, 14q32 $\rightarrow$ q11 inversions are also common. Involvement of immunoglobulin light chain loci (κ and λ) is also seen but to a lesser extent. In many cases, dominant translocations are seen without evidence of neoplasia, indicating that these rearrangements alone are not sufficient or may have no direct involvement in the transformation of normal cells. Indeed, in ataxia-telangiectasia, most rearrangements occur between TcR loci, and none studied thus far involve known oncogenes. Thus, ataxia-telangiectasia seems, at least in part, to involve faulty rearrangements of TcR loci, and the primary defect may occur in part of that process. In this respect, it is interesting that patients with this disorder are deficient in some aspects of DNA repair.

Superantigens

One novel aspect of T-cell receptor biology that has emerged recently is the so-called superantigen group. They have been found to be produced by pathogens as diverse as bacteria and mammalian retroviruses and may be even more widespread. It appears that antigens of this type bind to both MHC class II molecules and TcR $\alpha\beta$ receptors simultaneously and are generally able to stimulate most T cells that express a given $\alpha\beta$ sequence. Superantigens are not processed into peptides, nor do they bind to the normal antigen-binding site of the MHC molecule. Also, unlike peptide antigens, they are generally not affected by VDJ junctional sequences. Thus, they exhibit different properties and are generally able to stimulate many more T cells than a typical protein antigen (hence the "super" designation). Because a number of bacterial enterotoxins have these properties (such as *Staphylococcus* enterotoxin A, B, etc), it has been suggested that the mechanism of toxin-induced shock is a result of generalized T-cell stimulation and subsequent lymphokine release, but this idea is controversial. It is clear, however, that this phenomenon is so widespread that superantigens must provide pathogens with some selective advantage, perhaps to weaken the immune system by chronic overstimulation and thus hamper a specific response.

Conclusion

With the molecular probes now available for T-cell receptor genes and polypeptides and with some basic knowledge about how these genes and polypeptides may work, the way is open to explore how the expression of these molecules is orchestrated in vivo and how aberrations, such as neoplasia and autoimmunity, arise. In addition, an understanding of how T-cell–mediated immunity works in a healthy organism should prove useful in devising strategies for treating a wide variety of infectious diseases.

Selected Readings

Brenner MB, Strominger JL, Krangel MS. The γδ T cell receptor. **Adv Immunol.** 1988;43:133-192.

Davis MM. T cell receptor gene diversity selection. **Annu Rev Biochem.** 1990;59:475-496.

Davis MM, Bjorkman PJ. T-cell antigen receptor genes and T-cell recognition. **Nature.** 1988;334:395-402.

Herman A, Kappler JW, Marrack P, Pullen AM. Superantigens: mechanism of T-cell stimulation and role in immune responses. **Annu Rev Immunol.** 1991;9:745-772.

Janeway CA Jr. Self superantigens? **Cell.** 1990;63:659-661.

Toyonaga B, Mak TW. Genes of the T-cell antigen receptor in normal and malignant T cells. **Annu Rev Immunol.** 1987;5:585-620.

T-Cell Activation

4

Introduction

T lymphocytes recognize antigen when it is presented on the surface of other cells in association with products of the major histocompatibility complex (MHC). As a consequence of this recognition, T cells are activated to perform their effector functions, to express a number of new cell-surface molecules, and, under appropriate conditions, to proliferate. An important recent advance in cellular immunology has been the delineation of the molecules that comprise the T-cell receptor for antigen (TcR) and the molecular cloning of the genes that encode these molecules. This delineation has led to an understanding of the structural basis for the selective recognition of specific antigen by T cells. In addition, identification of the TcR and its associated surface molecule, CD3, has allowed investigators to begin unraveling the signaling events that mediate the T-cell response to antigen. Many of these signaling events are triggered by TcR-CD3 itself. This receptor complex, therefore, plays a central role both in the initiating cognitive event and in the ensuing signal transduction process.

It is important to bear in mind that physiologic T-cell activation occurs during cell-cell contact and thus differs fundamentally from the most carefully studied receptor-mediated events: the responses of cells to soluble ligands, such as hormones and growth factors. When two different cells come into contact, a variety of receptor-ligand interactions can occur. It is now known that a number of T-cell molecules bind to molecules on the surface of the antigen-presenting cell. For example, the ligand for the T-cell molecule CD2 is LFA-3, a molecule that is expressed on a wide range of cell types. In addition, CD4 binds to MHC class II molecules, CD8 recognizes MHC class I molecules, and LFA-1 can bind cell-surface molecules that have been designated ICAM-1 and ICAM-2 (Figure 26). (See Chapter 8 for a discussion of LFA, ICAM, and other adhesion proteins.)

Figure 26
Different receptor-ligand interactions during antigen recognition by T cells

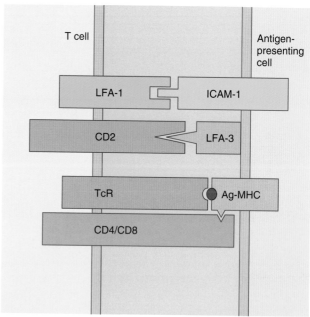

In addition to the critical binding of the TcR to antigen in association with an MHC molecule, receptor-ligand interactions occur that are not specific for a particular antigen. The interactions shown here enhance the avidity of the binding of the T cell to the antigen-presenting cell. CD2, CD4, and CD8 also influence the generation of intracellular signals that result from antigen recognition.

These additional receptor interactions serve two broad functions: (1) to promote binding of the T cell to the antigen-presenting cell, and (2) to modulate the signaling events that result from antigen recognition. Therefore, the activation of T cells by a specific antigen requires participation by the TcR-CD3 complex and also depends upon receptor-ligand interactions that are not specific for a particular antigen.

This chapter focuses primarily on the mechanisms of signal transduction by TcR-CD3, although the contributions of other cell-surface molecules are also considered. It is worth pointing out that the nomenclature for T-cell–surface molecules is a vexing problem for anyone who is not actively involved in the study of T cells. The nomenclature of these molecules was in a state of chaos throughout much of the 1980s, with any given molecule often receiving several different designations. To some extent, the confusion has been minimized by an increasing adherence to the classification established by the International Workshops on Human Leukocyte Differentiation Antigens. These workshops have assigned molecules a "cluster determinant" (CD) number, designations that, if uninspired, are at least uniform. In general, we will use the CD nomenclature. In certain instances, however, the CD assignments are not in general use, and the other designations have persisted.

TcR-CD3 Complex

Structure
The TcR is a disulfide-linked heterodimer that enables T cells to selectively recognize specific antigenic peptides bound to MHC molecules (the structure of the TcR is discussed in detail in chapter 3). The TcR is noncovalently associated with a complex of integral membrane proteins that has been designated CD3. There are five distinct CD3 polypeptides (γ, δ, ε, ζ, and η), which range in molecular weight from 16 to 26 kd. (The γ and δ polypeptides of CD3 are distinct from the TcR γ and δ chains and should not be confused with them.) CD3γ, δ, and ε are expressed only by

T cells. In contrast, CD3ζ can also be expressed by natural killer cells in association with CD16 (a receptor for the Fc region of IgG). An individual CD3 complex contains a single chain consisting of γ, δ, and ε together with either a disulfide-linked ζ-ζ homodimer or a ζ-η heterodimer.

The CD3 chains are not polymorphic and therefore cannot participate directly in the selective recognition of specific antigen. One function of the CD3 complex is to permit cell-surface expression of the TcR heterodimer. In addition, the weight of evidence indicates that the CD3 complex couples the TcR to signal transduction mechanisms. In other words, the flow of information that follows antigen recognition is from the TcR to CD3, and then from CD3 to the signaling pathways. TcR-CD3 couples to at least two distinct biochemical pathways that allow signal transduction: the polyphosphoinositide (PPI) pathway and the tyrosine kinase activation pathway (Figure 27).

TcR-CD3–Mediated PPI Turnover
PPI is a term used to refer to phosphorylated derivatives of phosphatidylinositol (PI), a phospholipid component of the plasma membrane. PI is phosphorylated initially to phosphatidylinositol 4-phosphate (PIP) and then to phosphatidylinositol 4,5-bisphosphate (PIP_2). Like PI, PIP and PIP_2 are found in the plasma membrane. A wide variety of cell-surface receptors in many different tissues use the hydrolysis of PPI to generate intracellular signals. Stimulation of these receptors activates a phospholipase C (PI-PLC) that hydrolyses membrane PPI. The key reaction is the breakdown of PIP_2, which yields two products with second messenger activity: inositol-1,4,5-trisphosphate ([1,4,5]IP_3) and diacylglycerol (DAG). (1,4,5)IP_3, which is water-soluble, binds to a specific channel-like receptor within the endoplasmic

Figure 27
Signal transduction by the TcR-CD3

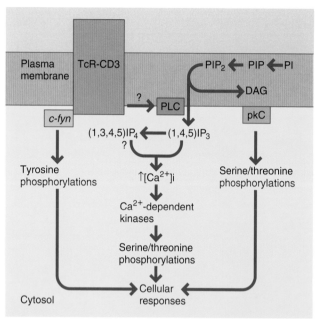

Stimulation of the TcR-CD3 activates two signaling mecha-nisms: *c-fyn* (a *src*-like tyrosine kinase) and inositol phospho-lipid turnover. The latter is due to TcR-CD3–mediated activation of a phospholipase C (PLC) that hydrolyses a membrane phospholipid, PIP_2. This reaction produces $(1,4,5)IP_3$, which in turn releases Ca^{2+} from internal stores. $(1,4,5)IP_3$ regulates an increase in $[Ca^{2+}]i$, possibly by acting in concert with its phosphorylated derivative, inositol-1,3,4,5-tetrakisphosphate (IP_4). The other product of PIP_2 hydrolysis is diacylglycerol (DAG), which activates pkC. The activation of *c-fyn*, Ca^{2+}-dependent kinases, and pkC is thought to result in the phosphorylation of key regulatory proteins and, in this way, to initiate a cascade of events that eventually culminates in a cellular response.

reticulum and stimulates the release of Ca^{2+} from that intracellular store. This release causes an increase in the concentration of cytoplasmic free Ca^{2+} ($[Ca^{2+}]i$) and the activation of Ca^{2+}-dependent kineses. The other product of PIP_2 hydrolysis, DAG, is an activator of protein kinase C (pkC) isoenzymes, a family of enzymes that phosphory-late protein substrates on serine and threonine residues. Increases in $[Ca^{2+}]i$ and in pkC activity act in synergy to cause a variety of receptor responses. In many instances, these responses can be mimicked by the combination of a Ca^{2+} iono-phore (an agent that allows extracellular calcium to enter the cell) and a biologically active phorbol ester. These pharmacologic agents bypass the PPI pathway and directly elicit increases in $[Ca^{2+}]i$ and in pkC activity. The combination of a Ca^{2+} ionophore and a phorbol ester (but neither agent alone) induces T cells to proliferate, an observa-tion supportive of the hypothesis that PPI turn-over has a key role in T-cell activation.

TcR-CD3–Mediated Increases in $[Ca^{2+}]i$

Stimulation of the TcR-CD3, either by appropri-ately presented antigen or by monoclonal anti-bodies (mAb) that bind to components of the receptor complex, leads to a sustained increase in the levels of $(1,4,5)IP_3$ and to an elevation in $[Ca^{2+}]i$ that is maintained for longer than 30 minutes. The initial component of the increase in $[Ca^{2+}]i$ is caused entirely by release of Ca^{2+} from internal stores and is almost certainly mediated by $(1,4,5)IP_3$. After 60 seconds of TcR-CD3 ligation, the increase in $[Ca^{2+}]i$ is dependent on the influx of extracellular Ca^{2+}.

There is no clear consensus as to the mechanism by which TcR-CD3 stimulation leads to an increase in the permeability of the plasma membrane to Ca^{2+}. Unlike neurons and other "excitable" cells, T cells do not appear to express voltage-gated Ca^{2+} channels (Ca^{2+} channels that open as a result of membrane depolarization). Patch-clamping studies demonstrate that T cells express voltage-insensitive channels that may conduct Ca^{2+} under physiologic conditions. One possibility is that $(1,4,5)IP_3$ regulates Ca^{2+} influx, either by directly affecting the plasma membrane channel or by indirectly increasing its ability to deplete intracellular Ca^{2+} stores. The addition of

$(1,4,5)IP_3$ greatly increases the probability of these plasma membrane channels opening, which raises the possibility that $(1,4,5)IP_3$ stimulates the influx of extracellular Ca^{2+} by binding to this channel. Support for this notion stems from the recent demonstration that the $(1,4,5)IP_3$ receptor within the endoplasmic reticulum is itself a Ca^{2+} channel.

TcR-CD3–Mediated Activation of pkC

In addition to releasing inositol phosphates, the hydrolysis of membrane inositol phospholipids by PI-PLC generates DAG, the physiologic activator of pkC. The activity of pkC is dependent upon phospholipid and Ca^{2+}. DAG increases the affinity of pkC for phospholipid and for Ca^{2+}, permitting pkC activation to occur at concentrations of Ca^{2+} that are within the intracellular range. The majority of pkC activity in unstimulated T cells is found in the cytoplasm. Following TcR-CD3 stimulation, there is a shift in pkC to a membrane-associated fraction, presumably a reflection of the formation of an active complex of pkC, DAG, phospholipid, and Ca^{2+}.

The link between TcR-CD3 stimulation and the activation of pkC has led to the hypothesis that pkC-mediated phosphorylation of certain proteins alters the functions of those proteins such that they in turn contribute to the cellular response. A potential target for TcR-CD3–mediated activation of pkC is *c-raf*, a cytoplasmic protooncogene that is phosphorylated on serine following the addition of phorbol esters to T cells. Like pkC, *c-raf* is a serine-threonine kinase. The enzymatic activity of *c-raf* is increased by serine phosphorylation, suggesting that pkC activation may lead to a complex cascade of phosphorylation events.

In addition to cytoplasmic substrates, pkC phosphorylates a number of cell-surface molecules that are involved in the response to antigen recognition, including CD3γ, CD3δ, CD4, and CD45. The functional consequences of these events are uncertain, but phosphorylation could alter either the signaling capabilities of these molecules or their interactions with ligand. It is also thought that pkC activation by TcR-CD3 modifies the adhesion molecule, LFA-1, leading to a conformational change in its structure and to an increase in affinity for its ligand, ICAM-1. The result is an increase in the avidity of the binding of the T cell to the antigen-presenting cell.

Coupling of TcR-CD3 to PI-PLC

In order to trigger the $[Ca^{2+}]i$ and pkC signaling pathways, TcR-CD3 must activate PI-PLC. The molecular basis by which TcR-CD3 communicates with PI-PLC, however, is not known. Studies of other systems indicate that guanine nucleotide-binding proteins (G proteins) couple receptors to PI-PLC in a manner that is analogous to the coupling of receptors to adenylate cyclase by G proteins. It is clear T cells express G proteins that can regulate the activity of PI-PLC, but it is not known whether TcR-CD3 uses these G proteins to activate PI-PLC. An alternative possibility is that PI-PLC is activated through tyrosine phosphorylation. This mechanism appears to be the one by which certain growth factor receptors stimulate PPI turnover within fibroblasts.

TcR-CD3–Mediated Activation of a Tyrosine Kinase

In addition to triggering PPI turnover, stimulation of TcR-CD3 activates a tyrosine kinase, leading to the phosphorylation of a number of proteins on tyrosine, including CD3ζ.

It should be noted that the great majority of protein phosphorylations within cells are on serine and threonine, that tyrosine phosphorylations are relatively rare, and that tyrosine kinases are intimately associated with cellular responses to growth factors and with malignant transformation. Thus, the link between TcR-CD3 signaling and activation of a tyrosine kinase is particularly interesting. Tyrosine kinases can be divided into two broad categories: growth factor receptors whose cytoplasmic domains have tyrosine kinase activity, and the *src* family of protooncogenes. The latter are cytoplasmic proteins that are associated with the inner surface of the plasma membrane and cannot communicate directly with external ligands. TcR-CD3–induced tyrosine phosphorylations appear to be mediated through p59[fyn], a *src*-like kinase.

TcR-CD3–Mediated Signaling Events and Subsequent Cellular Responses

The precise relationship between TcR-CD3–mediated signaling events and TcR-CD3–regulated cellular responses (eg, the production of lymphokines), and the relative roles played by PPI turnover and tyrosine phosphorylation in this process, remain uncertain and the subject of some controversy. This controversy stems in part from apparent biologic differences among the various models used to study T-cell activation in vitro. For example, studies of the human T-cell line Jurkat indicate that PPI turnover is necessary and sufficient for TcR-CD3–mediated production of interleukin-2 (IL-2), while tyrosine kinase activity is neither necessary nor sufficient. On the other hand, studies of 2B4 cells (a murine T-cell hybridoma) demonstrate that TcR-CD3–mediated production of IL-2 can occur in the absence of PPI turnover and, therefore, may be due entirely to the activation of a tyrosine kinase.

The Role of Other Receptors in T-Cell Activation

Because the primary physiologic role of T cells is to mount a response to foreign antigens, it makes intuitive sense that the cellular responses of T cells would be regulated by TcR-CD3. It came as a surprise, therefore, to find that stimulation of several other cell-surface molecules, such as CD2 and Thy-1, could activate T cells, raising the disconcerting possibility that T cells have the capacity to respond to stimuli that are not antigen-specific. However, further study of these "alternative" pathways of activation indicates that signaling by these molecules requires concomitant cell-surface expression of TcR-CD3 and, therefore, must be in some way regulated by TcR-CD3. Perturbation of certain other molecules, such as CD5, does not in itself activate T cells, but it does enhance TcR-CD3–mediated responses.

Taken together, these observations suggest that while physiologic T-cell activation requires participation of TcR-CD3, it is also influenced by the interactions between a variety of "accessory" molecules and their ligands. The physiologic signaling role of the accessory molecules may be to augment a TcR-CD3–mediated response, permitting activation despite suboptimal occupancy of TcR-CD3. A complete review of all potential accessory molecules is beyond the scope of this chapter. Instead, we will focus on several of the better understood examples.

CD2

The CD2 molecule is a 50-kd glycoprotein that is present on all mature T cells and on 95% of thymocytes. CD2 is also expressed by natural killer (NK) cells from all species, by mouse B cells, and by rat macrophages. The ligand for CD2 is LFA-3, a widely expressed cell-surface molecule. The interaction between CD2 and LFA-3 is thought to have a key role in establishing contact between T cells and potential antigen-presenting cells, perhaps permitting the T cell to "survey" the presenting cell for low concentrations of antigen and then to stabilize the cellular interaction so that T-cell activation can be initiated.

It is likely that CD2 also serves a signaling function, in addition to serving as an adhesion molecule. The cytoplasmic domain of CD2 is large and highly conserved between species, which are features expected of a molecule involved in transmembrane signaling. Consistent with this possibility, perturbation of CD2 by appropriate monoclonal antibody (mAb) stimulates T cells to proliferate. Thus, when stimulated by mAb (clearly not a physiologic ligand), CD2 can deliver all the signals required to activate resting peripheral T cells. This capacity of CD2 when bound by mAb to activate T cells is not shared by the great majority of other cell-surface molecules; binding of mAb to TcR-CD3 can activate T cells, but binding of mAb to other molecules generally does not. An important difference between the activation by anti-CD2 mAb and by anti–TcR-CD3 mAb is that the response to anti-CD2 requires the addition of pairs of mAb that react with particular regions of CD2. This observation raises the possibility that physiologic activation of CD2 requires interaction with two discrete regions of the CD2 molecule (and, possibly, with two separate ligands). Consistent with this possibility, LFA-3 substitutes for one of the required CD2 mAb and permits CD2-mediated activation in response to single CD2 mAb.

Stimulation of T cells by appropriate pairs of CD2 mAb activates PPI turnover and induces tyrosine phosphorylation. Gene transfer experiments, however, indicate that CD2 cannot signal in nonlymphoid cells. Thus, in order to couple to signaling pathways, CD2 must interact with molecules that are expressed by lymphoid cells but not by other cell types. Studies of mutant T-cell lines have carried this analysis further: CD2 cannot signal in T cells that fail to express TcR-CD3. Thus, CD2 must interact either with TcR-CD3 or with molecules that are functional only in the presence of TcR-CD3. It should be pointed out that TcR-CD3 cannot be the only receptor complex that regulates CD2 signaling. CD2 is functional in NK cells, but NK cells do not express TcR-CD3.

CD4 and CD8

The expression of CD4 and CD8 on mature T cells is mutually exclusive and divides T cells into two groups: those that recognize antigen in association with MHC class II molecules (generally helper T cells), and those that recognize antigen in association with class I molecules (generally cytotoxic T cells). Consistent with this dichotomy, CD4 binds to MHC class II molecules, and class I molecules are the ligands for CD8. CD4 and CD8 appear to serve dual roles as adhesion molecules and signal transducers. The cytoplasmic domains of both CD4 and CD8 are physically associated with p56^{lck}, a tyrosine kinase of the src family. Because the functions of CD4 and CD8 appear to be similar, only CD4 is considered in detail.

Analysis of T-cell hybridomas that have spontaneously lost expression of CD4 (called *CD4 loss variants*) demonstrates that CD4 is not absolutely required for antigen-mediated activation. Activation of the CD4 loss variants, however, requires substantially higher concentration of antigen than is needed to activate the original cell (wild type). Thus, CD4 appears to be important when occupancy of TcR-CD3 is relatively low. It is not clear whether the diminished response of the CD4 loss variants primarily reflects the loss of the adhesion function of CD4 or results from the absence of CD4-mediated signaling.

Studies with anti-CD4 mAb have led to conflicting conclusions as to whether CD4-mediated signaling augments or inhibits T-cell activation. A critical point appears to be whether CD4 and TcR-CD3 are in physical proximity when stimulated. For example, when anti-CD3 and anti-CD4 are immobilized on the same surface, the ensuing proliferative response is greater than the response to anti-CD3 alone. On the other hand, when anti-CD3 and anti-CD4 are immobilized on separate particles, the opposite effect is observed: the response is less than the response to anti-CD3 alone. This dichotomy is also observed when early signaling events (both tyrosine phosphorylations and PPI turnover) are studied. It is intriguing that CD4, presumably through effects on *lck*, can have dramatic effects on TcR-CD3–mediated production of inositol phosphates. This observation suggests that the tyrosine phosphorylations can regulate the ability of TcR-CD3 to couple to PI-PLC.

In light of the functional studies with CD4 mAb, it is important to understand the nature of the physical interactions, if any, between CD4 and TcR-CD3 during antigen recognition. One unanswered question is whether CD4 binds to the same MHC class II molecule that simultaneously interacts with the TcR (as shown schematically in Figure 27). If so, then CD4 could be viewed as a component of the TcR-CD3 complex. The results of several studies are consistent with this model, but there is as yet no conclusive proof of a physical association between CD4 and TcR-CD3.

CD45

CD45 (formerly known as the leukocyte common antigen) is expressed in high levels on all nucleated hematopoietic cells, including all mature T cells. A ligand for CD45 has not yet been identified, but it appears likely that one exists. There is a single gene for CD45, but through alternative RNA splicing the extracellular domain of CD45 varies among the different cell lineages.

In addition, the extracellular domain can vary during differentiation of a particular cell lineage. For example, naive CD4$^+$ T cells (ie, T cells previously unexposed to their recognized antigen) express CD45RA, whereas memory T cells express CD45RO. One hypothesis is that the different CD45 isoforms exist to permit interaction with a variety of different ligands.

Two recent observations indicate that CD45 has a major role in regulating the responses of T cells to antigen. First, the cell-surface expression of CD45 is required for murine T-cell clones to respond to specific antigen. Second, the cytoplasmic domain of CD45 (which is identical for all CD45 isoforms) displays striking homology to a tyrosine phosphatase that has been isolated from placenta. Subsequent studies using purified CD45 protein have established that CD45 itself has tyrosine phosphatase activity. Thus, one possibility is that CD45 regulates the tyrosine phosphorylations that result from TcR-CD3–mediated activation of p59^{fyn} or from CD4-induced activation of p56^{lck}. Although CD45 is a tyrosine phosphatase, the consequences of CD45 action may not necessarily be antagonistic to the tyrosine kinase pathways. For example, phosphorylation of src-like kinases on certain tyrosine residues inhibits their kinase activity. If CD45 prevents phosphorylation of these residues, then the effect of CD45 would be to promote tyrosine kinase activity.

Consequences of Activation

The functional consequences of T-cell activation depend upon the type of T cell involved. Activation of cytotoxic T cells causes the release of cytolytic granules and lysis of target cells. Activation of helper T cells, on the other hand, results in the production of lymphokines, such as IL-2. The latter process requires approximately 2 hours of sustained signal transduction and involves the transcriptional activation of previously silent genes. Activation of both cytotoxic T cells and helper T cells also results in the expression of fully functional receptors for IL-2, so that both types of T cells now can expand by proliferating in response to IL-2.

T-cell activation also induces a variety of other phenotypic changes, including the appearance of a series of new cell-surface molecules. Some of these molecules appear within hours, but others are expressed days after the stimulating event. Thus, T-cell activation is more properly viewed as a signal for further cellular differentiation and not simply as the response of a terminally differentiated cell.

Conclusion

PPI turnover and a src-like tyrosine kinase are activated when TcR-CD3 recognizes appropriately presented antigen (Figure 27). These signaling pathways probably regulate cellular responses by stimulating the phosphorylation of key regulatory proteins, thereby altering the function of these proteins. Although TcR-CD3 has a central role in T-cell activation, it is clearly not the only receptor involved in this process. A variety of other cell-surface molecules also influence the responses of T cells to antigen and contribute to the signaling process (Figure 28). While these molecules may deliver intracellular signals distinct from TcR-CD3–induced signals, it also appears that they have an important role in the modulation of TcR-CD3–mediated signaling.

This chapter has focused on the early events that appear to initiate the signaling process. Remarkable progress has been made in this area in the past decade. A major challenge of the future will be to determine how these intracellular signals in turn regulate the ensuing cellular responses.

Figure 28
Signal transduction by T-cell receptors

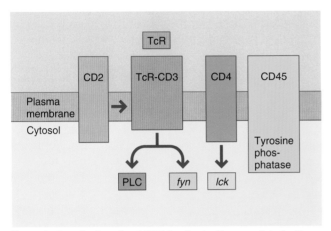

The cytoplasmic domain of CD4 is physically associated with the *src*-like tyrosine kinase, p56^{lck}. Ligation of CD4 can activate the kinase activity of p56^{lck} and, when CD4 and TcR-CD3 are in close physical approximation, can augment the ability of TcR-CD3 to induce tyrosine phosphorylations and to activate phospholipase C (PLC). The cytoplasmic domain of CD45 has tyrosine phosphatase activity. The cell-surface expression of CD45 is required for a T-cell clone to respond to antigen. It is likely, therefore, that CD45 has a major role in modulating the signaling response of T cells to antigen, presumably by regulating the tyrosine phosphorylation status of key proteins. Perturbation of CD2 can fully activate T cells, but CD2 does not appear to have intrinsic signaling capabilities. CD2-mediated signaling requires cell-surface expression of TcR-CD3, indicating that CD2 must interact with TcR-CD3 (or with molecules that are only functional in the presence of TcR-CD3) in order to signal.

Selected Readings

Makgoba MW, Sanders ME, Shaw S. The CD2-LFA-3 and LFA-1-ICAM pathways: relevance to T-cell recognition. **Immunol Today**. 1989;10:417-422.

Mustelin T, Altman A. Do CD4 and CD8 control T-cell activation via a specific tyrosine protein kinase? **Immunol Today**. 1989;10:189-192.

Weiss A, Imboden JB. Cell-surface molecules and early events involved in human T lymphocyte activation. **Adv Immunol**. 1987;41:1-38.

B-Cell Differentiation and Activation

5

Origin and Phylogeny

The name *B cell* derives from the avian bursa of Fabricius, the site of B-cell production in birds. In mammals, however, B cells are produced in hematopoietic tissues, first in the fetal liver and spleen and then in the bone marrow. B cells and their major products, antibodies, have been found in all vertebrates, including amphibians, reptiles, and cartilaginous and bony fish.

Like all other blood cells, B cells arise from pluripotent hematopoietic stem cells. Early in embryonic development, primitive mesenchymal cells migrate to the yolk sac, where they begin to differentiate into erythroid and myeloid cell lines. It is not until stem cells arrive at B-cell–specific microenvironments, such as the avian bursa of Fabricius, that differentiation along the B-cell pathway begins. During embryonic development, the liver is the major blood cell-forming tissue. In mice, the liver is the site of blood cell development from about day 11 of embryonic life until a few days after birth, when the bone marrow assumes this role. Studies of radioisotope-labeled B-cell precursors in bone marrow have suggested that the vast majority of B cells develop in the bone marrow within a 3-day span. It has been estimated that approximately 5×10^7 pre-B cells are produced per day. After leaving the bone marrow, most B cells quickly reappear in the spleen. A majority of these die in the spleen within a few days and a few recirculate.

Stages of B-Cell Differentiation

The major function of the B cell is to secrete antibody. Each clone of B cells expresses a unique antigen-binding immunoglobulin molecule on the cell surface and ultimately secretes antibody identical to this receptor. The stages of B-cell differentiation have been classified primarily according to the organization and expression of the genes for these immunoglobulins. For example, murine B-cell development, which provides a likely model for human B-cell development, can simply be divided into three stages. The first stage includes the commitment of pluripotent stem cells to the B-cell pathway, rearrangement of immunoglobulin genes, and expression of the antigen-specific receptor on the cell membrane. In the second stage, immunocompetent B cells (that is, B cells capable of binding and responding to antigen) migrate to the spleen and lymph nodes, where they accumulate and can respond to their specific antigens. In the third stage, these activated B cells multiply and differentiate into plasma cells that secrete large amounts of immunoglobulin (Ig).

Stem-cell differentiation into B cells probably occurs in the liver and spleen of fetal animals and in the bone marrow of adult animals. However, the earliest precursors of the B cell have been difficult to isolate and identify because of their heterogeneity and small numbers. Recently, however, a number of cell-surface markers have made it possible to isolate a population of cells within the bone marrow that appears to be the earliest renewable precursor of the B cell. These cells, isolated by a combination of positive immunoselection by electronic cell sorting and negative immunoselection by immune lysis, constitute only 0.5% of the total bone marrow population.

The molecular scheme of B-cell differentiation (Figure 29) has been established through the use of Abelson murine leukemia virus, which allows the transformation and immortalization of early pre-B cells in liver and bone marrow. The earliest event is the rearrangement of the D_H and J_H regions of the Ig gene in the stage preceding the pre–B-cell stage (see chapter 1). In this precursor of the pre-B cell, a functional IgM heavy chain (μ) is generated by further rearrangement that juxtaposes a variable region segment next to the D_H segment. At the next stage, the pre-B cell has an assembled $V_H D_H J_H C_H$ allele present as protein in the cytoplasm, but this allele is not yet expressed on the cell membrane, and therefore

Figure 29
Schematic representation of pre–B-cell development
according to immunoglobulin heavy and light chain gene
rearrangement and acquisition of differentiation antigens

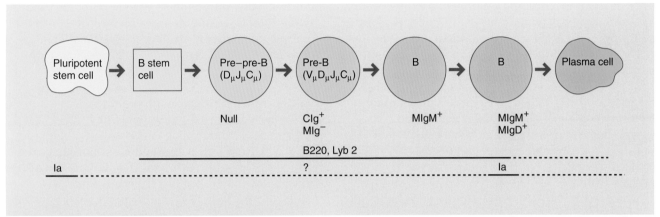

Lyb2 and B220 (Ly5) are differentiation antigens on murine B cells. Lyb2 has a molecular weight of 40 to 45 kd and is expressed on most peripheral and progenitor B cells, but its expression is lost on antibody-producing cells. B220 (Ly5) has a molecular weight of 220 kd on B cells and is expressed on all B-lineage cells from pre–pre-B cells to mature plasma cells. The functions of Lyb2 and B220 are not known. Ia indicates class II molecules. CIg is cytoplasmic immunoglobulin, and MIg is membrane immunoglobulin. Solid line indicates expression; broken line indicates no or questionable expression.

the pre-B cell cannot interact with antigen. Pre-B cells can be detected in fetal liver and constitute up to 10% of the cells in adult bone marrow. The transit time through the pre–B-cell stage is roughly 5 days in mouse fetal liver.

During the next stage of differentiation, pre-B cells may rearrange a κ and λ light chain. However, analysis of Ig genes in the transformed lines of pre-B cells indicates that not all pre-B cells successfully rearrange both a heavy chain gene and a light chain gene. The extent of wastage of pre-B cells whose development is abortive is not known. Those pre-B cells that do successfully undergo rearrangement of both the heavy and light chain genes assemble, express an IgM molecule on the cell membrane, and become mature B cells. The predominant population of resting immature B cells in the spleen requires further maturation after birth and is composed of cells that express both surface IgM and surface IgD containing a δ heavy chain. There is a large turnover of B cells, and the spleen and lymph nodes receive newly formed immature B cells daily.

The last stage of B-cell maturation occurs when a specific antigen and secondary factors from T cells and accessory cells activate the B cell to terminally differentiate to a plasma cell. Plasma cells divide and secrete immunoglobulin. During this terminal differentiation, further switching of heavy chain genes from the IgM class to other heavy chain isotypes may occur, resulting in secretion of other isotypes of immunoglobulins.

Cell-Surface Immunoglobulin

The surface immunoglobulin (sIg) molecules synthesized by each clone of a B cell are the antigen receptors for that clone. This mechanism was originally postulated by Paul Ehrlich in 1900, and evidence for it was acquired by Sell and Gell in the mid-1960s. These investigators demonstrated that antibodies against immunoglobulin determinants induced rabbit lymphocytes to proliferate and that antisera against either heavy or light chain determinants of sIg on antigen-specific B cells blocked the binding of antigen by those cells. These findings demonstrate that the effects of antigen binding to B cells can be mimicked by anti-Ig.

The use of lactoperoxidase-catalyzed radioiodination and anti-Ig antibodies tagged with fluorescein, ^{125}I peroxidase, or ferritin made it possible to directly label sIg. When used with light and electron microscopy, these techniques enabled researchers to identify sIg on B lymphocytes. The major sIgs expressed by B cells are IgM and IgD. A minor proportion of B cells express other classes (isotypes) of sIg such as IgG, IgA, and IgE. (The molecular structure of immunoglobulin is discussed in chapter 1.)

Developmental Changes in sIg
Surface Ig is crucial both in the initial recognition of antigen by a B-cell clone and in the activation of that clone. Studies of sIg on B cells during ontogeny have shown that neonatal mice have more surface IgM than adult mice and that the neonatal sIgM is more heterogeneous. The average amount of IgM declines gradually with age as cells express increasing amounts of sIgD. Most B cells in mature mice express both IgM and IgD, with one or the other surface Ig predominating. Two major subsets of B cells exist: those that express sIgM and little or no sIgD and those with higher amounts of IgD than IgM. B cells develop from a sIgM^{hi} sIgD$^-$ phenotype to a sIgM^{hi} sIgD^{low} phenotype and then to a sIgM^{low} sIgD^{hi} phenotype. During differentiation to plasma cells, sIgD is lost before sIgM so that large activated B cells and memory B cells (see page 65) are both largely IgD-negative.

sIg-Mediated Activation
Virtually all mature B cells express two and sometimes three different classes of sIg with the same antigen specificity. These receptor isotypes appear to have different roles in the activation and tolerance induction of B cells, as evidenced by the effects of isotype-specific (anti-μ and anti-δ) antibodies on B-cell proliferation and differentiation and on B-cell response to antigen or tolerogen. Because of these functional differences, B cells can be classified into two subsets on the basis of receptor isotypic phenotype.

The isotype-specific antibodies have been used to determine whether sIg can transmit a signal to the B cell. Both anti-μ and anti-δ antibodies can induce proliferation of Lyb5$^+$ B cells (see page 70) from mature mice, but not from mice under 4 weeks of age. This response is polyclonal and not antigen-specific. In general, the F(ab')$_2$ fragments of affinity-purified isotype-specific antibodies are required for this stimulation, most likely because the Fc portion of the antibody induces a negative signal upon interaction with Fc receptors on B cells. Binding of the anti-μ or anti-δ antibody to an insoluble matrix increases the proliferative capacity of the reagent. It is important to note that binding to sIg alone is not sufficient to produce proliferation. Cross-linking of sIg must also occur; thus, bivalent but not monovalent Fab fragments are mitogenic. It appears that sIg has a special function in signal transduction because antibodies to other B-cell surface molecules are not mitogenic. Binding anti-Ig (or antigen, in the more natural situation) to sIg is only the first step in the activation of the B cell. Antigen binding induces proliferation, but differentiation into Ig-secreting cells requires the presence of T-cell or other soluble factors.

Interestingly, anti-Ig reagents can cause both cell proliferation and inhibition of antigen-induced antibody production. Anti-Ig inhibits the secretion of IgM, IgG, and IgA antibody by antigen-driven cells. This apparent paradoxical behavior of anti-Ig reagents (ie, proliferation and inhibition of antibody secretion) may reflect the responses of different subsets of B cells or the independence of B-cell proliferation and differentiation to Ig secretion.

Isotype-specific antisera also have effects when injected into mice. Anti-μ treatment, especially if performed on neonatal mice, suppresses all classes of antibody, whereas anti-γ and anti-α inhibit only IgG and IgA responses, respectively. Anti-δ treatment leads to lack of sIgD expression, as well as to a modest decrease in sIgM expression. B cells from mice treated with anti-δ express increased levels of surface class II antigens. The functional effects of anti-δ treatment in vivo may be summed up by the statement that sIgD-positive B cells are important for the production of most antibodies, but that in the absence of sIgD$^+$ cells, sIgD$^-$ cells can compensate.

Tolerance Induction

B cells from adult and neonatal mice differ markedly in their abilities to be tolerized (that is, made tolerant to antigens and thus functionally inactivated). Immature B cells are extremely sensitive to cross-linking of sIg by anti-μ or anti-idiotypic antibodies, and such treatment results in a functional deletion of these B cells. Specific B-cell clones can be deleted by treating neonatal B cells with anti-idiotypic antibodies or specific antigen. In contrast, adult B cells are only temporarily inactivated by exposure to such agents.

Thus, it appears that cross-linking of sIg causes immature B cells to be tolerized and mature B cells to proliferate. Further differentiation to Ig secretion requires T-cell help. IgD appears to be important in the T-dependent B-cell response and in generating memory responses (see following discussions).

Effect of Mitogenic and Antigenic Stimulation

Ig Expression on B Cells
Human and murine B cells respond to a variety of mitogenic agents (Table 13), including certain lectins (carbohydrate-binding multimeric glycoproteins derived from plant and animal sources) that

Table 13
Polyclonal B-cell activators

Lipopolysaccharide (LPS)
Lipoprotein (LP)
Nocardia water-soluble mitogen
Polynucleotides
Purified protein derivative of tuberculin (PPD)
Dextran
Dextran sulfate
Pokeweed mitogen
Epstein-Barr virus (in humans)

bind preferentially to certain cells according to the carbohydrate groups displayed on the cell surface. Many of these compounds mimic the effects of specific antigens in that they dramatically stimulate B cells to proliferate and differentiate into Ig-secreting cells. Other agents (eg, lipopolysaccharides derived from bacterial cell walls, dextran sulfate, pokeweed mitogen, and purified protein derivative of tuberculin) are nonlectin mitogens and can also activate normal mouse B cells to differentiate into Ig-secreting cells.

B cells that bear IgM alone or IgM plus IgD secrete IgM and IgG antibody when treated with lipopolysaccharide (LPS). In contrast, B cells that bear only IgG will secrete only IgG and not IgM when treated with LPS. B cells from mice with the X-linked immunodeficiency (xid) defect, which is characterized by the absence of the Lyb5-bearing subset of B cells, respond poorly to mitogens, especially LPS. This finding is consistent with the observation that Lyb5$^+$ B cells are also responsible for the mitogenic response to anti-μ.

The Memory B Cell
When antigen and T-cell factors activate mature sIgM$^+$ sIgD$^+$ B cells to proliferate and increase their cell size, not all members of the B-cell clone differentiate into plasma cells. Some B cells lose sIgD and sIgM, acquire sIgG, and revert back to small lymphocytes. This subpopulation, called *memory B cells*, is long-lived and is more sensitive to subsequent triggering on reencounter with its specific antigen than are virgin B cells. Together with memory T cells, memory B cells are respon-

sible for the rapid kinetics, heightened response, and increased antibody affinity that occur on a second exposure to an antigen, the so-called secondary immune response. In general, sIgG$^+$ cells in the memory population are precursors for IgG-secreting cells, and sIgM$^+$ sIgG$^+$ memory cells produce both IgM- and IgG-secreting cells.

T-Independent and T-Dependent Antigens

As noted earlier, the resting B cell requires antigenic (or mitogenic) stimulation before it begins to secrete antibody. Some antigens activate B cells without T-cell help, but the majority of antigens require the assistance of T cells to trigger activation, differentiation, and proliferation.

T-Independent Antigens

There are two types of antigens that elicit B-cell response in the absence of any T-cell interaction and thus are termed T-independent (TI) antigens. Type 1 TI antigens induce antibody formation in both neonatal and adult B cells and activate B cells polyclonally. Type 2 TI antigens fail to activate B cells from neonatal mice, but they produce excellent antibody responses in adult B cells. Type 2 TI antigens generally are soluble polysaccharides and hapten conjugates of polysaccharides, such as Ficoll (a high–molecular-weight carbohydrate polymer), TNP-Ficoll (TNP is trinitrophenyl), and bacteria with a polysaccharide cell wall, such as *Brucella abortus* and LPS from *Escherichia coli* (Table 14). Type 2 TI antigens are not polyclonal activators. The ability of both type 1 and type 2 TI antigens to stimulate good responses in the congenitally athymic (nu/nu) mouse, which totally lacks T cells, indicates that TI antigen responses do not require the presence of T cells (Figure 30). Responsiveness to type 1 antigens distinguishes neonatal from adult B cells and B cells of xid mice from those of normal adult mice. Type 1, but not type 2, antigens can induce a

Figure 30
Model for T-independent (A) and T-dependent (B) antibody responses

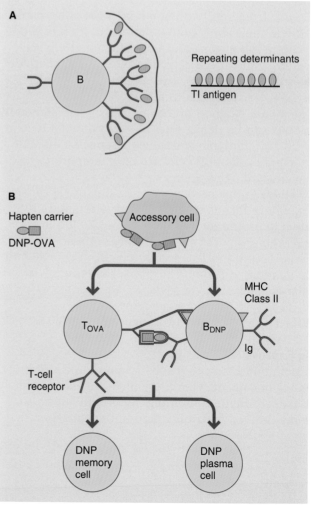

TI antigens typically contain repeating determinants. DNP-OVA is a typical TD antigen with the B cell recognizing the hapten DNP and the T cell recognizing the carrier protein ovalbumin (OVA).

response in xid mice, which have only Lyb5⁻ B cells, and in neonatal B cells. These results suggest that it is also the Lyb5⁻ B cells from normal adult mice that respond to type 1 but not to type 2 antigens. Although the double isotype-positive cell appears to account for most of the response, both sIgM⁺ sIgD⁻ and sIgM⁻ sIgD⁺ cells can respond to both types of TI antigens.

T-Dependent Antigens

Some immunocompetent B cells can complete their response to their specific antigens only in the presence of factors produced by T cells and macrophages. Many of these factors have now been identified and their genes isolated. A list of these factors and their functional effect on B cells is given in Table 15.

T-dependent (TD) antigens require the presence of T cells to elicit B-cell proliferation and differentiation to Ig-secreting cells (Figure 31). Primary responses to TD antigens, such as sheep red blood cells or keyhole limpet hemocyanin, can be obtained from most B-cell subsets. Thus, sIgM⁺ sIgD⁻, sIgM⁺ sIgD⁺, and sIgG⁺ subsets can respond to TD antigens in long-term adoptive transfer assays and in splenic focus assays. It is not clear, however, whether sIgD⁻ cells must acquire IgD before they can respond. The primary in vivo response of xid mice to TD antigens is much weaker than that of normal mice, although repeated immunizations improve the immune responses of xid B cells. However, compared with the isotype class and affinity of antibody produced by normal mice, antibody produced by xid mice has a marked deficiency of IgG2a and IgG3 subclasses.

Other B-Cell Surface Molecules

Although the hallmark of the mature B cell is the expression of membrane Ig, mature B cells also express many other membrane-surface components. These membrane-bound glycoproteins include receptors for complement components

Table 15
Factors that act on B cells

Factor	Other names	Molecular weight (in kd)	Functions
Interleukin-4	BSF-1 BCGF-1 BCDF-γ	18-20	Costimulator (with anti-IgM) of proliferation in resting B cells Increases volume of resting B cells Speeds entry into S phase Causes secretion of IgG1 and IgE by B cells Increases class II expression on resting B cells Increases Fc receptor for IgE on B cells
Interleukin-5	BCGF-II B15-TRF DL-TRF BCDF-μ	50	Costimulator (with dextran sulfate) of proliferation Stimulates IgG differentiation and IgG secretion Increases IL-2 receptors on B cells
Interleukin-1	LAF EP	17	Causes proliferation of B cells cultured at low density
Interleukin-2	TCGF	15-30	Low numbers of IL-2 receptors are present on B cells
Interferon-γ	–	40	Promotes Ig production by IL-2–stimulated B cells Causes B cells treated with anti-Ig to enter S phase Inhibits the actions of IL-4 on resting B cells
Interleukin-6	BSF-2 INF-β₂ HPGF	26	Promotes terminal differentiation of B cells into antibody-secreting cells

Figure 31
Serum antibody response to a thymus-dependent antigen

Serum
antibody
levels

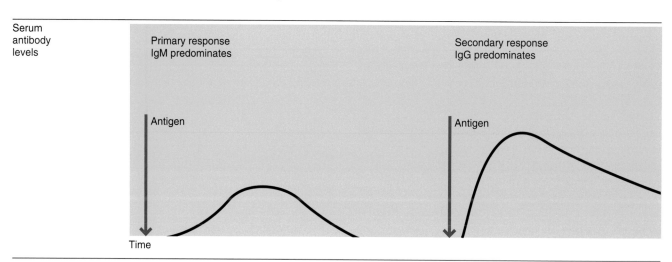

Primary response
IgM predominates

Antigen

Time

Secondary response
IgG predominates

Antigen

The primary response to a TD antigen is an IgM antibody. The
secondary response to repeat immunization occurs more
rapidly, is of higher magnitude, and is of the IgG class.

and for the Fc portion of IgG antibodies. An important type of surface molecule is the Ia or class II major histocompatibility complex (MHC) molecule. These molecules are glycoproteins encoded by the major histocompatibility complex (H-2 in the mouse, HLA in humans) and restrict T-cell recognition of antigen presented by accessory cells (see chapters 2 and 6). Class II molecules are required for collaboration between T and B cells in antigen-induced activation. B cells also express the products encoded in the H-2 K/D or HLA-A, B, and C regions (ie, the MHC class I antigens) and a number of so-called differentiation antigens.

The development of a large panel of monoclonal antibodies (mAb) that recognize surface markers on B cells has made it possible to study B-cell development and function at discrete stages of development. The most common surface markers in murine B-lineage precursor cells are listed in Table 16, grouped according to their distribution on cell types, and are described on the following pages. Most membrane molecules (eg, Lyb2 and Ly5) involved in the control of pre–B-cell development and function are also found on B cells at other stages of development, as well as on other cell lines. Although none of these markers is strictly stage-specific, antibodies against some of them have been extremely useful in defining precursors of mature B cells by depletion and enrichment of B-cell populations.

Table 16
B-cell surface markers

Marker*	Pre-B and B cells	T cells	Other hematopoietic cells
Group I			
Lyb2	Yes	No	No
Lyb5/3	Yes†	No	No
BP-1	Yes	No	No
Group II			
ThB	Yes	Yes	No
Ly1	Yes	Yes	No
IL-2R	Yes	Yes	No
TdT	Yes	Yes	No
Group III			
Ly5	Yes (220 kd)	Yes (200 kd)	Yes
Qa-2	Yes	Yes	Yes
Class II molecules	Yes	Yes‡	Yes
H-2 K/D	Yes	Yes	Yes
Mac-1	Yes	No	Yes (CR1)
Ly-17 (FcR)	Yes	Yes	Yes
LFA-1	Yes	Yes	Yes

*Markers are grouped according to their presence on B-lineage cells only (Group I), both B- and T-lineage cells (Group II), and a broader distribution on a number of other hematopoietic cells (Group III).
†Lyb5/3 is absent in xid mice.
‡Class II molecules are present on human T cells, but Ia antigens are not on murine T cells.

Ly5 Family of Glycoproteins

Many monoclonal antibodies have been generated to murine glycoproteins encoded by the Ly5 gene in the rat. This family of glycoproteins has been demonstrated on all hematopoietic cells, including T and B cells. Although a single structural gene encodes this family of glycoproteins, molecular size varies according to differential RNA processes in different tissues. B cells preferentially express the largest glycoproteins of this family (220 kd), T cells express somewhat smaller (200 kd) macromolecules, and myeloid cells express an intermediate-sized glycoprotein (205 kd). Several mAb to the Ly5 glycoprotein family recognize distinct epitopes on this macromolecule. Virtually all mature B cells, as well as precursor cells that develop rapidly into mature sIg⁺ B cells in culture, express the Ly5 molecule. The majority of Ly5⁺ cells in fetal liver and adult bone marrow have rearranged the Ig heavy chain gene. In contrast, most plasma cells are Ly5⁻. Pre-B cells and functional precursors of B cells in embryos younger than 16 days can be Ly5⁻. Recently, antibody to a Ly5 marker has been used to enrich a small fraction of pre-B cells in bone marrow, which are Ly5⁻ and which appear to be the very earliest renewable stem-cell precursors of the pre-B cell.

Surface Class II Molecules

Immature IgM⁺ B cells in the liver, bone marrow, and spleen of fetal and neonatal mice bear few or no class II molecules. By 2 weeks of age, the majority of B cells are class II-positive. Newly formed B cells in bone marrow appear to become class II-positive sometime after the acquisition of surface IgM and before the expression of surface IgD. Approximately one third of sIg⁻ Ly5⁺ cells are class II-positive. Although B-cell development in humans is similar to that in mice, one difference is that class II molecules in humans are expressed on both pre-B and B cells. Recent examination of a large panel of Abelson virus-transformed pre–B-cell murine tumor lines suggests, however, that the acquisition of surface class II molecules may not always follow the acquisition of sIg and that B-cell differentiation may branch, rather than follow a linear pathway. Recently, a factor secreted by T cells called B-cell stimulatory factor 1 or interleukin-4 (IL-4) was shown to increase the density of class II molecules expressed on B cells (see also chapter 7).

Lyb2

The Lyb2 differentiation marker is expressed exclusively on pre-B and mature B cells. It is a 45-kd monomeric glycoprotein that has two alleles. Antibody to Lyb2 inhibits the antibody response to a T-dependent antigen. It also mimics the effect of IL-4 and may be closely associated with, although not identical to, the receptor for IL-4.

Lyb5

Lyb5$^-$ cells appear earlier in development than do Lyb5$^+$ cells. In general, Lyb5$^-$ cells are easily tolerized, bear large amounts of sIgM, and cannot receive secondary signals from T cells and accessory cells. Lyb5$^+$ cells, on the other hand, are mature IgM$^+$ IgD$^+$ cells, are difficult to tolerize, can be activated by anti-Ig and type 2 TI antigens, and can interact with T cells and T-cell factors. Lyb5$^+$ B cells are absent in mice with the xid immune defect. Table 17 summarizes the properties of Lyb5 B-cell subsets.

LFA-1

LFA-1 belongs to the family of lymphocyte function-associated (LFA) antigens that mediate leukocyte adhesion and may serve to strengthen weak bonds between immune cells. This antigen is composed of a unique α chain and β chain common among members of the family (which, in addition to LFA-1, includes Mac-1 and p155/95). Some patients have been identified who are unable to make the β chain and thus do not have surface LFA-1. These individuals suffer from recurrent infections (see chapter 8).

Fc Receptor

Normal pre-B cells and all mature B cells bind immunoglobulin molecules by a receptor specific for the Fc portion of immunoglobulin, probably via a site in the C_H3 domain. Fc receptors (FcR) have also been described on T cells, macrophages, and human and rabbit B lymphocytes. Bone marrow stem cells and plasma cells are FcR-negative. While sIgM appears to be the earliest marker on murine B cells, FcR is acquired soon thereafter, followed by class II antigens, sIgD, and complement receptors (CR). Associations between FcR, sIg, MHC antigens, and CR have been postulated to occur at the cell surface and may be important in the activation or paralysis of the B cell. For example, because Fc binding produces a dominant inhibitory signal, anti-Ig antibodies can cause B-cell proliferation only if Fc binding is blocked.

Table 17
Summary of functional properties of Lyb5$^+$ and Lyb5$^-$ B-cell subsets

Lyb5$^-$ B cells	Lyb5$^+$ B cells
Appear early in development	Appear later in development
Easy to tolerize	Difficult to tolerize
Bear high sIgM	Bear low sIgM, high sIgD
Fail to respond to anti-IgM	Good mitogenic response to anti-IgM
Good response to type 1 TI antigen	–
Poor response to type 2 TI antigen	Good response to type 2 TI antigen
Can interact with T cells and T-cell factors in an MHC-restricted fashion	Can interact with T cells and T-cell factors in an MHC-unrestricted fashion
Present in xid mice	Absent in xid mice

Complement Receptor

Complement receptors have been identified on B cells from humans, guinea pigs, rabbits, and mice. However, not all B cells are CR-positive. There are at least two types of complement receptors, CR1 and CR2, for which the genes have been cloned. CR1 is expressed on B cells and erythrocytes and binds C3b, C4, and C5. CR2 is found only on B cells and binds C3d and C3b. In humans, CR2 is also the receptor for the Epstein-Barr virus. Complement receptors are expressed concomitantly with IgD and thus seem to characterize the mature immunocompetent B-cell population. Some memory cells and all plasma cells lose complement receptors. The function of these receptors remains a mystery, but CRs may facilitate cell interaction and cell cooperation and focus antigen more efficiently on the membrane. (See chapter 9 for a detailed discussion of complement.)

Ly1

Ly1, which originally was thought to be expressed only on T cells, is also expressed on a subset of B cells that may originate outside the bone marrow. Ly1-positive B cells are particularly prevalent in the peritoneal cavity. B cells that bear the Ly1 marker have a propensity to secrete autoantibodies and have been implicated in autoreactivity (see chapter 12).

Conclusion

The B lymphocyte is a critical player in the immune response. It contributes antibodies, the final effector mechanism for mounting the humoral immune response. In most species, the B cell originates from the bone marrow, but it must progress through a complicated developmental pathway of growth and differentiation before it reaches the antibody-secretion stage. B cells respond to factors produced by other immunocompetent cells, T cells, and macrophages. It is this interaction with other cells and products that results in activation, growth, and differentiation of B cells. Among the most important of these factors are the IL-4, IL-5, and IL-6 cytokines.

Selected Readings

Coffman RL, Seymour BWP, Lebman DA, Hiraki DD, Christiansen JA, Shrader B, Cherwinski HM, Savelkoul HFJ, Finkelman FD, Bond MW, Mosmann TR. The role of helper T-cell products in mouse B-cell differentiation and isotype regulation. **Immunol Rev.** 1988;102:5-28.

Kishimoto T, Hirano T. Molecular regulation of B-lymphocyte response. **Annu Rev Immunol.** 1988;6:485-512.

Miller JFAP, Mitchell GF. Cell-to-cell interaction in the immune response. I. Hemolysin-forming cells in neonatally thymectomized mice reconstituted with thymus or thoracic duct lymphocytes. **J Exp Med.** 1968;128:801-837.

Ovary Z, Benacerraf B. Immunological specificity of the secondary response with dinitrophenylated proteins. **Proc Soc Exp Biol Med.** 1963;114:72-76.

Paul WE, Ohara J. B-cell stimulatory factor-1/interleukin 4. **Annu Rev Immunol.** 1987;5:429-459.

Antigen Processing and Presentation

6

Introduction

Antigen presentation is the term used to describe the essential cellular and biochemical events that activate CD4 and CD8 T cells after an accessory or antigen-presenting cell (APC) binds an antigen. Antigen presented with protein molecules encoded by the major histocompatibility gene complex (MHC) must be recognized on the surface of the APC and bound by the T cells' antigen receptors before the T cells can be activated. However, CD4 and CD8 T cells recognize antigen differently. CD4 T cells recognize antigens presented with MHC class II molecules, also known as the *I-region–associated* or *Ia* molecules; the CD8 T cells recognize antigens presented with MHC class I molecules. CD8 T cells, which recognize MHC class I molecules, kill the target cells that present antigens, usually viral components. CD4 T cells generally express helper function and include the T cells that respond in delayed hypersensitivity, activate macrophages, and interact with B cells. Stimulation of the CD4 T cells is critical because these cells produce lymphokines with potent biological activities. This chapter primarily reviews antigen presentation to CD4 T cells.

Antigen Presentation to CD4 T Cells

The requirements for presentation have been studied best in culture where the reactivity of CD4 T cells to antigen is critically controlled. T cells neither bind protein antigen molecules in free solution nor are triggered by them. To be stimulated, CD4 T cells must attach to APCs bearing MHC class II molecules. Such APCs must take up the protein antigen and, in most cases, biochemically process the antigen, changing it in such a way that it can interact with MHC class II molecules. The CD4 T cells recognize the bimolecular complex of processed antigen linked to MHC class II molecules on the surface of the APC. A clear example of this recognition process can be demonstrated by exploring how T cells recognize antigen. T cells from a person immune to a microorganism will not bind to it, but the same T cells will bind to a macrophage that has ingested the microorganism. Historically, several lines of evidence indicate the requirements for an APC and a processing event in the immune response to proteins. For example, serum protein antigens such as albumin or gamma globulin are weakly immunogenic; however, their aggregation or polymerization results in their enhanced uptake by macrophages, which dramatically increases their immunogenicity. If macrophages containing a protein antigen are transferred from one syngeneic (genetically identical) person into another, the second person's response to the antigen is strong. This response to macrophage-associated antigens contrasts with the response to soluble antigen (antigen floating free in a solution and not associated with an APC), which is usually very weak and can even result in transitory tolerance.

Other important observations relate to the immune response to globular proteins by B cells or T cells. Usually, the antibody response to the protein antigen is directed to its conformational determinants, that is, to determinants displayed on the protein in its natural state. In its natural state, the molecule is folded, thus reducing the molecular distance between segments of the molecule; these juxtaposed segments constitute the antigenic determinant. These observations, therefore, indicate that most B-cell clones reactive to a protein antigen were selected before the unfolding or chemical alteration of the protein. In contrast, T cells recognize either denatured or native protein molecules that have been biochemically processed by the host. Thus, denatured proteins can trigger the delayed hypersensitivity reaction despite primary immunization with the antigen in its native state. The explanation for these observations has now become apparent (see discussion of the effects of antigen presentation beginning on page 76).

Steps in Antigen Presentation
APC presentation of antigen to CD4 T cells involves three steps:
- Uptake of the protein antigen.
- Biochemical processing of the antigen and its association with MHC class II molecules.
- Expression of molecules that stimulate the growth and differentiation of the CD4 T cells.

Uptake of the antigen: Protein uptake varies among the APCs. The macrophage takes up many microorganisms by direct contact through surface interactions that are not entirely defined. Some macrophage surface molecules are receptors for carbohydrates, such as the mannose receptor that binds to glycoproteins containing terminal mannose or fucose. Other surface structures of the macrophage bind to denatured proteins. The macrophage also has receptors for the immunoglobulin Fc fragment and for C3, which enable the macrophage to take up opsonized proteins. Thus, macrophages have the capability of binding to a wide range of molecules. In contrast, B cells preferentially take up antigens that bind selectively to specific immunoglobulin receptors (ie, antigens bind to B cells from a particular clone).

Antigen processing: Studies with microorganisms and with small globular proteins have defined the handling and intracellular processing stage. Protein antigen processing requires that the macrophage internalize the proteins in acidic intracellular vesicles. After processing, the immunogenic material appears on the plasma membrane associated with MHC class II molecules (Figure 32). The period of time from the initial binding to the surface of the macrophage to the internalization and final appearance of the active immunogenic structure on the cell surface is short, varying from 15 to 60 minutes. After this time, the macrophages can be lightly fixed with paraformaldehyde and still present the surface immunogen intact. Thus, judicious fixation will not destroy the immunogen.

With a defined globular protein, the meaning of processing can be explained biochemically. First, it is noteworthy that the number of epitopes recognized on a protein is limited. The nature of immunodominant epitopes (the epitopes recognized by the majority of T cells) varies according to the MHC haplotype to which the antigen binds.

Purified T cells, that is, either T-cell clones or hybridomas (T-cell hybridomas are made by cellular hybridization in which a thymoma is fused to activated T cells) derived from such clones, recognize linear sequences of amino acids either in a denatured protein or as small peptides. Some clones may recognize only whole peptides, while others may recognize a peptide sequence in a continuous sequence of amino acids. When synthetic peptides are used, usually 10 to 12 amino acids are required for T-cell recognition. Globular proteins, therefore, need to be unfolded and/or partially catabolized to generate the peptide sequences recognized by the CD4 T cell.

The requirements of processing are explained by the affinity of the processed peptide for MHC class II molecules. Isolated MHC class II molecules in free solution bind to peptides with affinity constants that are about 10^{-6} M. There is a strong relationship between the binding strength of a peptide for an MHC class II molecule produced by a given allele and the peptide's immunogenicity tested in vivo. For a given haplotype, those peptides that are immunogenic bind strongly to the MHC class II molecule, while the weakly immunogenic peptides bind much less strongly and consequently bind fewer molecules. These results imply that one important mechanism that determines if a T-cell response is made to a particular antigen is whether that antigen contains peptides or amino acid sequences capable of interacting with the MHC class II molecule. The T-cell receptor apparently interacts with both the MHC class II molecules and with some side chains of the amino acid residues of the antigenic peptide.

The initial observations about immune response (Ir) genes (genes that control immune response to specific antigens) were essential for our understanding of T-cell recognition of protein. Immune response genes were first defined by McDevitt and Benacerraf as the genes controlling the response to thymus-dependent antigens. Thymus-dependent antigens include proteins and peptides but not polysaccharides. The Ir genes were found in studies of synthetic peptides of limited heterogeneity and natural proteins administered in

Figure 32
Antigen presentation by B cells

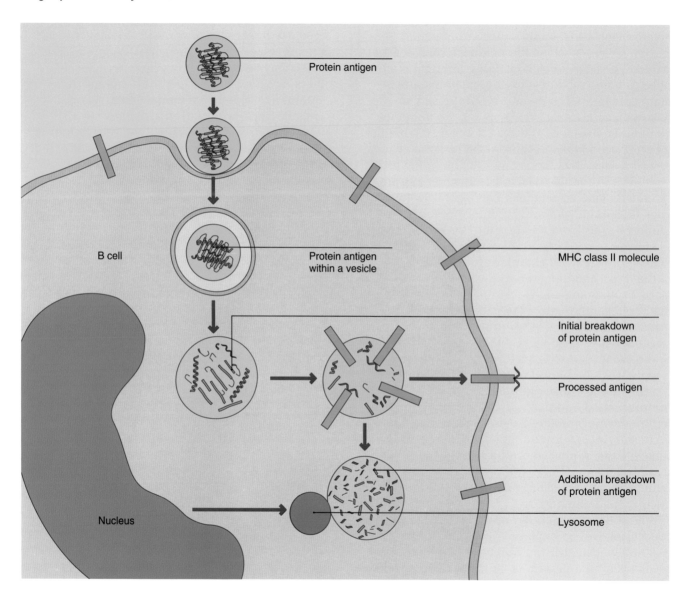

Protein antigen

B cell

Protein antigen
within a vesicle

MHC class II molecule

Initial breakdown
of protein antigen

Processed antigen

Additional breakdown
of protein antigen

Nucleus

Lysosome

limited amounts. Later the Ir genes were found to encode the MHC class II molecules. The in vivo action of Ir gene products, the MHC class II molecules, can now be best explained by their binding to peptides. Finally, it is noteworthy that isolated MHC class II molecules inserted in planar lipid membranes can bind a peptide antigen and trigger production of T-cell hybridomas. A hybridoma secretes IL-2 when the T-cell receptor it bears is engaged by processed antigen bound to an MHC class II molecule. (Hybridomas, however, do not require cofactors for growth.)

The binding of MHC class II molecules to peptides implies that the MHC class II molecules have a combining site with the power to discriminate among different peptides. A recent analysis of the crystal structure of an MHC class I molecule indicated that part of the first and second domains of the molecule's heavy chain forms a groove into which peptides can bind. The groove is formed by two α-helices that sit on a platform composed of a β-pleated sheet. The combining site is on the outermost part of the molecule capable of directly facing the T cell. Most of the amino acid residues responsible for the allelic polymorphism of the MHC class I molecule are found in this structure, either in the β-pleated sheet or in the α-helices. Some of the amino acid residues contact the peptide antigen in a process necessary for binding. The existence of a similar structure has been postulated for the MHC class II molecule (Figure 33).

How many different antigenic peptides bind to one MHC class II molecule? At any one time, only a single immunogenic peptide can bind to an MHC molecule. Many different peptides, however, can interact with that single binding site, and unlabeled peptides can compete with radioactive peptides to bind to a given MHC class II molecule. The finding that many different peptides can compete for a single binding site indicates that all these peptides can meet the conditions required for binding. Each peptide shares the property of being presented by the given MHC class II molecule. Attempts are being made to determine the common motif of peptides that bind to a given allele. For some MHC class II molecules, the presence of charged residues appears to be key, while for other MHC class II molecules, a combination of hydrophobic and hydrophilic residues in a particular sequence appears to be involved.

Among the peptides that bind to an MHC class II molecule are those derived from the normal catabolism of autologous proteins. For example, a self-peptide from mouse lysozyme competes effectively with a foreign peptide for presentation. Some self-antigens are associated with MHC class II molecules of macrophages in vivo. These observations raise several important issues, among them the question of whether self-antigens can be presented during autoimmune reactions. The binding of self-antigens raises the possibility of their competition with foreign antigens. Competition among antigens does occur, as is shown by results of concomitant immunizations with two strong immunogens: the response to one will be depressed. This phenomenon can also be observed in vitro when testing two unrelated antigens at the same time. It is likely that immunization overrides the possible competition from self-antigens by increasing the mass of effective immunogen available to the APC. Indeed, effective immunization requires aggregation of antigenic molecules (by incorporation in alum precipitates or in lipid droplets, for example) to increase the uptake of antigenic molecules by the macrophages.

The APCs that process proteins and peptides and present them to CD4 T cells include the monocytes and macrophages (cells from the mononuclear phagocyte system), B cells, and Langerhans dendritic cells. All these cells express MHC class II molecules that are essential for antigen presentation. Indeed, antibodies to MHC class II molecules inhibit antigen presentation. Furthermore, the extent of T-cell activation relates directly to the number of MHC class II molecules on the membranes of the APCs, as well as on the amount of antigen taken up.

Figure 33
The combining site of an MHC class II molecule

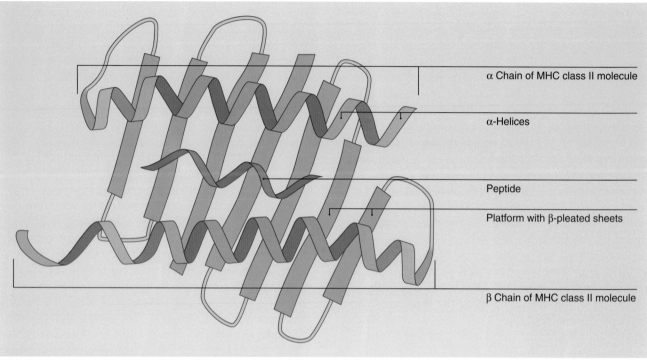

α Chain of MHC class II molecule

α-Helices

Peptide

Platform with β-pleated sheets

β Chain of MHC class II molecule

Adapted with permission from Bjorkman PJ, Saper MA, Samraoui B, Bennett WS, Strominger JL, Wiley DC. Structure of the human class I histocompatibility antigen, HLA-A2. *Nature.* 1987;329:506-512, © 1987 Macmillan Magazines Ltd.

The quantity of MHC class II molecules on monocytes and macrophages varies. Interferon gamma (IFN-γ), released by activated T cells during antigen presentation, binds to specific receptors on young mononuclear phagocytes and induces several changes, prominently the increased expression of MHC class II molecules. Thus, a strong immunogen introduced in vivo stimulates the appearance within a few hours of macrophages bearing large numbers of MHC class II molecules. In comparison, B cells constitutively express MHC class II molecules. Langerhans dendritic cells express large numbers of MHC class II molecules and are abundant in the epidermis and in T-cell–dependent lymphoid tissue.

Effects of Antigen Presentation
The effects of antigen presentation on both the APC and the T cell are reciprocal, and both cells are profoundly affected. The resting T cell binds firmly to the plasma membrane of the antigen-bearing APC and thereby causes changes in both. If the APC is a macrophage, it releases several cytokines, including interleukin-1 (IL-1) and tumor necrosis factor (TNF). IL-1 promotes T-cell activation, and both IL-1 and TNF have inflammatory properties. If the APC is a B cell, it will respond to other T-cell–secreted lymphokines and replicate and differentiate to an antibody-producing cell. Concurrent with changes in the APC, changes are also occurring in the T cell. After several hours, the T cell starts synthesizing DNA, secreting lymphokines, and expressing receptors for various cytokines. Because T cells both secrete IL-2 and express receptors for IL-2, IL-2 acts as an auto-

Figure 34
Course of *Listeria* infection

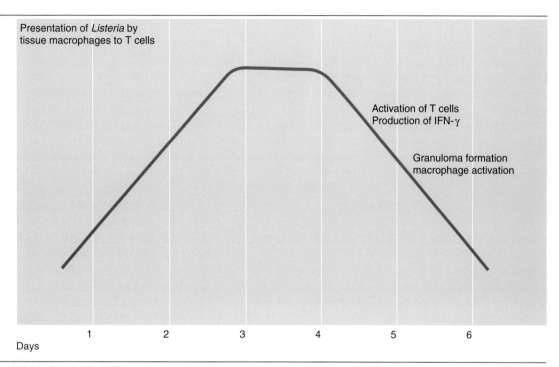

Growth of *Listeria*

Presentation of *Listeria* by tissue macrophages to T cells

Activation of T cells
Production of IFN-γ

Granuloma formation
macrophage activation

| 1 | 2 | 3 | 4 | 5 | 6 |

Days

Bacteria grow exponentially during the first 72 hours as *Listeria* antigens are presented to T cells. Activation of T cells causes secretion of interferon gamma, activation of macrophages, and inhibition of bacterial growth.

crine regulatory hormone and causes the cells to proliferate and become activated. In addition, other T cells secrete other lymphokines, including IFN-γ, which causes increased expression of MHC class II molecules on macrophages, and IL-4, which causes B cells to differentiate.

Activated macrophages: Activated macrophages are macrophages with increased metabolic activity and a heightened capacity to eliminate intracellular pathogens and tumors. Two classes of substances can increase the macrophages' microbicidal-tumoricidal effects: products of oxygen metabolism and cytotoxic factors such as TNF. Activation of macrophages and consequent resistance to many microorganisms also depend on the

response to IFN-γ, which is released by activated CD4 T cells following antigen presentation. IFN-γ not only activates macrophages but induces in nonlymphoid cells an antiviral response typical of all interferons.

The activated macrophage is essential for resistance to a range of intracellular pathogenic bacteria that includes *Mycobacterium tuberculosis* and *Listeria monocytogenes*. For example, the following scenario appears to occur during infection with *Listeria monocytogenes* in the mouse, an excellent experimental model that has yielded many insights (Figure 34). First, macrophages capture *Listeria* organisms and present some *Listeria* antigens to both CD4 and CD8 T cells, which rapidly proliferate and release IFN-γ. The IFN-γ attracts young monocytes that become activated and form a granuloma around the bacterial foci, and the immune granuloma curbs the growth of *Listeria*. Within 72 to 96 hours, *Listeria* growth diminishes and completely stops a day or two later (Figure 34). However, if IFN-γ is neutralized by an IFN-γ–specific monoclonal antibody, macrophage activation stops and *Listeria* grows uncontrolled. In this case, a single lymphokine, IFN-γ, is critical for activation of the macrophage. These interactions can be readily reproduced in culture.

Activation of other cells: An important feature of IFN-γ is that it also induces MHC class II molecules in cells other than macrophages, including connective tissue cells and endothelial and epithelial cells. This raises the possibility that this aberrant MHC class II expression, induced and maintained by prolonged immune stimulation, could stimulate the presentation of self-antigens to which no natural tolerance exists and could therefore cause autoimmunity. T cells directed to an autoantigen, for example a thyroid antigen, could be dormant in tissues because thyroid cells do not express MHC class II molecules. A chronic infection with prolonged secretion of IFN-γ could induce expression of MHC class II molecules in thyroid tissue and with it the capacity of the tissue to process and present self-antigens.

Antibody formation: Antibody formation requires antigen presentation, but in this case the B cell performs the antigen-presenting function. The surface-bound immunoglobulin molecules of the B cells bind the antigens. The B cells internalize and process these antigens, resulting in antigen fragments bound to MHC class II molecules on the surface of these cells (Figure 35). The CD4 T cells recognize the complex of antigen and MHC

class II molecules, triggering the reciprocal process of cell activation. The interaction between B and T cells illustrates the differences in antigen recognition between an antibody and a T-cell receptor. The immunoglobulin on a B cell binds directly to a circulating protein antigen in its native state. The antigen bound to surface immunoglobulin is then internalized and processed, and a fragment of the antigen associated with MHC class II molecules is presented to CD4 T cells. The T cells recognize the complex of fragments of antigen and MHC class II molecules and secrete several lymphokines, including IL-4, IL-5, and IL-6. These lymphokines appear to drive the growth and differentiation of B cells. The B cell eventually expands into clones that secrete soluble immunoglobulin molecules (antibodies) that will bind, as the initial B cell did, to the protein antigen in its native state.

Costimulators
During antigen presentation, the T cells recognize the peptide MHC class II complex, but that alone may not be sufficient to trigger the T cell to replicate. The T cell must interact with a second molecule that initiates the activation sequence. Among these costimulants is IL-1, which is secreted by activated macrophages. The IL-1 proteins are two molecules of about 17 000 daltons, termed *IL-1α* and *IL-1β*, that are encoded by two different genes with some similar nucleotide sequences. Both IL-1α and IL-1β have a wide range of biologic activities. In general, IL-1 has long-range hormonal effects responsible for some of the characteristic acute-phase responses to microbial infection. IL-1 produces fever by acting on the hypothalamus; induces liver cells to produce fibrinogen, complement components, and haptoglobin; and causes muscle wasting and leukocytosis.

How is IL-1 expressed on APCs? It is not constitutively expressed by the APC but is produced only after interaction of the APCs with antigens and T cells. The lipopolysaccharide molecules of microorganisms, particularly gram-negative bacteria, stimulate expression of IL-1. It is also produced in two ways when T cells interact with

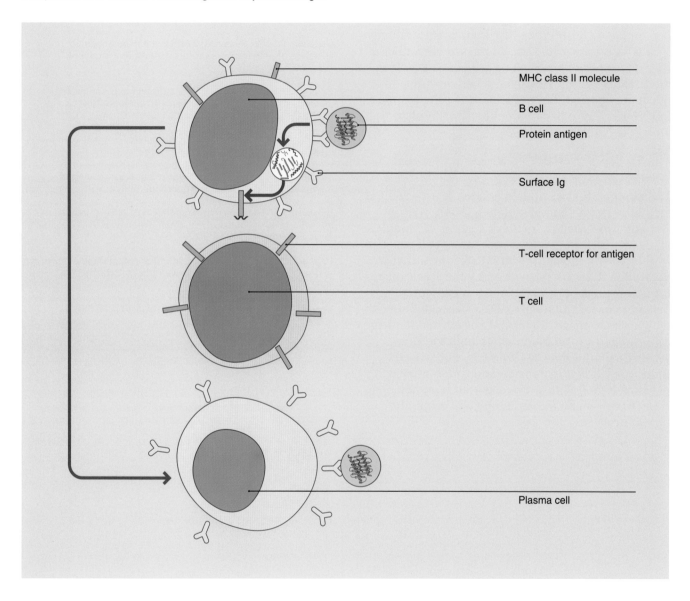

MHC class II molecule

B cell

Protein antigen

Surface Ig

T-cell receptor for antigen

T cell

Plasma cell

the macrophage or the B cell during antigen presentation, either by direct contact with the T cells or following the release of lymphokines. Tumor necrosis factor, or lymphotoxin, stimulates macrophages to produce IL-1. In turn, IL-1 induces T cells to produce IL-2 receptors and secrete IL-2. IL-1 also causes spontaneous growth of T cells in the thymus glands. However, it has recently become apparent that not all CD4 T cells respond to IL-1 and that other unidentified costimulator molecules are required.

Conclusion

The presentation of protein antigen is an essential step in selecting and stimulating CD4 T cells. Antigen presentation involves a series of complex steps in which the antigen-presenting cell processes the protein molecule and creates the antigenic determinant that is recognized by the T-cell receptor of a cloned CD4 T cell. Antigen presentation occurs in association with CD4 T-cell interactions with a macrophage, B cell, or Langerhans dendritic cell. Antigen presentation alters both the presenting cell and the CD4 T cell. The CD4 T cell undergoes clonal expansion and differentiates to produce lymphokines. The secreted lymphokines activate cell-mediated immunity and antibody formation.

Selected Readings

Benacerraf B, McDevitt HO. Histocompatibility-linked immune response genes. **Science**. 1972;175:273-279.

Benjamin DC, Berzofsky JA, East IJ, et al. The antigenic structure of proteins: a reappraisal. **Annu Rev Immunol**. 1984;2:67-101.

Buus S, Sette A, Grey HM. The interaction between protein-derived immunogenic peptides and Ia. **Immunol Rev**. 1987;98:115-141.

McDevitt HO, Benacerraf B. Genetic control of specific immune responses. **Adv Immunol**. 1969;11:31-74.

Mengle-Gaw L, McDevitt HO. Genetics and expression of murine Ia antigens. **Annu Rev Immunol**. 1985;3:367-396.

Schwartz RH. T-lymphocyte recognition of antigen in association with gene products of the major histocompatibility complex. **Annu Rev Immunol**. 1985;3:237-262.

Unanue ER, Allen PM. The basis for the immunoregulatory role of macrophages and other accessory cells. **Science**. 1987;236:551-557.

Unanue ER, Cerottini JC. Antigen presentation. **FASEB J.** 1989;3:2496-2502.

Introduction

The successful development of an immune response depends upon the efficient communication between macrophages and T and B lymphocytes. This communication is accomplished either directly through cell-cell contact or indirectly through the action of soluble cell products known as *cytokines*, which regulate nearly all phases of the immune response. Cytokines that participate in response induction are called *afferent cytokines*, and those that promote immune effector functions are known as *efferent cytokines*. Many of these molecules directly modulate the functional activities of immune cells, thereby promoting important immune processes such as antigen presentation and T-cell activation. Some cytokines can function as growth factors and thereby drive immune responses by inducing the proliferation of specific cell populations. Several cytokines can induce or increase the production of other cytokines, often in a reciprocal manner, and thus establish a mechanism of response amplification. Still other cytokines promote immune effector mechanisms that enhance host resistance to microbial pathogens and tumors or induce pathologic processes in the case of autoimmune reactions.

In the past, cytokines were classified by their cell of origin or by their suspected functional roles. Based on this convention, cytokines produced by lymphocytes became known as *lymphokines*, while those produced by monocytes and macrophages were called *monokines*. However, difficulties were encountered when attempts were made to identify cytokines solely on the basis of their functional activities. The nomenclature system based on function ultimately proved to be ineffective because (1) individual cytokines were found to be pleotropic (ie, they could induce different biologic responses in a wide range of target cell populations), and (2) different cytokines were found to induce identical functional activities in the same target cell population. A new nomenclature system, adopted in 1979, was based on the ability of cytokines to transfer information between leukocytes of distinct origins. Hence, with a few exceptions, specific cytokines are now referred to as *interleukins* and are designated as *IL-n*, where *n* is a number that currently ranges from 1 to 7.

Recently, largely through the use of state-of-the-art technologies, it has been possible to establish the molecular identities of many cytokines. Table 18 summarizes the pertinent characteristics of 11 distinct members of the cytokine family. In general, these components are proteins of modest molecular masses (between 10 and 50 kd) and have relatively simple structures (most consist of a single polypeptide chain). All are secreted in exceedingly low concentrations (on the order of 1 to 100 pg/mL), and most have been documented to produce their biologic effects by interacting with specific receptors at the surface of their target cells. The binding affinities (Ka) of these receptors are high (Ka = 10^9–10^{12} M^1), thereby permitting the induction of cellular responses at physiologic ligand concentrations. Thus, in many respects, cytokines can be considered the polypeptide hormones of the immune system.

The purpose of this chapter is to review the biology and biochemistry of three members of the cytokine family: IL-1, IL-2, and interferon gamma (IFN-γ). These components were chosen not only because they exemplify many of the different characteristics of the entire cytokine family, but also because their combined actions form an amplification mechanism that drives the immune response.

Interleukin-1

Historical Perspectives

The history of IL-1 dates back to 1948, when a soluble factor (termed *endogenous pyrogen*) was observed that produced a febrile response in rabbits. Twenty-four years later, another functional activity was detected in culture supernatants of adherent human or murine leukocytes that acted in concert with mitogenic lectins to stimulate

Table 18
Structural and functional characteristics of representative cytokines

Cytokine	Alternative designation	Cellular sources	Physiochemical properties	Functional activities	Human/murine specificity
IL-1α IL-1β	Endogenous pyrogen (EP) Lymphocyte-activating factor (LAF) Thymocyte-activating factor (TAF) Mitogenic protein (MP) Osteoclast-activating factor (OAF) Mononuclear cell factor (MCF)	Monocytes/macrophages Natural killer cells B cells T cells Endothelial cells Epithelial cells Fibroblasts Astrocytes Keratinocytes	Both forms share 20% sequence homology, are produced as a 32-kd intra-cellular pre-cursor, are released as soluble 32-kd full-length molecules or 17-kd mature molecules, and are nonglyco-sylated IL-1α appears as membrane IL-1 IL-1α pI = 5.0 IL-1β pI = 7.0	T-cell activation Induces IL-2 and IL-2 receptor expression Promotes B-cell growth and differentiation ↑ Cytocidal activities of CTL, NK, and macrophages Induces fever ↑ Acute-phase reactants ↑ Fibroblast growth ↑ Bone resorption	None
IL-2	T-cell growth factor (TCGF) T-cell–replacing factor (TRF) Killer helper factor	CD4+ and CD8+ T cells (murine T$_{H1}$) Immunocompetent thymocytes	Murine 25 kd Human 15.5 kd	Proliferation of T cells Proliferation of thymocytes Costimulates B-cell differentiation ↑ Lymphokine production by T cells ↑ CTL activity ↑ NK activity ↑ LAK cell activity	One way: human IL-2 can activate murine cells but not vice versa
IL-3	Mast cell growth factor (MCGF) Multiple colony-stimulating factor (multiple CSF) Burst-promoting activity (BPA) P-cell–stimulating factor	T cells (murine T$_{H1}$ + T$_{H2}$)	Murine 23 kd Human 23-25 kd Glycosylated	Supports growth of mast cells Supports growth and differentiation of multipotential stem cells and progeni-tors of monocytes, granulocytes, and erythroid and megakeryocyte lineages	Strict

Table 18
Structural and functional characteristics of representative cytokines (continued)

Cytokine	Alternative designation	Cellular sources	Physiochemical properties	Functional activities	Human/murine specificity
IL-4	B-cell–stimulating factor-1 (BSF-1) B-cell growth factor (BCGF) T-cell growth factor-2	T cells (murine T$_{H1}$)	Murine 15-20 kd Human 20 kd Glycosylated	Costimulates B-cell proliferation ↑ Proliferation of T cells and thymocytes ↑ Murine B-cell Ia antigens ↑ IgG1 and IgE production by murine B cells ↑ IgE receptors on B cells ↓ IgG2a production Activates macrophage cytocidal activity Induces class II molecules on macrophages	Strict
IL-5	B-cell growth factor II (BCGF-II) IgA-enhancing factor (IgA-EF) T-cell–replacing factor (TRF) Eosinophil colony-stimulating factor (EO-CSF)	T cells (murine T$_{H2}$)	Disulfide-bonded homodimer Murine 46-60 kd Human 30-60 kd Glycosylated	Costimulates B-cell growth ↑ IL-2 receptors on B cells ↑ IgA secretion by B cells Induces differentiation of eosinophils	None
IL-6	IFN-β_2 Hybridoma growth factor (HGF) B-cell stimulatory factor-2 (BSF-2) 26-kd protein Plasmacytoma growth factor	Mononuclear phagocytes Fibroblasts T cells (murine T$_{H2}$)	Murine 22-29 kd Human 19-34 kd Glycosylated	B-cell differentiation Stimulation of IgG secretion Induces growth of plasmacytomas Activates T cells Costimulates thymo-cyte proliferation Induces production of acute-phase reactants in hepatocytes	None

Table 18
Structural and functional characteristics of representative cytokines (continued)

Cytokine	Alternative designation	Cellular sources	Physiochemical properties	Functional activities	Human/murine specificity
IFN-γ	Macrophage-activating factor (MAF)	T cells (murine T_{H1}) Natural killer cells	Noncovalent homodimer Murine 40-50 kd Human 40-50 kd Glycosylated	↑ Ia/DR on mononuclear phagocytes and many other cells Activates nonspecific tumorcidal and microbicidal activities in macrophages ↑ Fcγ receptors on macrophages ↑ TNF/LT production ↑ Natural killer cell activity ↑ IgG2a production in murine B cells ↓ IgG1, IgE production in murine cells ↑ Antiviral activity ↑ Antiproliferative activity	Strict
Tumor necrosis factor-α (TNF-α)	Cachectin	Mononuclear phagocytes T cells (murine $T_{H1} + T_{H2}$) Natural killer cells	Murine 17 kd Human 17 kd Nonglycosylated	Cytolysis of tumor cells Induction of MHC class I antigens Synergy with IFN-γ for induction of MHC class II ↑ Respiratory burst activity in neutrophils	Partial (depending on which type of TNF receptor)
Tumor necrosis factor-β (TNF-β)	Lymphotoxin	T cells (murine T_{H1}) Natural killer cells	Murine 25 kd Human 25 kd Glycosylated Tends to aggregate	Same as TNF-α	Same as TNF-α
Granulocyte macrophage–colony-stimulating factor (GM-CSF)		T cells (murine $T_{H1} + T_{H2}$) Macrophages Endothelial cells Fibroblasts	Murine 23 kd Human 17-25 kd Glycosylated	Stimulates growth of macrophages and granulocytes from bone marrow precursors Activates macrophage cytocidal activity Induces Ia/DR on macrophages	Strict

proliferation of immature and mature populations of T cells. This activity was assigned a variety of names, including lymphocyte-activating factor (LAF), thymocyte-activating factor (TAF), and mitogenic protein (MP), based on the particular assay system used in different laboratories. In 1979, several laboratories agreed to use a common nomenclature system, and thus the comitogenic cytokine was renamed interleukin-1.

During the next 5 years, an intensive effort was made to unequivocally establish the molecular identity of IL-1. This goal was achieved by 1984 through biochemical purification of the human and murine IL-1α and IL-1β proteins and cloning of their genes. With the availability of purified recombinant IL-1 and IL-1–specific monoclonal antibodies, it became possible to identify IL-1 as the molecular species responsible for inducing both endogenous pyrogen and comitogenic functional activities. In 1985, the IL-1 receptor was identified by using radioligand binding techniques. (These techniques involve using a radioactive-labeled ligand, in this case IL-1, that binds to the receptor site, and measuring quantitatively the binding activity.) That same year, a third biologically active form of IL-1 was reported that was associated with plasma membranes of appropriately stimulated macrophage populations. Membrane IL-1 was not bound to IL-1 receptors but rather appeared to be directly attached to the cell surface. Finally, in 1988-1989 two distinct IL-1 receptors were identified and the cDNAs were cloned and expressed.

Measurement of IL-1

Traditionally, IL-1 is quantitated by its ability to induce a proliferative response in murine thymocytes. IL-1 shows neither strain nor species specificity in this assay system. The assay involves the coculture of 1×10^7 thymocytes/mL with serial dilutions of an IL-1 source and a constant amount of the lectin phytohemagglutinin (PHA). After 48 hours, the cultures are pulsed with ^{3}H-thymidine, and 24 hours later the amount of label incorporated into DNA is measured. One unit of IL-1 activity is defined as 10 times the reciprocal of the dilution of sample needed to produce a 50% maximal proliferative response. More recently, this assay has been improved by using the nontransformed IL-1–dependent T-cell line D10.G4.1. The modified assay offers higher levels of IL-1 sensitivity and lower amounts of biologic variation than the standard system.

Although functional assays for IL-1 offer the highest degree of sensitivity, they nevertheless suffer from two major drawbacks. First, they display a significant degree of biologic variability. Second, the assays can produce false-positive results because of the proliferative activities of other independent cytokines such as IL-2. For these reasons, considerable effort has gone into producing monoclonal antibodies to murine and human IL-1. The recent generation of these antibodies now permits the unequivocal identification of IL-1, either by specific inhibition of IL-1 functional activity or through the use of IL-1–specific immunoassays.

IL-1 Protein and Gene Structure

IL-1 activity is associated with at least two individual proteins, termed IL-1α and IL-1β. These proteins are the products of two distinct genes with similar organization that most likely arose during evolution as a result of gene duplication. The human and murine genes for both IL-1α and IL-1β have been cloned and expressed. The genes for the murine proteins have been localized to chromosome 2 and are linked to one another and to β_2-microglobulin. Human IL-1β has also been localized to chromosome 2, but no assignment has yet been made for human IL-1α. The IL-1α and IL-1β genes are structurally similar and contain 7 coding (exon) regions. These genes are somewhat unusual since they do not contain obvious coding sequences for signal peptides on the gene products. The IL-1α and IL-1β genes encode intracellular precursor protein molecules with molecular weights of 32 kd that consist of 271 and 269 amino acid residues, respectively. These proteins are subsequently processed by limited proteolytic digestion at residues 113 for human IL-1α, 115 for murine IL-1α, and 117 for human IL-1β. This cleavage liberates a 17-kd molecular fragment from the carboxy-terminus of each molecule, giving rise to the mature forms of IL-1. Depending on how the IL-1–producing cell is stimulated, IL-1α/β can be released as either the precursor or the mature form. Although both the precursor and mature forms of IL-1α can express functional activity, only the mature 17-kd form of IL-1β is active. The mature form of IL-1α is an acidic protein with an isoelectric point of approximately 5.0, whereas the mature form of IL-1β is a basic molecule with a pI of approximately 7.0. IL-1α and IL-1β display very little sequence homology with one another (20%), but each individual form is highly conserved across species lines (ie, human and murine IL-1α are approximately 60% homologous). Both forms of the cytokine are stable to extremes of temperature (−70° to +56°C) and pH (3.0 to 11.0). Moreover, both are relatively resistant to enzymatic degradation by trypsin, pepsin, and chymotrypsin, but they can be digested by pronase. Neither form is glycosylated.

Recently, a third form of IL-1 that is membrane-associated has been reported. Current evidence indicates that this form is closely related to IL-1α. Transfection of murine IL-1α cDNA into murine fibroblasts led to the expression of membrane IL-1 activity. No activity was detected when cells were transfected with IL-1β cDNA. Moreover, all the membrane-associated IL-1 activity expressed on murine macrophages was inhibited by a monoclonal antibody specific for IL-1α. Immunoprecipitation analysis of extrinsically labeled macrophage membranes indicates that membrane IL-1 is a 32-kd protein, suggesting that it most closely

resembles the intracellular precursor form of IL-1α. Since there appears to be only a single IL-1α gene and since neither the precursor nor mature IL-1 proteins contain transmembrane regions, it has been suggested that membrane IL-1 represents the nonprocessed form of IL-1α that is covalently attached to the plasma membrane.

IL-1 Biosynthesis

Although the macrophage is generally thought to be the major source of IL-1, several other cell types produce IL-1 activity (Table 18). Many are cells of the immune system including dendritic cells and B lymphocytes. However, nonimmunologic cells, such as endothelial cells, fibroblasts, and keratinocytes, can also produce IL-1–like functional activity. This latter observation suggests that immune responses may be influenced by other cellular effector systems.

IL-1 biosynthesis has been best studied in mononuclear phagocyte populations. Several stimuli can induce IL-1 in these cells either through direct contact or cytokine-induced mechanisms. Induction of both membrane IL-1 and soluble IL-1α and IL-1β occurs during antigen presentation. This process is T-cell–dependent, contact-mediated, and Ir gene-restricted. The magnitude of the IL-1 response is regulated by other cytokines. Tumor necrosis factor (TNF) has been suggested to play a major role in up-regulating IL-1 production in antigen-presenting macrophages. IL-1 can also be induced nonspecifically by a variety of microbial products, such as endotoxin or muramyl dipeptide; by immune complexes or activated complement fragments, such as C5a; or even as a result of adherence to plastic dishes in vitro.

Resting mononuclear phagocytes contain little or no IL-1 message or protein. However, stimulation causes a rapid increase in message levels for both forms of IL-1, and maximum levels of mRNA are reached after 1 hour. Production of IL-1 protein begins almost immediately after stimulation. The intracellular precursor proteins can be detected as

Figure 36
The lymphokine cascade

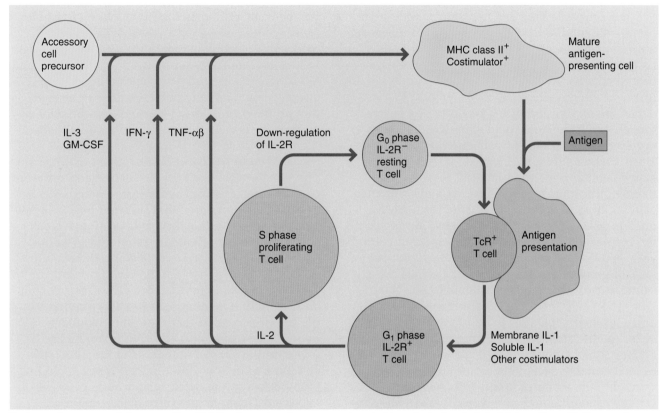

During antigen presentation, a resting (G_0) T cell receives two activation stimuli from an antigen-presenting accessory cell: occupation of the T-cell antigen receptor and a costimulatory activity such as IL-1. These signals drive G_0 phase T cells into early G_1 phase of the growth cycle. G_1 phase T cells express high-affinity IL-2 receptors (IL-2R) and secrete a variety of lymphokines, including IL-2. IL-2 interaction with its receptor causes the T cells to progress into S phase, where proliferation occurs. During the process, other lymphokines are derived that induce the growth and differentiation of additional antigen-presenting cells, thereby leading to the generation of more activated T cells and thus more lymphokines.

early as 30 minutes after stimulation, and the membrane form of IL-1 has been observed after 30 to 60 minutes, reaching maximum levels by 3 hours. Soluble IL-1 release from the cell is delayed approximately 1 hour and reaches maximum levels by 4 hours. In both the human and murine systems, IL-1β represents the predominant species of soluble IL-1 activity.

IL-1 Activities
IL-1 is perhaps one of the best examples of a pleotropic cytokine. It can affect a large variety of immune and nonimmune cells. Its action on cells of the immune system promotes both the induc-

tive as well as the effector phases of immune responses. Perhaps of greatest immunologic significance are the effects of IL-1 on T cells (Figure 36). Normal unstimulated T cells neither proliferate (ie, they are at the zero growth or G_0 phase of the cell cycle), nor do they produce lymphokines. However, both these functions are acquired in part through the actions of IL-1.

During antigen presentation, a T cell bearing the appropriate antigen receptor enters into intimate contact with an antigen-presenting cell that expresses MHC class II antigen. This contact causes the antigen-presenting cell to produce both membrane and soluble forms of IL-1. The IL-1 derived from antigen-presenting cells then binds to its receptor on antigen-stimulated T cells, thereby providing a signal that drives G_0 T cells into the G_1 phase of the growth cycle. Subsequently, IL-1 induces the expression of high-affinity IL-2 receptors on G_1 phase T cells and stimulates the cells to produce IL-2 and other T-cell–derived lymphokines such as IFN-γ, IL-3, and IL-4. Thus, this action sets in motion the first phase of the positive amplification system of the immune response.

In addition to its role in immune response induction, IL-1 can regulate the efferent phases of the response. IL-1 promotes antibody production and secretion by synergizing with B-cell growth and differentiation factors such as IL-4 and IL-6. It can directly interact with cytotoxic T cells, natural killer (NK) cells, and activated macrophages and augment their capacities to kill neoplastic target cells. Finally, under defined conditions, IL-1 can display direct cytocidal or cytostatic activity against certain susceptible tumor targets.

In addition, IL-1 profoundly influences the activity of nonimmune cell types. IL-1 can alter the function of cells of the central nervous system (CNS) and induce fever. This functional activity led to the early description of IL-1 as an endogenous pyrogen. It manifests this activity indirectly by inducing prostaglandin production from CNS cells that are in close proximity to the hypothalamic fever center. IL-1 also interacts with inflammatory cells by promoting chemotaxis and respiratory burst activity in neutrophils and inducing chemotaxis and prostaglandin production in monocytes. IL-1 can affect the function of connective tissue cells. It promotes fibroblast growth in vitro, which suggests that IL-1 may play an important physiologic role in wound healing. IL-1 promotes bone resorption by osteoclasts and has been identified as the molecule responsible for the action of the cytokine activity termed *osteoclast-activating factor (OAF)*. Finally, IL-1 can induce collagenase secretion by chondrocytes and synovial cells in vitro. This latter observation suggests that IL-1 may potentiate tissue destruction and therefore may play a role in the etiology of certain diseases such as rheumatoid arthritis.

Mechanism of Action of IL-1

The biochemical basis for IL-1 activity on different cell types is currently under investigation. Recent data have documented that IL-1 interacts with specific receptors on the surface of responsive cells. IL-1 receptors were initially identified in radio-ligand-binding experiments. These studies showed that cells responsive to IL-1 bound labeled, purified, recombinant IL-1 in a saturable, specific, and reversible manner. Competition binding experiments indicated that the same receptors bound either IL-1α or IL-1β. The receptors are expressed in limited amounts (100 to 5000 sites/cell) on a variety of different cell types, including thymocytes, splenocytes, lymph node cells, T-cell lines and T lymphomas, fibroblasts, epithelial cells, and endothelial cells. Two distinct IL-1 receptors have been identified. The type I receptor (IL-1RI) is an 80-kd single-chain glycoprotein expressed on T cells and fibroblasts. The type II receptor (IL-1RII) is a 60-kd single-chain glycoprotein that is expressed on B cells and myeloid cells. Both proteins bind ligand with high affinity (Ka = 1-10 $\times$ 10^9 at 4°C) and the cDNAs for both proteins from human and mouse have been cloned, sequenced, and expressed. It is noteworthy that normal heterogeneous T-cell populations generally express fewer than 200 IL-1 receptors/cell, which is a considerably lower expression than is seen on many nonimmune cells such as fibroblasts (1500 to 4000 sites/cell). Binding of ligand to the receptor leads to internalization of the receptor-ligand complex and the down-regulation of surface receptors. Concomitantly, cellular levels of cytosolic calcium and protein kinase C activity increase. A considerable effort is currently under way to define the role of the IL-1 receptors in mediating IL-1–dependent biologic activities.

Interleukin-2

Historical Perspectives

Interleukin-2 was first identified in 1976 as an activity found in culture supernatants of activated T cells that caused normal helper and cytotoxic T-cell populations to proliferate. This activity was given the name *T-cell growth factor (TCGF)*. In 1979, TCGF was found to be physicochemically similar to several other T-cell mitogenic activities and was renamed IL-2. The next 4 years saw an explosive growth of studies that defined the molecular structure of IL-2 and its receptor. Human and murine IL-2 were purified to homogeneity, and partial amino acid sequences were obtained. In 1981, purified preparations of radiolabeled IL-2 were used to define a high-affinity IL-2 receptor expressed on activated T cells. That same year, a monoclonal antibody (anti-Tac) was generated that reacted with a human T-cell activation antigen and inhibited binding of IL-2 to the IL-2 receptor. Just 2 years later, the IL-2 gene was cloned and sequenced. In addition, the Tac antigen was unequivocally identified as a component of the IL-2 receptor. This component was purified in 1984 and identified as an integral membrane 55-kd glycoprotein, and its corresponding gene was cloned and sequenced. By 1987, the complete structure of the high-affinity IL-2 receptor had been established through the identification of a second, 75-kd integral membrane protein that forms a noncovalent bimolecular complex with the 55-kd Tac component.

Measurement of IL-2

IL-2 is quantitated by its ability to induce a proliferative response in T cells. To facilitate this measurement, two IL-2–dependent murine T-cell lines have been derived: CTLL and HT-2. In this assay, 5×10^3 indicator cells are cultured for 24 hours with serial dilutions of an IL-2 source and then pulsed for 18 hours with ^{3}H-thymidine. T-cell proliferation is quantitated as a function of radiothymidine incorporation into cellular DNA. One unit of IL-2 activity is defined as the amount of lymphokine that induces 50% maximum thymidine incorporation. Highly purified IL-2 displays a specific activity of approximately 10^7 units/mg protein. Functionally, IL-2 displays partial species specificity. Although murine cells respond to both human and murine IL-2, human cells respond only to the human lymphokine.

IL-2 Protein and Gene Structure

Because IL-2 was the first cytokine to be purified and cloned, considerable information is now available about the gene and its corresponding protein. The IL-2 gene consists of four exon regions separated by one short and two long intervening sequences (introns). The human IL-2 gene is located on chromosome 4; the location of the murine gene has not been reported. The human gene codes for a protein of 133 amino acids with a predicted molecular weight of 15 420 daltons (d). This theoretical value is in close agreement with that observed for the purified natural material, which is 15 500 d. Natural human IL-2 is variably glycosylated and bears between 0% and 6% of oxygen-linked carbohydrate that includes a significant amount of negatively charged sialic acid. This postsynthetic modification results in multiple molecular forms and was the cause of some confusion in early attempts to purify IL-2. However, subsequent experiments using desialyated forms of IL-2 showed that all the activity could be attributed to a single molecular species with an isoelectric point of 8.2. The carbohydrate moieties on IL-2 are not required for expression of functional activity. The natural glycosylated protein and the recombinant nonglycosylated protein bind to IL-2 receptors with comparable affinities and display identical specific T-cell mitogenic activities. The structure-function relationships that exist within the IL-2 molecule have been extensively studied. The functional integrity of the molecule is heavily dependent on secondary and tertiary molecular structure. IL-2 activity is quickly lost upon removal of amino- or carboxy-terminal amino acid residues or upon reduction of a critical disulfide bond formed between cysteine residues at positions 58 and 105. Recently, the crystal structure of human IL-2 has been reported at a resolution of 3 angstroms. Although this resolution is less than optimum, it indicates that IL-2 consists structurally of six antiparallel α-helices without β secondary structure.

IL-2 Biosynthesis

IL-2 is produced predominantly by T cells and to a lesser degree by immunocompetent thymocytes. By using continuous T-cell lines and primary T-cell populations that were characterized by surface-marker analysis, IL-2 synthesis was documented in both helper (CD4$^+$) and cytotoxic (CD8$^+$) T cells. In the mouse, IL-2 synthesis has been ascribed to a subpopulation of helper T cells termed T_{H1}. Murine helper T cells have been functionally differentiated into two subsets on the basis of the lymphokines they produce. Certain lymphokines, such as granulocyte macrophage–colony-stimulating factor (GM-CSF), IL-3, and TNF-α, are produced by both T_H populations. However, the T_{H1} subset selectively produces IL-2, IFN-γ, and TNF-β (lymphotoxin), while the T_{H2} subset selectively produces IL-4 and IL-5. Based on the actions of the different lymphokines, it has been suggested that T_{H1} cells primarily regulate delayed-type hypersensitivity reactions and T_{H2} cells mainly promote humoral immunity. At the present time, no such division has been established among human helper T cells.

IL-2 is not constitutively produced by resting T cells. Unstimulated cells produce neither IL-2 message nor protein. Two physiologic signals are needed to induce IL-2 biosynthesis: antigen in the context of class II molecules and a costimulatory activity such as IL-1. Experimentally, these signals

can be replaced either by the combined pharmacologic stimuli of lectins or phorbol myristate acetate (PMA) and calcium ionophore. Concanavalin A (Con A) is the most commonly used lectin for murine cells, while PHA is most commonly used for human cells. Within an hour after stimulation, IL-2 mRNA begins to accumulate in the T cell. Message levels peak by 8 hours and then decline. The IL-2 message is rapidly translated, and the resulting protein is secreted immediately after synthesis. Extracellular IL-2 is first detected 4 to 6 hours after cell stimulation, reaches peak levels by 12 to 24 hours, and thereafter the levels decline. This decline is the net effect of the cessation of lymphokine biosynthesis and the cellular consumption of secreted IL-2 by the proliferating T cells.

IL-2 production is regulated by a variety of exogenous signals. Production is enhanced by compounds that tend to decrease cellular proliferation and prolong the G_1 phase of the growth cycle. IL-1, IFN-γ, and vasopressin are examples of these types of exogenous mediators. In contrast, IL-2 production is down-regulated by a variety of other agents that exert their effects either directly on the T cell or indirectly by influencing the activity of antigen-presenting cells. Perhaps the best examples of these types of compounds are glucocorticosteroids, cyclosporin A, and prostaglandin E_2 (PGE$_2$). Glucocorticoids such as dexamethasone and drugs such as cyclosporin A appear to exert their effects by inhibiting IL-2 gene transcription, thus directly ablating the capacity of the T cell to produce IL-2. In contrast, PGE$_2$ acts indirectly by inhibiting the function of antigen-presenting cells.

IL-2 Activities

Undoubtedly, the major activity of IL-2 is to act as a growth factor for T cells. It is mitogenic for both the helper and cytotoxic classes of T cells. IL-2–responsive T cells are those that have progressed into the early G_1 phase of the growth cycle. Responsiveness is now known to correlate with the expression of the high-affinity IL-2 receptor on the cell surface. The interaction of IL-2 with the G_1 phase T cell drives the cell into S phase, where proliferation begins (Figure 36).

IL-2 also regulates other aspects of T-cell function. It enhances the biosynthesis of other T-cell–derived lymphokines, such as IFN-γ, lymphotoxin, and B-cell growth and differentiation factors. Thus, IL-2 induces higher levels of lymphokines both by expanding the entire population of lymphokine-producing T cells and by increasing the biosynthetic capacity of each individual cell. This action establishes a positive feedback cycle that helps to amplify the immune response. In addition to its response-inducing functions, IL-2 can promote the efferent limb of the immune response by increasing the cytocidal activity of cytotoxic T cells, an action that is accomplished by the lymphokine's ability to promote growth and differentiation of cytotoxic T-lymphocyte (CTL) populations, as well as increase the cytolytic activity of individual CTL effector cells.

IL-2 affects other cells of the immune system. It has been reported to enhance the growth and differentiation of human and murine B cells. Although IL-2 is neither sufficient nor absolutely required to induce B-cell growth and differentiation, it can enhance the actions of other lymphokines, such as IL-4 or B-cell growth factor (BCGF). IL-2 increases the activity of cells that display natural killer activity, which has led to the development of a unique form of cancer therapy using peripheral blood mononuclear cells that have been activated by in vitro culture with IL-2 to express nonspecific tumoricidal activity. Because the origin of these cells remains poorly defined, they have been termed *lymphokine-activated killer (LAK)* cells.

Mechanism of Action of IL-2

A great deal is known about the biochemical mechanism of action of IL-2. To a large extent this information was gained through the study of the human IL-2 receptor. Figure 37 depicts the current model of this receptor. The human IL-2 receptor consists of two nonidentical glycopeptides. Both are integral membrane proteins, and both can

Figure 37
Schematic representation of the high-affinity human IL-2 receptor

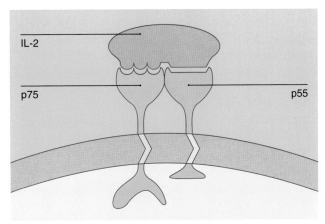

The receptor consists of two noncovalently associated subunits, each of which is an integral membrane protein. The larger subunit (p75) is responsible for ligand internalization and signal transduction. The smaller subunit (p55) modulates receptor affinity. The anti-Tac monoclonal antibody recognizes the p55 component.

bind IL-2. The larger chain (the p75 chain) is a 75-kd component that, in monomeric form, binds IL-2 with a $Ka = 8 \times 10^8$ M^{-1}. This chain appears to be responsible for internalizing the ligand-receptor complex and for producing the signals that eventually induce T-cell growth. This conclusion is drawn from experiments that identified a population of IL-2–responsive leukemic cells expressing only the p75 receptor component. The smaller subunit (termed p55) displays a molecular weight of 55 kd and was identified in 1981 as the low-affinity IL-2 receptor detected by the anti-Tac antibody. In monomeric form, p55 binds IL-2 with a $Ka = 7 \times 10^7$ M^{-1}. The major action of this subunit appears to be the modification of receptor affinity. Binding of IL-2 to cells expressing only p55 does not induce a proliferative response. Radioligand-binding studies have revealed that the two receptor subunits bind to distinct regions on the IL-2 molecule in a noncompetitive fashion. Thus, the association of the two chains results in the formation of a receptor complex that displays an affinity constant ($Ka = 8 \times 10^{10}$ M^{-1}) 100 to 1000 times greater than that observed for either individual chain. This affinity is sufficient to permit binding of IL-2 at physiologic lymphokine concentrations.

Regulation of cellular responsiveness to IL-2 occurs through alterations in the subunit composition of the IL-2 receptor complex. Resting T cells express little or no p75 and no p55. However, after T-cell stimulation by antigen and IL-1, mRNA for both receptor components is transcribed. High-affinity receptors appear at the cell surface, and expression of the receptor complex peaks at levels of 2 to 4×10^3 sites/cell between 2 and 3 days. Upon binding of IL-2 to the assembled αβ complex, the ligand-receptor complex is internalized, thereby reducing expression of high-affinity receptors on the cell surface. This event induces the cells to proliferate and differentially produce and express p55. Eventually, expression of monomeric p55 exceeds that of the receptor complexes by 5- to 10-fold. In this way, subsequent T-cell responsiveness to IL-2 is reduced. Surface expression of both high- and low-affinity receptors decreases during the next 6 to 10 days, and by day 12 all the T cells in the responding population have returned to the G_0 state.

Interferon Gamma

Historical Perspectives
IFN-γ belongs to a family of proteins that is related by an ability to protect cells from viral infection. Based on several criteria, the interferons are divided into three distinct classes: α, β, and γ. A summary of the distinguishing characteristics for the different interferons is presented in Table 19. IFN-α and IFN-β are classic interferons that are

induced as a direct result of viral infection of cells. They are largely differentiated by their cell of origin, their antigenic structure, and their primary amino acid sequence. It is of interest that IFN-α actually represents a family of at least 20 closely related proteins that are coded by distinct genes. The different forms of IFN-α share more than 70% sequence homology. Much less homology is seen between IFN-α and IFN-β. In contrast, IFN-γ is not induced directly by viral infection, but is induced by immune stimuli only. Although IFN-γ can induce antiviral activity in cells, it displays a 10- to 100-fold lower specific activity than either IFN-α or IFN-β. On the other hand, IFN-γ is 100 to 10 000 times more active as an immunomodulator than the other classes of interferons. Thus, IFN-γ is functionally and physicochemically distinct from IFN-α and IFN-β.

The history of the interferons dates back to 1957, when Isaacs and Lindenmann described a protein released from virally infected cells that protected naive cells (cells not yet exposed to antigen) from subsequent viral infection. They termed this protein interferon. Eight to 12 years later, a form of interferon activity was observed in supernatants of mitogen- or antigen-stimulated T-cell cultures. This activity was considered atypical because it was induced in the total absence of virus. In 1973, this unusual form of IFN was shown to be physicochemically and antigenically distinct from conventional virus-induced IFN and was termed immune IFN or type II IFN. This form was later renamed IFN-γ. Over the next 10 years, several lymphokine activities were identified that would eventually be attributed to IFN-γ. These activities included, among others: migration inhibition factor (MIF), defined by its ability to inhibit the directed migration of macrophages in an in vitro culture system; macrophage-activating factor (MAF), defined by its ability to activate nonspecific tumoricidal and microbicidal activities in monocytes/macrophages; and Ia-inducing factor (IAIF) or macrophage Ia-recruiting factor (MIRF), defined by its ability to induce expression of MHC class II antigens on macrophage cell surfaces. The turning point for IFN-γ research came in 1982, when the genes for human and murine IFN-γ were cloned and expressed, and the purified protein became available in substantial quantities. Using highly

Table 19
Characteristics of the interferons

Interferon	Cell source	Inducer	Physicochemical properties	Old nomenclature
IFN-α	T and B cells Macrophages	Viruses Polyribonucleotides	Acid stable Nonglycosylated 18-20 kd 20 genes	Leukocyte or type I IFN
IFN-β	Fibroblasts Epithelial cells	Viruses Polyribonucleotides	Acid stable Glycosylated 23 kd 1 gene	Fibroblast or type I IFN
IFN-γ	T cells NK cells	Antigens T-cell mitogens Bacterial products	Acid labile Heat labile Glycosylated 20-25 kd Homodimer 1 gene	Immune or type II IFN

purified recombinant IFN-γ and monoclonal IFN-γ antibodies, investigators rapidly established that IFN-γ is an important lymphokine responsible for inducing a variety of biologic responses in vitro in many different cell types. Over the next 4 years, studies were initiated to elucidate the mechanism of action of IFN-γ at the molecular level and to define its physiologic role in vivo. These efforts have resulted in the biochemical purification of the human and murine IFN-γ receptors. Moreover, it is now established that IFN-γ plays an obligatory role in promoting host defense against infectious agents in vivo.

Measurement of IFN-γ
IFN-γ is one of the most pleotropic of cytokines. As a result, a large variety of assays have been developed that can be used to quantitate IFN-γ. These assays all take into account the strict species specificity exhibited by human and murine IFN-γ. Perhaps the most commonly used assays are those that quantitate the antiviral activity of

IFN-γ. These assays measure either the reduction in viral yield from IFN-treated cells or the IFN-dependent protection of cells from the cytopathic effects of a virus. The latter, termed the *cytopathic effect (CPE) assay*, is particularly well suited for the rapid analysis of multiple IFN-containing samples. The assay is conducted in 96-well tissue culture plates in which 3×10^4 cultured cells, such as fibroblasts, are exposed for 24 hours to serial dilutions of the IFN source. The resulting monolayer is washed and then challenged with an excess dose of virus, such as vesicular stomatitis virus, sufficient to kill all the cells in the culture. Twenty-four to 48 hours later the viable cells remaining are quantitated immunohistochemically. A unit of IFN is defined as the reciprocal of the dilution needed to protect 50% of the cells from the cytopathic effect of the virus. When this value is normalized to an international IFN standard, the units are referred to as *international reference units (IRU)*. This assay displays a significant degree of sensitivity, but is unable to discriminate between the various forms of IFN. IFN-γ can be specifically identified in this system by determining the percentage of total antiviral activity inhibitable with neutralizing IFN-γ–specific monoclonal antibodies.

Other IFN-γ assays monitor the lymphokine's ability to regulate the function of immune cells. Two of the most commonly used assays quantitate IFN-γ–dependent induction of MHC class II molecules or nonspecific cytocidal activities in macrophages. These assays offer the highest level of sensitivity toward IFN-γ. However, specificity is again a problem because other cytokines, such as IL-4 or GM-CSF, can induce similar responses in the indicator cell population. Thus, it is necessary to immunochemically establish the identity of the active component with neutralizing monoclonal antibodies.

Finally, IFN-γ can be quantitated with monoclonal antibody immunoassays. Although these assays offer the lowest level of sensitivity, they offer the highest degree of specificity and are usually suitable to quantitate IFN-γ for most purposes.

IFN-γ Gene and Protein Structure

IFN-γ is encoded by a single gene that is composed of four exon and three intron regions. The gene for human IFN-γ has been localized to the long arm of chromosome 12 (the human IFN-αβ genes are located on the short arm of chromosome 9) and codes for a protein of 143 amino acids. The murine gene is located on chromosome 10 (the murine IFN-αβ genes reside on chromosome 4) and codes for a protein that is nine residues shorter. The genes for human and murine IFN-γ display 65% homology at the nucleotide level. However, the proteins are only 40% homologous. No significant homology has been detected between IFN-γ and IFN-α or IFN-β. The IFN-γ gene products are polypeptides of 17 (human) or 15 (murine) kd that assemble into a noncovalently associated homodimer. Each polypeptide chain contains two nitrogen-linked glycosylation sites that can be independently glycosylated, thereby giving rise to IFN-γ subunits of three different molecular weights (ie, 17, 20, and 25 for human IFN-γ). The differential combination of the three glycopeptides thus accounts for much of the observed heterogeneity in the fully mature molecule (ie, natural human IFN-γ displays molecular weights that range from 34 to 50 kd). Glycosylation is not important for expression of IFN-γ activity but is thought to influence the circulatory half-life of the molecule.

IFN-γ is exquisitely sensitive to extremes of heat and pH. These characteristics were originally used to differentiate it from the other interferons. IFN-γ rapidly loses activity when incubated below pH 4.0 or above pH 10.0. It also shows a time-dependent loss of activity when held at 56°C (half-life = 90 minutes). The protein can be inactivated by treatment with proteases. To a large extent, this inactivation is caused by the removal of 11 carboxy-terminal amino acid residues from the molecule, resulting in a fragment that binds to the IFN-γ receptor with a three-log lower affinity. Other experiments have confirmed the additional importance of the amino-terminal region of the molecule.

IFN-γ Biosynthesis

IFN-γ is produced by both CD4+ (helper) and CD8+ (cytotoxic) T-cell populations. In the mouse, the same helper T-cell subset that produces IL-2 also produces IFN-γ (T$_{H1}$). However, IL-2 and IFN-γ are not necessarily produced by the same cell. The stimuli that induce IFN-γ production by T cells are similar to those that induce IL-2: antigen in the context of MHC class I and class II molecules, T-cell mitogens such as Con A or PHA, or the combined pharmacologic stimuli PMA and calcium ionophore. In addition, T-cell–dependent production of IFN-γ is enhanced by products of activated T cells and macrophages. These agents include IL-2, hydrogen peroxide, and leukotrienes LTB$_4$, LTC$_4$, and LTD$_4$.

More recent studies have demonstrated that IFN-γ can also be produced by natural killer cells. The identity of NK cells has been established in the mouse and human by using a combination of surface marker, morphologic, and functional analyses. Mitogens appear to induce IFN-γ from populations of NK cells that have been expanded by IL-2. In addition, bacteria and bacterial products appear to stimulate IFN-γ production in naive NK cell populations. This latter observation suggests that NK-derived IFN-γ may be important in initiating pathways of host resistance to microbial infection.

Stimulation of T cells results in the induction of IFN-γ mRNA, which is first detectable in 6 to 8 hours, peaks by 12 to 24 hours, and then declines after 48 hours. Like IL-2, the IFN-γ protein is secreted immediately following biosynthesis. Extracellular IFN-γ can be detected as early as 8 to 12 hours after cell stimulation, reaches peak levels by 24 to 48 hours, and then slowly declines thereafter. Normal T cells express only limited numbers of IFN-γ receptors and therefore consume only limited quantities of IFN-γ. This observation in part explains why IFN-γ accumulates in stimulated T-cell culture supernatants, while IL-2 levels peak and then decline.

IFN-γ Activities

Although IFN-γ is a member of the interferon family and therefore can participate in nonimmune host antiviral responses, its greatest biologic importance undoubtedly resides in its immunomodulatory activities. IFN-γ modulates the function and differentiation of numerous cells of the immune system, and can promote both the afferent and efferent limbs of the immune response. Mononuclear phagocytes appear to be a primary target of IFN-γ action. Clearly one of the major roles for this lymphokine is the regulation of MHC class I and class II antigens on a variety of cell types, including the cells of the monocyte/macrophage lineage. This function is of primary importance to the inductive phase of the immune response because of the recognized role of class II molecules in binding processed antigen and presenting it to T cells. Human peripheral blood monocytes express HLA-DR but not HLA-DQ antigens. When placed in culture (and presumably when monocytes migrate into tissues and differentiate into macrophages), HLA-DR expression spontaneously decreases. Exposure of newly explanted monocytes to IFN-γ results in the maintenance of HLA-DR on the cell surface. Moreover, IFN-γ induces expression of HLA-DR and HLA-DQ anti-

gens on cultured monocytes/macrophages where MHC class II antigens have decayed. In the mouse, both circulating monocytes and peritoneal cavity macrophages are class II-negative, but these cells are induced to express both I-A and I-E class II antigens by IFN-γ. IFN-γ also promotes other afferent macrophage functions, including the enhancement of antigen-presenting activity by increasing levels of several intracellular enzymes and by enhancing production of tumor necrosis factor. The latter function may be particularly significant since TNF can induce or increase cellular production of IL-1.

IFN-γ has also been shown to regulate macrophage effector cell activities. It is unquestionably one of the major lymphokines responsible for activating nonspecific tumoricidal and microbicidal activities in macrophages. IFN-γ induces the expression of recognition structures on macrophages for target cells and promotes the elaboration of macrophage-derived cytocidal compounds, such as reactive oxygen and nitrogen intermediates and TNF. It has also been shown to promote the macrophage-mediated killing of a variety of intracellular and extracellular parasites both by altering the susceptibility of macrophage populations to infection and by inducing a variety of macrophage products that can kill microbial organisms. The physiologic relevance of IFN-γ–dependent macrophage activation has recently been demonstrated in animal models of infectious disease. Mice pretreated with neutralizing monoclonal antibodies to IFN-γ lost their ability to resist a sublethal challenge by a variety of microbial pathogens, such as *Listeria monocytogenes, Toxoplasma gondii,* and *Leishmania major.* Animals treated with control antibodies recovered normally from the infection. These experiments were some of the first to confirm the physiologic relevance of endogenously produced IFN-γ in an in vivo situation.

In addition to enhancing nonspecific macrophage cytocidal activities, IFN-γ increases expression of high-affinity Fc receptors on human and murine monocytes/macrophages, thereby enhancing the capacity of macrophages to participate in specific antibody-dependent cellular cytotoxicity reactions. IFN-γ can also enhance the biosynthesis of a variety of complement proteins (such as C3,

C4, and factor B) by macrophages and thus can promote humoral immunity through enhancement of complement activity.

In addition, IFN-γ exerts its effects on other cells of the immune system. It can regulate B-cell responses. Depending on the differentiation state of the B cell, IFN-γ can act as either a positive or negative regulatory signal. It antagonizes the activities of IL-4. Thus, in the mouse, IFN-γ inhibits IL-4–dependent class II induction on B cells. Moreover, it decreases production of IgG1 and IgE and up-regulates production of IgG2a. Very little is known about the effects of IFN-γ on T cells. Recent data suggest that IFN-γ may have an antiproliferative effect on murine T_{H2}. Thus, this one lymphokine may control humoral immunity by regulating the growth and differentiation of both T- and B-cell populations. IFN-γ enhances NK cell cytolytic function. However, the specific activity of IFN-γ for this particular function is equivalent to IFN-α and IFN-β.

Mechanism of Action of IFN-γ

Like the other cytokines discussed in this chapter, IFN-γ exerts its effects on cells through interaction with a specific cell-surface receptor. IFN-γ receptors have been detected on a variety of primary and cultured cells. In fact most cells, with the exception of erythrocytes, appear to express some level of IFN-γ receptor. The majority of radioligand analyses have detected only a single class of receptor that binds ligand with a moderately high affinity (2 to 20×10^9 M^{-1}). Although receptor expression is modest on most normal cells (200 to 10 000 sites/cell), certain tumor cell lines have been identified that express high levels of the receptor (25 000 to 50 000 sites/cell). The IFN-γ receptor binds IFN-γ in a species-specific manner. In addition, it does not react with either IFN-α or IFN-β. The analysis of the cell biology of this receptor on different cells has just begun. On most cells, receptor expression and affinity are not significantly modulated by external stimuli. At physiologic temperatures, ligand-receptor complexes formed at the cell surface are internalized, enter an acidic intracellular compartment, and dissociate. Free ligand is ultimately degraded, and free receptor enters an intracellular receptor pool and eventually recycles back to the cell surface. How-

ever, this recycling pathway appears to be inoperative in some tumor cells and possibly in T cells, where IFN-γ has been reported to down-regulate expression of its own receptor.

The IFN-γ receptor has recently been purified and cloned from both human and murine cell sources. The human receptor is a 90-kd component that contains a 65-kd polypeptide core and 25 kd of carbohydrate. The murine receptor is of similar size (95 kd). Receptor-specific monoclonal antibodies have been used to demonstrate that IFN-γ receptors on different cell types are similar, if not identical.

Very little is known about how the interaction of IFN-γ with its receptor ultimately induces a cellular response. It remains unclear whether the receptor stimulates intracellular signal transduction pathways or functions only to transport IFN-γ into the cell. Using somatic cell hybridization techniques, at least one other gene product was found to be necessary to confer biologic activity to the 90-kd IFN-γ binding protein. However, the identity of this component has not yet been established, and no information is available about how it functions.

Lymphokine-Dependent Amplification of the Immune Response

IL-1, IL-2, and IFN-γ in combination form the framework of a positive feedback cycle termed the *cytokine cascade* (Figure 36). This amplification system functions as the driving force of the immune response. Immune responses are initiated when two signals are provided to resting (G_0) T cells that bear the appropriate antigen receptor: antigen complexed with class II molecules and a costimulatory activity such as IL-1. These signals cause the responding T cells to progress into the early G_1 phase of the growth cycle. G_1 phase T cells produce both α and β chains of the IL-2 receptor, which assemble to form high-affinity IL-2 receptors at the cell surface. At the same time, stimulated T cells produce and release IL-2, together with a variety of other lymphokines, such as IFN-γ, GM-CSF, TNF-α, and TNF-β. The interaction of IL-2 with high-affinity IL-2 receptors drives the responding T-cell population through G_1 and into S phase, where proliferation begins. This interaction also leads to increased lymphokine production due to both the enhanced capacity of individual cells to produce lymphokines and the expansion of the entire lymphokine-producing T-cell population. Increased production of myelomonocytic growth factors, such as IL-3 and GM-CSF, results in increased availability of accessory cells, such as macrophages, that have antigen-presenting potential. Generation of IFN-γ leads to the up-regulation of class II antigens on the accessory cell surfaces. Enhanced production of TNF-αβ causes an up-regulation of both membrane and soluble forms of IL-1. Together these events increase antigen-presentation reactions, which in turn increase the number of activated T cells, thus giving rise to higher levels of lymphokines. This event completes the cycle, which now repeats itself many times over and results in the rapid and generalized progression of immune and inflammatory responses.

Conclusion

The study of the structure and function of cytokines progressed rapidly during the past 5 years. To a large extent, this progress reflects the advancement of technology in the areas of cell biology, biochemistry, and molecular biology. These advances have permitted, for the first time, the definition of a large number of cytokine activities on a molecular basis. Moreover, the advances have facilitated the production of highly purified materials in quantities of milligrams and grams; 10 years before only picogram amounts were available in unpurified form. Using highly purified protein preparations, investigators have been able to unequivocally delineate the function of individual cytokines and now have begun to elucidate their biochemical mechanisms of action. Perhaps most exciting of all are the recent attempts to use recombinant cytokines as therapeutic agents to treat a number of neoplastic, infectious, and autoimmune diseases. Over the next few years, additional insights will be gained about the functions and uses of cytokines in health and disease.

Selected Readings

Calderon J, Sheehan KCF, Chance C, Thomas ML, Schreiber RD. Purification and characterization of the human interferon-γ receptor from placenta. **Proc Natl Acad Sci USA**. 1988;85:4837-4841.

Dinarello CA. Biology of interleukin 1. **FASEB J**. 1988;2:108-115.

Dower SK, Urdal DL. The interleukin-1 receptor. **Immunol Today**. 1987;8:46-51.

Durum SK, Schmidt JA, Oppenheim JJ. Interleukin 1: an immunological perspective. **Annu Rev Immunol**. 1985;3:263-287.

Greene WC, Leonard WJ. The human interleukin-2 receptor. **Annu Rev Immunol**. 1986;4:69-95.

Mosmann TR, Coffman RL. Two types of mouse helper T-cell clone. **Immunol Today**. 1987;8:223-227.

Paul WE, Ohara J. B-cell stimulatory factor-1/interleukin 4. **Annu Rev Immunol**. 1987;5:429-459.

Pennica D, Shalaby MR, Palladino MA Jr. Tumor necrosis factors alpha and beta. In: Gillis S, ed. **Recombinant Lymphokines and Their Receptors**. New York, NY: Marcel Dekker Inc; 1987:301-317.

Smith KA. Interleukin-2: inception, impact, and implications. **Science**. 1988;240:1169-1176.

Vilček J, Gray PW, Rinderknecht E, Sevastopoulos CG. Interferon-γ: a lymphokine for all seasons. **Lymphokines**. 1985;11:1-32.

Integrins in Inflammation and the Immune Response

Introduction

During the inflammatory response, leukocytes are activated, migrate through tissue barriers, adhere to specific sites, and secrete soluble mediators. In the past few years, a large body of evidence has accumulated to support the hypothesis that adhesion receptors, defined as those receptors that mediate immune cell binding to extracellular matrix proteins or glycosaminoglycans and to other cells, are fundamental to each of these processes. This review focuses on the roles members of the adhesion receptor family play in the immune response.

Adhesion of any type of cell to the interstitial matrix or to other cells is a complex process that can be summarized as follows:

- Diverse adhesion receptors with unique structures and cell-specific expression mediate the phenomenon of cell adhesion.
- These receptors are expressed in a developmentally defined pattern and play a major role in morphogenesis during embryonic development.
- There is evidence both for cell polarity and for domains of increased focal membrane receptor density, which influence phenotypic effects and interaction with ligands.
- Receptor expression on individual cells can be altered by soluble mediators, which lead to increases or decreases in specific transcription rates.
- Receptor activities can be regulated by post-translational mechanisms that increase or decrease avidity of receptors for their ligands.
- Many adhesion receptors are expressed as two-chain heterodimers consisting of unique α and β chains. These chains can, in many instances, pair with not only one but several other chains. This results in different pairs of αβ heterodimers with unique ligand-binding properties.
- The receptors interact with specific intracellular and transmembrane proteins that modulate their activities.

The Adhesion Protein Families

In broad terms, three families of proteins are currently known to mediate adhesion of immune cells. (Table 20 lists these families and their members.) The families are defined by similarities in their amino acid sequences, as determined by cDNA cloning. The first family, the immunoglobulin superfamily adhesion proteins, has structural similarities to other members of the immunoglobulin superfamily. The second family, the selectins or LEC-CAMs, has a modular structure consisting of sequences similar to lectin binding, epidermal growth factor (EGF) receptorlike domains, and complement regulatory protein. The third family is the integrins, which are detailed in Table 21.

Integrins are expressed as noncovalently bound αβ heterodimers. Virtually every cell of all developmental lineages, in addition to cells important in the immune response, is believed to express at least one integrin. Many exciting observations have been made recently that have helped to increase our understanding of how integrins function in the immune response. In addition, some of the more recently understood general properties of integrins have been established through the use of immune cell models. For these reasons, this chapter focuses on integrins and their functions in the immune response. When specific important points about adhesion are raised, nonintegrin adhesion receptors will also be discussed.

Identification of Integrins

cDNA cloning and monoclonal antibody technology have been useful in characterizing and comparing specific integrin α and β chains derived from different sources. Many integrins were initially characterized as cell-surface receptors that allowed platelets, fibroblasts, tumor cell lines, or cells of endothelial or mesodermal origin to bind to matrix proteins. Matrix proteins include fibronectin, vitronectin, thrombospondin, laminin, collagen, fibrinogen, and von Willebrand factor. In many instances, specific binding of cells to a matrix protein could be demonstrated by purifying the protein and attaching it to glass or plastic. The binding was found to be cation-dependent. The divalent cations calcium and magnesium were generally used and are thought to be

Table 20
The three adhesion protein families

Family and members	Alternative name	Derivation of term
Immunoglobulin superfamily adhesion proteins		
LFA-2	CD2	Lymphocyte function antigen-2
LFA-3	CD58	Lymphocyte function antigen-3
ICAM-1	CD54	Intercellular adhesion molecule-1
ICAM-2	–	Intercellular adhesion molecule-2
ICAM-3	–	Intercellular adhesion molecule-3
VCAM-1	–	Vascular cell adhesion molecule-1
CD4	–	Cluster determinant-4
CD8	–	Cluster determinant-8
Selectins or LEC-CAMs		Lectin EGF (epidermal growth factor) complement–cell adhesion molecule
Mel-14	Lam-1 L-selectin	Named for the monoclonal antibody that defines this protein
ELAM-1	E-selectin	Endothelial leukocyte adhesion molecule-1
GMP-140	PADGEM P-selectin	Granule membrane protein-140
Integrins*		
αβ Heterodimers		

*See Table 21 for a complete list of integrin family members.

physiologically relevant. In some experimental systems, manganese has been used because this cation seems to markedly enhance receptor activity. Many matrix proteins are large enough and characterized in enough detail to allow the isolation of proteolytically derived fragments that still maintain cell adhesive properties. Purification of these fragments and the use of synthetic peptides derived from these regions allowed the specific amino acids within the matrix protein to which the cells bound to be characterized.

The prototypic use of this method was the purification of a fibronectin (Fn) receptor from fibroblasts and osteosarcoma cells. This type of assay allowed the identification of specific domains of Fn, a large (approximately 400 kd) homodimer, which mediate cell binding. Interestingly, several different regions of Fn bind cells. The integrin Fn receptor $\alpha_5\beta_1$ was found to interact specifically with a domain of Fn containing the tripeptide Arg-Gly-Asp (RGD, in single-letter code). Affinity chromatography, in which this cell-binding domain of Fn attaches to Sepharose, was used to characterize the receptor; the $\alpha_5\beta_1$ Fn receptor was purified and shown to consist of a 155-kd α chain and a 110-kd β chain (both nonreduced, ie, the intradisulfide bonds are still intact). Antibodies to the receptor complex were then made, the receptor was purified, protein sequence was obtained, and both chains of the receptor were cloned by Ruoslahti and colleagues. Similar methods were used to identify other integrins, such as vitronectin (Vn) receptors.

Interestingly, a different Fn peptide is involved in interaction with a distinct integrin $\alpha_4\beta_1$. Yet other Fn peptide sequences interact both with cells and with the glycosaminoglycan heparin. Although the cell-surface receptors have not yet been completely characterized, it is likely that they are cell-surface proteoglycans. At least one cell-surface proteoglycan, called syndecan, is known to bind Fn. The ability of multiple cell-surface receptors to bind a single extracellular matrix protein is a remarkable feature of cell adhesion. This feature raises the possibility that one important effect of cell binding to the extracellular matrix is that

Table 21
Integrin $\alpha\beta$ heterodimers

Heterodimers	Other designations	Ligands	RGD role	Immune cells expressed
$\alpha_1\beta_1$	VLA-1	Collagen, laminin	–	T cells, macrophages/monocytes
$\alpha_2\beta_1$	VLA-2, Ia/IIa, ECMRI	Collagen, laminin	–	B cells, T cells, macrophages/monocytes
$\alpha_3\beta_1$	VLA-3, ECMRII	Laminin, Fn	–	B cells, T cells, macrophages/monocytes
$\alpha_4\beta_1$	VLA-4, LPAM-2	Fn, cell-cell, HEV, VCAM-1	No	B cells, T cells, macrophages/monocytes
$\alpha_4\beta_7$	VLA-4$_{alt}$, LPAM-1	Peyer's patch, HEV	–	Mouse leukemic lines, mouse lymph node
$\alpha_5\beta_1$	VLA-5, Ic/IIa, Fn receptor	Fn	Yes	Pre-B cells, T cells, macrophages/monocytes
$\alpha_6\beta_1$	VLA-6, Ic/IIa	Laminin	–	T cells, macrophages/monocytes
$\alpha_6\beta_4$	VLA-6$_{alt}$	?	–	–
$\alpha_L\beta_2$	LFA-1	ICAM-1, ICAM-2	No	B cells, T cells, macrophages/monocytes, granulocytes
$\alpha_M\beta_2$	Mac-1, Mo-1, CR3	C3bi, fibrinogen, *Leishmania*, factor X, etc	?	Macrophages/monocytes, granulocytes
$\alpha_X\beta_2$	p150,95, CR4	C3bi?	No	Macrophages/monocytes, granulocytes
$\alpha_{IIb}\beta_3$	IIb/IIIa	Fn, fibrinogen, Vn, von Willebrand factor	Yes	–
$\alpha_V\beta_3$	Vn receptor	Vn, fibrinogen, von Willebrand factor, thrombospondin	Yes	B cells, macrophages/monocytes
$\alpha_V\beta_5$	Vn receptor (alt)	Fn, Vn	–	Macrophages/monocytes

several receptors, which are otherwise randomly distributed, aggregate within the plane of the membrane.

A second method for identifying integrins was indirect. Hemler and colleagues prepared monoclonal antibodies to antigens that appeared on activated T lymphocytes after weeks in culture. The antibodies identified a family called the VLAs (very late antigens). Although more recent studies have shown that the time course of expression of all VLAs does not follow this scheme, the nomenclature has remained.

A third method to identify integrins and integrin-associated proteins is to study the phenotypic cell changes that occur after the cells interact with a matrix protein or with other cells. One example is the characterization of proteins that mediate binding of macrophages and neutrophils to matrix proteins, a process that leads to increased phagocytosis of immunoglobulin and complement C3-coated targets. A second example is the characterization of receptors and their ligands that mediate attachment of cytotoxic T cells to targets. These integrins were initially identified by developing monoclonal antibodies that interfered with adhesion and cytotoxicity. The prototype molecule for this phenomenon is LFA-1 (lymphocyte function antigen-1). Of great interest, leukocyte adhesion deficiency (LAD), a naturally occurring deficiency of LFA-1 receptors, has been described (see page 109).

Structures of Integrins

Integrin Subfamilies

Table 22 includes a list of the known integrin α and β chains and their molecular weights under nonreducing conditions. This list continues to grow as new chains are identified by polymerase chain reaction (PCR) techniques. Historically, integrins have been grouped according to their β chain association. In this context, they have been known as the β_1 (VLA), β_2 (Leu CAM), and β_3 (cytoadhesin) subfamilies. More recently, the identification of several new β chains revealed that the strict association of α chains with a single β chain is not true in every case. For example, the α_V chain

Table 22
Individual integrin molecules

Chain	M_r (nonreduced)	α Chain Intervening sequences	Posttranslational cleavage
α_1	200 000	+	−
α_2	160 000	+	−
α_3	150 000	−	+
α_4	140 000	−	−
α_5	155 000	−	+
α_6	140 000	−	+
α_L	170 000	+	−
α_M	165 000	+	−
α_X	145 000	+	−
α_V	150 000	−	+
α_{IIb}	145 000	−	+
β_1	110 000		
β_2	90 000		
β_3	90 000		
β_4	210 000		
β_5	100 000		
β_6	100 000		
β_7	100 000		

was initially found to interact with β_3, but recently α_v has been found paired with β_1, β_5, and β_6. The significance of these diverse $\alpha\beta$ combinations is not clear. There is probably some alteration in ligand affinities, but all α_v-containing receptors seem to bind Vn. Perhaps more important, the different β chains provide different intracellular signals on ligand binding and different associations with cytoskeletal components. For example, $\alpha_v\beta_3$ appears to associate with focal contacts when cells are spread on a vitronectin surface but $\alpha_v\beta_5$ does not.

Figure 38 shows the known $\alpha\beta$ heterodimer associations. In some instances, where the β chain (for example β_6) has been isolated by PCR-derived cDNA cloning methods, all the α-chain associations have not yet been established. A recently cloned β_7 chain may be identical with β_p. The most complicated subfamily is the β_1 (VLA) family. The β_1 chain associates with at least seven unique α chains, α_1 through α_6 and α_v.

Table 21 lists the known $\alpha\beta$ heterodimers, other names by which they are commonly known, their cell distribution, and their known ligands. The ability of some receptors, for example $\alpha_v\beta_3$ and $\alpha_{IIb}\beta_3$, to interact with many different ligands of diverse structure is striking. Also notable is the ability of some receptors, for example VLA-4, to mediate both cell-matrix and cell-cell associations.

Integrin Molecular Structures

cDNA cloning analysis demonstrates that α and β chains share significant sequence identity, ranging from 20% to 60% with most in the 20% to 40% range. Several structural features common to each type of chain have been identified. α Chains have three or four domains with striking sequence homology to metal-binding domains. Such homology

is expected, given the divalent cation requirement for receptor function. Some α chains (Table 22) also have an intervening sequence of 180 to 200 amino acids, which probably plays a role in specific ligand binding. In addition, some α chains (Table 22) undergo a posttranslational proteolytic cleavage in the membrane-proximal region of the extracytoplasmic sequence. The role of cleavage is unknown, but it may serve to modulate ligand affinity or intracellular trafficking. β Chains have regions of high-cysteine content, and at least one disulfide bond is believed to stabilize a globular conformation of the β-chain head. The importance of the overall cysteine structure is reflected in the complete conservation of the 56 cysteines in the extracytoplasmic domains of the β_1, β_2, β_3, β_5, and β_6 chains (and 48 of 56 cysteines in β_4), in spite of significantly less conservation of amino acid sequence elsewhere.

To date, no integrin has been crystallized nor has its three-dimensional structure been solved. Therefore, our understanding of integrin structure is dependent on indirect protein modeling, cross-linking, and electron microscopic techniques. The primary experimental proteins upon which the integrin model is based are $\alpha_{IIb}\beta_3$, which is abundant on platelets, and $\alpha_5\beta_1$. Figure 39 illustrates one model of integrin structure.

Both α and β chains have short intracytoplasmic sequences of poorly understood function. The intracytoplasmic domains are believed to mediate interaction of receptor with the cytoskeleton rather than to play significant roles in heterodimer formation. They likely determine some aspects of ligand-specific interactions by the extracellular domain, a phenomenon that is discussed in more detail later. Although their roles are incompletely understood, the sequences of integrin (especially β chain) intracytoplasmic domains are almost completely conserved across species in which they have been examined. This nearly complete conservation is in contrast to extracytoplasmic sequences, which are only 80% to 90% conserved across species. In addition, recent experiments have demonstrated alternatively spliced intracytoplasmic sequences in the β_1 and β_3 molecules.

Figure 38
Known αβ heterodimer associations within the integrin family. cDNA cloning analysis has identified several β chains. Not all α-chain associations are known

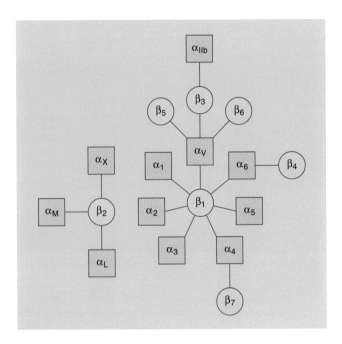

Figure 39
Model of an integrin based largely on studies of $\alpha_5\beta_1$ and $\alpha_{IIb}\beta_3$ heterodimers

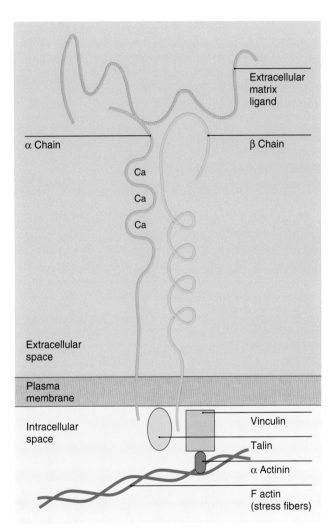

These alternatively spliced sequences are believed to function in the differential association of integrins with the cytoskeleton, in their efficiency as protein kinase substrates, and perhaps in ligand binding as well.

The gene structures of α and β chains are just beginning to be understood and are outside the realm of this chapter. Given the many sequence and domain similarities of α and β chains, their gene structures will likely share exon-intron organization similarities.

Functions of Integrins

General Ligand-Binding Properties

The known ligands for each integrin αβ heterodimer are listed in Table 21. The list is expected to grow as more is understood about the effects of cell background, other integrins, and alternative mRNA splicing on the binding properties of these receptors to ligands. To better explain the aspects of ligand binding, we will discuss a number of systems as models of these interactions. As more is understood about each integrin, many of these findings will likely become general rules within the family.

VLA-5 ($\alpha_5\beta_1$) is one of the best understood of the integrins, primarily because numerous investigators have studied its characteristics through the use of nonimmune cell models. The ligand for VLA-5 is Fn, which has many modular domains. Within the cell-binding domain is the tripeptide RGD. Peptides that contain RGD inhibit the ability of VLA-5 to bind Fn. Many of the ligands for integrins contain the RGD sequence, which inhibits the interaction of the receptor-ligand pairs. (See Table 21 for a list of individual receptors with known or postulated RGD interactions.) Why is the RGD sequence found in many ligand interactions with different receptors? One reason may be that RGD is in a different conformation in each ligand. Support for this hypothesis is demonstrated by studies of synthetic RGD peptides with side chains that constrain peptide flexibility in solution. Remarkable differences are seen in the ability of these constrained peptides to inhibit particular ligand-receptor pairs.

When RGD-Sepharose is used to purify proteins from placenta, $\alpha_v\beta_3$ is recovered and VLA-5 is not. RGD-Sepharose also purifies other types of less well-characterized integrins from neutrophils and monocytes.

As mentioned earlier, the interaction of integrins with their ligands is cation-dependent, and the relative ability of a receptor to bind its ligand varies with the cation used. For instance, manganese increases the apparent affinity of VLA-5 for Fn. In addition, studies have shown that the conformations of $\alpha_{IIb}\beta_3$, $\alpha_2\beta_1$, and $\alpha_M\beta_2$ change with different cations. It is also possible that different cations will stabilize preferred αβ heterodimers or that the use of different cations will alter the preferential use of integrins by cells.

Another striking characteristic of integrins is the apparent ability of a single αβ heterodimer to have many ligands. One example is $\alpha_4\beta_1$ (VLA-4). This receptor mediates adhesion of cells to other lymphoid cells, to the endothelial and follicular dendritic cell protein known as VCAM-1 (or INCAM-110), and to Fn through a different Fn peptide sequence present only in some forms of Fn. Interestingly, this domain is alternatively spliced in the Fn molecule, adding a further point at which integrin activities can be modulated. Whether VLA-4 interacts with all these molecules through a single site is unknown; however, more than one site is probably occupied, since binding to Fn and VCAM-1 can be discriminated with monoclonal antibodies and soluble Fn fragments.

Transmembrane Signals Mediated by Integrins

Outside the immune system, integrins have remarkable phenotypic effects on cells when interacting with their ligands. A few of these effects include myogenic cell differentiation, neural crest cell outgrowth and migration, and Drosophila wing and myospheroid stage development. The magnitude and complexity of such phenotypic effects suggest that specific transmembrane signals are delivered through integrins.

A current challenge in immunology is to understand the signaling mechanisms used by these receptors and the effects on immune cell function. Two models that address the issue are (1) the effects on T-cell function following the interaction of Fn, laminin, and collagen with VLA proteins, and (2) the effects of matrix proteins on phagocytic cell functions of chemotaxis and target ingestion (phagocytosis).

Signaling in T cells: T cells proliferate when the T-cell receptor (TcR) complex is engaged either by antigen-MHC molecules or experimentally by the use of monoclonal antibodies to CD3, which is part of the TcR complex (see chapter 3). Interestingly, the proliferative response to anti-CD3 antibodies is greatly augmented when T cells are cultured on Fn or on collagen-coated plates. In addition, the avidity of VLA-4 and VLA-5 for Fn and of VLA-6 for laminin is increased by TcR complex cross-linking. These findings suggest that the signal(s) mediated via VLA-4 and VLA-5 are very specific, and that there is considerable "crosstalk" among VLA-4, VLA-5, and the TcR complex. These findings also suggest that the activities of T cells can be modulated at sites of inflammation by interaction with matrix proteins. This effect is in addition to the likely increased adhesiveness of T cells to sites of inflammation mediated via VLAs.

Regulation of phagocytosis: In vitro phagocytic behavior of monocytes and neutrophils can be affected by a variety of extracellular matrix proteins. Phagocytic behavior is often mediated by integrin receptors. Since neutrophils and monocytes are normally circulating in the blood and are not in contact with the extracellular matrix, engagement of their extracellular matrix receptors is thought to be a mechanism through which the cells learn that they are out of the bloodstream and in an area of inflammation. Thus, extracellular matrix proteins and proteolytic fragments of these proteins help create the activated, inflammatory phenotype in phagocytic cells.

One of the best studied model systems for the functional effects of interaction of extracellular matrix with phagocytes is phagocytosis itself.

Early studies concentrated on the ability of extracellular matrix proteins to activate phagocyte complement receptors. Neutrophils and monocytes have two or three types of complement receptors, commonly called CR1, CR3, and p150,95 or CR4. These receptors recognize different domains of the C3 molecule and, on unactivated cells, none mediate phagocytosis. This finding suggests that foreign targets opsonized exclusively with C3 will be recognized by phagocytes and bound to their plasma membranes but will not be ingested. For many years it has been known that there are activation signals that will stimulate complement receptors to mediate ingestion of their bound C3-opsonized targets. The signals include cytokines, such as interleukin-4 (IL-4) and granulocyte macrophage–colony-stimulating factor (GM-CSF), and certain pharmacologic agents, such as phorbol esters. Because these activation signals neither increase Ia expression uniformly nor do they all activate the respiratory burst, phagocytic activation of C3 receptors on monocytes and macrophages must be distinguished from immunologic activation of monocytes. The primary cytokines involved in immunologic activation are tumor necrosis factor-α (TNF-α) and interferon gamma (IFN-γ), which have no effect on C3 receptor phagocytosis. (See chapter 7 for a complete discussion of cytokines.) It is now clear that phagocytic activation of monocyte C3 receptors is mediated by extracellular matrix proteins, including Fn, Vn, laminin, and collagen. Monocyte IgG-mediated phagocytosis (which is dependent on the receptors FcRI and FcRII) can also be enhanced by extracellular matrix proteins. Therefore, it appears that the phagocytic process is stimulated by monocyte or macrophage binding to extracellular matrix proteins.

For neutrophils, the phagocytic response to extracellular matrix is more complicated. Unactivated neutrophils are relatively inefficient at phagocytosis, and IgG-mediated ingestion is greatly enhanced by the exposure of neutrophils to extracellular matrix proteins. This effect is dependent on the RGD sequence in extracellular matrix proteins, and other RGD-containing proteins, such as fibrinogen and von Willebrand factor, also stimulate neutrophil IgG-mediated phagocytosis. In fact, synthetic peptides containing only the RGD sequence stimulate phagocytosis, provided the peptides contain several RGD sequences. This fact suggests that RGD is a sufficient recognition signal and that receptor clustering in response to the stimulatory protein is an important component of signal transduction from the integrin receptors for the extracellular matrix proteins to stimulate ingestion. However, neutrophil C3 receptors cannot be stimulated to ingest by extracellular matrix proteins alone. Stimulation appears to require another activation signal, such as the chemotactic peptide formylmethionyl leucylphenylalanine (fMLP) or the complement activation fragment C5a. The reason for this difference between monocyte and neutrophil C3 receptor function is not known. One hint may be that unactivated monocyte C3 receptors are capable of endocytosis of soluble C3 ligands, whereas neutrophil C3 receptors are not.

The integrin receptors involved in stimulating ingestion are not well defined. The results of studies of the binding of protein and synthetic peptide ligands suggest that β_1, β_2, β_3, and β_5 receptors are involved in ligand recognition on phagocytic cells. There is compelling evidence that a receptor immunologically related to β_3 or β_5 is involved in signal transduction for enhanced phagocytosis, which occurs on exposure to Fn, certain collagens, Vn, and von Willebrand factor. The α chain involved is not known but might be α_v. However, it is clear that laminin enhancement of ingestion does not occur through this receptor, but arises instead from interaction with $\alpha_6\beta_1$. Thus, at least two receptors on phagocytic cells are capable of mediating the extracellular matrix signal for enhanced ingestion.

The possible in vivo importance of extracellular matrix proteins activating phagocytosis has been illustrated in an animal model of newborn group B streptococcal septicemia. Group B streptococci are a major cause of morbidity and mortality among human newborns, particularly premature infants. In the animal model, which entails intranasal inoculation of bacteria into newborn rats, intravenous administration of Fn enhances survival. Improved survival correlates with increased neutrophil ingestion of the streptococci both in vivo and in vitro, which has been clearly demonstrated to result from activation of phagocytosis by Fn. Thus, activation of phagocytosis by extracellular matrix proteins is probably significant in host defense against bacterial infections.

Chemotaxis: In addition to increased phagocytosis mediated by matrix proteins, proteolytic fragments of Fn cause chemotaxis of monocytes but not neutrophils. These Fn fragments all contain the RGD sequence and are relatively large, suggesting that they may be ligands for $\alpha_5\beta_1$, which is present on monocytes but not neutrophils. Although this observation makes $\alpha_5\beta_1$ a candidate for the receptor mediating chemotaxis, the premise has never been proved. In fact, because $\alpha_5\beta_1$ is involved in focal contacts (see the discussion on regulation of integrin function on page 107), it may be an unlikely candidate for the chemotactic receptor. Laminin enhances the chemotactic responsiveness of neutrophils to fMLP, but is not a chemoattractant on its own. The possibility that other extracellular matrix proteins stimulate chemotaxis of neutrophils or monocytes has not been systematically investigated.

Respiratory burst: The effects of extracellular matrix components on the respiratory burst are complex. A well-performed and interesting series of experiments showed that when neutrophils adhere to a basement membrane made by endothelial cells, the fMLP-stimulated respiratory burst is greatly inhibited. The inhibition makes teleologic sense, because the respiratory burst is highly toxic to surrounding tissue and nonspecific in its targets. Thus, if neutrophils were fully active in the respiratory burst function as they migrated through the endothelium to a site of inflammatory injury, considerable vascular damage might result.

Vascular injury would be highly undesirable, since loss of vascular integrity would result, a potentially lethal condition. The same studies suggested that laminin is a major component of basement membrane responsible for inhibition of the respiratory burst, but that laminin alone could not completely reproduce the inhibition. In contrast, other investigators found that laminin added in solution will actually enhance the respiratory burst generated by fMLP. The discrepancy between the results of these studies has not been resolved, but it probably relates to whether the laminin is in solution or is insoluble on a surface. In this regard, Fn fragments in solution are also powerful stimulants of the neutrophil respiratory burst, but Fn on a surface does not stimulate respiratory burst activity.

Regulation of Integrin Function

Integrin function is also modulated by posttranslational changes and probably by molecules that associate with integrins in the extracytoplasmic and intracytoplasmic domains. One of the most intriguing aspects of integrin function is the recent recognition of "inside-out" regulation, ie, cell activation alters the affinity of integrin receptors for their extracellular ligands by the generation of intracellular second messengers. Inside-out regulation was first recognized by investigators who were examining C3bi binding by the integrin C3 receptor $\alpha_M\beta_2$, also known as Mac-1 or CR3. Phorbol esters were found to enhance neutrophil C3bi binding transiently, apparently unrelated to receptor expression. This phenomenon was later demonstrated more conclusively for the $\alpha_M\beta_2$-dependent processes of neutrophil aggregation and adhesion by careful separation of the kinetics of aggregation from increased receptor expression and by pharmacologic manipulations that inhibited increased receptor expression without affecting receptor activation and vice versa.

However, the most elegant demonstrations of the phenomenon of integrin activation in the immune system have come from studies of $\alpha_L\beta_2$ (LFA-1) on T cells. T-cell expression of $\alpha_L\beta_2$ is unaffected by activation, so the issues of quantitative versus qualitative change, which plagued the studies of $\alpha_M\beta_2$ on neutrophils, were not apparent. Moreover, the ICAM ligands for $\alpha_L\beta_2$ are clearly described, while the ligand for $\alpha_M\beta_2$ is less well understood. When T cells are activated by anti-CD3 antibodies, the avidity of $\alpha_L\beta_2$ on the cell for its ligand ICAM-1 is greatly and transiently increased. The molecular mechanism for the alteration in affinity is not understood and may represent receptor phosphorylation or receptor aggregation in the plane of the plasma membrane. Receptor phosphorylation has not been demonstrated in this system, but it has been observed for both β_1 and β_2 integrins under conditions that stimulate increased adhesion. The increased affinities of $\alpha_L\beta_2$ for ICAM and $\alpha_M\beta_2$ for C3bi are transient, which implies that the activation process is reversible. The reversibility might explain how cytotoxic T cells can kill multiple targets. Sequential killing of several target cells requires first tight $\alpha_L\beta_2$-dependent adhesion to one target and then release from that target in order to bind a second target cell.

One primary, well-explored role of integrins in many cells is to mediate attachment of the plasma membrane to the cell cytoskeleton. An important way in which attachment occurs is via the organization of focal adhesion plaques, which are sites of close apposition of the plasma membrane with the extracellular matrix. Focal adhesion plaques in nonimmune cells are well described. They are sites where stress fibers, which are long strands of filamentous actin, meet the plasma membrane. The interaction of actin with plasma membrane is not direct but is mediated by several other proteins, including talin, vinculin, and α-actinin, each of which can be localized by immunocytochemistry to focal adhesions. It is thought that integrins can interact directly with talin and possibly with vinculin. Thus, when integrins bind to extracellular matrix ligands, they can organize focal adhesions. Recent data suggest that the ability to organize focal adhesions is a property of the integrin β chains. Genetically engineered β_1 chains that lack intracytoplasmic domains do not localize to focal adhesions, even though the ability of the heterodimeric integrin to bind extracellular ligand is apparently unaffected. β_3 Chains also seem to mediate integrin inclusion in focal contacts, whereas β_5 chains do not. Other evidence suggesting a role for the intracytoplasmic domains of β_1 and β_3 in focal contact formation is the demonstration of direct binding of these chains to vinculin and the binding of vinculin, talin, and α-actinin to affinity columns made with peptides corresponding to the β-chain intracytoplasmic domains. No corresponding associations are apparent for the α-chain intracytoplasmic domains, and the functions of these peptides are not known. The role of the intracytoplasmic domain of β_2 in the activation-dependent change in ligand affinity has been tested for $\alpha_L\beta_2$. If the intracytoplasmic domain of β_2 is removed, increased affinity on cell activation does not occur. This finding suggests that affinity alterations and cytoskeletal attachment are closely related phenomena. The importance of focal contacts for the functioning of immune cells is not clear. Macrophages and neutrophils generally do not form stress fibers, but they do contain talin, vinculin, and α-actinin and therefore possess the potential for expressing focal contacts.

Integrins may also associate with other plasma membrane proteins, either spontaneously or with activation. One such protein, called IAP (integrin-associated protein), has been purified and partially characterized. IAP, a 50-kd glycosylated integral membrane protein, seems to associate with neutrophils, monocytes, and platelet β_3-like integrins upon activation. Antibodies to IAP inhibit β_3 and β_5 function in a variety of cell types, a finding that suggests that inhibition may be part of a signal transduction complex. However, the mechanism of action of IAP remains unknown.

Regulation of Integrin Expression

Integrin expression is cell-specific (Table 21). A number of other features are of relevance to immune cell function. During B- and T-cell ontogeny, expression of individual VLAs is regulated. The results of studies of murine B lymphopoiesis suggest that receptors for the cell-binding domain RGD and the heparin-binding domain II of Fn are differentially expressed. Human pre-B cells express VLA-5, whereas mature resting peripheral, tonsillar, or splenic B cells do not. In contrast, VLA-3 and VLA-4 are expressed throughout B-cell development. VLA-5 expression again increases in a subpopulation of cells when resting B cells are activated with *Staphylococcus aureus* Cowan 1 strain, a polyclonal B-cell activator. It is not yet known whether B cells, as well as T cells, can mediate similar transmembrane signals.

Expression of integrins on macrophages also is modulated by inflammation and inflammatory mediators. Studies with a mouse peritoneal cell model system have shown that VLA-5 expression is significantly increased on macrophages after inflammatory stimuli, such as thioglycollate, are instilled in vivo. The effect is specific for the α_5 chain, since levels of β_1 mRNA were unchanged. This finding suggests that the rate of α-chain expression primarily mediates levels of specific heterodimer expression. The α chains then use a pool of preformed β chains. This pool has been demonstrated with fibroblast model systems. The VLA-5 increase is not likely to be due to IFN-γ. The cytokine transforming growth factor-β (TGF-β) has also been shown to increase VLA-5 expression by fibroblasts and probably has similar effects on immune cells.

Another model of integrin regulation is found in memory T cells, which have an increased β_1 (CD29) expression relative to resting (or naive) T cells. The increased expression is accounted for by increases primarily in VLA-1 and VLA-2 expression. This phenotype is believed to correlate with activated T cells found in inflammatory sites, such as in the synovial fluid of patients with rheumatoid arthritis. Although the extent of commitment of cells to a memory or naive phenotype has been challenged, it is of great theoretical interest that these VLAs might play a significant role in cell trafficking and in organ-specific immunity. This possibility is underlined by the recent finding that $\alpha_4\beta_P$ is a lymphocyte receptor for Peyer's patch endothelium.

Clinical Aspects of Integrins

Deficiency Disorders

Perhaps the best model of in vivo integrin function is the deficiency of integrin expression identified in a number of human kindred. A human genetic disease characterized by frequent bacterial infections has been recognized for about 10 years. The clinical characteristics of affected individuals include, in addition to frequent infections, failure to resorb the umbilical stump and a leukocytosis with a predominance of neutrophils, even at times when infection is not present. These patients lack expression of the β_2 integrins on their leukocytes. The disease, now termed *leukocyte adhesion deficiency* (LAD), is the manifestation of genetically heterogenous defects, including point mutations in β_2, deletions in β_2, and splicing defects in β_2. In general, severely affected persons express less than 1% of normal levels of β_2 integrins, and moderately affected persons express 1% to 10% of normal levels. Cutaneous infections in LAD patients are characterized by a lack of infiltration of neutrophils and by a delayed and deficient appearance of monocytes into the sites of infection.

Despite the critical role of LFA-1 ($\alpha_L\beta_2$) in many T-cell functions in vitro, patients with LAD are rarely troubled by infections caused by viruses or intracellular pathogens, which suggests that lymphocytes may use other adhesion mechanisms to overcome the defect created by β_2 deficiency. Recent data suggest that monocytes possess alternative modes for adhering to endothelium and for emigrating into inflammatory sites as well. The recognition that both monocytes and lymphocytes express $\alpha_4\beta_1$, which can recognize the endothelial ligand VCAM-1, may explain this alternative pathway for recognition and emigration.

The lack of $\alpha_4\beta_1$ expression on neutrophils may explain why LAD manifests itself primarily as a neutrophil defect. However, even neutrophils may possess alternative mechanisms for emigration into inflammatory sites, at least in some tissues. An elegant set of experiments showed that in an animal model of pneumococcal pneumonia, neutrophils emigrated into the infected lung normally in the absence of β_2 function.

Patients with severe genetic β_2 deficiency have been treated with bone marrow transplantation to combat the lethal nature of the infections they acquire so easily. β_2-Deficient patients accept partially allogeneic bone marrow grafts more readily than do other bone marrow recipients, and the success of this therapy in patients with the β_2 defect has been high. The efficacy of allogeneic grafts in this special circumstance suggests that the absence of LFA-1 actually down-regulates the immune response. This supposition led to clinical trials in which anti–LFA-1 is used to treat bone marrow recipients who have normal expression of β_2; although results are preliminary, the studies indicate that anti–LFA-1 may improve marrow engraftment in such patients.

Prospects for Therapy

Because adhesive events are involved so ubiquitously in immunologic and inflammatory phenomena, considerable attention and effort have gone into developing methods for inhibiting adhesive interactions as a way of modulating or abrogating the ill effects of inflammation. Relatively recently, reperfusion of ischemic tissue has been recognized as the cause of morbidity and mortality in a variety of circumstances. Reperfusion injury has been implicated in death from hypovolemic or septic shock, in the adult respiratory distress syndrome, in extension of myocardial infarction, in acute failure of transplanted organs, and in frostbite, to name a few clinical situations. Reperfusion injury is at least partially due to factors released from ischemic tissue that attract neutrophils, causing the neutrophils to adhere and emigrate into the injured tissue. Neutrophil degranulation and respiratory burst are responsible for much of the tissue injury that occurs on reperfusion.

Antibodies to β_2 integrins have been used in several animal models to inhibit neutrophil adhesion and emigration. Survival from experimentally induced hypovolemic shock can be improved, and necrosis from chemical or thermal injury can be limited by systemic administration of anti-β_2 antibodies. In a canine model, the size of a cardiac infarction that occurred after thrombosis and reperfusion was also decreased by such a protocol.

Perhaps one of the most interesting studies involved a model of bacterial meningitis in rabbits. Anti-β_2 antibodies prevented neutrophil accumulation in the infected cerebrospinal fluid (CSF) and also prevented the CSF increases in protein and decreases in glucose that are characteristic of meningitis. The chemical changes in the CSF that occur in meningitis are indicative of breaches in the blood-brain barrier. Although neutrophils have an obvious host defense function in meningitis, loss of the blood-brain barrier is associated with many of the late complications, such as hydrocephalus in pediatric patients. Thus, it is possible that judicious inhibition of neutrophil function with the appropriate use of antibiotics may be an ideal way to treat bacterial meningitis in infants and children.

Therapy with anti-β_2 antibodies has not yet reached the clinical trial stage in humans, but there is reason to believe that agents that block β_2 function will be useful in a variety of clinical circumstances.

Selected Readings

Albelda SM, Buck CA. Integrins and other cell adhesion molecules. **FASEB J**. 1990;4:2868-2880.

Hemler ME. VLA proteins in the integrin family: structures, functions, and their role on leukocytes. **Annu Rev Immunol**. 1990;8:365-400.

Hogg N. The leukocyte integrins. **Immunol Today**. 1989;10:111-114.

Ruoslahti E, Pierschbacher MD. New perspectives in cell adhesion: RGD and integrins. **Science**. 1987;238:491-497.

Springer TA. Adhesion receptors of the immune system. **Nature**. 1990;346:425-434.

The Complement System

Overview

Introduction
The complement system consists of at least 29 proteins engaged in the defense of the body. Following the course of this regiment by diagrams is sometimes like trying to track infantrymen on a field of furious battle. Nonetheless, an understanding of the complex mechanisms of the complement system will assist the reader in grasping how most humans can live well beyond birth, despite the continual barrage of microorganisms and infecting elements that assault the body. Additionally, knowledge of the system's normal operation aids in researching and treating defects that occur along genetic and acquired fronts.

In its simplest description, the complement cascade provides both an independent immune system and an adjunct to the antibody system. It possesses the ability to independently attack and amplify its components when confronting a foreign particle. Additionally, when antibodies are synthesized against and bind to an invading element, the complement system becomes activated to assist in this defensive process.

Investigation of the complement system originated just before the turn of the 20th century. About the same time Marconi was perfecting the wireless telegraph to lay the foundation for global communications, researchers such as Jules Bordet and Paul Ehrlich were discerning the inner communications of the immune system. These and other researchers found both heat-labile and heat-stable elements in serum that worked synergistically to eliminate microorganisms. The heat-inactivatable fraction of serum was termed *complement*. Because all individuals possessed complement, it was considered to be "nonspecific." In contrast, the heat-stable elements, or antibodies, were specific in being directed against particular pathogens and were found in high concentrations following infection. Now it is evident that complement and antibody are two independent but overlapping humoral recognition and effector systems that developed to protect the host from infections.

Table 23
Molecular weights and concentrations of complement proteins in plasma

Component	Molecular weight	Serum concentration (µg/mL)
Classical pathway		
C1q	410 000	150
C1r	90 000	100
C1s	85 000	50
C4	206 000	300
C2	117 000	15
Alternative pathway		
Factor B	90 000	225
Factor D	25 000	3
Properdin	110 000-220 000	25
Both pathways		
C3	190 000	1200
Terminal components		
C5	185 000	85
C6	128 000	60
C7	120 000	55
C8	150 000	55
C9	79 000	60
Regulators		
C1 inhibitor (C1 INH)	105 000	275
Factor I	88 000	35
Factor H	150 000	500
C4-binding protein (C4bp)	560 000	250
S protein	84 000	500
Anaphylatoxin inactivator	310 000	35

Functions of Complement
Current research has identified 29 components in the complement system; 20 of these patrol plasma and other body fluids (and constitute about 5% of total serum protein), while 9 are membrane-bound (Tables 23 and 24). Although most circulat-

Table 24
Complement membrane proteins*

	Molecular weight	Tissue distribution
Regulators		
DAF	70 000	All peripheral blood cells, epithelial and endothelial cells, fibroblasts
MCP	45 000-70 000	Similar to DAF but not found on erythrocytes
HRF	65 000	Widely distributed; probably similar to DAF and MCP
MIRL	20 000	
Receptors		
CR1	190 000-280 000	Erythrocytes, monocytes/macrophages, B cells, some T cells, neutrophils, eosinophils, kidney podocytes
CR2	140 000	B cells, some T cells
CR3	150 000/90 000	Monocytes/macrophages, neutrophils, some lymphocytes
C3aR	?	Mast cells, basophils
C5aR	?	Granulocytes, monocytes

*Abbreviations: DAF is decay-accelerating factor; MCP is membrane cofactor protein; HRF is homologous restriction factor (also called C8-binding protein); MIRL is membrane inhibitor of reactive lysis (also called CD59); CR1, CR2, and CR3 are complement receptors types 1, 2, and 3; C3aR and C5aR are receptors for C3a and C5a.

ing complement proteins are synthesized in the liver, some are made by monocytes, macrophages, fibroblasts, and other cells. This local synthesis of components may contribute to the initiation of the inflammatory process at extravascular sites.

Following activation, the complement system functions in two major ways, as illustrated in Figure 40:

- Complement modifies foreign membranes as its components swarm onto microorganisms, such as bacteria and viruses. While this may lead to disruption of the membrane's integrity (lysis), the more important function of complement is to promote *opsonization* (literally, "to prepare for ingestion"), which refers to the coating of membranes or particles with complement components. Host cell receptors for these proteins subsequently bind and help clear complement-coated complexes.

- Complement promotes inflammation by releasing anaphylatoxins and chemotactic factors. Complement components that elicit body reactions resembling anaphylaxis are termed *anaphylatoxins*. They work primarily by triggering the release of histamine and other mediators from mast cells and basophils. The resulting contraction of smooth muscle and dilation of blood vessels facilitate the exudation of plasma and cells into an area of infection. *Chemotactic factors* serve to attract phagocytic cells to a site of inflammation.

In these two ways, the complement system promotes the destruction of microorganisms. In autoimmune diseases, however, complement can similarly produce inflammation and destroy host cells and tissues through phagocytosis or lysis.

Pathways of Complement Activation

In performing its defensive role, complement possesses several interesting features. First, its reaction sequence behaves like a biologic cascade or waterfall in which one element assists in activating the next step. Second, the complement

Figure 40
Functions of complement

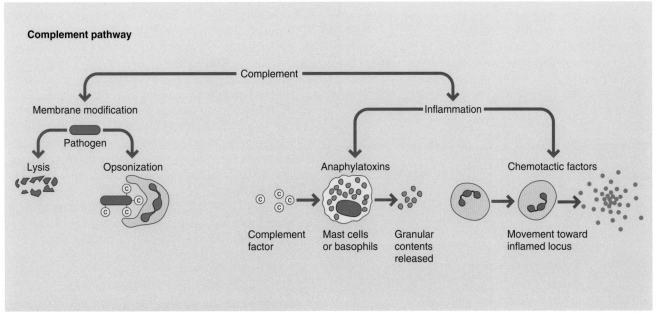

Complement pathway

Complement

Membrane modification

Pathogen

Lysis

Opsonization

Inflammation

Anaphylatoxins

Chemotactic factors

Complement factor

Mast cells or basophils

Granular contents released

Movement toward inflamed locus

The primary function of complement is to alter microbial membranes by lysis or opsonization. Additionally, complement factors promote inflammation by causing the release of histamine from certain cells and/or by attracting phagocytes to the site of inflammation.

system consists of two pathways that are triggered independently, yet merge in a common route.

One system, termed the *classical pathway*, becomes activated when antibody binds to antigen, such as viruses and bacteria. Antibody, therefore, defines the target. Its binding initiates a series of reactions in the complement system designed to rid the body of these invaders. As such, complement assists antibody as an efficient effector arm of the humoral immune system and, in fact, derived its name from this function.

Another route of complement activation is termed the *alternative pathway*. In this system, it is not necessary for the host to have had prior contact with (and thus have made antibody against) the microbe. Instead, a constant "trickle" of an activated component keeps this powerful system always on guard. Thus, the alternative pathway plays a surveillance role in the non-immune host and forms its own primitive immune system capable of recognizing and destroying foreign substances.

Amplification of components occurs only in the presence of foreign material. This fundamental and essential role of the alternative pathway is best illustrated when gram-negative bacteria enter the serum of a nonimmune host. Within a few

Figure 41
Structure of *Escherichia coli* as seen in scanning electron micrographs before and after killing by complement

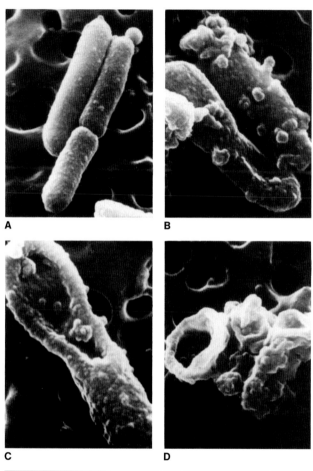

A

B

C

D

(**A**) Intact bacteria.
(**B**) and (**C**) Bacteria killed by purified complement proteins in the absence of lysozyme. Note the dramatic surface expansion and membrane blebbing.
(**D**) Bacteria killed by the combined action of complement and circulating lysozyme. Lysozyme degrades the peptidoglycan layer resulting in morphologic breakdown of the typical bacterial structure.

Reproduced with permission from Schreiber RD, Morrison DC, Podack ER, Müller-Eberhard HJ. Bactericidal activity of the alternative complement pathway generated from 11 isolated plasma proteins. *J Exp Med*. 1979;149:870-882.

minutes, the alternative pathway can deposit 2 million particles on the foreign surface to facilitate phagocytosis or lysis (Figure 41).

Nomenclature
Although complement was first identified in 1894 as a functional entity, it was not until the 1960s that its biochemical complexity began to be appreciated. Primarily because of technologic advances in the purification of proteins, more information has been uncovered since 1970 than in the preceding 70 years. Components have been named as they have been elucidated, leading to some inconsistencies in terminology. However, there is now a general pattern of reference:

- Components of the classical pathway are designated as C1, C2, C3, etc, for the most part in the order that they are activated in the cascade. Components of the alternative pathway are designated as *factors* with capital letters, such as factor B and factor D.
- Components cleaved by proteolysis are described by the suffixes *a*, *b*, etc (ie, C3a, C3b). The "b" fragment may directly combine with a target membrane and continue the cascade, while the "a" fragment is liberated and promotes the inflammatory response. (In the past, the terminology for C2 was just the opposite, but in this review we follow the general pattern of the rest of the components. The reader should be aware, however, that the nomenclature for C2 is not standardized and therefore both terminologies are found in the literature.)
- Most complement components circulate in an inactive, or zymogen, form. When a complement factor becomes activated, it may be designated by a bar placed over the term for the component, eg, $\overline{C1}$.

Figure 42
The binding of antibody to antigen (in this case on the membrane of a microbe) initiates the classical pathway that consists of four functional steps

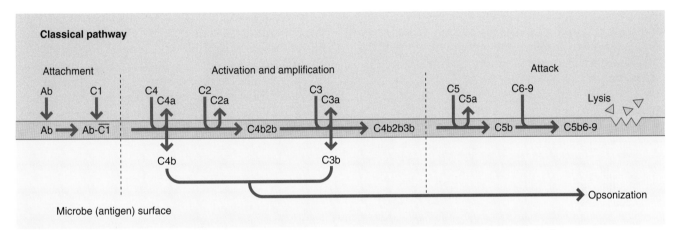

Classical pathway

Attachment — Activation and amplification — Attack

Microbe (antigen) surface

(Step 1: Attachment) Binding of the C1 complex to the Fc portion of antibody initiates the cascade.
(Steps 2 and 3: Activation and Amplification) Activated C1 cleaves C4 and then C2. A single C1 protein can activate numerous C4 components. C4b fragments attach covalently to the membrane where they serve primarily as opsonins. Some may bind C2b to form the C3 convertase (C4b2b), which proteolytically activates C3. After binding to the membrane, most C3b fragments act as opsonins. A few may form the C5

convertase (C4b2b3b). During the activation process, pro-inflammatory peptides, C4a, C3a (and later, C5a) are proteolytically cleaved from the parent component.
(Step 4: Attack) The complement-coated microbe is "attacked" (1) by host cells, which possess complement receptors that bind and ingest complexes via the C4b and C3b fragments (opsonization), and (2) by the membrane attack complex, which causes lysis.

Adapted with permission from Liszewski MK, Atkinson JP. The role of complement in autoimmunity. In: Bigazzi PE, Reichlin M, eds. *Systemic Autoimmunity*. New York, NY: Marcel Dekker Inc; 1991:13-37.

The Classical Pathway

The classical pathway was the first to be discovered. It serves primarily as a self-assembling series of components that are activated when antibody binds to antigen. When attached to antigen, IgM and most subclasses of IgG activate the classical pathway. In contrast, IgA, IgD, and IgE do not cause such activation.

Functionally, the classical pathway can be defined by the four A's: attachment, activation, amplification, and attack (Figure 42).

Attachment
Attachment, the linkage of the humoral immune system to complement, is the first stage of the classical pathway. It begins when a component of

the C1 complex, termed *C1q*, becomes attached to the Fc portion of an antibody molecule that has bound to antigen. In this way, C1q connects the humoral immune system to the classical pathway.

The C1 complex, with a molecular mass of approximately 750 000 daltons (d), is a noncovalently bound complex consisting of a single C1q and the calcium-dependent tetramer, C1s-C1r-C1r-C1s (C1r$_2$-C1s$_2$). An interesting feature of C1q is its fine structure (Figure 43). This molecule contains 18 polypeptide chains of three distinct types that are organized into a complex resembling a bouquet of flowers. There are six peripheral globular portions connected by collagenlike fibrillar strands to a central structure. The globular domains of C1q bind to the Fc portion of antibody. This interaction initiates the activation of the $C1r_2$-$C1s_2$ complex to continue to the next phase of the complement cascade.

Activation

In the activation stage, complement components with specific protease activity are produced. These subsequently activate other complement proteins to continue the cascade. C1r is cleaved by an autocatalytic mechanism when C1q binds to antibody. (Autocatalysis is a reaction that gradually accelerates because some of the products of catalysis are themselves catalytic agents.) This activated C1r then cleaves C1s, causing its activation. C1r and C1s are serine proteases with limited substrate specificity.

Circulating C4 is the next component in the series (Figure 42). It has a molecular mass of approximately 200 000 d and exists as three peptide chains linked together by disulfide bonds. C4 becomes activated when C1s cleaves C4 into two fragments. The larger fragment (C4b) may bind covalently to the nearby cell surface, while the smaller fragment (C4a) drifts away. C4a is a weak anaphylatoxin. Because of the enzymatic nature of C1s, many C4 molecules are activated. Some C4 molecules covalently attach to the particle surface near the site of antibody, some bind to antibody, and some enter the aqueous extracellular environment (fluid phase), where they rapidly become inactivated. The C4b fixed to the membrane forms a cluster, or complement-fixing site, around the area where antibody is bound. The cluster of C4b molecules becomes the site at which the complement cascade continues. C4b also serves as a ligand (opsonin) for complement receptors.

In addition to cleaving C4, C1s activates C2, the next component of the cascade. C2 binds C4b and then is cleaved by C1s. C2, a single polypeptide chain of about 117 000 d, is cleaved into two fragments: the smaller fragment (C2a) diffuses away; the larger fragment (C2b) is a serine protease and binds to C4b. C4b2b is a surface-bound bimolecular enzyme complex. C4b anchors the complex to the complement-fixing site, serves as a cofactor in the sense that it binds C2b, and positions the next component, C3. It is the critical function of C4b2b, termed the *C3 convertase*, to cleave and thereby activate C3.

Amplification

Amplification, the next step in the series, refers to the buildup of enzyme complexes and opsonic fragments on a target. This critical phase revolves around the component C3 (Figure 42). This 190 000-d glycoprotein consists of two disulfide-linked chains. When plasma C3 interacts with C4b2b, a small fragment (C3a) is released. C3a is a moderately potent anaphylatoxin. The larger fragment (C3b) either attaches covalently to the membrane or diffuses away to become inactivated. Membrane-bound C3b serves two purposes: the majority facilitate phagocytosis by C3b receptor-bearing host cells (ie, opsonization), and some interact with C4b2b to form a C5-splitting enzyme.

During C3 activation, the complement cascade becomes amplified. From one experimental system, it was estimated that each activated C1 molecule generated approximately 30 bound C4b molecules and up to six membrane-bound C4b2b complexes. Each C4b2b yielded approximately 200 bound C3b components, but only two to three activated C5 molecules. Therefore, each activated C1 complex gave rise to about 1200 molecules of C3b for opsonic purposes and approximately 12 to 18 molecules of C5b to initiate the membrane attack complex (see page 118).

Figure 43
The structure of C1q

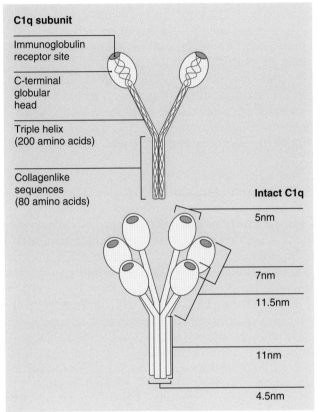

A

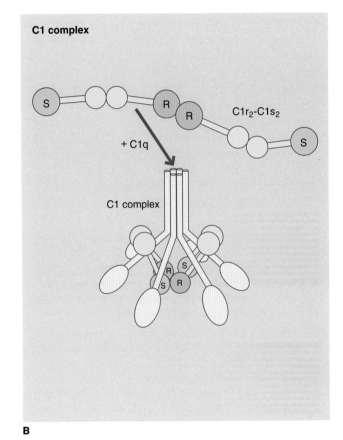

B

(**A**) Eighteen peptide chains are formed into three subunits of six chains each. Each subunit consists of a Y-shaped pair of triple helices joined at the stem and ending in a globular head. The receptors for the attachment to immunoglobulin complexes are situated in the globular heads.

(**B**) The model proposed for the C1 complex may be formed by placing the rodlike, inverted S-shaped $C1r_2$-$C1s_2$ complex across the C1q arms, then bending each end of the $C1r_2$-$C1s_2$ complex around two opposite C1q arms so that both C1s catalytic domains come into contact with the centrally located catalytic domains of C1r.

Adapted with permission from Colomb MG, Arlaud GJ, Villiers CL. Activation of C1. *Phil Trans R Soc Lond [Biol]*. 1984;306:283-292.

From the estimates it should be evident that the major goal of the complement system is the deposition of C3b on a foreign surface. The opsonic C3b targets the destruction of the particle to which it is bound by serving as a ligand for C3b receptors on phagocytic cells.

Attack

Another method of foreign cell destruction by complement occurs by assembly of the membrane attack complex (MAC), which can disrupt the integrity of the cell membrane (Figure 42). The MAC commences when C5 binds to C3b on target cells and becomes activated when the C5 convertase (C4b2b3b) cleaves C5 into two fragments. C2b again serves as the protease. The larger fragment (C5b) remains loosely attached to the C3b, while the smaller C5a is released into the fluid phase where it acts as a potent chemotactic factor and anaphylatoxin.

C5b, in contrast to C4b and C3b, does not display covalent binding capabilities upon activation; however, it is able to associate with biologic membranes and has binding sites for C6 and C7. This trimolecular complex (C5b67) becomes associated with the cell membrane, possibly through phospholipid binding sites within C7. Subsequently, C8 and C9 join the C5b67 complex. (Note that this buildup of terminal components does not involve proteases, as do the early components.) The MAC components C5 through C8 are sufficient to lyse a cell. It is C9, though, that markedly accelerates the lytic capacity of the C5-8 complex. Although as many as six C9 components may bind along with a C8, a single C9 molecule may be enough to mediate cell lysis. The actual mechanism of lysis is not enzymatic but involves the insertion of the MAC into the membrane forming a lesion (hole).

The Alternative Pathway

Although the classical pathway was discovered first, it is likely that the alternative pathway evolved first. Evidence for the existence of this system arose from the experiments of Louis Pillemer and associates. In a *Science* article appearing in 1954 (Vol. 120, pages 279-285), they described a novel protein in serum, called *properdin* (from the Latin word *perdere*, meaning "to destroy") that would bind to bacteria and yeast, triggering complement activation *without antibody*. A scheme of complement activation was proposed that involved components different from those of the classical system. At the time, relatively inexact methods of protein purification and characterization existed. Many immunologists disputed the findings and pointed to the presence of contaminants of antibody or classical components in the preparations.

Reportedly despondent over a continuing reluctance of the scientific community to accept his proposal, Pillemer committed suicide in 1957 with a buffer containing a barbiturate that was widely used in complement research. It was not until the 1970s that the individual components were purified and incubated together to demonstrate unequivocally the existence of a functional alternative pathway.

Four plasma proteins are directly involved in the alternative pathway: C3, factor B, factor D, and properdin (occasionally called factor P).

The alternative pathway provides a natural, immediately available line of defense. Again, it does not require specific antibodies against an infectious agent to be effective. The most remarkable aspect of the alternative pathway is its ability to recognize "foreignness" and quickly amplify on such targets. For example, if any of a wide variety of pathogens are placed in nonimmune human serum, they rapidly become coated with C3b. The alternative pathway mediates this protective response and acts as an independent immune system, comparable in many respects to the antibody-dependent system, which can also separate self from nonself.

Figure 44
C3 and the alternative pathway

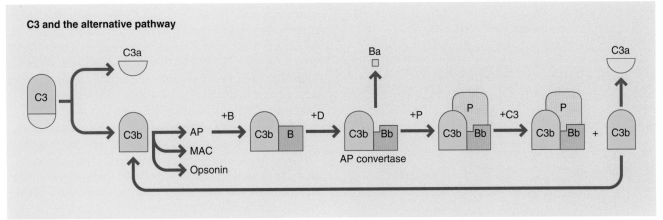

C3 and the alternative pathway

In addition to its important roles in eliciting the membrane attack complex (MAC) and serving as an opsonin, complement component C3 may trigger the alternative pathway (AP). Deposited C3b binds factor B to produce C3bB. Factor D, a serine protease of plasma, cleaves factor B (but only if it is bound to C3b) to release Ba, thereby forming the alternative pathway C3 convertase, C3bBb. The attachment of properdin (P) stabilizes the complex. As the convertase generates more and more C3b, the amplification loop further accelerates the activation of C3 and therefore the deposition of C3b on the target. Note that the initial C3 that is activated to C3b may be derived from the classical pathway or from the spontaneous "tickover" of this protein.

The central enzyme complex of the alternative pathway is C3bBb. Like the classical pathway C3 convertase (C4b2b), this bimolecular enzyme complex splits C3 to form C3a and C3b (Figure 44). The alternative pathway convertase forms as C3b binds covalently to the substrate and then binds serum factor B. Factor B, if associated with C3b, is subsequently cleaved at a single Arg-Lys bond to produce the fragments Bb and Ba by a serine plasma protease, factor D. The convertase is stabilized when properdin attaches to it. As the convertase cleaves more C3 to C3b, an amplification loop is set in motion in which large amounts of C3b are deposited on the foreign surface. The C3b may initiate the MAC, serve as opsonin, or generate more convertases.

Thus, C3 serves as a critical component for both the alternative and classical pathways (Figure 45). Regardless of which pathway generated the C3b, its subsequent involvement in opsonization or activating the MAC is identical.

What is not clear in the activation of the alternative pathway is the source of the initial C3b. In an immune host this could come from activation of the classical pathway. In other words, C3b deposited by the classical pathway could bind factor B and thereby trigger the alternative pathway. In this sense, the alternative pathway is a feedback loop for depositing more C3b on a target that has been identified by antibody.

However, the alternative pathway also forms in the absence of classical pathway activation and consequently must have its own means of generating C3b. Most investigators favor the hypothesis that low levels of C3b or a C3b-like molecule are continuously generated in the body. This turnover of C3 provides the starting material for the alternative pathway. However, the mechanism underlying C3b turnover has not been elucidated. It could arise enzymatically via endogenous proteases cleaving C3 to C3a and C3b. It also could arise nonenzymatically. The thioester bond within the α chain of C3 is unstable and with spontaneous hydrolysis would generate $C3(H_2O)$ (also known as iC3, since the thioester bond has become inactivated). This species behaves just like C3b in that it can bind to substrates and interact with factor B. Whether $C3(H_2O)$ binds directly to substrates and then binds factor B or first forms a fluid-phase $C3(H_2O)Bb$ convertase to cleave C3 is not clear.

Control of the Complement System

Strict regulation of the complement system is essential in preventing host cells and tissues from being destroyed (Table 25). Control is needed at several points to prevent amplification in the fluid phase and on host tissue. For example, activated components diffuse away from the site of activation, C3b and C4b deposit on self as well as foreign tissue in an inflammatory locus, and the C3 turnover phenomenon provides constant (although low) levels of activated C3 that binds indiscriminately to host as well as foreign targets.

Figure 45
A simplified diagram of the classical and alternative pathways of the complement system

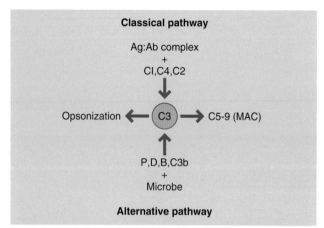

C3 is the central component of both cascades. When activated, it promotes the opsonization (and subsequent phagocytosis) or leads to the formation of the MAC.

Reproduced with permission from Liszewski MK, Atkinson JP. The complement system and immune complex diseases. In: Stein JH, ed. *Internal Medicine*. 3rd ed. Philadelphia, Pa: Little Brown & Co; 1990:1635-1642.

Table 25
Complement regulatory proteins

Component	Location	Function Decay-accelerating activity*	Cofactor activity†	Substrate
C4bp‡	Plasma	+	+	C4b
Factor H	Plasma	+	+	C3b
DAF	Membrane	+	−	C4b/C3b
MCP§	Membrane	−	+	C3b/C4b
CR1	Membrane	+	+	C3b/C4b

Component	Location	Function	Substrate
C1 inhibitor	Plasma	Inactivates C1	C1r/C1s
S protein	Plasma	Blocks fluid-phase MAC	C5b67
MAC inhibitorsII	Membrane	Blocks MAC on host cells	C8
Anaphylatoxin inactivator	Plasma	Degrades C4a, C3a, C5a	C4a, C3a, C5a
Factor I	Plasma	Degrades C3 convertases with cofactor	C3b, C4b

*Decay-accelerating activity refers to the ability to dissociate the convertases.
†Cofactor activity indicates participation of the regulators with factor I to cleave and thereby inactivate C3b and C4b.
‡C4bp can bind to C3b, as well as C4b, although factor H is probably the major C3b-binding protein of plasma.
§MCP can bind to C3b and C4b, but its binding to C4b is with a lower affinity.
IIMAC (membrane attack complex) inhibitors are HRF and MIRL (Table 24).

In order to control the complement system, regulation occurs primarily during the activation, amplification, and membrane attack steps.

Activation of the Classical Pathway

The C1 complex is rapidly inactivated by the C1 inhibitor, which is a single-chain, heavily glycosylated protein of about 100 000 d that binds to both C1r and C1s. This causes C1r and C1s to dissociate from the C1 complex. Protection against this regulator is temporarily afforded when C1 is bound to antibody. Thus, the C1 inhibitor does not block appropriate activation but degrades fluid-phase C1 and prevents excessive consumption by antigen-antibody complexes.

Classical and Alternative Pathway C3 Convertases

The generation of C3 convertases amplifies the complement system. Consequently, the opportunity exists for destruction not only of foreign cells, but also of host cells. To prevent this, the body has engineered a series of functionally, structurally, and genetically related plasma and membrane glycoproteins. These proteins provide strict control of convertase activity in order to focus its activity on pathologic substrates. Regulation is exerted in three ways: (1) Inhibition of the formation of the C3 convertases. (2) Acceleration of the decay of already formed convertases. (3) Proteolytic cleavage and thereby inactivation of C4b and C3b components of the convertase.

The two major regulatory activities are called *decay-accelerating activity*, which is the displacement of the protease (C2b or Bb) from the C3 convertase, and *cofactor activity*, which is the proteolytic attack on C4b and C3b in association with factor I, a serine protease. The latter activity can take place only when a cofactor protein has first bound to C4b or C3b. Some regulatory proteins possess only decay-accelerating activity or cofactor activity, while other proteins have both activities. In addition, some regulatory proteins have specificity for C3b or C4b, while other proteins have specificity for both C3b and C4b.

Cell membrane regulators are decay-accelerating factor (DAF), membrane cofactor protein (MCP), and complement receptor type 1 (CR1).

Plasma control proteins for this step are factor I, C4-binding protein (C4bp), and factor H.

- DAF is a glycolipid-anchored membrane glycoprotein that both prevents the assembly of C3 convertase and promotes dissociation of C2b from C4b or Bb from C3b in preformed complexes. DAF is expressed on a variety of different cells.
- MCP is a recently discovered membrane glycoprotein that serves as a cofactor for the proteolytic inactivation of C4b and C3b by factor I. MCP exists on a wide variety of cells (with the notable exception of erythrocytes). The ubiquitous presence of MCP and DAF on most cells of the body indicates their importance as biologic sentries preventing complement activation on autologous tissues.
- CR1 is present on most peripheral blood cells. Its primary function is to bind C3b-bearing immune complexes. As a regulator, it prevents excessive complement activation by such complexes.
- Factor I (C3b inactivator) is a plasma protein that cleaves C4b or C3b, but only in the presence of a cofactor, such as C4bp, MCP, or CR1.
- C4-binding protein, as its name suggests, binds C4b. C4bp is a spiderlike plasma protein (560 000 d) that can combine with up to six molecules of C4b to prevent its coupling to C2. In addition to dissociating the preformed convertase by displacing C2b, C4bp serves as a cofactor for the proteolytic inactivation of C4b by factor I.
- Factor H is analogous to C4bp in its role as regulator of C3/C5 convertases. Factor H not only binds to C3b but also acts as a cofactor in the presence of factor I to permanently inactivate C3b. Factor B regulates fluid-phase C3b and assists DAF and MCP in the control of C3b deposited on host tissue.

In summary, a number of plasma and membrane proteins regulate the amplification step of the classical and alternative pathways. They accomplish this goal by preventing assembly of the convertase, by dissociating already formed convertases, and/or by inactivating C4b or C3b so that they can no longer form the convertase. These regulators do not block complement activation on foreign tissue but localize the process to the membrane of the infectious particle; that is, they prevent activation in host fluids and on host tissues.

The Membrane Attack Complex

Control of the MAC is exerted by a plasma inhibitor known as S protein and several membrane proteins. The C5b67 complex can insert not only into foreign particles but also into host cells and tissues. To restrict this capability to the site of desired complement activation, S protein couples to the binding site on C5b67 complex, preventing its effective participation in the membrane attack sequence. Further, two membrane proteins of host cells bind to C8 and block the attachment of C9. These membrane proteins are homologous restriction factor (HRF) and membrane inhibitor of reactive lysis (MIRL). Inhibitory proteins are present to prevent the development of fluid-phase MAC (via S protein) and to block complement lysis of host tissue (via HRF and MIRL).

Biologic Action of Complement Components

Fragments liberated during complement activation mediate fluid-phase reactions that produce inflammation. Additionally, membrane-fixed components are ligands for receptors on peripheral blood cells and tissue macrophages.

Circulating Complement Fragments

C3a, C4a, and C5a are low–molecular-weight ($\approx$10 000 d) fragments that bind to specific receptors on mast cells and cause them to "fire." Biologically active mediators such as histamine are released, causing increased vascular permeability, contraction of smooth muscle, and local edema. C4a possesses mild spasmogenicity, while C3a and C5a are more potent spasmogens. C3a and C5a bind to receptors on neutrophils, monocytes, mast cells, and basophils. The firing of these receptors, in turn, leads to cell movement and release of granule constituents. Importantly, C5a induces the directed migration (chemotaxis) of leukocytes into an area of inflammation.

Complement Receptors

Receptors of the complement system bind substrates containing C3b and C4b. This allows the cellular attachment and, in some cases, subsequent ingestion of C3b/C4b-bearing material.

When a pathogen invades the body, the complement system may become activated along the classical or alternative pathways. In the immune host, antibodies "swarm" onto the microorganism, initiating the classical cascade and deposition of C4b and C3b. In the nonimmune host in whom no antibodies are present, the alternative pathway produces C3b to "coat" the pathogen.

Following activation of complement, some pathogens are destroyed as the terminal complement components in the membrane attack complex lyse the invader. More commonly, however, microorganisms are dealt a lethal blow by opsonization. That is, as the cascades amplify, many C3b molecules are produced that bind to the microorganism's surface. Complement receptors located on host cells bind and clear such opsonized particles. Tumor cells and soluble immune complexes may be processed in a similar fashion.

Complement receptor type 1 is the receptor for human C3b/C4b and is present on most peripheral blood cells (Table 24). In tissue sites, CR1 on neutrophils and monocytes promotes the internalization and subsequent digestion of the complexes.

Figure 46
Complement receptor type 1 (CR1) on erythrocytes (E) is the pivotal player in removing immune complexes (IC) from the circulation

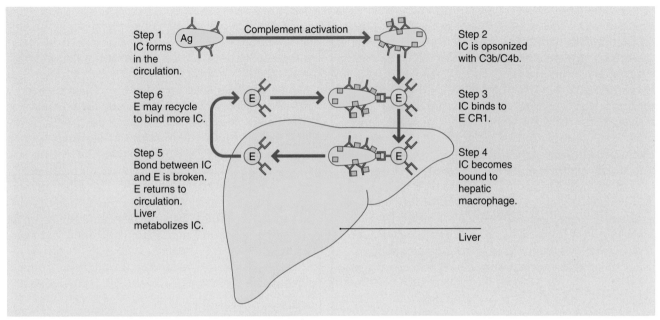

Step 1
IC forms in the circulation.

Complement activation

Step 2
IC is opsonized with C3b/C4b.

Step 6
E may recycle to bind more IC.

Step 3
IC binds to E CR1.

Step 5
Bond between IC and E is broken. E returns to circulation. Liver metabolizes IC.

Step 4
IC becomes bound to hepatic macrophage.

Liver

In this model, the CR1 on the erythrocytes binds circulating IC and transports it to the liver (or spleen), where it is transferred to hepatic macrophages. The erythrocytes then return to the circulation (possibly without the receptor).

Reproduced with permission from Liszewski MK, Atkinson JP. The role of complement in autoimmunity. In: Bigazzi PE, Reichlin M, eds. *Systemic Autoimmunity*. New York, NY: Marcel Dekker Inc; 1991:13-37.

CR1 on erythrocytes plays an especially important role in the handling and removal of immune complexes (Figure 46). Erythrocyte CR1 binds intravascular immune complexes (via C3b and C4b) and transports them to the liver and spleen. Macrophages in these organs strip off complexes (and possibly the receptor) from the erythrocyte surface. Subsequently, the erythrocyte returns to the circulation ready to shuttle again.

CR1 is a glycoprotein composed of a single polypeptide chain. It has an unusual polymorphism in that there are four codominantly inherited allelic forms with substantially different molecular weights. The two most common species are type A (220 000 d) and type B (250 000 d); the two rarer forms are type C (190 000 d) and type D (280 000 d). These four products all bind C3b.

Complement receptor type 2 (CR2) primarily binds C3b degradation fragments, termed *C3d* or *C3dg* (Figure 47). This receptor is detectable on 80% to 90% of B cells. In addition to its C3d-binding site, CR2 also contains a binding site for the Epstein-Barr virus, which allows entry and infection of B cells by this virus. Along with CR1 on B cells, CR2 facilitates the localization of immune complexes to B-cell–rich areas of spleen and lymph nodes.

Complement receptor type 3 (CR3) binds primarily to another breakdown product of C3, called *C3bi*. CR3 is found on cells such as macrophages/monocytes and certain lymphocytes. It is a two-chain protein that is part of a larger family of adherence-promoting molecules termed *integrins* (see chapter 8). Deficiency of CR3 is associated with severe infections that begin in childhood.

Recent research has also uncovered the presence of receptors for C1q as well as for factor H. B lymphocytes, neutrophils, and monocytes possess both types of these receptors. Their functional role is unknown.

Genetics and Common Structural Features of the Complement System

Genetics

The discovery of charge and/or size variants of complement components in the mid-1960s provided the impetus for investigating the genetics of complement proteins. Genetic variation was first noted for C3 because it was the easiest protein to study due to its abundance in serum. Shortly thereafter, polymorphic variants and genetic deficiencies of other complement proteins were discovered. New developments in tissue culture systems, cell-free translation (ie, the in vitro mRNA translation to protein on ribosomes), and recombinant DNA technology have accelerated the study of the structure, expression, and function of complement genes and their genetic variations. In some cases, these allelic deviations or deficiencies provide the basis for various illnesses (see page 127).

To date, the largest clustering of genes encoding human complement components has been found on the long arm of chromosome 1. The so-called regulators of the complement activation (RCA) family consist of the complement regulatory and receptor genes: CR1, CR2, DAF, MCP, factor H, and C4bp. The close linkage of these six complement components parallels their similar functions as regulatory and/or receptor proteins that bind C4b/C3b.

Additionally, a structural feature called a *short consensus repeat (SCR)* is found on these and other complement proteins that interact with C4b/C3b. The SCR consists of a unit of approximately 60 amino acids. Within this segment lie approximately 6 to 10 highly conserved amino acids at predictable locations (Figure 48). The existence of these internal repeating units points to common ancestral genes that have undergone gene duplication and exon shuffling during continued specialization (Table 26). A second clustering of complement component genes is found on chromosome 6 and consists of factor B, C2, and C4 (see chapter 2).

Special and Common Structural Features

Taken as a whole, the complement system is a diverse set of proteins that function as a potent yet carefully controlled means of host protection. Several special structural features are noteworthy when various aspects of the complement system are reviewed (Table 27).

At the attachment phase of the classical pathway, the C1q molecule initiates the cascade when it binds to the Fc portion of antibodies attached to

Figure 47
Metabolism of C3

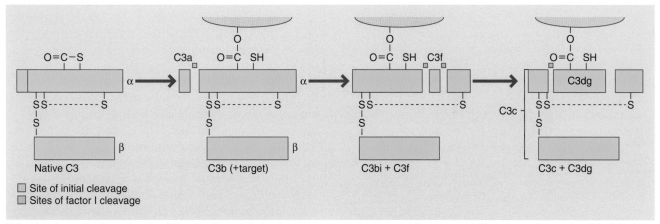

Site of initial cleavage
Sites of factor I cleavage

Following the activation of native C3, a small peptide is cleaved from the parent molecule (C3a) and the thioester moiety is altered, allowing it to bind target surfaces. Inactivation of C3b proceeds while factor I, along with cofactor proteins, sequen-
tially degrade the molecule. Complement receptors bind the various breakdown fragments to promote clearance of the foreign particle.

Adapted with permission from Hebert LA, Cosio FG. The erythrocyte–immune complex–glomerulonephritis connection in man. *Kidney Int.* 1987;31:877-885.

Figure 48
The short consensus repeat (SCR) unit

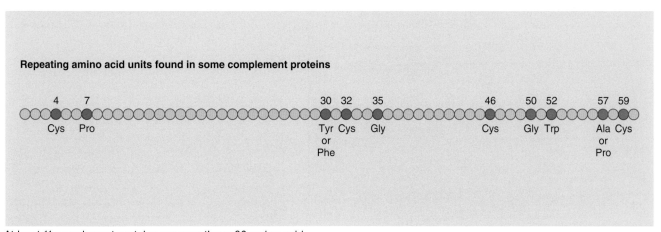

At least 11 complement proteins possess these 60 amino acid repeating units. The amino acids shown are conserved in almost all of the repeats.

Table 26
Short concensus repeat (SCR) family

Protein	SCR units	Chromosome
Plasma components		
C1s	2	12
C1r	2	12
C2	3	6
C6	2	?
C7	2	?
Factor B	3	6
C4bp*	56	1
Factor H	20	1
Factor I	1	4
Membrane components		
CR1†	30	1
CR2	16	1
DAF	4	1
MCP	4	1
Noncomplement proteins		
β_2 glycoprotein-1	5	?
IL-2 receptor	2	10
Factor XIII	10	1

*C4-binding protein has eight SCRs on each of seven identical chains.
†CR1 possesses seven SCRs within a so-called long homologous repeat; there are four such units with two additional SCRs (ie, 30 altogether).

Table 27
Some special structural features of complement proteins*

Structural feature	Protein*	Function
Collagenlike strands	C1q	Scaffolding for globular domains that interact with the Fc region of antibody
Serine proteases (of limited specificity)	C1r, C1s, C2, factor B, factor D	Cleavage and thereby activation of other complement components
Thioester bonds	C4, C3	Covalent attachment to substrates
Short concensus repeat (SCR, 60 amino acids)	C1r, C1s, C2, C6, C7, DAF, MCP, CR1, CR2, C4bp, factors B, H, and I	Binding domains for C3b and C4b
Hydrophobic domains	C5, C6, C7, C8, C9	Insert into biologic membrane

*Many of these proteins with similar structural features are homologous molecules having arisen by gene duplication or evolved from a common ancestral protein: for example, C1r and C1s; C2 and B; C4 and C3; factor H, MCP, DAF, C4bp, CR1, and CR2; C6 and C7; and C8 and C9.

an antigen. The unusual collagenlike stalk of C1q (Figure 43) provides the scaffolding for the globular heads, which interact with the complement-fixing sites on immunoglobulins.

Five complement proteins (C1r, C1s, C2, factor B, and factor D) are all precursors of serine proteases of very limited and focused substrate specificity (eg, C1r cleaves only C1s which, in turn, cleaves and activates only C4 and C2). C2 and factor B are structurally related protease precursors that cleave both C3 and C5. Factor D is a serine protease that exists in plasma in an active form; however, it cleaves a substrate (factor B) only when factor B is bound to C3b.

The thioester bond of C3 and C4 provides a highly reactive area on the molecule that can form covalent attachment to substrates (such as the membranes of microorganisms). This bond is formed between a thiol group of a cysteinyl residue and a gamma-COOH group of a glutamyl residue. Upon cleavage of C3 to C3b and C4 to C4b, the activated C3b and C4b react with cell-surface amino groups to form amide linkages or with hydroxyl groups to form ester linkages.

The importance of the reactive versatility of the thioester bond is illustrated especially by C4. There are two forms of C4 termed *C4A* and *C4B*. They are the products of two closely linked and highly homologous (more than 99% at the amino acid level) genes. The few amino acid differences are found near the thioester bond and give rise to different functional abilities. Thus, C4A binds more efficiently to amino groups, while C4B shows enhanced affinity for hydroxyl groups. This reactive diversity allows the complement system to interact with a wider variety of microbes, thus conferring a biologic advantage.

As described, a family of structurally related complement proteins possesses short repeating amino acid units (Figure 48). Thus far, 25 proteins have been found that contain varying numbers of

Table 28
Complement deficiencies and associated diseases

Component	Number of patients with homozygous deficiency	Number of patients with associated diseases	
		IC diseases*	Infections
Classical pathway			
C1q	15	14	Fewer than 20% with bacterial infections
C1r/C1s	8	6	
C4	16	14	
C2	66	38	
Alternative pathway			
Factor D	2	–	Most with bacterial infections
Factor B	0	–	
Properdin	4	–	
Both pathways			
C3	11	8	10 with severe bacterial infections
Terminal components			
C5	12	1	9 with *Neisseria*
C6	17	2	10 with *Neisseria*
C7	14	1	6 with *Neisseria*
C8	14	1	8 with *Neisseria*
C9	Many	None	Healthy
Regulators			
C1 inhibitor	> 500	2%	Hereditary angioedema
Factor I	5	1	4 with bacterial infections
Factor H	2	1	–

*IC (immune complex) diseases include SLE, SLE-like syndromes, glomerulonephritis, vasculitis.

Modified from Schifferli JA, Peters DK. Complement, the immune-complex lattice, and the pathophysiology of complement-deficiency syndromes. *Lancet.* 1983;2:957-959.

these tandemly arranged repeats (Table 26). In the complement system, these proteins share the functional feature of interacting with C3b and/or C4b.

Finally, hydrophobic domains are present on all proteins of the membrane attack complex. The obvious utility for such a feature is to facilitate insertion into and thus disruption of the membranes of microorganisms.

Clinical Aspects of Complement

Deficiencies of Complement Components

The study of complement deficiencies has provided clues to understanding the functioning and importance of the complement system (Table 28). For the most part, deficiencies are rare and inherited as autosomal recessive conditions. Particular-

ly striking is the association between immune complex diseases and the deficiencies of certain complements, such as C1, C4, and C2. Approximately 90% of individuals with C1q, C1r/C1s, and C4 deficiencies have systemic lupus erythematosus (SLE). More than 50 C2-deficient individuals have been described, approximately half of whom exhibited SLE or a related illness. Moreover, even partial deficiencies of C4 predispose an individual to SLE. Such disease states may arise from the failure to efficiently clear circulating immune complexes, especially those containing infectious particles. There is also an increased frequency of infections in patients with deficiencies of these early components of the classical pathway.

Genetic deficiencies have been noted for other complement components. A C3 deficiency is the most life-threatening of the "complete" deficiency states. It is associated with severe, recurrent infections that begin soon after birth. Such severe ramifications attest to the important role C3b plays as an opsonin of infectious particles. Deficiency of C5-8 is associated with *Neisseria gonococcus* or *N meningococcus* infections, but affected individuals are otherwise surprisingly healthy. These data indicate that the C5-9 lytic system may have evolved to assist the host against this particular group of organisms. It should be noted that severe gram-negative infections like *Neisseria* are also associated with deficiencies of the alternative pathway, especially properdin.

Deficiencies of Inhibitors

C1 inhibitor deficiency: Hereditary angioedema was the first complement deficiency state recognized in clinical medicine. This familial syndrome of recurrent episodes of swelling (angioedema) has been known since the turn of the century. It is inherited in an autosomal codominant fashion. In 1961, patients with hereditary angioedema were discovered to be deficient in the C1 inhibitor (C1 INH). In this deficiency, activated C1 is not regulated and, as anticipated, C4 and C2 are chronically low. (Additionally, the edema that occurs may be mediated by a small peptide liberated during the degradation of C2.)

Usually the attacks of swelling first occur in adolescence and continue throughout life. The reason for their episodic nature is unclear, although physical trauma is one precipitating factor. The swelling develops over a 4- to 6-hour period and persists for approximately 2 days before spontaneously resolving. The swelling is nonpainful, nonpruritic, nonerythematous, and nonpitting. It commonly involves the extremities, face, and gastrointestinal tract. Occlusion of the airway secondary to laryngeal swelling was formerly a cause of death in about one third of these patients.

Afflicted individuals have reduced (less than 25% of normal) functional activity of the C1 INH. Analysis of the C1 INH at the protein and DNA levels indicates that various genetic defects can be responsible for the deficiency. The disease process can be prevented by infusions of plasma (a source for C1 INH) or the purified protein. Also, it is partially controlled by antifibrinolytic agents. Of great interest is the fact that upon the administration of androgens, most patients with this deficiency develop increased levels of C1 INH, with some patients achieving normal levels. In addition, the C4 and C2 levels become normal. If the medication is stopped, C1 INH levels decrease and the swelling episodes return. The mechanism whereby androgens exert their effect is unknown, but presumably it represents an androgen-responsive element in the regulatory portion of the C1 INH gene.

Factor I and factor H deficiencies: For the most part, factor I and factor H deficiencies are similar, although more data are available for factor I. These deficiencies are inherited as autosomal recessive traits. Affected individuals experience recurrent infections, and some also have hemolytic anemia and urticaria (hives). C3 is synthesized normally, but turnover is rapid because the alternative pathway cannot be adequately controlled. Severe pyogenic infections are a consequence of the markedly decreased C3 levels. In this respect, the clinical syndrome is similar to that seen in patients with inherited deficiency of C3. The hemolytic anemia probably represents the deposition of C3b on erythrocytes which, in turn, cannot be inactivated because the inhibitor is

Figure 49
Structure of DAF membrane glycoprotein

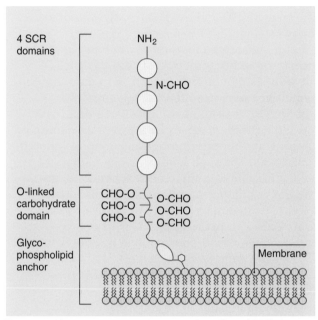

This model is based on the biochemical studies of DAF glycosylation and the glycophospholipid anchor. The one asparagine-linked oligosaccharide (N-CHO) is shown at the border between short consensus repeats (SCR) 1 and 2 (the four contiguous SCRs are shown as circles). The serine- and threonine-rich region is the probable site of extensive glycosylation (O-CHO). O-linked units may also be attached in the repeat domains. The carboxy-terminal hydrophobic region of DAF is replaced posttranslationally with a glycophospholipid anchor.

Adapted with permission from Medoff ME, Lublin DM, Holers VM, Ayers DJ, Getty RR, Leykam JF, Atkinson JP, Tykocinski ML. Cloning and characterization of cDNAs encoding the complete sequence of decay-accelerating factor of human complement. *Proc Natl Acad Sci USA*. 1987;84:2007-2011.

absent. The recurrent urticaria may be explained by the increased amounts of C3a that are produced. As expected, plasma infusions temporarily alleviate the clinical symptoms and C3 levels return to normal.

DAF and MAC Deficiencies
Paroxysmal nocturnal hemoglobinuria (PNH) is an acquired hemolytic disorder characterized by spontaneous episodes of red cell lysis. Erythrocytes, leukocytes, and platelets from these patients can be shown in vitro to have an increased sensitivity to lysis by complement. One cause of the increased sensitivity to lysis is a deficiency of decay-accelerating factor. In fact, in some forms of PNH, the hemolytic process can be largely corrected in vitro by supplying DAF to the cells. DAF is a particularly interesting protein because it has a glycolipid tail (called a "greasy foot") rather than the usual hydrophobic peptide to anchor it to a membrane (Figure 49). Patients with PNH are also deficient in membrane inhibitors of the membrane attack complex. MAC inhibitors are also attached to membranes by a glycolipid tail. It is likely that the defect in PNH is related to the biosynthesis of the glycolipid tail, thereby accounting for deficiencies of similarly anchored proteins.

Individuals deficient in C1 INH, factor H or I, or DAF all have disease states in which there is increased complement turnover with associated deleterious effects on the host. This fact dramatically points to the critical role of these components in regulating the complement system.

Complement in Acquired Disease
Infectious diseases: The complement system evolved in order to protect the host from microbes. Its role in protecting the host can be illustrated by the example of bacterial infection in the lung. In the nonimmune host, specific antibody is not present. Consequently, during the first few days of pulmonary infection, the major host defenses consist of "baseline" phagocytosis by macrophages in the lung and the facilitation of this phagocytosis by the alternative pathway.

Alternative pathway C3 convertase is formed and C3b is deposited on the bacteria. Amplification occurs and the bound C3b interacts with C3b receptors on macrophages and granulocytes. The production of C3a and C5a causes an influx of plasma (a source of more complement) and phagocytic cells. The goal of the immune system in this early stage is to localize the infection to one lobe of the lung and prevent its spread to other organs via the bloodstream. Depending on the virulence of the bacteria and the status of the host's immune system, the infection could be eliminated at this step.

During the first few days, bacteria are phago-cytosed (albeit rather inefficiently) and degraded, and antigenic fragments are presented by macro-phages to lymphocytes. In several more days, IgM and IgG antibodies specific for the bacteria are synthesized by B cells. The antibody binds to the organisms and activates the classical pathway. The combination of large quantities of antibody, complement activation, and the influx of more and more phagocytes leads to efficient killing of the bacteria. Consequently, the illness resolves. Because most of the activating and inhibiting components of complement are acute-phase proteins, and the synthesis of these components increases in response to inflammatory stimuli, such as interleukin-1, complement blood levels rise during such an infection. Although comple-ment participates actively in this process, the quantity required for controlling a local bacterial infection is so small that no decrement in the blood level can be detected. However, other systemic infections, such as malaria and certain viral diseases that produce large amounts of antigen, may be accompanied by decreased complement levels.

Immune complex-mediated diseases: If the host's immune system produces autoantibodies or an excessive amount of immune complexes, the complement system naturally becomes activated.

Surprisingly, and as yet unexplained, antibodies to self-tissue are produced in a wide variety of diseases. Autoimmune targets include red cells, platelets, tissues (eg, the thyroid and pancreas), and cell-surface proteins, such as acetylcholine receptors. In some autoimmune diseases, such as SLE, excessive amounts of immune complexes are present. The nature of the antigen in these immune complexes is usually unknown.

In any event, the binding of antibody to either foreign or self-tissue activates the destructive capabilities of complement. Thus, in autoimmune hemolytic anemia, antibody and complement combine to destroy host red cells. In other situa-tions, the problem arises because of an excessive quantity and inappropriate deposition of immune complexes. Although host cells have a variety of means to control complement activation (especi-ally the regulatory proteins), the presence of excessive quantities of autoantibodies or immune complexes can overcome this protective system and produce tissue damage that, in part, is medi-ated by the complement system.

Measurement of Complement
Most hospitals offer laboratory tests for C4, C3, and factor B, as well as the so-called CH_{50}, or total hemolytic complement (THC), assay. C3, C4, and factor B are antigenic measurements. Such tests are simple and useful and do not require special precautions for sample handling. Their disadvan-tage is that they are static measurements and do not assess function of the complement component. Nevertheless, in most cases there is an excellent correlation between the antigenic and hemolytic activities for complement components.

In the total hemolytic complement assay, sheep erythrocytes are coated with a rabbit antibody. This particulate immune complex is incubated with dilutions of human serum. The reciprocal of the dilution of serum that lyses 50% of these antibody-coated erythrocytes is the THC activity or CH_{50}. All nine components of the classical pathway must be present in at least 50% of their normal concentrations in order to give a normal whole complement titer. In individuals who are totally deficient in C9, the CH_{50} levels are 30% to 50% of normal. In contrast, complete deficiencies of the other components result in a very low or zero whole complement titer.

In some diseases, such as systemic lupus erythematosus, in which there are large amounts of circulating immune complexes, measurement of complement levels assists in the diagnosis as well as the evaluation of therapy. As the complement system interacts with these immune complexes, the utilization of complement components may outstrip their synthesis by the liver. Consequently, low serum levels result. In fact, about 50% of patients with SLE have low complement levels at diagnosis, and approximately two thirds develop low levels during the course of the disease. If treatment is effective, the complement levels usually return to normal. If the complement levels subsequently decrease, this may be a signal that the disease is becoming active again. Thus, the complement values, particularly antigenic determination of C4 and C2, can be utilized to monitor patients with SLE. Decreased complement levels may also be indicative of certain forms of vasculitis (usually mediated by immune complexes), some forms of hemolytic anemia, and cryoglobulinemia (most cryoglobulins are immune complexes that precipitate in the cold).

Conclusion

The important role played by complement for host defense becomes evident when examining the diseases associated with complement deficiencies. Consequently, assessment of serum complement levels provides helpful information necessary to evaluate and treat a variety of human illnesses.

Selected Readings

Atkinson JP, Eisen HN. The complement system. In: Davis BD, Dulbecco R, Eisen HN, Ginsberg HS, eds. **Microbiology**. 4th ed. Philadelphia, Pa: JB Lippincott Co; 1990:385-404.

Frank MM. Complement in the pathophysiology of human disease. **N Engl J Med**. 1987;316:1525-1530.

Hourcade D, Holers VM, Atkinson JP. The regulators of complement activation (RCA) gene cluster. **Adv Immunol**. 1989;45: 381-416.

Reid KB. Activation and control of the complement system. **Essays Biochem**. 1986;22:27-68.

Ross GD, ed. **Immunobiology of the Complement System: An Introduction for Research and Clinical Medicine**. Orlando, Fla: Academic Press Inc; 1986.

Ross SC, Densen P. Complement deficiency states and infection: epidemiology, pathogenesis and consequences of neisserial and other infections in an immune deficiency. **Medicine (Baltimore)**. 1984;63:243-273.

Rother K, Rother U, eds. **Hereditary and Acquired Complement Deficiencies in Animals and Man. Progress in Allergy**. Vol 39. New York, NY: Karger; 1986.

Rother K, Till GO, eds. **The Complement System**. New York, NY: Springer-Verlag; 1988.

Whaley K, ed. **Methods in Complement for Clinical Immunologists**. New York, NY: Churchill Livingstone; 1985.

Immediate Hypersensitivity and Allergy

10

Introduction

The immune system has evolved to combat a variety of organisms that are potentially harmful to vertebrates. However, the same components of the immune system that are effective in protection can, under certain circumstances, actually cause injury to the host. Initial exposure to an agent that is not intrinsically harmful to the host produces no clinically apparent illness. Subsequent exposure to that agent, however, initiates an immune reaction that produces tissue injury. These immune responses are known as the *hypersensitivities*. One example of hypersensitivity is "hay fever," which is a response to ragweed pollen. Ragweed pollen is not in itself harmful to the host, but the immune response to ragweed pollen proteins can lead to conjunctivitis, rhinorrhea, and/or asthma. The individual with allergic rhinitis feels miserable because of the immune response to ragweed rather than from any intrinsically harmful properties of ragweed pollen itself.

Several different immune mechanisms are responsible for the hypersensitivities. Antibodies, immune cells, or a combination of both can result in the various hypersensitivities. Gell and Coombs classified the hypersensitivities into four types, according to the responsible mechanisms (Table 29).

- Type I hypersensitivity, also known as *immediate*, *atopic*, and *anaphylactic hypersensitivity*, is mediated by IgE antibodies in combination with mast cells, which supply the chemical mediators.
- Type II hypersensitivity, which is now broadly defined as *anti–membrane antibody hypersensitivity*, is mediated by the reaction of antibodies (with or without complement) and cell-surface antigens.

- Type III hypersensitivity, or *immune complex hypersensitivity*, is mediated by a combination of antibody and complement.
- Type IV hypersensitivity, also termed *cell-mediated* or *delayed-type hypersensitivity*, is mediated predominantly by T cells and macrophages, although other cells also may play a role.

This chapter details type I (immediate) hypersensitivity. Antimembrane, immune complex, and delayed hypersensitivity reactions are discussed in chapter 11.

IgE in Immediate Hypersensitivity

IgE-mediated immune responses are appropriate to defend the host against foreign organisms, particularly parasites. However, IgE-mediated reactions may be detrimental when they are inappropriately mounted against innocuous foreign antigens, in which case they are termed immediate hypersensitivity or allergic responses. Antigens that stimulate allergic reactions are known as *allergens*.

IgE antibodies are preferentially formed in response to parasitic antigens or allergens. Although low in concentration, IgE antibodies bind with high affinity to specific receptors (FcεRI) on mast cells and basophils. Antigen cross-linking of IgE molecules and the receptors to which they attach initiates the release or production of a variety of cellular mediators. The mediators begin a series of physiologic events that lead to allergic diseases, such as allergic rhinitis, asthma, and urticaria, but they may also help to confer specific protective immunity against parasites.

The structure of IgE and the organization of the gene encoding the V, D, J, and constant exons of the epsilon chain are similar to other immunoglobulin classes (see chapter 1). The IgE molecule (which is approximately 190 000 daltons) is composed of four polypeptide chains: two ε heavy chains, and a pair of either κ or λ light chains. The four chains are covalently linked by disulfide bonds. The light chains are common to all immunoglobulin classes, but the ε heavy chains are unique to IgE. Each ε chain is heavily glycosylated

Table 29
Gell and Coombs classification of hypersensitivity states

Type	Synonyms	Time course at second challenge	Humoral host factors		Effector cell	Physiologic role	Pathologic consequences
			Ig	Comple-ment			
I	Atopic Anaphylactic	Immediate (minutes)	IgE	−	Mast cell initially; eosinophils, neutrophils, monocytes, and lymphocytes may be recruited later	Destruction, expulsion of parasites	Allergies Asthma Rhinitis Urticaria Angioedema Anaphylaxis
II	Antimembrane	Intermediate (hours)	IgG IgM	±	Polymorpho-nuclear cell	Clearance of small particulate organisms (eg, bacteria), lysis of virally infected cells	Hemolytic anemia Transfusion reaction Goodpasture's syndrome (anti-basement membrane antibody) Graves' disease (anti-thyroid-stimulating hormone antibody) Myasthenia gravis (anti-acetylcholine receptor antibody)
III	Immune complex	Intermediate (hours)	IgG IgM	++	Polymorpho-nuclear cell	Clearance of soluble antigens and viruses	Systemic lupus erythematosus Poststreptococcal glomerulonephritis Serum sickness Arthus reaction
IV	Cell-mediated Delayed	Delayed (1-2 days)	No	−	T cell, macro-phage, polymor-phonuclear cell, basophils, NK cells, goblet cells	Containment of poorly catabo-lized or continu-ously replicating organisms, par-ticularly intra-cellular parasites, and viruses	Allograft rejection Graft vs host reaction Contact dermatitis (poison ivy)

Figure 50
Diagram of quaternary structure of the IgE molecule

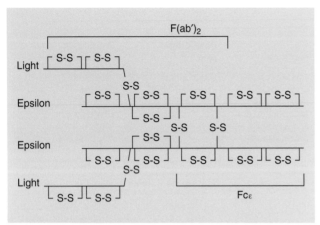

The four polypeptide chains are linked by four interchain disulfide bonds. Sixteen intrachain disulfide bonds are present, two in each $C_\varepsilon 1$ domain and one in all other domains. The fragment Fcε produced by papain digestion and the fragment $F(ab')_2$ resulting from pepsin digestion are illustrated.

Adapted with permission from Bennich H, von Bahr-Lindstrom H. Structure of immunoglobulin E (IgE). In: Brent L, Holborow J, eds. *Progress in Immunology II*. Vol I. Amsterdam, Holland: North Holland Publishing Co; 1974:49-58.

and contains five domains (V_ε, $C_\varepsilon 1$, $C_\varepsilon 2$, $C_\varepsilon 3$, and $C_\varepsilon 4$), each with at least one intradomain disulfide bond (Figure 50). The IgE molecule can be proteolytically digested near the hinge region of its Y or T shape to yield two antigen-binding $F(ab')_2$ fragments and one Fc fragment. The Fc fragment contains the $C_\varepsilon 2$, $C_\varepsilon 3$, and $C_\varepsilon 4$ domains of the two ε polypeptide chains.

The most unique property of the IgE molecule is its ability to bind selectively with very high affinity to mast cells and basophils. The reason for this highly selective binding is that mast cells and basophils have specific receptors, termed *FcεRI*, for IgE. (The R stands for receptor, and the I indicates that it is high affinity; a low-affinity receptor on other types of cells is noted as II.) The ability of IgE to bind to FcεRI on mast cells and basophils allows extremely small concentrations of specific IgE antibodies to unleash the rapid and potent immediate hypersensitivity reaction in the presence of specific antigens.

Another characteristic of IgE antibodies is that they are usually synthesized in extremely low concentrations (0.18 to 0.35 μg/mL in normal humans) by a subset of B cells. IgE antibodies are biochemically less heterogeneous than antibodies of other classes and appear to have a more limited repertoire of antigen-combining sites. Because IgE antibody responses in mammals are particularly strong against parasite antigens, it is believed that the major evolutionary function of immediate hypersensitivity is to provide a defense against parasites.

IgE antibodies are also produced against many common allergens (Table 30). Antibodies are made against pollen proteins because pollen tubes developing on moist mucosal surfaces may, in some undefined way, simulate a parasitic invasion. IgE antibodies are made against a protein in fecal particles from the nearly ubiquitous house dust mites (*Dermatophagoides pteronyssinus* and *D farinae*), which are related evolutionarily to parasites, but these mites are "parasitic" only in the sense that they feed on shed epidermal scales. Certain nonprotein chemicals (eg, drugs) and certain proteins derived from animal dander, molds, foods, and Hymenoptera stings can elicit IgE antibody formation.

The FcεRI Receptor

The presence of IgE antibody activity was first inferred from the Prausnitz-Küstner (P-K) reaction. The injection of serum from Küstner, who was allergic to fish, into Prausnitz's skin caused Prausnitz to develop a local hive at the injection site when he ate fish. Passive cutaneous anaphylaxis (PCA) is a similar test used in experimental animals. Both P-K and PCA reactions depend on the ability of IgE antibody to bind specifically to receptors on mast cells or basophils.

Binding Affinity

Detailed studies have been carried out on human IgE binding to human basophils and on rat IgE binding to rat mast cells and to rat basophilic leukemia cell cultures. In both species, IgE binding

Table 30
Common allergens in immediate hypersensitivity reactions

Respiratory symptoms
Tree, grass (*Lol p* I), and weed pollens
Cat antigen 1 (*Fel d* I) and other animal dander antigens
Dust mite fecal pellet antigens (*Der p* I, *Der f* I) and cockroach
    antigens
Mold spores

Urticaria and angioedema
Medications and other chemicals
Foods and food additives
Tree, grass, and weed pollens
Cat antigen 1 and other animal dander antigens
Insect venom

Gastrointestinal symptoms
Foods

Anaphylaxis
Drugs
Insect venom
Foods

to cell-surface receptors is a reversible reaction, consistent with the simple bimolecular forward reaction and the first order reverse reaction:

$$\text{IgE} + \text{receptor} \underset{k_{-1}}{\overset{k_1}{\rightleftarrows}} \text{IgE} - \text{receptor complex}$$

The forward rate constant (k_1), estimated at 10^5 L/mole per second at 37°C, is not unusual for biologic reactions. In fact, it is not the k_1 but rather the extremely low concentrations of IgE in serum that explain why IgE binding to FcεRI requires long "latent" periods (several hours) after intradermal injection in vivo during P-K and PCA reactions. The reverse rate constant (k_{-1}) is extremely small, less than 10^{-5} per second. The extremely slow dissociation of IgE from FcεRI (half-life is at least 27 hours) and the ability of dissociated IgE to rebind to its receptor both help to explain the observations that passive sensitization (ie, binding of injected IgE in P-K or PCA reactions or transfused IgE antibodies) may persist for weeks.

The equilibrium constant (a measure of affinity derived from k_1/k_{-1}) is extremely high, at least 10^{10} L/mole. The high-affinity interaction of IgE and

FcεRI appears to have some degree of species specificity. Human IgE binds only to human and primate FcεRI. However, rat IgE and mouse IgE bind not only to rodent Fcε receptors but also to human FcεRI.

Mast cells and basophils express large numbers of FcεRI receptors on their surfaces. It is estimated that human basophils have 40 000 to 100 000 receptors per cell and that each rat mast cell has 300 000. Both unoccupied and occupied FcεRI are diffusely distributed on the cell membrane.

FcεRI Structure

The IgE receptor is composed of four polypeptide chains: one α chain, one β chain, and two identical γ chains (Figure 51). The α chain is a heavily glycosylated, largely extracellular subunit that appears to bind a single IgE molecule. The β chain is not glycosylated and spans the membrane four times. The pair of γ chains probably form a disulfide-linked homodimer. The α, β, and two γ chains associate noncovalently via their membrane-spanning regions, and the assembly of $\alpha\beta\gamma_2$ (or at least of $\alpha\gamma_2$) is required for expression on the cell surface. The genes encoding α and γ are closely linked on chromosome 1 in both the human and the mouse. The α chain of FcεRI is a typical member of the immunoglobulin gene superfamily and is more homologous to Fc receptors for IgG than are other members. The α chain is unusual because two exons encode its NH_2-terminal "signal sequence," which allows for alternative mRNA splicing to produce some receptors that may become functional only upon proteolysis. (Proteolysis may occur during degranulation or any other inflammatory event that releases proteases.)

Another type of receptor for IgE is the FcεRII or CD23 receptor, which is found on B cells, eosinophils, and macrophages. This receptor has a lower affinity for IgE and appears to play a role in the synthesis of IgE and in IgE-mediated parasite destruction.

Figure 51
A model of FcεRI, the tetrameric high-affinity receptor for IgE, expressed uniquely on mast cells and basophils

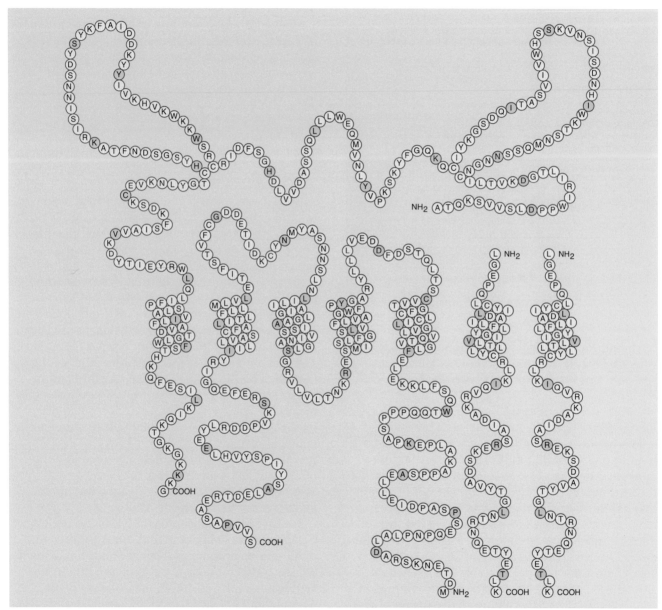

The α subunit is at the left with its large extracellular IgE-binding domain at the top. The β subunit with its four transmembrane domains is in the center. The pair of γ subunits are at the right. The γ subunits are likely to be disulfide-bonded to each other; otherwise, the subunit interactions probably occur between the seven hydrophobic membrane-spanning regions. Every tenth residue is colored.

Reproduced with permission from Blank U, Ra C, Miller L, White K, Metzger H, Kinet J-P. Complete structure and expression in transfected cells of high affinity IgE receptor. *Nature.* 1989;337:187-189, © 1989 Macmillan Magazines Ltd.

Cross-Linking of FcεRI

The combination of the exceedingly low concentration of antigen-specific IgE and the extremely high-affinity constant of IgE for its receptor (FcεRI) allows this immunoglobulin to function selectively as a cell-surface–bound molecule. In this way, the IgE-mediated immediate hypersensitivity response is fundamentally different from events that are mediated by IgG, IgA, and IgM. The sequence of events (Figure 52) in immediate hypersensitivity is:

- An allergen (or antigen capable of stimulating an IgE response) stimulates production of IgE antibodies from B cells. Various factors generated from T cells, such as interleukin-4 (IL-4), are involved in IgE synthesis.
- IgE diffuses to and binds tightly to the FcεRI receptors on mast cells and basophils.
- Re-exposure to the antigen allows the allergenic molecule to bind and cross-link two surface-bound IgE molecules.
- Since each IgE molecule is bound tightly to an FcεRI receptor, the cross-linking event automatically brings together two FcεRI receptors, which triggers the mast cell or basophil to release within minutes a variety of preformed mediators stored in granules and to synthesize other mediators (Figure 53).

Mediators

Mediators of the allergic response are usually classified as preformed mediators and mediators generated de novo at the onset of the response.

Preformed Mediators

Histamine (5-β-imidazolylethylamine) is formed selectively in mast cells, basophils, and gastric enterochromaffin cells. Large quantities of histamine (approximately 2×10^{13} molecules/mast cell) are stored preformed in basophilic staining granules, probably complexed with heparin. Histamine is synthesized from histidine by the enzyme histidine decarboxylase. Histamine acts rapidly, within minutes, to dilate and increase permeability of small blood vessels, to contract bronchial and intestinal smooth muscle, and to cause itching. Such effects appear to largely involve histamine type 1 (H_1) receptors and can be inhibited by H_1-type antihistamines (eg, chlorpheniramine). Histamine

Figure 52
Model of the immediate hypersensitivity response illustrating the roles of the mast cell and basophil, IgE antibody, and antigen

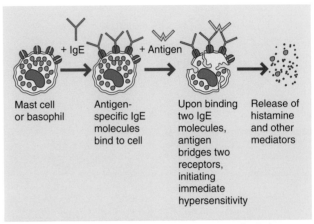

| Mast cell or basophil | Antigen-specific IgE molecules bind to cell | Upon binding two IgE molecules, antigen bridges two receptors, initiating immediate hypersensitivity | Release of histamine and other mediators |

IgE binding does not morphologically alter the cells. Subsequent addition of antigen bridges receptor-bound IgE molecules and initiates cell degranulation, resulting in the release of histamine and other substances that mediate various physiologic effects.

Reproduced with permission from Sullivan TJ, Kulczycki A Jr. Immediate hypersensitivity responses. In: Parker CW, ed. *Clinical Immunology.* Philadelphia, Pa: WB Saunders Co; 1980:115-142.

Figure 53
Morphologic alterations in rat mast cells during the release of inflammatory mediators

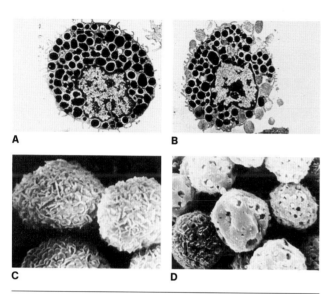

A   B

C   D

(**A**) A transmission micrograph of a normal rat mast cell demonstrating electron-dense cytoplasmic granules. (Magnification × 13 000.)
(**B**) A rat mast cell 15 minutes after stimulation of mediator release by concanavalin A. Membrane fusion and release of granule contents predominantly involve the peripheral rank of granules. (Magnification × 11 000.)
(**C**) Scanning electron micrograph of normal rat mast cells demonstrating abundant microridges over their surfaces. (Magnification × 9000.)
(**D**) Ten minutes after initiation of mediator release, many microridges have disappeared from the mast cells and numerous pores have appeared. (Magnification × 7000.)
(Courtesy of Dr. David Lagunoff, St. Louis University, St. Louis, Missouri.)

Reproduced with permission from Sullivan TJ, Kulczycki A Jr. Immediate hypersensitivity responses. In: Parker CW, ed. *Clinical Immunology.* Philadelphia, Pa: WB Saunders Co; 1980:115-142.

also increases gastric acid production via H_2 receptors, which can be inhibited by H_2-type antihistamines (eg, cimetidine). Histamine can also increase mucus secretion and is chemotactic for eosinophils.

The proteolytic enzymes tryptase and chymase are also contained within granules. These enzymes are complexed with histamine and acidic heparin. The proteases released during the exocytosis of granules may contribute to the manifestations of the immediate hypersensitivity response by generating kinins and activating additional FcεRI.

Heparin and other proteoglycans are large sulfated macromolecules within granules. The acidity of heparin accounts for granules staining with basic dyes. After exocytosis from cells, heparin may slow the diffusion and degradation of histamine and proteases.

Newly Synthesized Mediators

Leukotrienes are newly generated products formed from arachidonic acid, a 20-carbon polyunsaturated fatty acid derived from the hydrolysis of phospholipids by phospholipase A_2 or phospholipase C and diacylglycerol lipase (Figure 54). The enzyme 5-lipoxygenase becomes activated when mast cell FcεRI receptors are cross-linked, and it adds an oxygen atom to carbon 5 of arachidonic acid, converting it to 5-hydroperoxyeicosatetraenoic acid (5-HPETE), which then can form the unstable epoxide leukotriene A_4 (LTA_4). LTA_4 can be hydrated to form LTB_4, which strongly attracts neutrophils and stimulates production of superoxides (Table 31). LTA_4 also can covalently attach to the sulfhydryl group of glutathione (glutamyl-cystinyl-glycine) to form leukotriene C (LTC_4). Removal of the γ-glutamyl residue from LTC_4 yields LTD_4. Subsequent removal of glycine yields the relatively less active LTE_4. LTC_4 and LTD_4 are extremely powerful constrictors of bronchioles (100- to 1000-fold more potent than an equivalent number of histamine molecules). Like histamine, LTC_4 and LTD_4 increase permeability of small blood vessels, constrict smooth muscle, increase mucus production, and cause itching. In contrast to histamine, leukotrienes produce a much slower

Figure 54
Newly generated mediators synthesized from membrane-derived arachidonic acid: leukotrienes, prostaglandins, hydroperoxyeicosatetraenoic acids (HPETEs), and hydroxyeicosatetraenoic acids (HETEs)

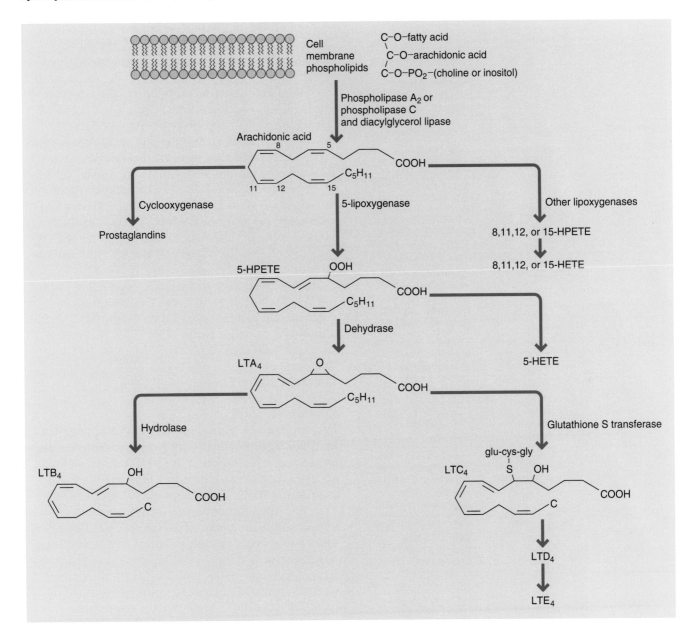

Table 31
Some mediators of immediate hypersensitivity

Mediator	Structure	Physiologic/ immunologic effects
Preformed mediators		
Histamine	5-β-imidazolylethyl-amine	↑ Microvascular permeability, constricts smooth muscle, itching, ↑ gastric acid, ↑ mucus secretion, attracts eosinophils
Tryptase, chymase	Proteins (enzymes)	Proteolytic action
Heparin	Proteoglycan (high MW)	Binds histamine within granules, ↑ anticoagulation, slows the release of mediators?
ECF-A	Val-gly-ser-glu Ala-gly-ser-glu	Chemotaxis of neutrophils and eosinophils
Newly generated mediators		
LTB_4	Leukotriene	Chemotaxis of neutrophils and eosinophils, stimulates superoxide production
LTC_4, LTD_4, LTE_4	Derivatives of LTA_4 and glutathione	↑ Microvascular leakage, constrict smooth muscle, itching, ↑ mucus secretion
HPETEs, HETEs	Oxygenated products of arachidonic acid	Chemotaxis of neutrophils and eosinophils
PAF	1-alkyl-2-acetyl-glycerol-3-phosphocholine	↑ Microvascular permeability, constricts bronchi, chemotaxis for eosinophils, aggregates platelets
PGD_2	Prostaglandin	↑ Microvascular leakage, contracts smooth muscle, chemotaxis

onset of bronchoconstriction but effect a long duration, which accounts for their previous designation as the "slow-reacting substance of anaphylaxis" or SRS-A.

The enzyme cyclooxygenase converts arachidonic acid into various prostaglandins. Prostaglandin D_2 (PGD_2), found in mast cells but not in basophils, can produce increased permeability and smooth muscle contraction (like histamine) but does not cause itching.

Platelet-activating factor (PAF) (1-alkyl-2-acetyl-glycerol-3-phosphocholine) is produced by mast cells, monocytes, and platelets. After the arachidonyl group of phosphatidylcholine is removed to form lysophosphatidylcholine, acetylation forms PAF. Like histamine, PAF causes increased permeability of small blood vessels, bronchoconstriction, and chemotaxis for eosinophils, but PAF can also cause aggregation of platelets. (Viruses and irritants can trigger asthma attacks, in part by damaging epithelial cells, which release PAF and initiate chronic inflammation.)

Furthermore, a large variety of cytokines, including IL-1, IL-2, IL-3, IL-4, IL-5, IL-6, granulocyte macrophage–colony-stimulating factor (GM-CSF), and tumor necrosis factor (TNF), can be synthesized by mast cells.

Effector Cells

Eosinophils
Eosinophils are commonly found in tissues after immediate hypersensitivity responses to parasites or allergens. Eosinophils are preferentially attracted by histamine and PAF, but they are attracted nonpreferentially (ie, along with neutrophils) by LTB_4 and other chemotactic factors, such as eosinophil chemotactic factor of anaphylaxis (ECF-A). The eosinophilic granules stain with the acid dye eosin, because their crystalline core is composed largely of major basic protein (MBP), the protein with the highest isoelectric point (pI over 10) in mammals. Granules also contain eosinophil peroxidase, β-glucuronidase, histaminase, and basic proteins, such as eosinophil cationic protein (ECP) and eosinophil-derived neurotoxin.

One evolutionary function of the eosinophil is to act as an effector cell in killing parasites. Mast cells release chemoattractants and mediators of permeability that attract eosinophils to sites of parasitic invasion. After eosinophils bind (via FcεRII and other Fc receptors) to IgE and IgG antibodies that are attached to parasitic antigens, the granules release their contents (eg, MBP, ECP, peroxidase), which are toxic to parasites. However, the release of eosinophil granules can be damaging to host tissue in allergic diseases; for example, MBP causes epithelial damage to the bronchial lumen in asthma.

Neutrophils and Mononuclear Cells
LTB_4, ECF-A, and other mediators also rapidly attract neutrophils as well as eosinophils and basophils to sites of allergic reactions. Subsequently, lymphocytes and monocytes may infiltrate the tissue sites. The mediators released from mast cells, other resident cells, and infiltrating inflammatory cells together appear to cause the *late-phase reaction* occurring 3 to 24 hours after the onset of the allergic response. The late-phase reaction accounts for the persistence of hyperresponsiveness of bronchi or nasal congestion long after allergen challenge.

It is believed that late-phase reactions play an important role in the chronicity of allergies, especially chronic asthma, by increasing the individual's sensitivity to allergens so that hypersensitivity becomes self-perpetuating. The apparent mechanism for chronic allergic reactions involves the production of additional functional FcεRI receptors by proteases and the release of histamine-releasing factors from neutrophils, which elicits another round of mast cell degranulation.

Activation Sequence of Immediate Hypersensitivity

From an evolutionary point of view, the immunologic and physiologic events mediated by IgE make sense in order to defend mammals against parasites. Many parasites can cross the barriers of the skin, the respiratory mucosa, or the gastrointestinal mucosa within minutes. One encounter with a given parasite leads to IgE antibodies directed against some of its antigens. The IgE antibodies then bind to mast cells, which are especially numerous in mucosal surfaces and skin. A second attempt by the parasite to penetrate a skin/mucosal boundary leads to a parasite-derived antigen binding to one cell-bound IgE molecule and then to an adjacent IgE molecule. The occupied FcεRI receptors are thus cross-linked, which activates the mast cell to release mediators with unprecedented biologic amplification; one allergen molecule binding two IgE molecules may prompt the release of up to 10^{13} histamine molecules, as well as other classes of mediators.

The evolutionary purpose of the immediate hypersensitivity response may be to confer protection against parasitic invasion. Preformed mediators increase permeability of the capillaries almost immediately, producing localized swelling, hives, or angioedema, which limits the ability of the parasite to penetrate the barriers. Similarly, itching may trigger the appropriate physiologic response to scratch off a penetrating parasite. In addition to localized swelling during parasitic invasion of the bowel wall, transudation of fluid and increased peristalsis also occur and serve to expel the parasites. Since larval forms of many parasites invade from pulmonary capillaries into alveoli, the lower respiratory tract is equipped to respond to IgE-mediated stimuli by causing bronchoconstriction and increased mucus secretion (both barriers to parasite motion), which prompt coughing to expel the invaders.

Similar responses, more delayed in onset and more prolonged in duration, are caused by other mediators. The late phase of all of these reactions involves chemotactic attraction of eosinophils, monocytes, and other cells that have specific mechanisms adapted for killing parasites. Mast cells and basophils have extremely acidic molecules such as heparin in their granules that bind positively charged histamine. Acidic proteins and histamine may be directly toxic to parasites. The recruited eosinophils release major basic protein onto parasites to damage or destroy them. Macrophages secrete a variety of proteolytic enzymes that are toxic to parasites.

One disadvantage of the immediate hypersensitivity response (even when it is directed against an appropriate parasitic antigen) is that carried to the extreme, massive mediator release may lead to such increased permeability and edema that death can result from anaphylaxis.

Another drawback of the immediate hypersensitivity response is that some persons (atopic individuals) inappropriately produce significant quantities of IgE antibodies in response to innocuous substances, such as pollens, molds, fecal pellets of house dust mites, or allergenic proteins from pets. Seasonal encounters with pollen may lead to seasonal allergic rhinitis. Perennial exposure to dust mite products may lead to perennial rhinitis or asthma. Contact or systemic exposure to these and other allergens may lead to hives or angioedema.

Allergic Rhinitis

Allergic rhinitis is a common condition that has been estimated to affect up to 20% of the U.S. population. Its most bothersome symptoms include sneezing, rhinorrhea, and nasal congestion. Often it is associated with itching of the eyes, nose, and palate and with sneezing "jags." These associated symptoms, which usually indicate histamine release, help to classify the rhinitis as allergic. Allergic rhinitis can occur as a seasonal condition (eg, rhinitis in spring from tree pollen or in autumn from ragweed pollen) or as a perennial

problem (eg, chronic rhinitis from dust mite antigen, cat antigen, or cockroach antigen), and either form can be confused with a viral cold.

The nasal mucosa is normally an efficient filter of particles larger than 5 μ. It warms and moistens air, and it produces a mucus blanket containing lysozyme for nonspecific bacterial killing and IgA for specific action against pathogens. In all individuals the nasal mucosa (and to a lesser extent, tracheal and bronchial mucosa) can filter out pollen grains, mold spores, dust particles containing mite fecal antigens, cat dander, or other allergens. In atopic individuals, one or more proteins eluted from the moistened particles are locally absorbed, which stimulates an IgE response. IgE antibodies are bound to basophils in nasal secretions and to mast cells on the mucosal surface. Reexposure to the protein allergen causes rapid (within minutes) release of preformed mediators and production of newly formed mediators, which account for symptoms. After experimental nasal challenges, both immediate reactions (involving predominately mast cells) and delayed reactions 1 to 2 days later (involving mainly basophils) can occur.

On physical examination, the nasal mucosa is typically moist and swollen, especially the inferior and middle nasal turbinates. Excessive watery secretions may be present anteriorly. When postnasal drainage (containing histamine) is reported, erythema anterior to the tonsillar pillars is often present, along with edema of the uvula. Injected conjunctivae are commonly found.

Untreated allergic rhinitis can be complicated by sinusitis, nasal polyps, otitis, or middle ear effusions. Overuse of nasal decongestants can result in a paradoxical worsening of congestion, termed *rhinitis medicamentosa*. Proper therapy requires a combination of avoiding the allergens and administering antihistamines, oral decongestants, intranasal steroids, intranasal cromolyn, and/or immunotherapy.

Asthma

Asthma is a disease involving reversible obstruction and hyperactivity of parts of the tracheobronchial airway. It is characterized by one or more of the following symptoms: wheezing, cough, dyspnea, and chest tightness. The prevalence of asthma has been estimated at 3% to 7% of the population. Most cases are caused by allergens and involve IgE antibody. However, many other factors can acutely worsen the hyperreactive airway and are viewed as triggers of attacks. Common triggers in addition to allergens are physical exertion, cold or dry air, viral infections, and irritants, such as cigarette smoke, SO_2, and ozone.

As in allergic rhinitis, asthma can occur when particles containing allergens settle on the mucosa of the tracheobronchial tree and initiate IgE-mediated reactions from mucosal mast cells. The mediators released cause airway abnormalities, such as bronchospasm, bronchial edema, increased mucus production, and chronic inflammation. Since some of the initially produced mediators are chemoattractants to inflammatory cells, especially eosinophils, the integrity of the bronchial mucosa may become disrupted because of the highly basic MBP from eosinophils. Inflammation may result from proteases and secondary mediators, and the bronchial lumen may become narrowed or occluded by tenacious mucous plugs containing eosinophils.

Inhalation challenge studies involve measuring forced expiratory volume in 1 second (FEV_1) before and after an allergen is inhaled. In asthmatic individuals, inhalations of allergens cause immediate and/or delayed reduction in forced expiratory volume. Chronic decreases in FEV_1 result from continuous allergen exposure or from late-phase reactions with chronic inflammation. Normally, one requirement for the diagnosis of asthma is to demonstrate reversibility of the airway obstruction after medication or environmental improvements are instituted. However, years of inadequate treatment may result in irreversible chronic obstruction.

The onset of asthma in cat-sensitive asthmatics may be rapid because potent allergen is present on extremely small particles. Dust mite asthma is probably slower in onset and in resolution. In one study, it required months in a mite-free environment for 10 mite-sensitive asthmatic children to obtain complete resolution of their asthma.

Urticaria and Angioedema

Urticaria is a common condition that has been reported to occur at least once in 12% to 16% of college students and medical patients. Urticaria (hives) can be serious if it is the harbinger of a life-threatening anaphylactic reaction or a symptom of an underlying illness, or if it becomes a chronic condition. In many cases, both urticaria and angioedema are present at the same time.

A hive is an intensely itchy skin lesion consisting of a raised, blanched, circular wheal surrounded by an erythematous flare (Figure 55). The wheal is caused by increased vascular permeability, which allows leakage of plasma into the connective tissue. The reddish flare can be blanched by pressure and represents dilation and engorgement of blood vessels in the superficial dermis. Typically, an urticarial lesion develops over a period of minutes and lasts 4 to 6 hours. Multiple hives are common.

Angioedema involves the deeper layer of dermis and causes less itching. It often appears as a single area of diffuse local swelling that may burn, tingle, or itch. Angioedema of the larynx may be life-threatening because it can cause airway occlusion.

Figure 55
Two hives consisting of 1 × 1 cm wheals surrounded by erythema

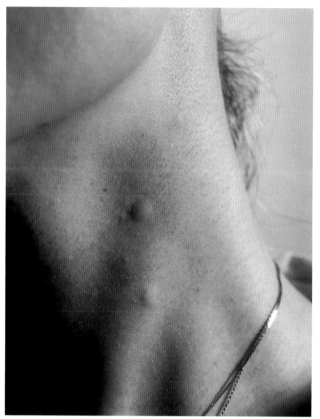

These hives resulted from a double-blind challenge with an artificial sweetener. (The challenge procedure was described in: Kulczycki A. Aspartame-induced urticaria. *Ann Intern Med.* 1986;104:207-208.)

Often, an individual will experience a transient episode of hives for which the cause cannot be reliably determined. The allergen can arrive at dermal mast cells by a variety of routes, eg, inhalation, ingestion, absorption through the skin. Allergic reactions to drugs (see following discussion) are a major identifiable cause of urticaria or angioedema. Drug-induced urticaria/angioedema usually improves within days of eliminating the offending medication. A variety of foods may cause hives or sometimes severe angioedema, including fish, seafood, eggs, peanuts, true nuts, milk, wheat, and soy protein. Food additives implicated in severe reactions include aspartame, sodium benzoate, bisulfites, monosodium glutamate, and dyes.

Tree, grass, or weed pollens sometimes cause seasonal urticaria along with seasonal rhinitis. Common chemicals, such as the paraben preservatives found in shampoos, lotions, sunscreens, ointments, and medications, may cause contact urticaria. Cat dander and epithelial antigens from other animals (inhaled or contacted) may be a cause of episodic or chronic urticaria.

Urticaria or angioedema can occur in chronic infections such as *Trichophyton* infections of the feet. Urticaria may be a manifestation of a serious disease, such as serum sickness, collagen vascular disease, mastocytosis, or vasculitis. Urticaria and angioedema may result from physical stimuli, such as cold, heat, pressure, vibration, light, exercise, or increased core body temperature. Angioedema may also occur in the hereditary disorder C1 esterase inhibitor deficiency (see chapter 9).

Drug Allergy and Anaphylaxis

Low–molecular-weight drugs differ from other allergens because they (or one of their derivatives) must react with a protein in order to function as an allergen. Penicillin is a common cause of drug allergy because some of its metabolites (especially the penicilloyl derivative) readily conjugate to proteins and initiate allergic reactions.

After the term *prophylaxis* was applied to the protective effect of immunization, the term *anaphylaxis* (against protection) was coined to describe sea anemone stings, which stimulate

IgE responses at initial exposure and can be fatal in a second exposure. Systemic anaphylaxis results from extensive and rapid mediator release. Extreme increases in vascular permeability and edema produce life-threatening anaphylactic shock. Extremes of bronchoconstriction or laryngeal swelling may cause death from anaphylactic asphyxia. Pulmonary edema and hyperinflation, urticaria, or angioedema may also occur.

Anaphylactic reactions can result from drugs, Hymenoptera stings, foods (commonly fish, seafood, peanuts, and nuts), and other allergens. Emergency lifesaving treatment requires administering epinephrine and limiting further exposure to the antigen.

Diagnostic Tests

The most convenient, rapid, and sensitive method for evaluating antigen-specific IgE in allergic diseases is the direct skin test. Test solutions of common allergens are applied to the skin via scratches, punctures, or intradermal injection. A positive reaction produces a wheal-and-flare reaction, usually within 20 minutes.

Alternative in vitro methods of measuring antigen-specific IgE antibodies include the radioallergosorbent test (RAST). In the RAST, allergens attached to solid supports (eg, discs) are incubated first with a patient's serum and, after washing, with radiolabeled anti-IgE antibody. The amount of radioactivity bound to the solid disc after washing is a good measure of the quantity of antigen-specific IgE in the patient's serum. However, direct measurement of serum IgE is less sensitive (and more expensive) than direct skin testing in the clinical setting.

Total IgE serum concentrations are usually below 1 µg/mL in humans. Because the normal range of total IgE is broad, and because there is a considerable overlap in levels of normal individuals and allergic individuals, total IgE is seldom a useful test. However, total IgE levels may occasionally be clinically useful because they are elevated in most cases of invasive parasitism, allergic bronchopulmonary aspergillosis, and atopic dermatitis combined with asthma.

A suspected food allergy may be corroborated by skin tests (prick or scratch tests), by in vitro testing for specific IgE antibodies, or by excluding the suspected food in "elimination diets" and provocative challenge with specific foods (ideally by using double-blind challenges). However, skin testing and provocative challenges can be dangerous and should be carried out by skilled physicians in settings with adequate life support facilities.

Treatment of Allergic Diseases

In many cases, pharmacologic agents are available to temporarily reduce allergic symptoms. In allergic rhinitis, antihistamines can reduce sneezing and rhinorrhea and β-sympathomimetics can decrease nasal congestion. In asthma, β-sympathomimetic drugs and theophylline usually reduce bronchial edema and bronchospasm. In urticaria, antihistamines can counteract itching and hive formation. Apart from relief of symptoms, such measures may also be important in preventing complications, such as hypoxia in acute exacerbations of asthma and middle ear or sinus infections in severe allergic rhinitis.

However, these treatment strategies are sometimes inadequate because a variety of pharmacologic mediators and physiologic processes are involved. A single antagonist may block only one of the mediators, and a single agonist may influence only a few physiologic consequences. More importantly, symptom relief may mask the underlying process and allow it to progress. Long-term symptomatic treatment of asthma may allow underlying allergic mechanisms to produce extensive damage to the bronchial or sinus lumen and cause chronic inflammatory changes and even irreversible changes.

With chronic or severe allergic problems, it is important to use additional therapeutic strategies that are directed toward:
- Eliminating exposure to the allergens.
- Modifying the immune response by immunotherapy.
- Inhibiting mast cells from releasing mediators.
- Reducing the chronic inflammation.

Since most asthma results from exposure to antigens derived from house dust mites, cats, or cockroaches, elimination of the allergen source is the treatment of choice. For example, clinical studies have shown that encasing pillows and mattresses and removing bedroom carpeting (or treating it with chemicals such as benzyl benzoate) significantly reduce mite exposure and the symptoms of mite-induced asthma.

Immunotherapy, consisting of regular subcutaneous injections of allergens for about 5 years, is mandated for systemic reactions to bee and wasp stings to prevent fatal anaphylactic reactions. Immunotherapy is also effective and widely used in treating allergic rhinitis and asthma.

Cromolyn, steroids, and other medications appear to decrease the release of mediators from mast cells. Steroids also inhibit allergic and inflammatory reactions by decreasing vascular permeability and cellular infiltration. Corticosteroids, especially inhaled steroids, play an important role in decreasing chronic (late-phase) allergic reactions.

Selected Readings

Frew AJ, Kay AB. Eosinophils and T-lymphocytes in late-phase allergic reactions. **J Allergy Clin Immunol**. 1990;85:533-539.

Gleich GJ. Eosinophils, basophils, and mast cells. **J Allergy Clin Immunol**. 1989;84:1024-1027.

Kaplan AP, ed. **Allergy**. New York, NY: Churchill Livingstone; 1985.

Kulczycki A, Atkinson JP. Urticaria and angioedema. In: Wedner HJ, Korenblat P, eds. **Allergy, Theory and Practice**. 2nd ed. New York, NY: Grune and Stratton; 1992.

MacGlashan D, Lichtenstein LM. Mast cell and basophil derived mediators of allergic disease. In: Lessof MH, Lee TH, Kemeny DM, eds. **Allergy: An International Textbook**. Chichester, England: John Wiley & Sons, Ltd; 1988.

Metzger H, Alcaraz G, Hohman R, Kinet J-P, Pribluda V, Quarto R. The receptor with high affinity for immunoglobulin E. **Annu Rev Immunol**. 1986;4:419-470.

Platts-Mills TAE, Chapman MD. Dust mites: immunology, allergic disease, and environmental control. **J Allergy Clin Immunol**. 1987;80:755-775.

Types II, III, and IV Hypersensitivity States

11

Introduction

Whereas IgE antibodies mediate immediate (type I) hypersensitivity, other classes of antibodies, complement, and T cells mediate other types of hypersensitivity. Because of the properties of these different components, each hypersensitivity state results in a distinct type of tissue damage. This chapter describes the type II, type III, and type IV hypersensitivities of the Gell and Coombs classification.

Antimembrane (Type II) Hypersensitivity

Type II hypersensitivity reactions are mediated by the binding of antibody with a molecule on a cell or basement membrane. Physiologically, antibody binding to a cell surface evolved to rapidly clear bacteria and other particulate organisms from the circulation, either by directly lysing the organism or by promoting phagocytosis through opsonization. In type II hypersensitivity states, antibodies bind to antigens on the surface of autologous (self) or allogeneic (genetically distinct) cells. Depending in part on the cell-surface molecule recognized, the activation of the complement system, and the participation of other cells, there can be several different outcomes (Figure 56).

- If the cell-surface molecule is a receptor molecule, antibody binding to the receptor can mimic the natural ligand (eg, Graves' disease) or prevent the ligand from binding to its receptor (eg, myasthenia gravis).
- Antibody attached to the cell can bind to the Fc receptor on a macrophage and cause the cell to be phagocytosed.
- Antibody attached to the cell can bind through its Fc portion to K cells (which include natural killer cells, cytotoxic T lymphocytes, monocytes, and macrophages that express Fc receptors for IgG), and the K cell lyses the antibody-coated cell. This phenomenon has been termed *antibody-dependent cell-mediated cytotoxicity* (ADCC).
- The complement system can be activated, leading to deposition of C3b on the cell surface. The cell is then bound by C3b receptors on macrophages and phagocytosed.
- The complement system can be activated to its terminal stage, and the antibody-coated cell is lysed.

Antireceptor Antibodies

Myasthenia gravis is an autoimmune disease in which muscles weaken, and the weakness increases as the muscle is used. It is caused by an antibody directed against the acetylcholine receptor (AChR) on the muscle end-plate at the neuromuscular junction (Figure 57). A minor proportion of antibodies attach to the AChR, which blocks the neurotransmitter acetylcholine from binding to its receptor, and thus prevents normal triggering of the muscle end-plate action potential by a nerve impulse. However, most anti-AChR antibodies, both with and without complement activation, cause the receptors to degrade more rapidly than they can be synthesized. The muscle end-plate becomes disorganized and has fewer receptor molecules. The available receptors are occupied quickly, and subsequent nerve impulses are not transmitted to the muscle end-plate. The result is the characteristic pattern of myasthenia gravis, that is, weakness and fatigue brought on by exertion and relieved by rest.

Graves' disease is a hyperthyroid condition in which an autoantibody is produced against the thyroid receptor for thyroid-stimulating hormone (TSH), which is released by the pituitary. Normally, the binding of TSH to its receptor on the thyroid causes this organ to release the two thyroid hormones, triiodothyronine (T_3) and thyroxine (T_4). In addition to their effects throughout the body, T_3 and T_4 operate through a negative-feedback mechanism on the hypothalamus to decrease secretion of TSH by the pituitary. In Graves' disease, the binding of anti-TSH receptor antibody to the TSH receptor mimics TSH binding. However, because the antibody, rather than ligand, is engaging the TSH receptor, the negative-feedback mechanism becomes inoperative. TSH levels are greatly reduced, but the binding of antibody to the receptor drives the thyroid gland to produce more T_3 and T_4, resulting in a hyperthyroid state (Figure 58).

Figure 56
Possible different outcomes as a result of antibody binding to a cell-surface molecule

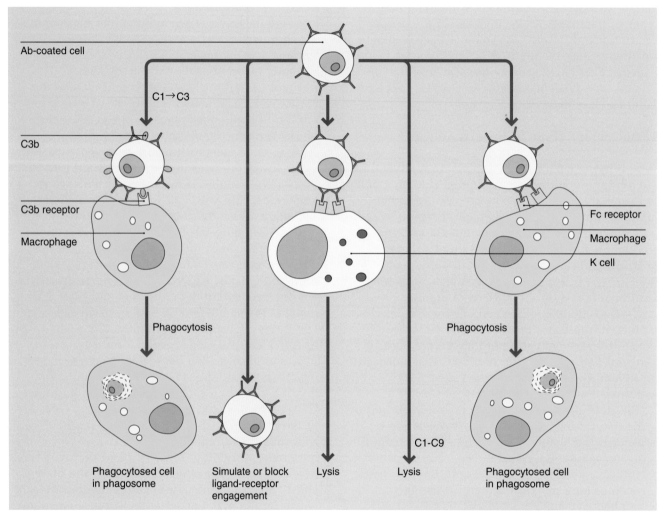

Ab-coated cell

C1→C3

C3b

C3b receptor

Macrophage

Fc receptor

Macrophage

K cell

Phagocytosis

Phagocytosis

C1-C9

Phagocytosed cell in phagosome

Simulate or block ligand-receptor engagement

Lysis

Lysis

Phagocytosed cell in phagosome

A cell to which antibody has bound may be: (1) phagocytosed through receptors for C3b (upper left) or the receptors for the Fc region of antibody (upper right); or (2) lysed by cells bearing Fc receptors for IgG (including NK cells, CTLs, macrophages, and monocytes), which, in their role in ADCC, have been termed K cells (bottom right); or (3) lysed by activation of the full complement sequence (bottom middle). In addition, antibodies bound to the cell surface can simulate the ligand by engaging the receptor or prevent ligand from engaging the receptor (bottom left).

Figure 57
Antibodies against acetylcholine receptors in myasthenia gravis

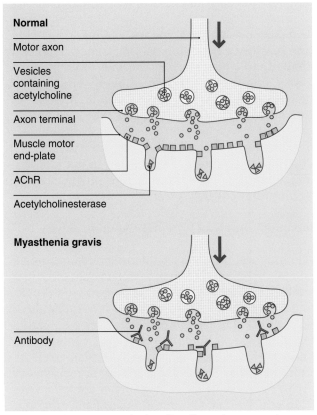

Normal

Motor axon

Vesicles containing acetylcholine

Axon terminal

Muscle motor end-plate

AChR

Acetylcholinesterase

Myasthenia gravis

Antibody

In the normal neuromuscular junction, the motor axon releases acetylcholine, which binds to the acetylcholine receptor (AChR) on the muscle end-plate, and causes the muscle to contract. In myasthenia gravis, antibodies bound to the AChR prevent acetylcholine from binding and also reduce the number of acetylcholine receptors. As a result, the ability of the muscle to respond to repeated stimulation is decreased.

Figure 58
Antibodies to the TSH receptor in hyperthyroidism

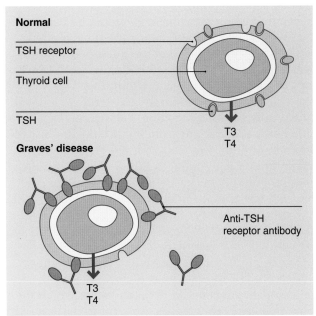

Normal

TSH receptor

Thyroid cell

TSH

T3
T4

Graves' disease

Anti-TSH receptor antibody

T3
T4

Normally, TSH released by the pituitary binds to the TSH receptor on thyroid cells, causing the thyroid gland to release T_3 and T_4. T_3 and T_4 operate through a negative-feedback loop to reduce the production of TSH. In Graves' disease (hyperthyroidism), anti-TSH receptor antibody mimics TSH, causing the thyroid gland to release T_3 and T_4. Because no feedback loop is operative, the blood levels of T_3 and T_4 are increased.

Anti-RBC Antibodies

In autoimmune hemolytic anemia, antibodies are produced against an individual's own red blood cells (RBCs). The production of such autoantibodies can be spontaneous in diseases such as systemic lupus erythematosus or can be triggered by infections or by penicillin, quinidine, methyldopa, and other drugs that are adsorbed to the cell surface. Autoantibody binding to the cell activates complement, causing either direct lysis of the cells or, more commonly, accelerated removal of RBCs from the circulation. The mechanism for this latter event arises from the interaction of cell-bound antibody and C3b with the Fc and C3b receptors on macrophages in the spleen and liver. Similar antibodies can be elicited against platelets, causing immune thrombocytopenia purpura (ITP).

Exposure of an Rh-negative (Rh−) mother to the blood cells of an Rh-positive (Rh+) fetus, which is usually greatest during delivery, can result in the production of anti-Rh antibodies in the mother. These are IgG antibodies and can cross the placenta. In subsequent pregnancies in which the blood cells of the fetus are Rh+, these maternal antibodies can react with and lyse the blood cells of the fetus. The released hemoglobin is catabolized to bilirubin, but the fetal liver is too immature to further metabolize the bilirubin. The accumulation of bilirubin can produce jaundice, brain damage, and death. This condition, termed hemolytic disease of the newborn or *erythroblastosis fetalis*, can now be prevented by administration of anti-Rh antibodies to the mother immediately after the delivery of the first Rh+ fetus. Anti-Rh antibodies suppress the active production of antibodies by the mother. Although the precise mechanism of suppression is unknown, the passively administered antibodies may either block Rh antigens on the blood cells or eliminate the Rh+ blood cells from circulation before they can sensitize the mother (Figure 59).

Transfusion of incompatible blood can also result in antibody production. Antibodies against erythrocyte antigens of the ABO system tend to be IgM, which is highly efficient in activating the complement system and causing lysis because of the many combining sites on this large molecule.

During subsequent transfusions with similarly incompatible blood, the antibodies can cause massive hemolysis, transfusion reaction, and even death. Today, cross-matching techniques have made life-threatening transfusion reactions rare.

Anti–basement Membrane Antibodies

Goodpasture's syndrome results from a circulating antibody to a basement membrane component of kidney and lung tissue. The antibody binds to glomerular and alveolar-capillary basement membrane and activates complement. The ensuing damage to the basement membrane causes pulmonary hemorrhage, hematuria, and proteinuria. Linear deposits of IgG accumulate in the kidney (Figure 60) and may cause severe progressive glomerulonephritis.

Immune Complex (Type III) Hypersensitivity

The humoral immune system responds to foreign antigen by generating IgM and, subsequently, IgG antibodies that bind to the foreign antigen, leading to the formation of immune complexes. The development of immune complexes is thus a desirable end result. Most immune complexes containing IgG and/or IgM in turn activate complement. During complement activation, large fragments of the third and fourth components of complement (C3b and C4b) are bound to the antigen and, to a lesser extent, to the antibody. The deposited C4b and C3b influence the solubility of the immune complex and serve as ligands for receptors on peripheral blood cells and tissue macrophages. Thus, immune complexes are maintained in a soluble state so that they adhere to and, in some cases, are ingested by cells bearing Fc and complement receptors. This scavenging system evolved to protect the host by eliminating soluble

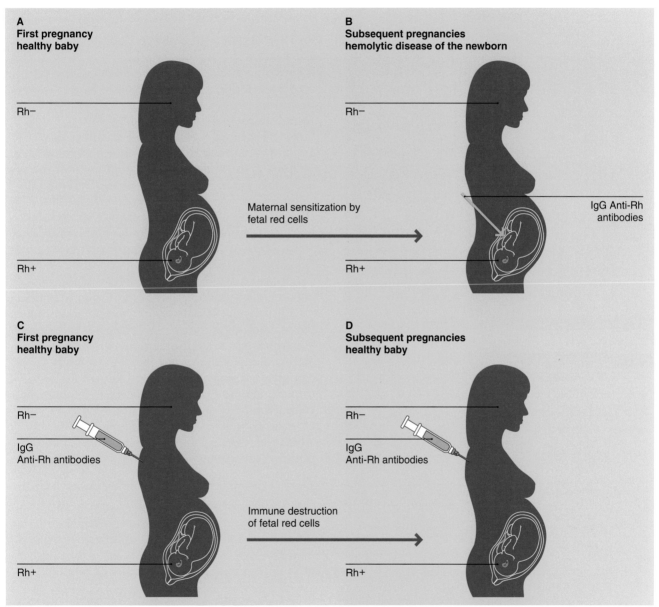

A
First pregnancy
healthy baby

Rh−

Rh+

Maternal sensitization by
fetal red cells

B
Subsequent pregnancies
hemolytic disease of the newborn

Rh−

IgG Anti-Rh
antibodies

Rh+

C
First pregnancy
healthy baby

Rh−

IgG
Anti-Rh antibodies

Immune destruction
of fetal red cells

Rh+

D
Subsequent pregnancies
healthy baby

Rh−

IgG
Anti-Rh antibodies

Rh+

(**A**) During a pregnancy in which the mother is Rh− and the
fetus Rh+, fetal erythrocytes sensitize the mother, who
produces anti-Rh antibodies. The maximum risk of sensitization
occurs during delivery, when large numbers of the infant's
erythrocytes escape through the placenta into the mother's
blood. First pregnancies are not usually harmful to the infant.
(**B**) During subsequent pregnancies, maternal IgG anti-Rh
antibodies cross the placenta and lead to the destruction of the
infant's Rh+ erythrocytes. Intrauterine death or severe hemolytic
anemia of the newborn child can result.

(**C**) Administration of anti-Rh antibodies prevents sensitization
of the mother by destruction of Rh+ fetal erythrocytes that enter
the maternal circulation.
(**D**) The antiserum, produced by human volunteers, is administered shortly after delivery of the baby (the time of maximum
risk of sensitization). The maternal erythrocytes are Rh− and
are unaffected by the anti-Rh serum. Destruction of the Rh+
erythrocytes (or the coating of their antigenic sites) by the
antibody blocks maternal sensitization. The antibody must be
administered after delivery or termination of all subsequent
pregnancies to prevent isoimmunization of the mother.

Figure 60
Tissue sections stained with fluorescein isothiocyanate-labeled rabbit anti–human immunoglobulin G

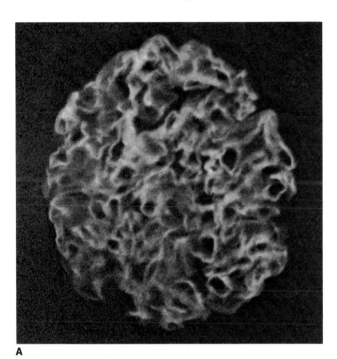

A

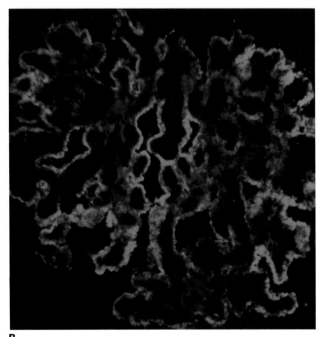

B

(**A**) Linear localization of IgG in anti–basement membrane glomerulonephritis.
(**B**) Granular or "lumpy-bumpy" localization of IgG in immune complex nephritis.

antigens and viral particles from the circulation. Illnesses, such as some forms of arthritis and glomerulonephritis, may result when immune complexes are in excess or are not properly cleared.

Primate Erythrocyte Immune Complex Clearance Mechanism

Immune complexes that form in tissue are processed locally by leukocytes. Although a pathologic lesion may develop at this site, the immune complex is usually isolated and destroyed and, therefore, does not enter the circulation. If antibody and antigen interact in the circulation, a potentially more dangerous situation faces the host. This interaction may occur in autoimmune states, as well as in any disease in which the soluble antigen (possibly derived from an infectious particle) gains access to the circulation. The subsequent deposition of immune complexes in a vessel wall can induce an inflammatory response and thereby destroy vascular integrity and adversely affect the function of the tissue to which the vessel supplies blood. The deposition of immune complexes in the glomerulus of the kidney illustrates this type of pathologic process.

To process IgM and IgG complexes that fix complement, a system evolved known as the primate immune complex clearance mechanism. Within seconds of the interaction of IgM or IgG with antigen, thousands to millions of C3b molecules can deposit on the immune complex. Erythrocytes from primates and nonprimate platelets possess complement receptor type one (CR1), which is a C3b/C4b-binding glycoprotein. The immune complex bearing C3b/C4b can attach to the erythrocyte via the CR1 receptor, allowing the removal of "free" immune complexes from blood. As a result, immune complexes are prevented from becoming trapped in organs of relatively high blood flow per unit mass of tissue (eg, kidneys, lungs, and skin). In addition, the receptor plus factor I, a serum serine protease (see chapter 9), can process some of the bound C3b. The modified C3b can react with other receptors on fixed macrophages in the spleen and liver. As the erythrocyte bearing the immune complexes traverses the liver, the immune complexes, and possibly the receptor as well, are stripped away and the "cleansed" erythrocyte returns to the circulation. Thus, in humans, the erythrocyte via its C3b receptor serves as a "sump, processing station, and shuttle" for immune complexes.

If the immune complex clearance mechanism is functioning inefficiently or is overwhelmed by an excess of immune complexes, tissue injury can result as they are deposited in undesirable locations. For example, immune complexes deposited in the synovial tissue that lines a joint may cause an inflammatory reaction (arthritis). Small peptides released by complement activation cause fluid and cells to accumulate, and the joint becomes swollen and painful. As leukocytes ingest the immune complexes, they release degradative enzymes that may damage normal joint tissues. If the process becomes chronic, the joint can be destroyed.

In a similar manner, the renal glomeruli and pulmonary alveoli can be damaged. Recent experiments in a primate model indicate that immune complexes that inefficiently bind complement have a greater likelihood of being deposited in the kidney and lung. Similarly, if the complement system is deficient or if there are too few or poorly functioning complement receptors, the host is at greater risk for developing immune complex–mediated disease.

Two types of experimental models of immune complex disease, both of which have clinical correlates, have been developed. Immune complex disease can be defined according to the anatomic site of immune complex formation: (1) In the circulation, antibody can interact with soluble antigen forming immune complexes that may deposit in any vessel, but appear to accumulate especially in tissues with large filter areas, such as the kidney, lung, and skin. (2) In tissues, antibody may react with antigen that is secreted or injected locally.

Circulating Antibody-Antigen Complexes

Acute serum sickness: The animal model of acute or "one-shot" serum sickness (Figure 61) is usually demonstrated in rabbits. In humans, acute serum sickness involves predominantly skin (urticaria and angioedema), the kidney (glomerulonephritis), blood vessels (vasculitis), and joints (arthralgia and arthritis). It occurs 7 to 14 days after the injection of a large quantity of a heterologous serum protein. Serum sickness–like reactions have followed the administration of antibiotics (particularly penicillin) and foreign serum. In the early 1900s, heterologous (usually horse) hyperimmune sera were used to treat various infectious diseases, especially those of childhood, such as diphtheria. The immune response to the foreign protein resulted in immune complex formation and the disease commonly called serum sickness. Recently, heterologous monoclonal antibodies and polyclonal antibodies, such as equine anti–thymocyte globulin, have been used to treat immunologic conditions, such as bone marrow failure and transplant rejections, and serum sickness has resulted.

Chronic serum sickness: The experimental model of chronic serum sickness requires daily injections of heterologous protein antigen in doses sufficient to maintain the antigen in slight excess over antibody. In the rabbit, glomerulonephritis develops within 5 weeks. In this model, disease does not develop if antigen is not in excess, if the animal does not make an immune response, or if an excess of either antigen or antibody is present. Human illnesses that may represent chronic serum sickness–like reactions include systemic lupus erythematosus, some forms of glomerulonephritis (Figure 60), and certain infections such as viral hepatitis, in which foreign antigen is chronically present.

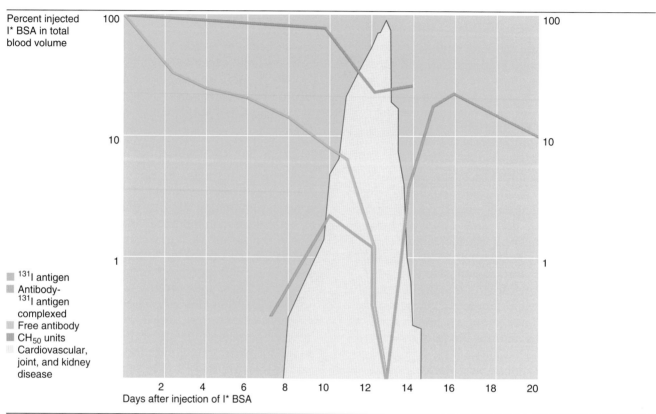

Percent injected
I* BSA in total
blood volume

- ¹³¹I antigen
- Antibody-
  ¹³¹I antigen
  complexed
- Free antibody
- CH₅₀ units
- Cardiovascular,
  joint, and kidney
  disease

Days after injection of I* BSA

The sequence of events after injection of 250 mg I*BSA/kg body weight in rabbits. (I*BSA is bovine serum albumin tagged with radiolabeled iodine.) Elimination of ^{131}I antigen is indicated by a red line, and antigen-antibody complexes are plotted as the percent of total I*BSA injected (green line) related to the log scale at left. The amount of circulating free antibody (blue line), level of total complement (CH$_{50}$ units) plotted as percent of normal (purple line), and incidence of cardiovascular, joint, and kidney disease (grey shaded area reaching 100% on day 13) relate to log scale at right.

Figure 61b
Composite of serial circulating immune complex (^{125}I-C1q binding) and complement levels (percent of normal) in a serum sickness patient who received 10 days of anti-thymocyte globulin

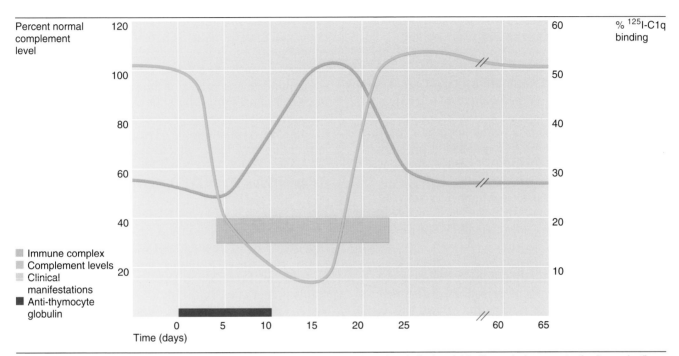

Percent normal complement level

% ^{125}I-C1q binding

Immune complex
Complement levels
Clinical manifestations
Anti-thymocyte globulin

Time (days)

Symptoms are shown by the hatched bar. They were most severe at about day 15 and consisted of fever, malaise, cutaneous eruptions, arthralgia, and gastrointestinal disturbances.

Note the similarity of this illness in humans to the "one-shot" serum sickness model in rabbits (Figure 61a).

Based on data from Lawley TJ, Bielory L, Gascon P, et al. A prospective clinical and immunologic analysis of patients with serum sickness. *N Engl J Med.* 1984;311:1407-1413; and Bielory L, Gascon P, Lawley TJ, et al. Human serum sickness: a prospective analysis of 35 patients treated with equine antithymocyte globulin for bone marrow failure. *Medicine.* 1988;67:40-57.

Several factors influence the course of both acute and chronic serum sickness, including the nature of the antigen (type, quantity, and valence), the antibody response (qualitative and quantitative aspects), hemodynamic factors (eg, high blood pressure), vascular factors (permeability of blood vessels), and complement and complement receptors.

Tissue Deposition of Antibody-Antigen Complexes

The Arthus reaction is an example of a local vasculitic process that appears within a few hours of the subcutaneous release or injection of a soluble antigen into a host who has preformed precipitating IgG antibody. Antibody and antigen form immune complexes that are deposited in and around local blood vessels, where they activate complement and cause vasculitis. IgG, an intact complement system, and neutrophils are necessary to mediate the reaction.

Examples of Arthus reactions in humans include too frequent administration of tetanus toxoid and some forms of thyroiditis. Inflammation of synovial tissue in rheumatoid arthritis is also probably an Arthus-type reaction.

Detection of Immune Complexes

Immune complexes accompany most infectious illnesses and chronic inflammatory conditions of both known and unknown etiology. At present, measurement of immune complexes in clinical medicine is of limited utility. More than 30 different types of tests have been developed to measure immune complexes, but not one is entirely satisfactory. It is hoped that these assays will be refined to permit identification of the offending antigen in the complex.

Clinical assays that measure complement and cryoglobulin levels are widely used in clinical medicine and do provide information relative to the presence of immune complexes. Immune complexes may activate the classical complement pathway, causing a measurable reduction in circulating components (C1, C4, C2, and C3). Mixed cryoglobulins (usually containing IgG, IgM, C3, and an antigen) are immune complexes that precipitate in the cold and thus are a direct measure of an important subset of immune complexes. Mixed cryoglobulins are found in a variety of infectious, inflammatory, lymphoproliferative, and connective tissue diseases.

Delayed-Type (Type IV) Hypersensitivity

The classic delayed-type hypersensitivity (DTH) skin reaction is caused by a cellular immune response to an antigen in an immune individual. In the original immune injury scheme proposed by Gell and Coombs, all hypersensitivity responses that take more than 12 hours to develop were classified as delayed hypersensitivity responses. The cutaneous delayed hypersensitivity response (type IV hypersensitivity of Gell and Coombs) is now defined as a local cell-mediated immune reaction that is elicited by antigen administered subcutaneously. This immune response results in edema, congestion, and an accumulation of cells (predominantly mononuclear leukocytes) at the injection site that peaks 24 to 48 hours after antigen challenge. Macroscopically, this response is manifested as erythema (redness) and induration (swelling) of the skin at the site of injection (Figure 62).

Unlike other hypersensitivity responses, DTH is mediated exclusively by T lymphocytes. It can be experimentally transferred by immune cells but not by any class of specific antibody. The T cells that orchestrate the response to experimentally administered antigens are currently believed to be the same T cells that participate in protective immune responses. The cells and the effector molecules involved in the development of DTH responses probably carry out similar functions in the elimination of invading microorganisms.

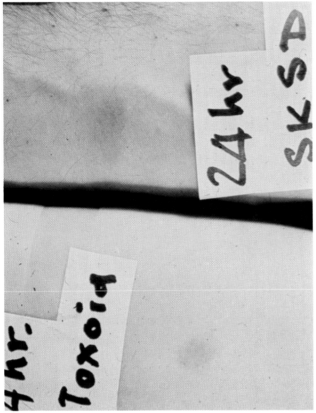

Figure 62
Positive results of a delayed-type hypersensitivity skin test

Note swelling and erythema.

Classification of DTH Reactions

At least four different types of delayed hypersensitivity reactions have been defined by clinical and morphologic criteria.

Jones-Mote hypersensitivity: Jones-Mote hypersensitivity, also called cutaneous basophil hypersensitivity, is an atypical form of DTH characterized by an infiltration of inflammatory cells rich in basophils. The skin swelling associated with the response peaks 24 hours after antigen challenge. The antigens that elicit this atypical response are usually weak immunogens, and the Jones-Mote hypersensitivity reaction is usually greatest if the second exposure to the antigen occurs 7 to 10 days after the initial exposure.

Contact hypersensitivity: Contact hypersensitivity is characterized clinically by an eczematous response of the skin to the sensitizing allergen. The response typically peaks 48 to 72 hours after exposure to the antigen. Contact allergens are often small, chemically reactive molecules that attach to skin proteins and serve as haptenic groups capable of sensitizing T cells. The prototype contact allergen among North Americans is the oleoresin in poison ivy and poison oak, but other molecules, such as nickel and latex components, frequently elicit contact responses. The eczematous skin lesion is characterized microscopically by infiltration of the epidermis by mononuclear cells (monocytes/macrophages and T cells), which causes destruction of the epidermis and leads to vesicle formation, discoloration, crusting, and sloughing of the skin. The major histocompatibility complex (MHC) class II–positive epidermal Langerhans cell is believed to be the critical antigen-presenting cell for induction and elicitation of contact hypersensitivity.

Classic DTH reaction: The classic delayed hypersensitivity response is the tuberculin-type hypersensitivity elicited by intradermal administration of the purified protein derivative of *Mycobacterium tuberculosis* cultures. Purified proteins from a number of microorganisms (eg, *Mycobacterium leprae*, *Leishmania tropica*) induce similar reactions in sensitized individuals. The response is characterized by redness and induration of the skin at the site of antigen inoculation and peaks 48 to 72 hours after challenge. Microscopically, this response is characterized by dense infiltration of the dermis by mononuclear cells (monocytes/macrophages and lymphocytes), with extensive accumulation of mononuclear cells around small blood vessels (perivascular cuffing). The perivascular accumulation of mononuclear cells reflects a local egress of cells from the vessels. The response begins to wane by 4 to 6 days postchallenge, with the loss of macrophages preceding the loss of lymphocytes from the site.

Granulomatous hypersensitivity: Perhaps the most clinically important hypersensitivity response, granulomatous hypersensitivity is characterized by the formation of granulomas composed of epithelioid macrophages, lymphocytes, fibroblasts, and, in many instances, giant cells. The cause of granulomatous hypersensitivity is believed to be antigens that the immune system is unable to clear, which produce a chronic persistent cellular immune response. Persistent T-cell stimulation results in the sustained activation of macrophages, which causes the activated macrophages to differentiate into epithelioid cells. Giant cells are believed to be either terminally differentiated forms of epithelioid macrophages that have undergone nuclear division without separation of daughter cells or syncytia formed as a result of fusion of epithelioid cells. Granulomatous hypersensitivity is seen in a variety of disease states, including infections (eg, tuberculosis, leprosy, parasitic infestations), exposure to environmental agents (eg, zirconium and beryllium salts), and diseases of uncertain etiology (eg, sarcoidosis, Wegener's granulomatosis). Less frequently, granulomatous reactions are produced by foreign bodies and antigen-antibody complexes through poorly understood mechanisms. Severe granulomatous reactions are often associated with extensive tissue destruction, hence the importance of this response as an injury mechanism.

Mechanisms of DTH

Delayed hypersensitivity is a manifestation of cell-mediated immunity. Clinically detectable T-cell response to antigen in the skin normally requires induction or "priming" of the T cells through prior exposure to the antigen. Priming is most easily understood as a selective expansion of T cells directed toward the antigen or allergen. However, there is some evidence that unlike naive T cells, memory T-cell precursors may more rapidly and vigorously undergo the differentiation and activation event associated with the expression of T-cell effector activity. Thus, the inductive phase of the DTH response can be thought of as both an expansion of antigen-specific memory T-cell precursors and as a change in the state of activation of the memory T-cell precursors, which allows for a more rapid and vigorous response to subsequent challenge with antigen.

The elicitation of DTH response requires a complex interaction between $CD4^+$ MHC class II-restricted helper T cells and MHC class II-expressing antigen-presenting cells displaying the processed antigen (see chapters 2 and 6). Class II-positive B cells, follicular dendritic cells, and macrophages can serve as presenting cells for antigens that are localized to peripheral lymphoid tissue (eg, regional lymph nodes). In the skin, MHC class II-positive macrophages and the class II-positive epidermal dendritic cells (Langerhans cells), in particular, appear to be the important antigen-presenting cells in inducing local delayed-type hypersensitivity responses.

Some evidence indicates the existence of at least two distinct subsets of helper T cells, T_{H1} and T_{H2}, in the mouse. These two T-cell subsets secrete different constellations of lymphokines and appear to interact preferentially with different antigen-presenting cell types (see also chapters 6 and 7). One intriguing possibility is that the T_{H1} cell, which secretes lymphotoxin (tumor necrosis factor [TNF-β]), interferon gamma (IFN-γ), and interleukin-2 (IL-2) in response to antigenic stimulation, primarily interacts with class II-positive macrophages as antigen-presenting cells. Since macrophages are the principal effector cells in the delayed hypersensitivity response, the T_{H1} cell may be the CD4$^+$ cell that orchestrates the DTH reaction. The T_{H2} cell, on the other hand, secretes IL-4 and appears to utilize class II-positive B cells as presenting cells. Therefore, this T-cell subset would be involved with the induction of humoral immune responses and would not participate directly in DTH responses. Developed from studies in experimental animals, this intriguing model has received increasing support from studies in human subjects.

The initial event in the delayed hypersensitivity response is the activation of macrophages/monocytes. The activation can occur as a result of direct interaction of antigen (eg, microorganisms or their cell-wall products) with the macrophage/monocyte or through the action of lymphokines (particularly lymphotoxin and IFN-γ) derived from activated T cells. Macrophage activation leads to the synthesis and local release of two protein cytokines, interleukin-1 (IL-1) and tumor necrosis factor-α (TNF-α), and to the formation of products of arachidonic acid metabolism, notably the lipoxygenase product leukotriene B$_4$ (LTB$_4$) and the cyclooxygenase product prostaglandin E$_2$ (PGE$_2$). (See chapter 7 for a discussion of lymphokine and other cytokines.) PGE$_2$ is a potent vasodilator that enhances blood flow and serves to increase access of circulating cells to the site of antigen deposition. IL-1, TNF-α, and LTB$_4$ interact with vascular endothelium to promote the adherence of circulating neutrophils, monocytes, and lymphocytes to postcapillary venules. IL-1 and LTB$_4$ are extremely potent chemotactic agents and presumably promote the accumulation of blood leukocytes at the site of the delayed response. It should be evident that the early events in macrophage activation can lead to the early inflammatory response associated with the DTH reaction.

The second essential element in the expression of DTH is the recognition of the processed antigen–class II molecule complex on the antigen-presenting cell by the receptor on CD4$^+$ T cells. The engagement of the antigen receptor leads to a cascade of events that culminates in the activation and proliferation of the T cells (see chapters 6 and 7). One of these events is the release of a variety of lymphokines by the activated CD4$^+$ T cells. Critical among these are lymphotoxin and IFN-γ, which are the major macrophage-activating factors (MAF) that lead to the release of IL-1, TNF-α, and other monokines by the activated monocyte/macrophage. Because lymphotoxin and IFN-γ can also up-regulate the expression of class II molecules on tissue macrophages, vascular endothelial cells, keratinocytes, and tissue fibroblasts, T-cell activation can, as a result of IFN-γ release, lead to increased numbers of MHC class II-positive cells with antigen-presenting capacity. Such cells can serve to amplify the T-cell response by providing a further source of processed antigen–class II complexes for presentation to T cells.

Several other lymphokines play an important role in the expression of DTH. Macrophage migration inhibition factor (MIF) activity independent of IFN-γ has been identified. MIF inhibits random migration of monocytes/macrophages and likely promotes the accumulation of mononuclear phagocytes at the site of the cellular immune response. IL-2 and IL-4 are the predominant lymphocyte-specific autocrine growth factors for the murine CD4$^+$ T_{H1} and T_{H2} T cells, respectively. Local release of these factors stimulates the proliferation of activated T cells. IL-2 is also a potent chemotactic factor for mononuclear cells.

Other lymphokines, including IL-5 and IL-6, appear primarily to regulate B-cell activation and proliferation. Several lymphokines (eg, lymphotoxin) have been implicated as inducers of epithelioid changes in activated macrophages and as promoters of the formation of giant cells from epithelial macrophages. They also can act as potent chemotactic factors for basophils.

The clinical and histologic manifestations of the delayed hypersensitivity reaction (ie, erythema, induration, mononuclear infiltration, perivascular cuffing) can be understood as a complex interaction between specifically sensitized CD4+ T cells and other cell types. It is probable that direct cell-to-cell interaction is an essential facet of this reaction. In addition, it is becoming evident that many of the effector activities of these cells are mediated through the action of diffusible cytokines. Recombinant DNA technology will provide better understanding of the mechanism of action of cytokines, and the cloned gene products may be used to augment or inhibit the expression of the cellular immune responses in the body.

Cell-Mediated Cytotoxicity

Studies in which defined populations of antigen-specific immunocytes have been adoptively transferred into nonimmune recipients implicate CD4+ T cells as the primary mediators of the chronic inflammatory response that is associated with delayed hypersensitivity reaction. Activated CD4+ T cells orchestrate the response by releasing a variety of lymphokines in response to antigenic stimulation. As described elsewhere (see chapter 4), a second major population of T cells functions in cellular immune responses. This subset is the killer or cytotoxic T lymphocyte (CTL) which has the capacity to directly destroy cells expressing the foreign target antigen to which the CTL is directed.

Until recently, the expression of cell-mediated cytotoxic activity has been considered to be the exclusive property of T cells bearing CD8 cell-surface molecules. In the mouse, the expression of the cell-surface CD8 marker on a T cell is strongly correlated with the expression of cytolytic activity, whereas in humans, killing by both CD8+ and CD4+ effector T cells has been well documented. It appears that in humans, the nature of the antigenic stimulus (ie, the type of virus or tissue graft) in part dictates whether CD4+ or CD8+ CTLs will predominate in the cytolytic response. In most persons, CD8+ T cells apparently make up the majority of CTLs generated in response to a given antigen.

Like helper T cells, CTLs usually exist in the peripheral blood or peripheral lymphoid organs as small T cells (ie, quiescent precursor lymphocytes) that lack cytolytic machinery. Engagement of the T-cell antigen receptor on the CTL precursor by peptide MHC complex leads to activation of the precursor (Figure 63). The membrane-associated and intracellular events resulting from receptor engagement and activation are similar to the activation of helper T cells (see chapter 6). An important consequence of CTL precursor activation is the clonal expansion of the precursor into a number of daughter cells that undergo differentiation into active effector CTLs. The proliferation and differentiation of CTL precursors appear to require the action of soluble factors that provide proliferative and differentiative signals. A number of cytokines, including the T-cell products IL-2 and IFN-γ, have been implicated as important CTL differentiation factors. However, the role of these and other T-cell products in CTL differentiation is not completely understood.

The fully differentiated CTL is a large, blastlike lymphocyte that possesses the cellular machinery to induce target cell lysis. Killing by the activated CTL involves irreversible damage to the target cell cytoplasmic membrane. The damage is mediated by pore-forming proteins similar to the membrane attack complex of complement formed by C6, C7, C8, and C9 (see chapter 9). These pore-forming proteins are contained in granules located in the cytoplasm of activated CTLs and are released by the CTL during killing. Also present in or associated with the granules are other toxic molecules, such as lymphotoxin (TNF-β) and serine proteases, which are also released during the killing event. These factors may mediate intracellular damage to the target cells.

The process of target cell recognition and lysis by CTL can be divided into discrete steps. The first step is binding of the CTL to the target cell. This binding step appears to be mediated by several antigen-independent nonspecific adhesive molecules on the CTL surface that recognize acceptor structures on the target cell surfaces. One of the most important of these cell adhesion molecules (CAMs) is lymphocyte function-associated antigen-1 (LFA-1), a member of the integrin family of CAMs displayed on the surface of cells of hematopoietic-lymphoreticular origin (see chapter 8). Binding of this molecule to the target cell acceptor structure is necessary for CTL binding and for subsequent recognition and target cell lysis. Whether LFA-1 binding is purely adhesive or also results in the transduction of a signal in the CTL is not yet clear.

The second step in CTL-mediated lysis is recognition of the antigenic moiety on the target cell surface by the CTL antigen receptor. Engagement of the receptor leads to a cascade of membrane-associated events (ie, Ca^{2+} flux) and intracellular events (ie, protein phosphorylation), resulting in the expression of T-cell effector activity. CTL activation leads to the rapid movement of cytoplasmic granules with their lytic contents to the side of the CTL that binds the target cells. Rapid granule exocytosis follows with the release of the pore-forming proteins and other lytic factors into the site of CTL target cell contact (Figure 64).

Figure 63
CTL precursor differentiation

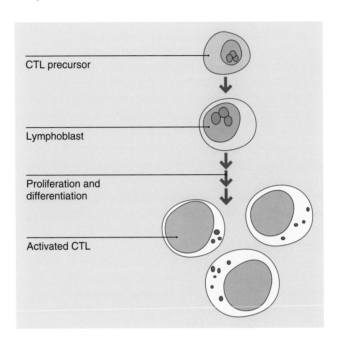

Figure 64
Granule exocytosis in CTL-mediated lysis

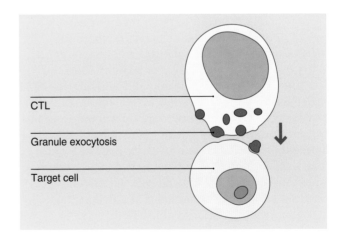

The final step in the cytolytic process is the destruction of the target cell. As suggested previously, target cell destruction apparently involves both the target cell membrane and its intracellular contents. Pore-forming proteins are present in the CTL granule as protein monomers that are released as a result of degranulation into the intercellular space between the CTL and the target cell. The monomers intercalate into the target cell membrane and coalesce to form a transmembrane pore that allows lymphotoxins and proteases released from the granule to enter the target cell and fragment the DNA. The initial binding and recognition events associated with CTL-mediated lysis occur rapidly (in less than 10 minutes) at body temperature of 37°C. The actual destruction of the damaged target cell takes up to several hours.

CTLs have been implicated as important cellular immune effectors in allograft rejection and in the recognition of virally infected cells and tumors. Virus-specific CTLs are MHC-restricted in their recognition and killing of virally infected cells. The antigen receptor on the CTL recognizes a complex of self-MHC molecules and viral antigen. We now know that the CTL antigen receptor does not recognize intact viral polypeptides on the infected cell surface, but like the receptor on helper T cells, the CTL antigen receptor sees a complex of MHC molecules and fragmented (processed) forms of viral antigen (see chapter 6). Alloantigen-specific CTLs utilize an antigen receptor similar to that of helper T cells and MHC-restricted CTLs (see chapter 3). However, alloantigen-specific CTLs are not MHC-restricted in their recognition of grafted tissue bearing foreign MHC molecules; instead, these CTLs appear to recognize the foreign MHC molecule directly. A possible explanation for the difference between alloreactive and MHC-restricted CTLs is that the recognition of alloantigen represents a cross-reaction of a self–MHC-restricted CTL directed to foreign (eg, viral) antigen with a non–self-MHC molecule-peptide complex present on the allograft.

The MHC locus products that restrict CTL recognition of the host's infected cells and are recognized by CTLs directed to grafted tissues are predominantly MHC class I molecules. These molecules are present on most cells of the body. Consequently, MHC class I-restricted CTLs can survey a diverse array of body cell types in their search for abnormal cells. Likewise, many different cell types in an allograft can serve as targets for activated alloantigen-specific (ie, MHC class I-reactive) CTLs.

Natural Killer Cells and Lymphokine-Activated Killer Cells

Natural killer (NK) cells are a unique subpopulation of lymphocytelike cells that constitutively express lytic activity (ie, without specific activation of precursor cells by an antigen). The NK cells constitute a small population in peripheral blood (fewer than 5% of total blood leukocytes) and lymphoid tissues. NK cells have been identified in vitro by their ability to kill a variety of tumor cell types and virally infected cells in a non–MHC-restricted fashion. The molecular structure of the NK receptor is currently unknown. NK cells appear not to use a conventional T-cell antigen receptor for target cell recognition, since their receptor genes are in a germline (that is, nonrearranged) configuration.

NK cells are large granular lymphocytes with characteristic cytoplasmic granules that are morphologically similar to the granules in activated CTLs. They are believed to destroy target cells by a mechanism similar to CTLs in which pore-forming proteins and other toxins are released.

At present, the in vivo role of NK cells in immunity is not clear. Their ability to kill virally infected cells and tumor cells in a nonspecific fashion makes them prime candidates for playing a surveillance role in the elimination of any abnormal cells in early infection or tumor development. Experimental studies in which cloned NK populations were transferred into infected or tumor-bearing animals suggest that NK cells can function in the body to eliminate virus or tumor. In addition, recombinant preparations of lymphokines that enhance NK activity in the test tube also increase the host response to viral infection and tumor formation.

A recent advance in the immunotherapy of tumors has been the use of lymphokine-activated killer (LAK) cells. LAK cells are derived from lymphocytes obtained from peripheral blood of tumor patients. The lymphocytes are activated in vitro with autologous tumor cells in the presence of high concentrations of IL-2. The LAK cells are then transfused back into the patient who provided the lymphocytes. To date, there has been some success in using LAK cells to slow tumor development and spread in some patients, but the mechanism of action in the body is unclear.

Conclusion

Hypersensitivity occurs when an immune response, which normally would protect the host from an invading organism, is activated against an agent that is not intrinsically harmful, and the normal mechanisms employed by the immune response induce morbidity in the host. The entire gamut of immune responses can evoke hypersensitivity, and four types have been defined according to the involvement of IgE, IgG, IgM, complement, or T cells. Upon second or subsequent contact with the antigenic agent, manifestations are observed within minutes to days and can be as minor as a skin rash, as devastating as an autoimmune disease, or as catastrophic as anaphylaxis. Treatment for hypersensitivity states includes removal of the offending agent, interference with physiologic mediators, and suppression of the immune response.

Selected Readings

Bielory L, Gascon P, Lawley TJ, Young NS, Frank MM. Human serum sickness: a prospective analysis of 35 patients treated with equine anti-thymocyte globulin for bone marrow failure. **Medicine**. 1988;67:40-57.

Dixon FJ, Cochrane CC, Theofilopoulos AN. Immune complex injury. In: Samter M, Talmage DW, Frank MM, Austen KF, Claman HN, eds. **Immunological Diseases.** Vol I. 4th ed. Boston, Mass: Little, Brown & Co; 1988:233-259.

Engel AG. Myasthenia gravis and myasthenic syndromes. **Ann Neurol.** 1984;16:519-534.

Hebert LA, Cosio FG. The erythrocyte-immune complex-glomerulonephritis connection in man. **Kidney Int**. 1987;31:877-885.

Lawley TJ, Bielory L, Gascon P, Yancey KB, Young NS, Frank MM. A prospective clinical and immunologic analysis of patients with serum sickness. **N Engl J Med.** 1984;311:1407-1413.

Schifferli JA, Ng YC, Peters DK. The role of complement and its receptor in the elimination of immune complexes. **N Engl J Med.** 1986;315:488-495.

Schifferli JA, Taylor RP. Physiological and pathological aspects of circulating immune complexes. **Kidney Int.** 1989;35:993-1003.

Wall JR, Kuroki T. Immunologic factors in thyroid disease. **Med Clin North Am**. 1985;69:913-936.

Introduction

Readers of this book have probably concluded by now that the major problems in immunology have been solved. This book has detailed the structures of antibodies and T-cell receptors, the mechanisms for generating the diversity of the immune repertoire, the molecular basis of antigen recognition, and how cells of the immune system interact. In contrast, autoimmunity, the topic of this chapter, is a bulwark of ignorance confronted by an army of unanswered questions. Once relegated to an obscure corner and referred to by a scornful "so-called," autoimmunity is now the Cinderella of immunology. Two new scientific journals carry its name, and it has become a prominent and often exclusive topic of numerous national and international meetings. It has generated excitement not only among clinicians, pathologists, and immunologists, but even among molecular biologists. The reason for all this attention may be that autoimmunity is one of the last unsolved problems in immunology.

Evolution of Ideas About Autoimmunity

The major issues in autoimmunity have their roots in the theories of the immune system elaborated by Paul Ehrlich at the turn of the century. After finding that goats make isoantibodies when immunized with red cells from other goats, but never autoantibodies against their own erythrocytes (Figure 65), Ehrlich formulated his dictum of *horror autotoxious*. As early as 1900, he emphasized that the immune system must have a mechanism that prevents autoreactivity. If it did not, he thought the result would be incompatible with life. Unfortunately, Ehrlich's ideas about autoimmunity were overinterpreted, and the very idea that autoimmunization might cause a disease was dismissed, often with disdainful disregard of evi-

dence to the contrary. Under the guise of science, opinion stalled progress for half a century, but then several key experiments began the renaissance that continues with undiminished vigor to the present day.

One of the most influential investigations of the era of revival that began 50 years after Ehrlich was the demonstration by Ernst Witebsky (who, ironically, was a scientific "grandson" of Ehrlich, having been trained by one of Ehrlich's own pupils) and Noel Rose (then a medical student in Buffalo) that normal rabbits immunized with bovine thyroglobulin developed not only anti-thyroglobulin antibodies, but also a thyroid lesion exactly of the type described by Hashimoto (Hashimoto's disease). This discovery made it apparent that, despite Ehrlich's stricture, autoimmunization can indeed occur and that autoimmune disease could be induced experimentally. The results also showed that a normal animal can produce autoantibodies if the mechanisms that prevent their formation are outmaneuvered. Immediately after Witebsky and Rose's experiments, Doniach and Roitt in London demonstrated the presence of antithyroglobulin autoantibodies in human patients with Hashimoto's disease, thus adding weight to the impact of the Witebsky-Rose experiment.

Another noteworthy event, which preceded the work on autoimmune thyroiditis, occurred in 1945 when Coombs, Mourant, and Race developed the antiglobulin test. This simple method of detecting anti–red cell antibodies (Figure 66) revolutionized blood group serology, made safe blood transfusions possible, and allowed the accurate diagnosis of maternal-fetal isoimmunization, ie, Rh disease of the newborn (see chapter 11). Moreover, because the test is equally applicable to isoantibodies and autoantibodies, it definitively established the existence of autoimmune hemolytic anemia in which opsonic autoantibodies prepare the patient's own red blood cells for premature destruction by macrophages. The pathogenic mechanism of autoimmune hemolytic anemia, implied by the antiglobulin test, led William Harrington (then at the Barnes Hospital in St.

Figure 65
Ehrlich's early experiment with autoimmunity

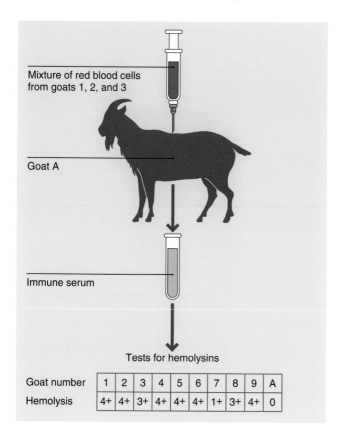

Mixture of red blood cells from goats 1, 2, and 3

Goat A

Immune serum

Tests for hemolysins

Goat number	1	2	3	4	5	6	7	8	9	A
Hemolysis	4+	4+	3+	4+	4+	4+	1+	3+	4+	0

Figure 66
Coombs' antiglobulin test

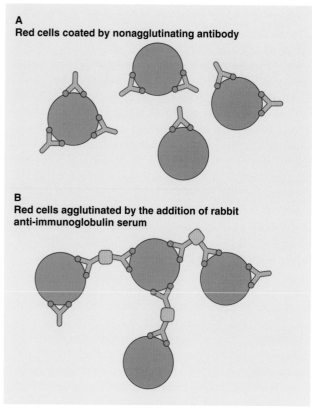

A
Red cells coated by nonagglutinating antibody

B
Red cells agglutinated by the addition of rabbit anti-immunoglobulin serum

(**A**) Erythrocytes are coated by nonagglutinating antibody.
(**B**) Erythrocytes are agglutinated by addition of rabbit anti-immunoglobulin serum.

Louis) to subject himself to an infusion of plasma from a patient with idiopathic thrombocytopenia. The result was dramatic: within hours of the infusion, Harrington's platelet count plunged to dangerous levels, thus establishing for the first time that autoantibodies can indeed be the direct cause of a human illness.

But Harrington's bold experiment did not erase the pejorative label "so-called autoimmune disease," and the discoveries of rheumatoid factor and of antinuclear and anti-DNA antibodies in the early 1950s only led to further doubts. Were these serologic findings merely epiphenomena, explaining nothing about the basis of rheumatoid arthritis, systemic lupus erythematosus, and similar mysterious disorders (ie, the "connective tissue" diseases)? Only after the Bielschowskys at the University of Otago discovered the New Zealand Black (NZB) mouse was the reality of autoimmune diseases finally established. This mouse (Figure 67) provided the first example of a spontaneous autoimmune disease in an animal and a model that could be manipulated, bred, analyzed, and dissected. Nevertheless, the NZB mouse was a disappointment; it only developed autoimmune hemolytic anemia and it had an unusual lymphoproliferative disorder. However, by crossing NZB mice with the NZW (white) strain developed by the Bielschowskys, it was possible to raise an F_1 hybrid animal with all the features of severe lupus nephritis (Figure 68). This work showed that there is a genetic basis not only for autoimmunization, but also for particular autoimmune diseases. Because the NZW strain develops no discernible evidence of an autoimmune disease, it also is apparent that normal animals carry within them suppressed information that can determine the outcome of an inherent susceptibility to autoimmunization.

After a decade of such extraordinary advances, it seemed that the only remaining problem was the development of a theoretical framework to account for the two major functions of the immune system: to defend against a world of hostile organisms and to avoid autoimmunization.

Figure 67
NZB mouse

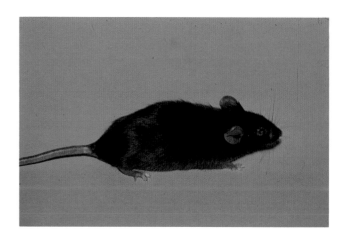

Figure 68
Lupus nephritis in the (NZBxNZW)F₁ mouse

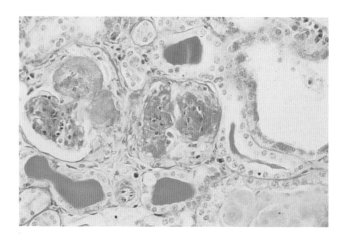

That question was first taken up in 1953 by McFarlane Burnet who, with Frank Fenner, formulated the issue in its simplest form: self and nonself. Ray Owen's experiment, published in the same year as the description of the antiglobulin test, had a substantial impact on their thinking. He had observed that dizygotic cattle twins, which are joined by a common placental circulation, commingled in their circulation each other's red cells without any trace of isoantibodies. "This raises the suggestion," Burnet and Fenner wrote, "that the process by which self-pattern becomes recognizable takes place during the embryonic or immediately postembryonic stages." In other words, the ability to distinguish between self (autoantigens) and nonself (exogenous antigens) is engraved on the organism during fetal life. For this process, Burnet and Fenner used the term *tolerance*. Burnet later elaborated on this theme as follows:

- The role of the thymus is to eliminate potentially autoreactive lymphocytes.
- Autoimmunization arises with the appearance of a *forbidden clone*, a mutant lymphocyte that escapes thymic surveillance.

Natural Autoantibodies

Long before the impact of Burnet's theories about autoimmunity was felt, an undercurrent of research began that would eventually bring into question his idea of forbidden clones. The topic of those investigations was the presence of autoantibodies in the serum of normal animals: natural autoantibodies. As early as 1920, observations began appearing in the literature about reactions of normal serum with extracts of various organs and tissues. The findings attracted little notice because of doubts about immunologic specificity and the purity of the antigens. However, Pierre Grabar of l'Institut Pasteur, the inventor of immunoelectrophoresis, did take them seriously. In the 1950s, he brought these strange observations into focus with an ingenious theory: natural autoantibodies are immunologic housekeepers that cleanse the body of cell debris and worn-out proteins (Figure 69).

Figure 69
Pierre Grabar's notion of the "housekeeping" function of natural autoantibodies

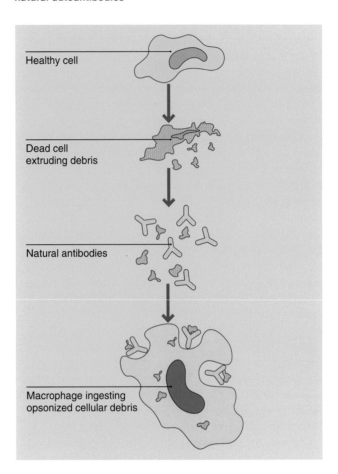

Healthy cell

Dead cell extruding debris

Natural antibodies

Macrophage ingesting opsonized cellular debris

Work on natural autoantibodies continued in Paris under the direction of Stratis Avrameas. With refined techniques and purified antigens, his group was able to show that normal human serum contains autoantibodies against a broad panel of autoantigens, including thyroglobulin, transferrin, DNA, and even albumin. The autoantibodies the investigators found were present in low concentrations, they were almost always of the IgM class, and they cross-reacted extensively with other antigens in the test panel. Later, using the hybridoma technique, several groups of investigators were able to "capture" monoclonal natural autoantibodies from normal adult, newborn, and even from germfree mice and normal humans. Notably, monoclonal natural autoantibodies were also obtained from athymic nude mice, thus showing that their production is an inherent property of the B-cell compartment, and their presence in newborn mice demonstrates that this property resides in the preimmune repertoire of antibodies. A surprising aspect of natural autoantibodies is their frequency. About 25% of hybridomas from unimmunized healthy mice produce monoclonal autoantibodies, but since the measurable frequency depends on the number of autoantigens in the test panel, the real frequency is probably even higher. With a typical test panel, the most common reaction occurs with single-stranded DNA, but autoantibodies against cytoskeletal proteins (eg, vimentin and actin), thyroglobulin, pancreatic islet cells, and other endocrine organs are also frequent. Like their counterparts in serum, these monoclonal autoantibodies are IgM, highly cross-reactive (polyspecific), and bind to autoantigens with only low avidity.

Parallel investigations revealed that monoclonal paraproteins, the immunoglobulins produced by patients with Waldenström's macroglobulinemia or multiple myeloma, often have autoimmunity activity. About 10% bind to DNA, an additional 10% bind to the I antigen of red cells (cold agglutinins), and another 10% are rheumatoid factor. Others bind to antigens of the lupus-related ribonucleoprotein antigen (RNP), and a surprising number bind to a glycoprotein in peripheral nerve. Some patients who produce autoantibody paraproteins have an autoimmune disease, such as chronic hemolytic anemia (cold agglutinin disease), cryoglobulinemia (monoclonal rheumatoid factor), and peripheral neuropathy (monoclonal antinerve antibodies). These clinical observations suggest that the natural autoantibody-producing B cells of the preimmune repertoire are susceptible to malignant transformation and that, once transformed, they secrete large amounts of immunoglobulin into the circulation.

All this leads to the conclusion that natural autoantibodies are not, as Burnet proposed, forbidden. On the contrary, natural autoantibodies dominate the preimmune B-cell repertoire, and they do so without any intervention from T cells because even athymic mice produce them. An interesting source of natural autoantibodies is a subpopulation of B cells with the CD5+ (also termed Ly1 and Leu-1) surface marker. Large numbers of these lymphocytes are found in the fetus, but some adult B cells are also CD5+. Their numbers increase in patients with rheumatoid arthritis and in NZB mice. In vitro and in the absence of T cells, CD5+ B cells spontaneously produce rheumatoid factor as well as antibodies against single-stranded DNA, thyroglobulin, and pancreatic islet cells. About one third of human B-cell lymphomas are CD5+, which may explain the associations between malignant lymphoproliferative diseases and autoimmune diseases.

Germline Origins of Autoantibodies

In the context of immunologic tolerance and the body's apparent need to avoid autoimmunization, it may seem odd that autoantibodies against DNA, thyroglobulin, islet cells of the pancreas, and acetylcholine receptors (all associated with serious and even potentially lethal diseases) are found so commonly in the normal antibody repertoire.

Figure 70
Synthesis of immunoglobulins with idiotypic markers of lupus anti-DNA antibodies

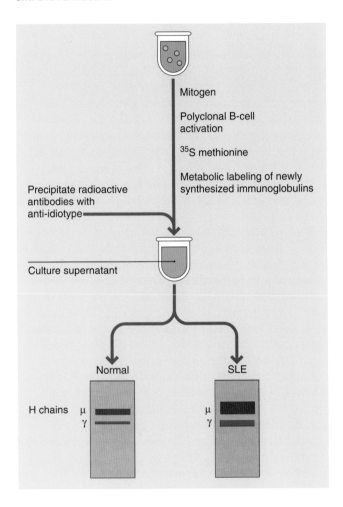

Mitogen

Polyclonal B-cell activation

^{35}S methionine

Metabolic labeling of newly synthesized immunoglobulins

Precipitate radioactive antibodies with anti-idiotype

Culture supernatant

Normal

SLE

H chains μ γ

However, the presence of such antibodies in normal serum is consistent with the vast repertoire of B cells. In a 30-gram mouse, the molecular mechanisms of immunoglobulin V gene recombination (discussed in chapter 1) have the potential to yield 100 million different antibody combining sites. Among those many variable regions there surely will be some, if not many, with the capacity to bind to antigenic surfaces on autoantigens. In other words, it is inevitable that the randomly joined V_H and V_L gene segments will encode immunoglobulins with autoantibody specificities.

These ideas about autoantibodies of the pre-immune repertoire imply that the origins of pathogenic autoantibodies can be traced back to the germline. In other words, we all have the genetic potential to form lesion-producing autoantibodies. Three lines of evidence support this idea:

- The binding specificities of monoclonal natural autoantibodies against DNA and acetylcholine receptor resemble those of monoclonal antibodies derived by the hybridoma technique from patients with systemic lupus erythematosus (SLE) and myasthenia gravis, respectively.

- Idiotypic markers of monoclonal anti-DNA antibodies from patients with SLE have also been found in anti-DNA antibodies obtained from normal people. Furthermore, in vitro stimulation of normal B cells by a polyclonal activator leads to the synthesis of anti-DNA antibodies with an idiotypic marker of lupus anti-DNA antibodies (Figure 70).

- Structural analyses of anti-DNA antibodies from humans and mice with SLE and of human rheumatoid factor have shown that some are encoded by unmutated germline V genes or by V genes that differ only slightly (one or two nucleotides) from known germline genes.

T Cells and Autoantibodies

What accounts for the absence of immune lesions in a normal person who possesses the same immunoglobulin V genes and who can produce autoantibodies with the same binding specificities and idiotypes as a patient with an autoimmune disease? To begin to answer this question, it is necessary to recall that natural autoantibodies are normally produced only in small amounts, that they are of the IgM isotype, and that their avidity for autoantigens is low. In an autoimmune disease, by contrast, large amounts of high-avidity IgG autoantibodies are usual. Nonetheless, IgM antibodies also can be pathogenic, as seen in the case of pathogenic monoclonal paraproteins. The antibodies that cause the hemolytic anemia of cold agglutinin disease and the cold agglutinins in normal serum are both IgM antibodies with specificity for the I antigen of erythrocytes. However, patients with cold agglutinin disease produce 1000 to 100 000 times more autoantibody than normal persons. A mass action effect, therefore, can render IgM autoantibodies pathogenic.

IgG autoantibodies are more likely to be pathogenic than IgM autoantibodies, not only because of their higher avidity for autoantigens, but also because they tend to have certain physical properties that favor interactions with tissues. For example, IgG anti-DNA antibodies, which have a net positive charge, are preferentially deposited in renal glomeruli. What mechanism converts the low-avidity IgM precursors to high-avidity IgG antibodies? In the usual immune response to exogenous antigens, B cells whose immunoglobulin receptors best fit the immunogen are preferentially selected for growth, a process that involves immunoglobulin gene switching (from IgM to other isotypes) and extensive V gene mutation (Figure 71) (see chapter 1). This mechanism, termed affinity maturation of the antibody response, depends on signals, ie, lymphokines, from T cells (see chapters 5 and 7). The major restraining in-

fluence on the potential of the B-cell compartment to produce pathogenic autoantibodies is, therefore, the T-cell compartment. This principle has been demonstrated in the MRL-lpr/lpr mouse, an animal that develops a rapidly lethal form of systemic lupus erythematosus. Thymectomy carried out early in life, before pathogenic autoantibodies appear, completely prevents the disease. Studies of splenic B cells from normal mice and from lupus-prone mice have shown almost identical proportions of autoantibody-producing cells, but in lupus-prone mice the absolute numbers of such cells are 10- to 20-fold higher. These data suggest that the B-cell population of lupus-prone mice expands in unison by the process of polyclonal B-cell activation (Figure 72). A major, but not exclusive, factor in the proliferation and differentiation of so many B cells is a set of growth and differentiation signals produced by activated T cells. As previously emphasized, the most common autoantibody specificity in the preimmune B-cell repertoire is anti–single-stranded DNA, so it is now apparent why precisely that specificity occurs in highest abundance in the serum of lupus-prone mice: it represents the dominant binding specificity of the preimmune autoantibody repertoire.

Recent structural studies have shown that anti-DNA antibodies from MRL-lpr/lpr mice contain mutations of the type found during affinity maturation of the immune response. Within a single animal, the mutated antibodies could be traced to a single B-cell clone. These results strongly imply that the same mechanisms of antigen selection and V gene mutation that occur during the normal

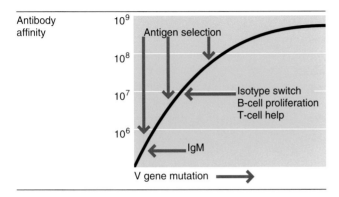

Figure 71
Maturation of the immune response

Antibody affinity

10^9

Antigen selection

10^8

10^7 — Isotype switch
B-cell proliferation
T-cell help

10^6

IgM

V gene mutation →

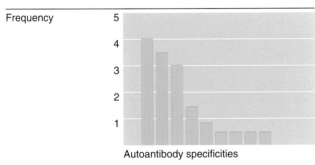

Figure 72
Frequency of autoantibody specificities before and after activation of polyclonal B-cell activation

Normal preimmune repertoire

Frequency

5

4

3

2

1

Autoantibody specificities

Polyclonal B-cell activation

Frequency

50

40

30

20

10

Autoantibody specificities

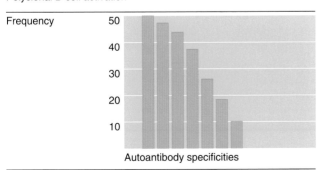

immune response are also important in autoimmunization. The process of autoimmunization in MRL-lpr/lpr mice may begin with polyclonal B-cell activation but, ultimately, clonal selection dominates the disorder.

Thus, for one important autoimmune disease, SLE, the driving force by which B cells produce pathogenic autoantibodies consists of T cells. Even more interesting is that in all examined strains of lupus-prone mice, an unusual population of T cells that lacks conventional T-cell surface markers appears concordantly with the production of cationic anti-DNA antibodies. These are exactly the kind of anti-DNA antibodies that are thought to constitute the main set of autoantibodies that cause nephritis (nephritogenic autoantibodies). Thus, T cells have at least three roles in the pathogenesis of certain autoimmune diseases (Figure 73):

- They trigger polyclonal B-cell activation.
- They convert low-affinity IgM autoantibodies to high-affinity IgG autoantibodies.
- They shift subpopulations of those IgG autoantibodies into a set with physical properties that enable the induction of particular kinds of tissue lesions.

One of the major challenges in autoimmunity research is to discover the genetic mechanisms for these remarkable events and to define their causes at the molecular level. Even if the concepts just reviewed are not generally applicable, it is still important to understand how autoantibodies of particular specificities come to dominate events in individual patients. Of two patients with systemic lupus erythematosus, why does nephritis develop in one and immune thrombocytopenia in the other if polyclonal B-cell activation is the thematic disturbance in both cases? Why does patient A develop SLE and patient B rheumatoid

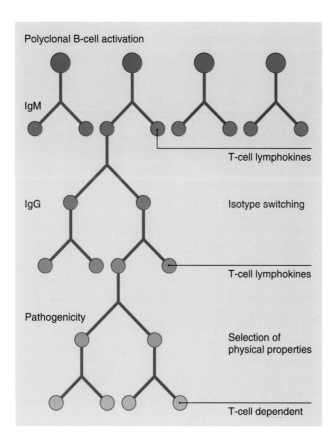

Polyclonal B-cell activation

IgM

T-cell lymphokines

IgG

Isotype switching

T-cell lymphokines

Pathogenicity

Selection of
physical properties

T-cell dependent

arthritis? For that matter, why does the NZB mouse develop autoimmune hemolytic anemia, whereas the (NZBxNZW)F₁ hybrid dies of lupus nephritis?

Autoantigens

Up to now, the major emphasis in this chapter has been on endogenous factors that may initiate the production of autoantibodies. The germline origin of autoantibodies, the process of polyclonal B-cell activation, and the influence of T cells on the development of pathogenic autoantibodies are important considerations, but they say nothing about the role, if any, of immunogenic stimuli in autoimmunization. The reason for this silence is ignorance. Double-stranded DNA, for instance, is not immunogenic, even in lupus-prone mice with a genetic program to spontaneously produce antibodies against double-stranded DNA.

Autoantibodies have an unusual feature: their immunochemical specificities for autoantigens almost always entail conserved regions which are structural features (eg, peptide sequences or antigenic surfaces) of a molecule that recur in many species. The anti-DNA autoantibodies of SLE and rheumatoid arthritis are an example. Human autoantibodies to thyroglobulin bind to human, bovine, and horse thyroglobulin; amazingly, human anti–acetylcholine receptor antibodies also bind to receptors of the electric eel. An illuminating comparison is the difference between transfusion-induced erythrocyte isoantibodies and anti–red cell autoantibodies: the former are strictly specific for erythrocyte alloantigens (eg, antigenic variants of the Rh blood group system), whereas the latter almost always bind to an unidentified antigen present on all normal human red cells.

It appears, therefore, that if we are irreversibly tolerant of self-antigens, then the tolerogenic determinants must be self-specific. How the immune system discriminates between self-specific and conserved regions of a molecule is mysterious but, by whatever mechanism, it *does* make the distinction, and the immune system allows for the possibility of autoimmunization by retaining the capacity to respond to conserved structures. This brings us back to Witebsky and Rose who induced autoimmune thyroiditis by immunizing rabbits with bovine thyroglobulin. In their model, the resulting autoantibodies also reacted with rabbit thyroglobulin, and the bovine thyroglobulin initiated the development of autoimmune thyroiditis in the rabbit. This principle applies to all examples of organ-specific autoimmune diseases, whether experimentally induced in animals or spontaneously occurring in humans. It is the reason why serologic assays for autoantibodies in all human autoimmune diseases successfully employ animal or even bacterial antigens. Now the connection is clear between the immune lesions of rheumatic carditis and infection by group A hemolytic streptococci. The bacteria elaborate an antigen (streptococcal M protein) that cross-reacts with the myosin in fibrils of the human heart. The go-between, therefore, is a conserved sequence present both in the bacterial organism and the cardiac cell.

Major Histocompatibility Complex (MHC) Antigens and Autoimmunization

Progress in elucidating the mechanism of MHC-restricted antigen recognition has been substantial (see chapters 2 and 6). It is now clear that T cells recognize only a fragment of the native immunogenic protein. Such a peptide, produced by limited proteolytic digestion within antigen-presenting cells, forms a trimolecular complex with an MHC class II molecule and the receptor on a helper T cell. The peptide fragments bind directly to the class II molecules, which present them to the antigen receptors of T cells. Moreover, the same

region of the class II molecule can bind to different immunogenic peptides. These findings support the concept that immunogenic proteins contain two functional components: the *aggretope*, which binds to the MHC molecule, and the *epitope*, amino acid residues that interact with the T-cell receptor. Aggretopes of peptides that interact with the same class II molecule may share amino acid patterns.

If the immunogenicity of a protein depends on particular features of the antigenic surface formed by the class II peptide complex derived from the protein, then either self-specific peptides lack aggretopes that can bind to self class II molecules (unlikely as a generality) or, more likely, the immune system purges or suppresses T cells that can recognize self-peptide class II epitopes. Conserved peptides, by contrast, should bind to class II molecules because they are immunogenic. Indeed, to eliminate recognition of conserved sequences would not be a sound evolutionary strategy for the immune system. In that event, its repertoire would contain an intolerable number of blanks or holes. Even so, the extensive polymorphism of MHC class II glycoproteins implies that the capacity to respond to conserved peptides varies within a population. Having the "right" MHC phenotype can be good luck when it confers protective immune responses, but that same phenotype portends bad luck when it permits immune responses against conserved peptides that cross-react with self structures. This is the theoretical basis of the association between MHC phenotypes and autoimmunization.

However, the actual situation is vastly more complicated than the theory implies. The main problem is that, in most cases of autoimmunization, the source of the antigen recognized by the sanctioning MHC structure is unknown. For example, an inbred mouse that uniformly develops autoimmune type I diabetes (the nonobese diabetic mouse) has a particular structural variation in its class II molecule. This mutant molecule must be a key element in the development of diabetes in the animal, because when the corresponding variant gene is inserted into the germline of mice of a normal strain, these animals also develop autoimmune diabetes (Figure 74). How that unique structural alteration allows the T cells of the animal to destroy its own pancreatic islet cells is not understood. Nor do we understand how a particular variant of HLA-DR3 permits the development of insulin-dependent diabetes mellitus in humans (see chapter 2). The best current guess is that inflammation or infection initiates the process by inadvertently exposing an intracellular protein to the immune system. In this model, the inflammation also induces expression of class II molecules on the target organ, thereby allowing T cells to recognize the released antigen.

There is another layer of complexity. Imagine a bacterial infection in which the "right" MHC complex permits a vigorous immune response, with immunoglobulin V gene mutations that lead to the usual process of affinity maturation of antibodies. In principle, one of these mutations could change the specificity of an antibacterial antibody, converting it to an autoantibody. Exactly that kind of mutation has been documented with a monoclonal mouse antibody against the bacterial antigen phosphocholine. This particular monoclonal antibody, S107, protects mice against lethal streptococcal infection. A point mutation caused the replacement of a single amino acid in the heavy chain of the antibody, changing its specificity from antiphosphocholine to anti-DNA. In this example, a random process (mutation) nullified the beneficial effects of the "right" MHC by converting a protective antibody into an autoantibody.

Figure 74
Development of autoimmune diabetes in normal mice following insertion of a variant MHC gene

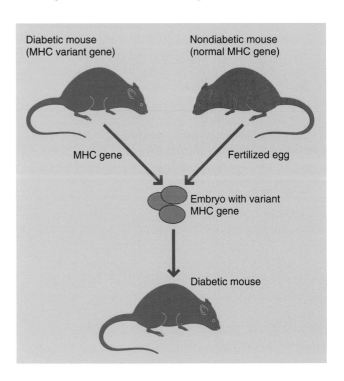

Conclusion

Research in autoimmunity started at the beginning of the 20th century with Ehrlich's goats, but soon thereafter it lapsed into a state of dormancy because of rigid adherence to dogma. Today it thrives, fed by remarkable advances in immunology, but research also draws strength from other disciplines, molecular biology in particular. It seems highly likely that many of the fundamental problems in this field will be solved before the end of the 20th century. What remains? We need to know much more about:

- The organization and control of expression of human immunoglobulin V genes, particularly those that seem to be recurrently involved in specifying the structures of autoantibodies.
- How the MHC confers susceptibility to autoimmunization and how T-cell receptors collaborate in that permissiveness.
- Which T-cell lymphokines are relevant to polyclonal B-cell activation and affinity maturation of autoantibodies.
- Whether immunogens are really involved in "spontaneous" autoimmunization (the type seen clinically) and, if so, which are the relevant ones.
- What role, if any, idiotypic networks have in originating or controlling autoantibody production: are they merely entertaining chess games or do they have pathogenic relevance?

These five fundamental issues are at the core of autoimmunity. Their solutions will prove not only intellectually satisfying, but will surely lead to improved clinical management and prevention of an extraordinary variety of human diseases.

Selected Readings

Burnet FM, Fenner F. **The Production of Antibodies**. Melbourne, Australia: MacMillan & Co; 1949.

Rose NR, Herskowitz A, Neumann DA, Neu N. Autoimmune myocarditis: a paradigm of post-infection autoimmune disease. **Immunol Today**. 1988;9:117-120.

Rossini AA, Mordes JP, Like AA. Immunology of insulin-dependent diabetes mellitus. **Annu Rev Immunol**. 1985;3:289-320.

Schwartz RS. Autoantibodies and normal antibodies: two sides of the same coin. **The Harvey Lect**. 1987;81:53-66.

Schwartz RS, Datta SK. Autoimmunity and autoimmune diseases. In: Paul WE, ed. **Fundamental Immunology**. 2nd ed. New York, NY: Raven Press; 1989:819.

Strominger JL. Biology of the human histocompatibility leukocyte antigen (HLA) system and a hypothesis regarding the generation of autoimmune diseases. **J Clin Invest**. 1986;77:1411-1415.

Introduction

The immunodeficiency diseases are a diverse group of disorders that are characterized by increased susceptibility to recurrent or chronic bacterial, fungal, and viral infections. Primary immunodeficiency diseases are usually caused by genetic or developmental defects that result in the absence or dysfunction of one or more components of the immune system. Secondary immunodeficiency diseases can result from immune system impairment caused by malnutrition, malignant neoplasm, infectious agents, cytotoxic drugs, or metabolic disease. The clinical manifestations of primary and secondary immunodeficiency diseases are similar, but secondary immunodeficiency diseases occur more commonly than do primary immunodeficiency diseases.

This chapter will discuss only a selection of the primary immunodeficiency diseases. More than 50 well-characterized immunodeficiency disorders are known and they can be subdivided into five major groups:

- Antibody deficiency diseases
- Combined immunodeficiency diseases, in which there is a paucity or dysfunction of both antibody and T cells
- Immunodeficiency associated with other major defects
- Complement deficiencies
- Phagocytic cell defects.

Development of the Lymphoid Immune System

Most immunodeficiency diseases result from the absence or malfunction of B lymphocytes or T lymphocytes, or both. Our knowledge of the development of the lymphoid immune system provides some understanding of those diseases. Conversely, careful study of patients with primary immuno-

deficiency diseases has contributed to a better understanding of the function and significance of components of the immune system.

Both T and B cells arise from pluripotent stem cells of mesenchymal origin. B-cell differentiation begins in the human fetal liver at 8 to 9 weeks of gestation (see chapter 5). In later fetal life and after birth, B-cell maturation and hematopoiesis occur in the bone marrow. Pre-B cells, the first identifiable cells of B-cell lineage, can be identified by their cytoplasmic μ chains (Figure 75). At that stage of differentiation, rearrangement of variable (V), diversity (D), and joining (J) region genes with μ constant (C) region genes on chromosome 14 generates clonal diversity. Successful heavy chain rearrangement is followed by similar rearrangement of κ light chain genes on chromosome 2 or of λ light chain genes on chromosome 22 (see chapter 1). Functional gene rearrangement results in the progression of the pre-B cell to the immature B-cell stage in which monomeric IgM is expressed on the cell membrane. Shortly thereafter, membrane-bound IgD is expressed; most mature B cells express both surface IgM and IgD. Subsequently, some daughter cells of each B-cell clone undergo isotype switching, in which the variable region that was originally associated with the μ and δ constant region genes is translocated next to another heavy chain gene with the deletion of intervening sequences.

The generation of antibody isotype diversity was thought to be entirely independent of T cells; however, a class of "switch T cells" is now known to at least facilitate the process. Antigen-specific B-cell activation and terminal differentiation into antibody-secreting plasma cells requires interaction of B cells with both antigen and T cells that recognize the major histocompatibility complex (MHC) class II molecule–antigen complex on the B-cell surface. In the conversion of B cells to plasma cells, surface-bound immunoglobulins are lost, and the plasma cell synthesizes and secretes thousands of Ig molecules per second. Normally, plasma cells do not divide; they die after a few days. When exposed to antigen, only a fraction of

Figure 75
B-lymphocyte differentiation in humans

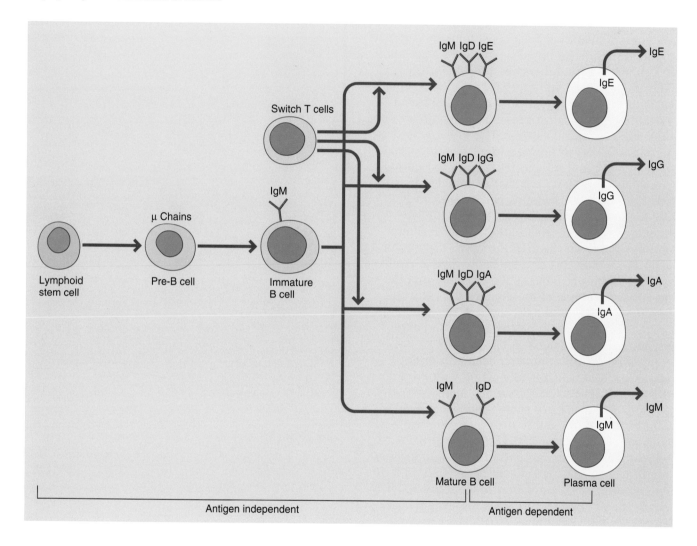

the cells produced by a given B-cell terminally differentiate to the plasma cell stage; the remaining cells become memory cells that will terminally differentiate after subsequent exposure to
antigen. Circulating B cells constitute 5% to 15% of
the total peripheral blood lymphocyte population.

T cells arise from the same pluripotent stem
cells as do B cells and other hematopoietic cells.
Cells destined to become T cells (ie, prothymocytes) begin to localize in the fetal thymus during
the eighth week of gestation. The thymus itself is
an epithelial organ derived from the endodermal
elements of the third and fourth pharyngeal
pouches adjacent to cells that eventually develop
into the parathyroid glands and the calcitonin-
producing cells of the thyroid. The epithelial
thymus descends caudad into the mediastinum
and enlarges as a result of the influx of lymphoid
cells. Prothymocytes first enter the thymic cortex
and proliferate rapidly. As they migrate into the
medullary portions of the thymus, the cells differentiate into functionally distinct T-cell subpopulations. Differentiation occurs only in the intrathymic microenvironment.

Intrathymic differentiation occurs in three
stages, each of which is associated with the expression of characteristic surface membrane glycoproteins (Figure 76). In stage I, early thymocytes
constitute approximately 10% of thymic lymphoid
cells and express the CD2 (T11) glycoprotein,
which has the unusual property of binding sheep
erythrocytes. The CD2 glycoprotein is a structure
essential for T-cell activation. Stage II thymocytes
constitute 50% of intrathymic cells, express CD2
as well as the glycoprotein CD1 (T6), and simultaneously display the CD4 (T4) and CD8 (T8)
glycoproteins. In stage III, the final stage of intrathymic differentiation, CD1 is lost and the T-cell
receptor for antigen (the TcR-CD3 complex)
is expressed. TcR-CD3, which permits antigen-
specific activation of the T cell, consists of a

Figure 76
**Differentiation of thymocytes and T lymphocytes in the human
thymus**

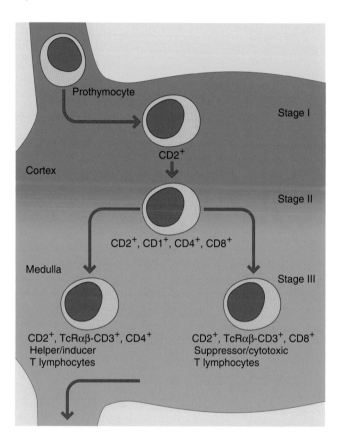

heterodimer, TcR αβ or TcR γδ, and five CD3 molecules (see chapters 3 and 4). The TcR αβ and TcR γδ molecules are similar to immunoglobulin molecules because they impart antigen specificity to the complex, being composed of several V, J, and D genes, as well as C region genes that are rearranged in a manner similar to the immunoglobulin genes. The CD3 molecules are invariant but essential for T-cell activation. At stage III, some T cells lose the ability to express either CD4 or CD8, segregating mature thymocytes into two separate T-cell subpopulations: the CD2$^+$, TcR αβ-CD3$^+$, CD4$^+$ cells, designated helper/inducer T cells, and the CD2$^+$, TcR αβ-CD3$^+$, CD8$^+$ cells, called suppressor/cytotoxic T cells. TcR αβ receptors bind to antigen in association with either MHC class I or class II molecules, although with lower avidity than when they bind to antibody-combining sites. The CD4 glycoprotein binds to MHC class II molecules and stabilizes the binding of T-cell receptors to antigens presented with class II molecules. The CD8 glycoprotein binds to MHC class I molecules and stabilizes the binding of T-cell receptors to antigen presented with class I molecules. Although the expression of CD4 by different populations of T cells has been associated with helper/inducer functions and the expression of CD8 has been associated with suppressor/cytotoxic functions, exceptions exist. The true function of CD4 and CD8 appears to be in MHC recognition and antigen presentation.

Intrathymic differentiation is an inefficient process with a substantial number of cell deaths. The surviving mature T cells are immunologically competent and move from the medulla of the thymus to the thymus-dependent peripheral lymphoid tissue in lymph nodes, spleen, and the gastrointestinal and respiratory tracts. Because T cells recirculate through the blood and lymphatic channels to a much greater extent than B cells, T cells are relatively easily depleted by intentional or accidental thoracic duct drainage (eg, chylothorax). T cells constitute 60% to 80% of the peripheral blood lymphocyte population.

Antibody Deficiency Diseases

X-Linked Agammaglobulinemia

The largest group of immunodeficient patients is made up of those whose synthesis of antibodies is defective. X-linked agammaglobulinemia (XLA) is the prototype of the antibody deficiency diseases. Patients with XLA characteristically suffer recurrent infections with encapsulated gram-positive bacteria (eg, *Streptococcus pneumoniae, Staphylococcus aureus*) and some gram-negative bacteria (eg, *Haemophilus influenzae, Neisseria meningitidis*) because specific antibody plays a pivotal role in immunity to these organisms. Such infections as pneumonia, meningitis, and septic arthritis appear shortly after the patient's maternal IgG has been depleted, when the child is about 6 to 12 months of age.

Patients with XLA have virtually a complete absence of all serum immunoglobulin isotypes and subclasses, are unable to synthesize specific antibodies, and lack plasma cells in lymph nodes, spleen, bone marrow, and the mucosa of the gastrointestinal and respiratory tracts. No mature or immature B cells are present in the peripheral blood or lymphoid tissues, but pre-B cells are detectable in the bone marrow. In contrast, T-cell counts are normal in the peripheral blood and lymphoid tissues, and delayed hypersensitivity reactions, as well as other T-cell–mediated immunologic functions, are intact.

The primary defect in XLA is in the transition of pre-B cells to immature B cells. The pre-B cells of normal people contain small amounts of cytoplasmic μ chain, but in XLA patients the pre-B cells contain an abnormally short μ chain lacking part of the heavy chain variable region. The μ chain messenger RNA also appears to be truncated.

Additional evidence suggesting that the defect in XLA is intrinsic to cells of the B-lymphocyte lineage comes from studies of X chromosome gene expression in female XLA carriers. Investigators used X-linked polymorphisms and restriction fragment length polymorphisms (RFLP) to demonstrate that immunologically normal female carriers of XLA have mature B cells that each contain an active X chromosome expressing only the genes on the X chromosome that does not bear the XLA gene (Figure 77A). Thus, the pre-B cells that contain an active X chromosome carrying the XLA gene do not contribute to the mature B cells in female carriers. However, the T cells and granulocytes from XLA carriers express genes on both X chromosomes, indicating that the XLA gene defect is selectively lethal to cells of the B-cell lineage.

The differential X chromosome gene expression in B lymphocytes of XLA carriers has been used to identify carriers of the disease. RFLP analysis of X chromosome inactivation is based on the finding that the DNA of the inactivated X chromosome is methylated and is differentially degraded by methylation site-specific endonucleases (Figure 77B). With RFLP analysis, carriers can be detected even when the pedigree is limited. When several males in two or more generations of a pedigree have been affected, RFLP analysis of the X chromosome can identify carriers. Using a series of X chromosome RFLPs for the analysis of several large XLA pedigrees, investigators found the XLA gene in the proximal region of the long arm of the X chromosome. However, the XLA gene itself has not been identified or cloned, and precise prenatal diagnosis is not yet possible.

Immunoglobulin Deficiency With Hyper-IgM

Immunodeficiency with hyperimmunoglobulinemia M (hyper-IgM) is another antibody deficiency disease in which normal B-cell differentiation is perturbed. Hyper-IgM was first detected in young boys and family studies suggested X-linked inheritance. However, the disorder has been reported to occur in young girls; late-onset cases have also occurred. Thus, the disorder may be genetically heterogeneous. Patients synthesize and secrete large amounts of IgM but no IgG or IgA. IgD may be synthesized by the patients' B cells, but it is not secreted. Like patients with XLA, patients with hyper-IgM are antibody-deficient and suffer frequent pyogenic infections. In addition, these patients have a striking predilection for neutropenia and lymphoproliferative diseases.

Immunodeficiency with hyper-IgM is a defect in isotype switching. The B cells of affected patients express surface IgM and IgD, and circulating plasmacytoid cells spontaneously synthesize and secrete IgM. However, the B cells do not bear surface membrane IgG, IgA, or IgE, and synthesis of these immunoglobulins cannot be induced with antigens or polyclonal B-cell stimulators, such as pokeweed mitogen or Epstein-Barr virus. The results of early studies suggested that the primary defect was intrinsic to cells of the B-cell lineage, since coculture of B cells from these patients with normal T cells did not restore the B cells' ability to synthesize IgG and IgA. However, analysis of the DNA from B-cell lines derived from hyper-IgM patients demonstrated no defects in IgG structural genes or in switch regions. Moreover, a T-cell clone derived from a patient with Sézary syndrome, a T-cell leukemia, facilitated isotype switching in the B cells of patients with immunodeficiency with hyper-IgM. That observation strongly suggests that the primary defect in hyper-IgM syndrome is not in the B-cell lineage, but is due to the absence or malfunction of switch T cells. This T-cell subpopulation is apparently rare in the normal peripheral blood lymphocyte pool, a fact that explains the inability of normal peripheral blood T cells to facilitate isotype switching.

Common Variable Immunodeficiency

Common variable immunodeficiency (CVI) is a group of diseases in which antibody deficiency can develop at any age and occurs with equal frequency in both sexes. Familial clustering of CVI has been observed and relatives of CVI patients tend to have other immunoglobulin deficiencies,

Figure 77
Patterns of expression of X-linked genes in the mature B-cell populations of a normal female and a female carrier of X-linked agammaglobulinemia (XLA)

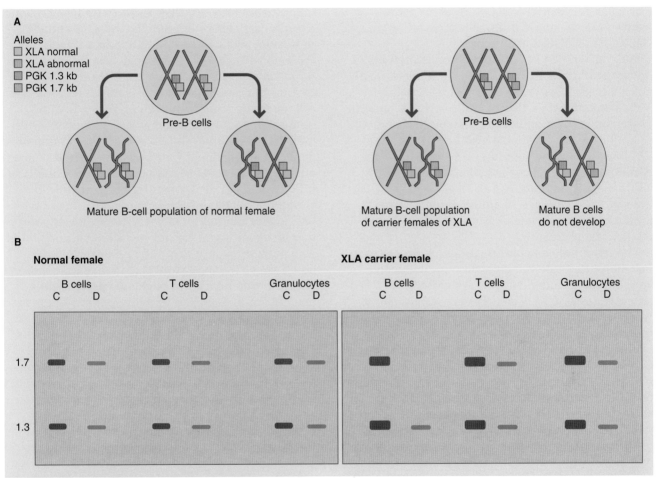

(**A**) In the normal female, the mature B-cell population includes cells with active X chromosomes derived from either X chromosome of the parent cell. In the female carrier of XLA, the mature B cells express the genes on only the X chromosome that does not carry the abnormal XLA gene. Inactivation of the X chromosome is random in somatic cells.

(**B**) The restriction fragment length polymorphism (RFLP) pattern of DNA from B lymphocytes, T lymphocytes, and granulocytes from a normal female and a female carrier of XLA. Both women are heterozygous for an X-linked phosphoglycerate kinase (PGK) polymorphism in which one allele has a 1.3-kb fragment and the other a 1.7-kb fragment. Because the DNA of the inactivated X chromosome is heavily methylated, identi-

fication of alleles on the inactive X chromosome was performed by digestion with an endonuclease specific for methylated DNA. Control (C) and endonuclease digested (D) RFLP patterns from each cell population of the normal female and XLA carrier are shown. Note that the 1.7-kb allele is eliminated in the DNA from the B cells of the XLA carrier. The elimination indicates that the 1.7-kb allele is located primarily on an inactivated X chromosome and that no mature B cells were derived from cells in which the X chromosome remains active. In the other cell populations from the carrier and in all cell populations from the normal female, the PGK genes from both chromosomes are equally expressed.

most commonly IgA deficiency. Patients are particularly susceptible to bacterial infections similar to those seen in patients with XLA, although the onset of infections is less dramatic. Some patients with CVI suffer from chronic sinus and pulmonary infections for many years before immunodeficiency is suspected. Chronic diarrhea, often due to *Giardia lamblia*, is common.

Patients with CVI have serum concentrations of immunoglobulins that are lower than normal, but not necessarily as low as those of XLA patients. Most patients with CVI respond poorly to immunization, but occasionally some make small amounts of antibody. Some patients also have subnormal T-cell counts and impaired T-cell function. Autoimmune diseases occur in up to one third of all CVI patients, particularly those patients with T-cell defects; the incidence of autoimmune disease in their first-degree relatives is greater than that in the general population.

The immunologic characteristics, clinical manifestations, and inheritance pattern of common variable immunodeficiencies are extremely heterogeneous. CVI is clearly not a single entity with a single cause. Patients can be classified into three groups. The largest group comprises patients who have an intrinsic B-cell defect that results in few or no B lymphocytes, B cells incapable of responding to T-cell–derived B-cell differentiation factors, and B cells that synthesize but do not secrete immunoglobulins. In the second group, the predominant defect is in immunoregulatory T-cell function (ie, defective helper/inducer function or excessive suppressor cell activity). Although immunoregulatory T-cell defects are present in many CVI patients, including those with intrinsic B-cell defects, T-cell abnormalities are the cause of immunodeficiency in only a small proportion of patients. In the third group, patients have autoantibodies to T cells and B cells, an abnormality found in only a few patients with CVI.

Other Immunoglobulin and Antibody Deficiencies

More limited immunoglobulin and antibody deficiency diseases include selective IgA deficiency, IgA deficiency associated with deficiency of immunoglobulin subclasses IgG2 and IgG4, selective deficiencies of IgG subclasses, and antibody deficiency without immunoglobulin deficiency. Patients with clinically significant immunoglobulin deficiencies cannot make antibody and usually require immunoglobulin replacement therapy (see following discussion). However, patients with immunoglobulin deficiencies not associated with antibody deficiency should not be given immunoglobulin replacement therapy. An example of such a disorder is transient hypogammaglobulinemia of infancy (THI). THI is a self-limited disorder in which infants have subnormal levels of serum IgG, low or normal levels of IgA, and usually normal levels of IgM. T-helper/inducer cell function is also subnormal, but THI patients have both B cells and T cells and can synthesize and secrete antibodies normally. The hypogammaglobulinemia usually resolves by the time the patient is 2 years of age. While these children have hypogammaglobulinemia, they rarely suffer severe infections, although mild viral upper respiratory tract infections may occur more often than in normal children. Because children with THI produce antibodies, immunoglobulin replacement therapy is not recommended.

Treatment of Antibody Deficiency

Therapy for patients with antibody deficiency consists of passive immunization with antibodies from normal people. Immunoglobulins containing antibodies are injected either intramuscularly or intravenously. The immunoglobulins are prepared from the plasma of more than 2000 normal blood donors after it has been screened for hepatitis viruses and the human immunodeficiency virus (HIV), and the pooled plasma is purified by the Cohn fractionation procedure. Immune serum globulin contains IgG, IgA, and IgM in both monomeric and polymeric (aggregated) forms. The aggregates are removed from immune serum globulin intended for intravenous administration to eliminate the risk of anaphylactic reactions from the activation of complement by aggregated IgG and IgM.

For treatment of antibody deficiency with the intramuscular immunoglobulin preparation, patients usually receive 100 mg/kg every 3 to 4 weeks. Only limited amounts of immunoglobulin can be given intramuscularly because injection of large volumes causes severe pain. In contrast, much more immunoglobulin can be injected intravenously, and patients usually receive 400 mg/kg every 3 to 4 weeks. Therapy with intravenous immunoglobulin is now the treatment of choice for patients with antibody deficiency syndromes.

Combined Immunodeficiency Diseases

The combined immunodeficiency diseases include disorders in which both antibody-mediated immunity and T-cell function are defective. Their causes are diverse and in many instances the primary defect is unknown.

Severe combined immunodeficiency disease (SCID) is a group of disorders, rather than a single entity, and is best defined as any disorder in which antibody-mediated and T-cell–mediated immune responses to specific antigens are severely impaired or absent. Although the causes of these disorders are heterogeneous, their clinical manifestations are very similar. Onset occurs in early infancy because maternal transplacental immunoglobulins cannot compensate for defective T-cell function. Characteristically, infants fail to gain weight or to grow normally. Chronic diarrhea is common, and *Candida* infections involve the skin, the oropharynx, and the gastrointestinal tract. Because T-cell function is defective, opportunistic infections with organisms normally of low pathogenicity are a hallmark of SCID. Interstitial pneumonitis due to *Pneumocystis carinii* is common.

In addition, patients with SCID are exquisitely susceptible to infections with large DNA viruses (including cytomegalovirus, herpes simplex, Epstein-Barr virus, and varicella) that are almost always fatal. Severe, life-threatening disease can result from inoculation with attenuated viruses used for routine immunization. Live oral poliomyelitis vaccine can produce paralytic poliomyelitis. Inoculation with bacille Calmette-Guérin (BCG) or smallpox vaccine invariably causes death from disseminated disease produced by these attenuated organisms. Virtually every microbe is a potential pathogen for children with SCID, few of whom live beyond 2 years of age without specific treatment to correct their immunodeficiency.

Most infants with SCID have substantial deficiencies of lymphocytes in their peripheral blood because of the virtual absence of circulating T cells. Some SCID infants also lack circulating B cells, although a substantial number do have detectable B cells. All organs are profoundly depleted of lymphoid cells. The thymus is considerably reduced in size and consists primarily of epithelial cells; Hassall's corpuscles are also absent (Figure 78). The infants cannot synthesize specific antibodies in response to immunization with any antigen, and cutaneous delayed-type hypersensitivity reactions cannot be elicited. In vitro T-cell responses to both antigens and lectins (eg, phytohemagglutinin and concanavalin A) are absent (see chapter 5). Because the T cells of SCID patients cannot recognize or kill histoincompatible cells, blood transfusions often produce graft-versus-host reactions as a consequence of immunologic attack by the donor lymphoid cells. Similarly, maternal lymphoid cells introduced into the child prenatally or perinatally can also cause a graft-versus-host reaction.

Inheritance of severe combined immunodeficiency disease can be either autosomal recessive or X-linked recessive. The primary pathogenetic defect is known for only a few forms of the disease. In patients who lack both T and B cells,

Figure 78
Thymus tissue

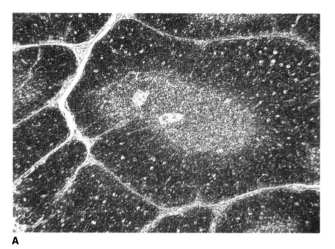

A

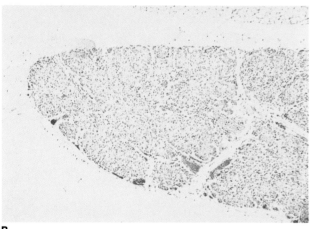

B

(A) Thymus from a normal child (hematoxylin-eosin, magnification × 63).
(B) Thymus from a patient with severe combined immunodeficiency disease (SCID). The intensely blue-staining thymocytes and T lymphocytes which are obvious in A (top) are absent from the thymus of the SCID patient in B (bottom).

development or maturation of lymphoid stem cells appears to be defective. In other patients, SCID results from enzyme deficiencies in which toxic metabolites interfere with normal lymphocyte maturation. Severe combined immunodeficiency can also result from failure of cells to express cell-surface structures critical for antigen-specific immune responses.

Approximately 50% of patients with autosomal recessive SCID have a deficiency of the enzyme adenosine deaminase (ADA). A ubiquitous enzyme in mammalian tissues, ADA facilitates the catabolism of adenosine to inosine and of deoxyadenosine to deoxyinosine (Figure 79). In the absence of ADA, deoxyadenosine accumulates and is converted to deoxyadenosine triphosphate (dATP) in lymphoid cells, which have extremely active kinases. The dATP accumulates in immature T cells because they are relatively deficient in nucleotidases capable of destroying dATP. Accumulated concentrations of dATP in lymphocytes can be 1000-fold the normal concentrations. dATP is a potent inhibitor of ribonucleotide diphosphate reductase, the enzyme responsible for the conversion of ribonucleotides to deoxyribonucleotides, which are essential precursors for DNA synthesis. Thus, ADA deficiency ultimately inhibits DNA synthesis in immature T cells, resulting in their failure to proliferate and differentiate. The selectivity of ADA deficiency for cells of the lymphoid system and the exquisite sensitivity of developing T cells appear to be related to the differential distribution of enzymes that metabolize purines. Other possible metabolic consequences of ADA deficiency include the inhibition of methylation of DNA due to accumulation of S-adenosylhomocysteine. This compound inhibits donation of methyl groups and ultimately lymphocyte proliferation.

Purine nucleoside phosphorylase (PNP) deficiency is another cause of SCID. The PNP enzyme is required for the catabolism of inosine, deoxyinosine, guanosine, and deoxyguanosine. Accumulated deoxyguanosine triphosphate is particularly toxic to dividing T lymphocytes, and suppressor T cells are unusually sensitive. B cells and serum immunoglobulin concentrations are normal until late stages of the disease.

Figure 79
Purine metabolism

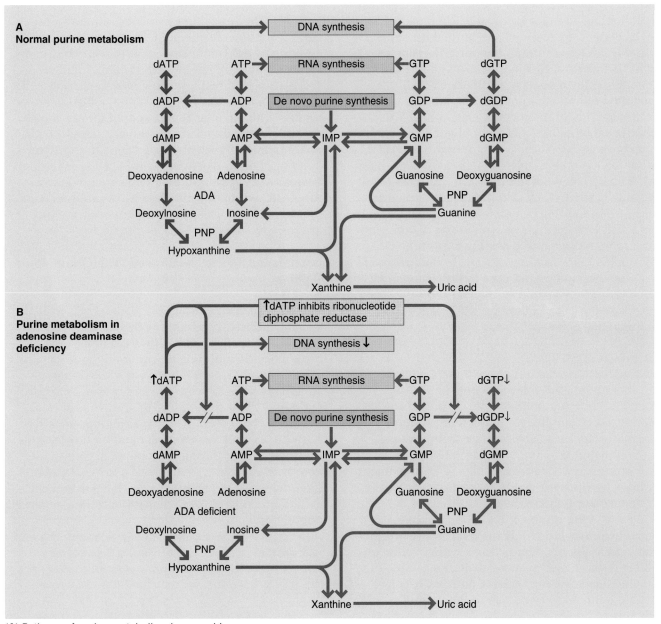

A Normal purine metabolism

B Purine metabolism in adenosine deaminase deficiency

(**A**) Pathway of purine metabolism in normal humans.
(**B**) Purine metabolism in patients with adenosine deaminase
(ADA) deficiency associated with severe combined immuno-
deficiency disease. PNP is purine nucleoside phosphorylase.

Failure to express the products of MHC class II molecules (HLA-DR, DP, and DQ) on the surfaces of lymphocytes and monocytes is a form of SCID that is *termed* MHC class II deficiency. In contrast to patients with other types of SCID, those with MHC class II deficiency have normal numbers of T and B cells and normal lymphocyte responses to lectins in vitro. However, these patients cannot generate antigen-specific antibody or T-cell–mediated immune responses. The failures are due to the inability of monocytes, macrophages, B cells, or other cells to present antigens to CD4+ T cells because MHC class II expression is absent. In the patients' cells, mRNA is not synthesized for the α and β chains of the HLA-DR, DP, or DQ loci. Patients with MHC class II deficiency appear to lack a DNA-binding protein called regulatory factor-X (RF-X) that binds to a promoter region common to both the α and β chain genes of the DR, DP, and DQ loci. Binding of RF-X to the promoter regions is necessary for gene transcription. MHC class II deficiency is an autosomal recessive disease, and the gene coding for RF-X is not linked to the MHC.

Treatment of SCID

Histocompatible bone marrow transplantation is the therapy of choice for all forms of severe combined immunodeficiency disease. In patients with SCID, a lymphocyte population is either absent or has an intrinsic defect that prevents normal maturation and/or differentiation. Thus, engrafting normal stem cells should correct the defects, because normal bone marrow contains the necessary lymphoid stem cells.

However, the principal limitation in bone marrow transplantation is the availability of histocompatible donors. The extreme genetic polymorphism of the major histocompatibility complex in humans (see chapter 2) limits potentially compatible bone marrow donors to the patient's immediate family and specifically to the patient's siblings. Transplantation with nonidentical bone marrow would cause a potentially fatal graft-versus-host reaction. On the average, only one in four siblings would be expected to be MHC-identical with the patient. Consequently, a signifi-

cant number of patients have no MHC compatible donors. However, methods that deplete bone marrow of mature T cells permit transplantation of haploidentical parental bone marrow to SCID patients. The procedure has been generally successful for most forms of SCID, although reconstitution of ADA-deficient SCID patients has met with only limited success when haploidentical T-cell–depleted bone marrow has been used.

Some ADA-deficient patients have also been treated with enzyme replacement therapy, most recently with adenosine deaminase treated with polyethylene glycol. Recently, "gene therapy" has been applied to ADA-deficient SCID by inserting a normal ADA gene into a patient's own bone marrow cells and then reinfusing the treated marrow into the patient. The results of this new therapy are not yet known.

Immunodeficiencies Associated With Other Major Defects

Wiskott-Aldrich Syndrome

Wiskott-Aldrich syndrome (WAS) is an X-linked disorder characterized by the triad of eczema, thrombocytopenia, and susceptibility to infections (Figure 80). During the first year of life, patients usually become ill with severe eczema, diarrhea, and otitis. They suffer a broad spectrum of infections with both gram-positive and gram-negative bacteria, as well as with yeast and viral infections. Bleeding due to thrombocytopenia accounts for approximately 30% of the deaths in WAS patients. The incidence of leukemia and Hodgkin's disease is higher among WAS patients than in the general population.

Patients with WAS have elevated serum IgA and IgE, normal IgG, and decreased IgM concentrations. Catabolism of all immunoglobulin classes is

Figure 80
Patient with the Wiskott-Aldrich syndrome

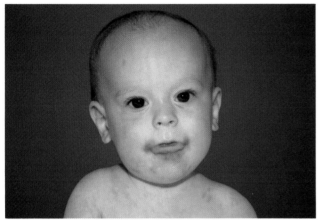

This child has characteristic severe eczema and petechiae due to thrombocytopenia.

Figure 81
Ocular telangiectasias on the bulbar conjunctivae of a patient with ataxia-telangiectasia

Photograph courtesy of Immunology Branch, National Cancer Institute.

greater than normal. Patients with WAS are unable to make antibodies to polysaccharides and thus lack antibodies to blood group antigens, as well as to the capsular polysaccharides of bacteria. That inability may partially account for the patients' increased susceptibility to infection. T-cell deficiency increases with age.

The basis for the numerous clinical and immunologic manifestations of WAS is unclear; however, sialophorin (a 115 000-kd membrane glycoprotein) is deficient in T cells, and glycoprotein Ib is deficient in platelets. Deficiencies of these glycoproteins might be responsible for the rapid clearance of platelets and T cells by the spleen, ultimately resulting in both thrombocytopenia and T-cell depletion. Neither the defects in polysaccharide antibody synthesis and hypercatabolism of immunoglobulins nor the clinical manifestation of eczema have been explained. Successful immunologic reconstitution has been achieved with bone marrow transplants.

Ataxia-Telangiectasia
Ataxia-telangiectasia (AT) is an autosomal recessive syndrome with prominent neurologic, dermatologic, and immunologic manifestations.

Progressive cerebellar ataxia is usually apparent when the child begins to walk. By the time the child is 4 to 8 years old, multiple collections of tortuous, small blood vessels (telangiectasias) appear on the bulbar conjunctivae (Figure 81) and on the skin. The frequency of sinus and pulmonary infections among AT patients is greater than among the general population and, ultimately, chronic lung disease and bronchiectasis develop. The infections result directly from antibody-mediated and cell-mediated immunodeficiency.

The incidence of neoplastic diseases among white AT patients is 60-fold greater than among age-matched controls. The incidence of lymphomas among whites with AT is 250-fold greater, and the incidence of leukemia is 70-fold greater. The incidence of lymphoreticular malignancies among black AT patients may be even higher. The median age of death is 17 years; cancer is the leading cause of death and pulmonary disease is the second most common cause. Patients with AT have a higher prevalence of chromosomal breakage with translocations and are abnormally sensitive to damage by X-irradiation (but not to damage by ultraviolet light). Serum concentrations of α-fetoprotein, a so-called oncofetal antigen, are elevated in 97% of AT patients, and its measurement is the single best laboratory test for the diagnosis of the disease.

The immunologic abnormalities in patients with AT involve both B lymphocytes and T lymphocytes. IgA and IgE deficiency, as well as substantially decreased concentrations of the IgG2 and IgG4 subclasses, occur in most patients. Specific antibody synthesis is poor, and hypogammaglobulinemia occurs in about half of the patients. Patients commonly produce autoantibodies, particularly anti-IgA antibodies. In patients with AT, the thymus is hypoplastic, and T-cell deficiency and dysfunction cause decreased cutaneous delayed hypersensitivity reactions and impaired responses in vitro to specific antigens and lectins. The immunologic and neurologic defects worsen with age.

Defects in repair of damaged DNA and the regulation of DNA synthesis may be central to the pathogenesis of ataxia-telangiectasia. After X-irradiation or exposure to a radiomimetic drug, normal cells significantly decrease their rate of DNA synthesis, but cells from patients with AT do not. The defects may impair the normal gene rearrangement required for assembly of functional immunoglobulin and T-cell receptor genes, as well as for isotype switching. Interestingly, AT patients have deficiencies of those immunoglobulins (IgA, IgE, IgG2, and IgG4) in which heavy chain genes

are farthest from the V region genes. In the lymphocytes, the loci of the immunoglobulin supergene family are the most common sites at which translocations occur. The most frequent site for translocation is at chromosome position 14q12, which is the location of the T-cell receptor α chain gene. Translocation of that gene and its associated enhancer regions close to oncogenes such as c-myc can result in reactivation of the oncogene and may be related to the unusually high incidence of cancer in patients with AT. A similar mechanism of gene dysregulation is thought to cause serum levels of α-fetoprotein to remain elevated in patients with AT. (Normally the α-fetoprotein gene is expressed only during fetal life and disappears within the first year of birth.) The incidence of cancer, particularly breast cancer, is greater among relatives of AT patients than among the general population, and heterozygous carriers of the defect are more sensitive to X-irradiation. At least five genes may cause AT. Three of the AT genes have been mapped to chromosome position 11q22-23.

No satisfactory treatment for ataxia-telangiectasia is currently available. Immunoglobulin replacement therapy appears to help to decrease the frequency and severity of sinopulmonary infections. Aggressive measures directed toward immunologic reconstitution (eg, bone marrow transplantation) are inappropriate in light of our inability to modify the patients' inexorable neurologic deterioration.

DiGeorge Syndrome

Congenital thymic hypoplasia occurs as part of the DiGeorge syndrome, which consists of hypocalcemic tetany, congenital heart disease, unusual facial features, and increased susceptibility to infections. Hypocalcemia results from congenital hypoparathyroidism. Abnormalities in the aortic arch (truncus arteriosus, interrupted aortic arch, and tetralogy of Fallot) are the forms of congenital heart disease most commonly associated with the syndrome. Underdevelopment of the mandible, resulting in a fish-shaped mouth, low-set ears, and ocular hypertelorism, are characteristic facial features.

The severity of the immunologic effects associated with the DiGeorge syndrome varies, depending upon whether the syndrome is partial or complete. In the complete syndrome, the thymus is totally absent and there is a profound paucity of circulating T cells. Patients do not have cutaneous delayed hypersensitivity reactions, and they do not have in vivo or in vitro T-cell–dependent immune functions, such as lymphocyte proliferative responses to antigens. Circulating lymphocytes bear only determinants characteristic of prothymocytes (ie, CD10); the determinants characteristic of mature T cells (eg, CD3, CD4, and CD8) are lacking. Although the patients have B cells, immunoglobulin levels can be low and antibody synthesis defective.

In the partial form of DiGeorge syndrome, there is a small remnant of thymus that is structurally and functionally normal. T-cell deficiency is not as severe as it is in the complete DiGeorge syndrome, and with time immunodeficiency becomes less severe as the thymic remnant releases more mature T cells. The patients have immunoglobulins and antibodies. Approximately 70% of patients with DiGeorge syndrome have the partial form of the disease.

DiGeorge syndrome results from abnormal embryonic development of the tissues derived from the third and fourth pharyngeal pouches, which include the parathyroid glands and the thymus. The aortic arch develops from the fourth branchial arch adjacent to the pharyngeal pouch; the cartilage from which the mandible is derived ultimately arises from tissues immediately cephalad to this area. The primary defect in DiGeorge syndrome is thought to be the failure of neural crest mesenchyme to migrate normally into the pharyngeal pouch area and the consequent absence of the inductive interactions required for the development of the epithelial components of the thymus and parathyroids. Without the appropriate inductive environment created by thymic hormones and epithelial cell-surface determinants, migration of lymphoid cells into the thymus and subsequent thymocyte and T-cell maturation fail to occur.

Transplantation of fetal thymus glands, implantation of thymus in a micropore chamber, or injection of thymic hormones have been reported to correct the immunologic defects in patients with DiGeorge syndrome. Whether these procedures reconstitute immune function is difficult to determine, because most patients have the partial form of disease in which immunologic function spontaneously improves with time. The treatment methods have generally not been successful in patients with the more severe complete form of the disease. Recently, a patient with severe DiGeorge syndrome was successfully treated with a histocompatible bone marrow transplant. Mature postthymic T cells in the donor bone marrow probably restored immune function.

Complement Deficiencies

The complement system is a key element in host defenses against infection. Proteins of the complement system lyse bacteria directly, amplify the inflammatory response, recruit phagocytic cells, and facilitate phagocytosis and killing of microorganisms through opsonization. The complement system, including the classical and alternative pathways, regulatory proteins, and complement receptors, are reviewed in detail in chapter 9. Here we shall discuss only those defects that increase susceptibility to infection and thus should be considered immunodeficiency diseases.

Complement defects that increase susceptibility to infection are rare and constitute only 2% of all primary immunodeficiency diseases. Terminal complement component deficiency produces a clinical syndrome characterized by recurrent disseminated neisserial infections, such as meningococcemia, meningococcal meningitis, or disseminated gonococcal infections. Patients with the deficiency also have a high rate (6.3%) of relapse of the infections and a high recurrence rate (45%). Consequently, terminal complement component deficiency must be considered a diagnostic possibility in any patient with relapsing or recurrent neisserial infections. Deficiencies of the terminal complement components C5, C6, C7, and C8 are clinically significant; C9 deficiency is not associated with susceptibility to infection. All the terminal complement component deficiencies have an autosomal recessive pattern of inheritance. *Neisseria* are usually lysed and killed by the assembly on the bacterial cell wall of membrane attack complexes by the sequential addition of C5b, C6, C7, C8, and C9. The membrane attack complexes form transmembrane lesions in the bacterial cell membrane. The C5b-C8 complex alone can lyse the bacterium. Because C9 is not absolutely necessary, patients with C9 deficiency are asymptomatic.

However, gram-positive bacteria cannot be readily lysed by the terminal complement components and must be destroyed by phagocytosis and intracellular killing. C3 and its cleavage products, C3b and C3bi, play important roles in opsonization since phagocytic cells have complement receptors (CR) for C3b (CR1) and C3bi (CR3). Any condition that results in C3 deficiency or inappropriate C3 activation can significantly impair host defenses. Patients with C3 deficiency suffer recurrent infections, such as meningitis, bacteremia, pneumonia, and peritonitis; *Neisseria meningitidis* and *Streptococcus pneumoniae* are common pathogens. Factor I deficiency results in a secondary C3 deficiency because of inappropriate activation of the alternative pathway. Factor I cleaves C3b to C3bi, thus regulating the concentration of the C3-cleaving enzyme C3bBb. Factor I-deficient patients suffer the same types of infections as do C3-deficient patients.

Children with a deficiency of CR3 on leukocytes suffer severe pyogenic bacterial infections, such as pneumonia, osteomyelitis, gingivitis, and skin infections. These children have persistent leukocytosis and a history of delayed separation of the umbilical cord. In addition to its role in phagocytosis, CR3 is also important in adherence to cell surfaces. In patients with the CR3 deficiency syndrome, neutrophil phagocytosis and adherence are defective, and monocyte and lymphocyte functions related to adherence are abnormal. The syndrome has an autosomal recessive pattern of inheritance. CR3 deficiency is readily diagnosed by the use of specific monoclonal antibodies to demonstrate the absence of CR3 on neutrophils and monocytes.

Deficiencies of the early components (C1, C4, and C2) of the classical pathway are associated with the clinical picture of autoimmune disease, such as systemic lupus erythematosus–like syndromes or glomerulonephritis, and generally are not considered in the differential diagnosis of recurrent infections.

Treatment for the complement deficiency disorders associated with recurrent infection is not satisfactory. Replacement of the missing components is not feasible because of their short half-lives. Immunization with antipneumococcal and antimeningococcal vaccines is helpful, however, and antibiotic prophylaxis may also reduce the frequency of infections.

Phagocytic Cell Defects

Phagocytes function by adhering to the vascular endothelium, migrating through the blood vessel wall, moving toward a chemoattractant, recognizing and ingesting opsonized particles, forming a phagolysosome, and killing the ingested microbe. Defects in one or more of those essential processes can cause phagocyte dysfunction and increase susceptibility to infection.

Chronic Granulomatous Disease

Chronic granulomatous disease (CGD) is the best known and most extensively studied of the 15 or more primary phagocyte dysfunction disorders. Because of a defect in nicotinamide-adenine dinucleotide phosphate (NADPH) oxidase, the phagocytes of patients with CGD lack the respiratory burst that normally accompanies particle ingestion and thus cannot generate the toxic oxygen derivatives, such as the superoxide anion, hydroxyl radical, and hydrogen peroxide, required to kill ingested bacteria. The defect is expressed in both neutrophils and monocytes. Patients are particularly likely to have infections with catalase-positive organisms that can break down the hydrogen peroxide produced by the organism. *Staphylococcus aureus* is the most common cause of infections in patients with CGD, followed by *Aspergillus, Chromobacterium, Pseudomonas,* and *Nocardia.* Abscess formation is a clinical hallmark of the disease; in the absence of neutrophil function, monocytes and macrophages wall off bacteria to form a granuloma. The most common sites of abscesses are the subcutaneous tissues, lymph nodes, liver, bone, and lung. Infections begin during the first year of life, but some patients survive into early adulthood; life expectancy has improved with the aggressive use of antibiotics.

The classic and most common form of CGD is inherited as an X-linked recessive disease, although autosomal recessive and autosomal dominant variants have been reported. Patients with CGD have a defect in the activation of NADPH oxidase. Consequently, superoxide anions, hydroxyl radicals, and hydrogen peroxide are not generated. NADPH oxidase is composed of multiple subunits, including flavoprotein, cytochrome b-245, and quinones. Patients with X-linked CGD lack the cytochrome b-245, but patients with CGD that is not linked to the X chromosome do not. The gene for cytochrome b-245 has recently been cloned. A normal respiratory burst is required to reduce nitroblue tetrazolium (NBT), a dye, and to produce neutrophil chemiluminescence. Tests for the reduction of NBT and for chemiluminescence are used to confirm the diagnosis of CGD. Female carriers of X-linked CGD have half the normal concentrations of NBT dye reduction.

Chédiak-Higashi Syndrome

Chédiak-Higashi syndrome (CHS) is a phagocyte dysfunction characterized by frequent infections, partial oculocutaneous albinism, and the development of a lymphomalike accelerated phase of the disease. CHS is readily diagnosed by the appearance of giant lysosomal granules in neutrophils and in other cells. The primary defect appears to be abnormal microtubule function that decreases chemotaxis and impairs killing of ingested microorganisms because of delayed fusion of the phagosome with the abnormal giant lysosomes.

Neutrophil-Specific Granule Deficiency

Deficiency of neutrophil-specific granules is a rare disorder associated with frequent infections. Neutrophil microbicidal activity and chemotaxis are impaired.

Hyperimmunoglobulinemia E Syndrome

Hyperimmunoglobulinemia E (HIE) syndrome, as its name implies, is characterized by extraordinarily high concentrations of serum IgE (more than 2000 IU/mL), persistent eosinophilia, and frequent skin and sinopulmonary infections. Cold subcutaneous abscesses with minimal inflammatory response that are caused by *S aureus* are common.

A variable chemotactic defect is thought to be caused by inhibition of chemotaxis by histamine. High concentrations of IgE antibody to *S aureus* and *Candida albicans* have been found in patients with HIE syndrome and may contribute to mast cell degranulation and release of histamine, which impair neutrophil chemotaxis.

Treatment of Phagocytic Defects

Aggressive antibiotic therapy is the mainstay of treatment for patients with phagocytic cell defects. Prophylactic antibiotic therapy has effectively reduced the frequency of infections among patients with CGD and HIE syndrome. Recently, interferon gamma injections have been shown to reduce the frequency and severity of infections in CGD patients. Some patients with CGD have received bone marrow transplants, and gene therapy may be possible in the future.

Conclusion

The immunodeficiency diseases continue to challenge investigators to determine their pathophysiology and to develop innovative therapy. The disorders cover a broad spectrum of immunodeficiency, from those that are minor to those that are life-threatening. In some instances, treatment has been successfully accomplished through replacement of abnormal cells with histocompatible normal cells by bone marrow transplantation. The application of molecular biology to these diseases provides new insights into their causes and offers new hope for treatment, including gene therapy.

Selected Readings

Asherson GL, Webster ADB. **Diagnosis and Treatment of Immunodeficiency Diseases**. Oxford, England: Blackwell Scientific Publications; 1980.

Buckley RH. Immunodeficiency diseases. **JAMA**. 1987;258:2841-2850.

Fauci AS, Goldstein RA. Foreword: Symposium – childhood immunodeficiency disorders. **Clin Immunol Immunopathol**. 1986;40:1-2.

Rosen FS, Cooper MD, Wedgwood RJP. The primary immunodeficiencies. **N Engl J Med**. 1984;311:235-242, 300-310.

Savilahti E, Ruuskanen O, eds. Special Issue on Immunodeficiencies. **Ann Clin Res**. 1987;19:219-402.

Scientific Group on Immunodeficiency. Primary immunodeficiency diseases: report of a WHO-sponsored meeting. **Immunodefic Rev**. 1989;1:173-205.

Stiehm ER, ed. **Immunologic Disorders in Infants and Children**. 3rd ed. Philadelphia, Pa: WB Saunders; 1989.

Acquired Immunodeficiency Syndrome (AIDS)

14

Introduction

The acquired immunodeficiency syndrome (AIDS) is an infectious disorder characterized by life-threatening opportunistic infections, malignant neoplasms (in particular, Kaposi's sarcoma [KS] and lymphomas), and disorders of the central nervous system (CNS). In the United States, the disease occurs most commonly in homosexual or bisexual men, persons exposed to contaminated needles or blood products, and their sexual partners. Both AIDS and a spectrum of related syndromes are believed to be caused by the human immunodeficiency virus (HIV), a retrovirus first identified in 1983. From 1981 through 1990, more than 161 000 cases meeting full diagnostic criteria for AIDS were reported in the United States (Figure 82).

The laboratory findings in symptomatic HIV-infected patients reflect a disturbance of the cell-mediated arm of the immune system, as manifested by anergy to recall skin-test antigens and the failure of T lymphocytes to respond normally to a variety of stimuli in vitro. Characteristically, the helper-inducer ($CD4^+$) subset of T cells is depleted and there is a relative increase of suppressor-cytotoxic ($CD8^+$) T cells, particularly early in the course of infection, which reverses the normal ratio of $CD4^+$ to $CD8^+$ T cells. Depletion of $CD4^+$ T cells renders the patient unable to mount an effective immune response and thus appears to be indirectly responsible for many of the clinical manifestations of disease.

Epidemiology and Transmissibility of AIDS

More than half the AIDS patients in this country are homosexual or bisexual men (Figure 83). That proportion has remained relatively constant since the outbreak was first noted in 1981, but it is expected to decline largely because of behavioral changes in this risk group. Another 24% of patients have been IV drug users (ie, persons who injected illicit drugs intravenously) who presumably were exposed to the AIDS virus by contaminated needles. A substantial increase in the number of cases among IV drug users is anticipated. Approximately 3% of AIDS patients contracted the disease through transfusion of blood or blood products contaminated with the AIDS virus. However, the implementation of routine blood bank screening programs in 1985, coupled with better education of prospective donors, has led to self-deferral by people likely to transmit HIV, which has dramatically reduced the risk of recipients contracting AIDS via blood or blood products.

To date, approximately 6% of AIDS patients in the United States appear to have been infected during intimate heterosexual contact. Despite that low percentage, heterosexual intercourse is an unequivocal means of transmitting the virus, as reflected by a major epidemic in Central Africa that has affected an equal number of men and women, primarily through heterosexual contact. The number of affected heterosexuals in the United States will certainly rise with time, but the likely rate and extent of the spread of HIV infection in the heterosexual population is uncertain. A major potential source of HIV spread to heterosexuals is the IV drug-using population. The majority of perinatally infected babies are born to HIV-infected mothers who are IV drug users.

There is no evidence at this time that the AIDS virus can be transmitted through public swimming pools, spas, hot tubs, showers, or toilets used previously by an infected individual, or through casual contact with an AIDS patient or other HIV carrier in such places as a theater, a store, or the workplace. Therefore, it is not surprising that no documented cases of HIV transmission by the aerosol route have been reported. Similarly, there is no evidence that AIDS can be contracted from dishes, food, or personal objects touched by a

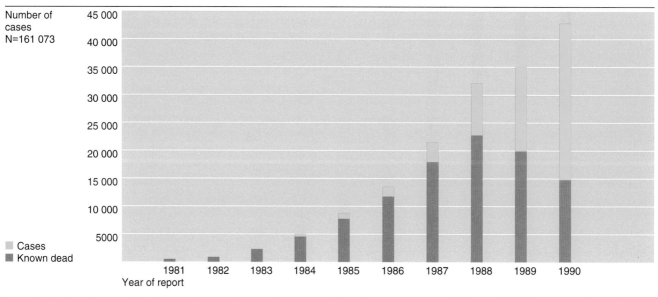

Number of cases
N=161 073

Cases
Known dead

Year of report

patient or carrier. With few exceptions, the available evidence indicates that transfer of semen or blood, either through anal or vaginal intercourse or through parenteral inoculation, is required to transmit the virus. Nonetheless, virtually all body fluids of infected individuals, including saliva and tears, may contain viable virus, albeit in much lower concentrations than in blood or semen. Epidemiologic studies indicate that the transmission of AIDS follows a pattern similar to that of hepatitis B, which is transmitted, for the most part, sexually and parenterally. In rare cases, however, hepatitis B has been transmitted through saliva exposure. Moreover, the mode of transmission in at least 5% of the reported AIDS cases remains unknown.

Despite the overwhelming disease manifestations seen in patients with full-blown AIDS, HIV is not efficiently transferred from one person to another. This inefficiency is reflected in the very few infections that have been definitely linked to occupational exposure among US health-care workers. Occupational exposure refers not only to the direct care of HIV-infected patients and handling their food, blood, bedpans, and so forth, but also to numerous incidents of direct exposure to potentially infected body fluids. For example, more than 2000 instances have been reported in the United States in which health-care workers received penetrating needle-stick–type injuries involving infectious materials. Many of these people have been monitored for several years, but only a handful have been infected with the AIDS virus. The few well-documented cases of HIV infection attributable to occupational exposure in clinical or laboratory settings underscore the importance of strict compliance with recommended procedures for handling potentially infectious

Figure 83
Reported adult and adolescent cases of AIDS by exposure category, United States, 1990

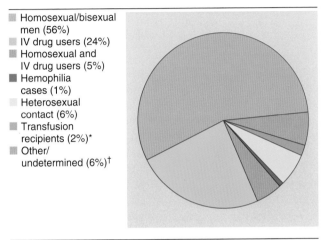

- ▦ Homosexual/bisexual men (56%)
- ▦ IV drug users (24%)
- ▦ Homosexual and IV drug users (5%)
- ▪ Hemophilia cases (1%)
- ▫ Heterosexual contact (6%)
- ▦ Transfusion recipients (2%)*
- ▦ Other/ undetermined (6%)†

*Includes 14 transfusion recipients who received blood screened for HIV antibody, and 1 tissue recipient.
†"Other" refers to 4 persons who developed AIDS after exposure to HIV-infected blood within the health-care setting, as documented by evidence of seroconversion or other laboratory studies. "Undetermined" refers to patients whose mode of exposure to HIV is unknown. This includes patients under investigation; patients who died, were lost to follow-up, or refused interview; and patients whose mode of exposure to HIV remains undetermined after investigation.

Centers for Disease Control. Summary of notifiable diseases, United States 1990. *MMWR.* 1991;39(53):16.

materials. Most of the cases could have been prevented by strict adherence to recommended precautions.

Recently, the issue of possible transmission from infected health-care providers to patients has become extremely controversial. In one case, an infected dentist appears to have transmitted HIV to patients, as judged by comparative analysis of the viruses isolated from the dentist and the patients. However, it has been suggested that the route of transmission involved inadequately sterilized dental instruments, which had been used in dental procedures on both patients and the dentist. It still seems that with stringent adherence to fundamental principles of disinfection, the risks of transmission from an infected health-care worker to patients are negligible, except perhaps in the most invasive of clinical procedures.

There are no documented cases of HIV infection transmitted by mosquito bite, despite the fact that the virus can survive for at least 2 days in mosquitoes. Although not definitive, the absence of documented cases suggests not only that intimate blood or sexual contact is usually required for infection, but also that the concentration of virus to which a subject is exposed is a critical factor. Host factors, such as pre-existing venereal diseases (especially chancroid or genital ulcers), also appear to play a role in susceptibility. In particular, HIV penetrates immunologically activated CD4+ T cells more efficiently than resting T cells, and activated HIV-infected CD4+ T cells produce large amounts of virus whereas resting T cells do not. Consequently, persons who are frequently exposed to other infectious agents may be more likely to have an aggressive clinical course. Finally, the results of recent studies suggest that HIV undergoes mutation and/or selection in infected hosts, becoming more biologically aggressive over time. This finding may explain why patients in advanced clinical stages of HIV infection appear more efficient at transmitting the virus than are patients in earlier, asymptomatic stages.

Clinical Manifestations

Within days to weeks after infection with HIV, patients may develop an acute mononucleosislike or flulike syndrome characterized by fever, malaise, and pharyngitis. This syndrome most often resolves spontaneously after days or weeks, but it can evolve into a persistent generalized lymphadenopathy or develop into full-blown AIDS in a matter of months. Some patients infected with HIV experience no symptoms whatsoever for several years. The vast majority exhibit either this latter pattern or rapidly recover from their acute flulike symptoms and enter a prolonged asymptomatic phase.

After varying periods of latency, however, the symptoms and signs of AIDS or HIV infection develop, including fever, weight loss, diarrhea, neurologic disorders, secondary infectious diseases, or cancers. Among the most common, but by no means the only, infectious disorders are candidiasis, *Pneumocystis carinii* pneumonia, herpes simplex or cytomegalovirus infection, chronic cryptosporidiosis, toxoplasmosis, and *Mycobacterium avium* infection. In infants with AIDS, pyogenic infections with *Haemophilus influenzae* or *Streptococcus pneumoniae* are also frequent. Lymphocytic interstitial pneumonia is a particularly common clinical manifestation in HIV-infected pediatric patients, although the exact pathogenic basis of the disorder remains unclear.

Malignant neoplasms are another important group of clinical manifestations in AIDS. Malignant lymphomas, typically of unusual histologic phenotypes such as Burkitt's lymphoma and immunoblastic lymphoma, are common tumors in AIDS patients. Extranodal presentations are characterized by a striking frequency of CNS involvement and an extraordinarily aggressive clinical course with poor response to conventional therapy. During the first years of the AIDS epidemic, KS (often in an unusual and clinically aggressive form) accounted for a significant proportion of malignant tumors occurring in AIDS patients. However, in recent years, the incidence of KS among newly diagnosed AIDS patients has declined for unknown reasons. Some investigators have speculated that environmental cofactors may be important in the development of KS. KS is relatively common among homosexual and bisexual men with AIDS, whereas it is distinctly rare among persons infected through transfusion or contaminated needles. Furthermore, there is a small group of AIDS patients who have a limited indolent form of KS. These observations led some investigators to propose that KS is not a true malignant neoplasm, but is a reversible hyperplasia related to exposure to environmental cofactors in the setting of HIV infection. Recent data suggest that the induction and excessive secretion of certain cytokines, notably interleukin-6 and oncostatin, may play an important role in triggering and maintaining the proliferation of cells that comprise KS lesions.

Although the full extent of neurologic disorders in AIDS patients has been recognized only recently, perhaps half of all HIV-infected patients eventually manifest symptoms of dementia, subacute encephalitis, aseptic meningitis, or peripheral neuropathy. Significant neurologic disease may be the primary, and sometimes the sole, manifestation of HIV infection. Some patients may have profound neurologic disease, despite the apparent absence of other symptoms and despite apparently intact immunity.

In an attempt to relate the prognostic significance of the varying clinical and laboratory findings in HIV-infected patients, a number of clinical staging systems have been developed. Most staging systems consist of sets of increasingly severe symptoms and signs associated with decreasing absolute CD4+ T-cell counts. It should be emphasized that despite the grim long-term prognosis for patients with HIV infection, both the rate of clinical progression and the specific manifestations of disease are highly variable. Improvements in supportive care and prophylactic interventions, such as the use of pentamidine in aerosol form to prevent pneumocystis pneumonia, have extended survival for many patients.

Natural History of HIV Infection

In addition to the more than 161 000 reported cases of full-blown AIDS in this country, perhaps three to five times as many patients have symptomatic conditions related to HIV infection. In addition, there are between 1 and 2 million asymptomatic HIV-infected persons, many of whom are unaware that they are infected. They represent a major potential source of new infections since they are capable of transmitting the virus to others. Over a 5-year period, approximately 20% to 30% of asymptomatic HIV-infected persons are expected to develop AIDS, and an additional 20% or 30% will manifest one of the lesser AIDS-related conditions. Perhaps 50% will remain asymptomatic "carriers" for 5 years, but recent studies suggest that most of these persons will eventually develop AIDS or other significant HIV-associated disease as the clinical follow-up period is extended beyond 10 years. There is reason to believe that infected persons remain infected, and potentially infectious, for their lifetimes. Among those who become symptomatic, the time from initial exposure to the virus to the onset of symptoms ranges from several days to 10 years or more.

HIV Genes and Proteins

The retrovirus responsible for AIDS and its related conditions was discovered in 1983 by French investigators who called it "lymphadenopathy-associated virus" (LAV). The key to elucidating its etiologic role in AIDS was the ability to propagate the virus in a semipermissive cell line, a feat accomplished in 1984 by a group of American investigators who called their isolate "human T-cell lymphotropic virus type-III (HTLV-III)" in an effort to emphasize its similarity with two other human retroviruses, HTLV-I and HTLV-II. Because LAV and HTLV-III are nearly identical, a consensus nomenclature for the virus was subsequently adopted, and the virus is now designated *human immunodeficiency virus*. Numerous clearly distinct but related isolates of HIV have subsequently been cultured and characterized by various investigators. As will be discussed later (see page 199), another distantly related form of HIV has been isolated in West Africa.

The propagation of large quantities of the virus in cell lines not only facilitated the development of an HIV antibody test (see discussion of clinical laboratory testing on page 203), but also led rapidly to the cloning of viral genes, elucidation of the entire nucleotide sequence of the approximately 10-kb genome, and identification of most of the proteins encoded by HIV genes. Such work also provided a partial understanding of the viral life cycle. After the virus binds to its cell-surface receptor, the viral envelope fuses with the plasma membrane and the virion contents enter the cytoplasm (Figure 84). Like other retroviruses, the HIV genome consists of single-stranded RNA that, upon release into the cytosol of susceptible cells, is reverse transcribed into double-stranded DNA forms by the virally encoded enzyme reverse transcriptase, which is packaged in each infectious virion. The DNA forms are later integrated into the host genome. Expression of the integrated proviral genome is governed in part by the long terminal repeats (LTRs) present at both ends of the coding region of the virus.

The viral gene structure and organization indicate that HIV is a member of the lentivirus family, a group of nontransforming cytopathic retrovi-

Figure 84
Electron microscopic visualization of HIV entry into T cells

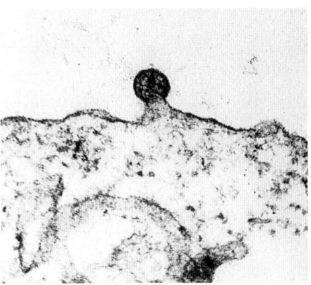

Reproduced with permission from Stein BS, Gowda SD, Lifson JD, Penhallow RC, Bensch KG, Engleman EG. pH-independent HIV entry into CD4-positive T cells via virus envelope fusion to the plasma membrane. *Cell*. 1987;49:659-668, © Cell Press.

Figure 85
Genetic structure of HIV includes the nine genes identified thus far, which are arranged along the viral DNA (top) and flanked by the long terminal repeats (LTR)

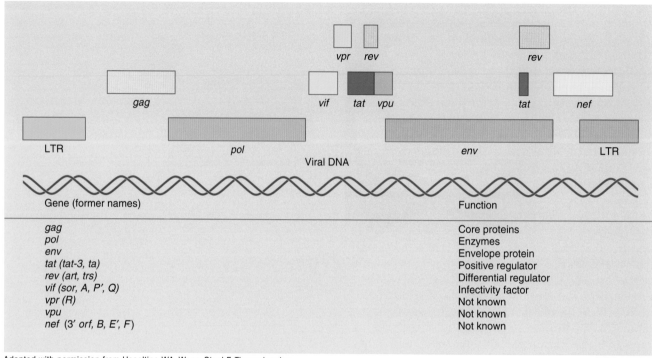

Gene (former names)	Function
gag	Core proteins
pol	Enzymes
env	Envelope protein
tat (tat-3, ta)	Positive regulator
rev (art, trs)	Differential regulator
vif (sor, A, P', Q)	Infectivity factor
vpr (R)	Not known
vpu	Not known
nef (3' orf, B, E', F)	Not known

Adapted with permission from Haseltine WA, Wong-Staal F. The molecular biology of the AIDS virus. *Sci Am*. 1988;259:52-62, © Scientific American Inc., George V. Kelvin.

ruses (Figure 85). HIV is distinct from both HTLV-I and HTLV-II, which are transforming human retroviruses; HTLV-I is etiologically associated with lymphocytic malignancies. In addition to the usual retroviral genes encoding gag (core protein), pol (reverse transcriptase, integrase, and protease), and env (envelope glycoprotein) products, HIV has at least six additional genes, the functions of which are not completely understood at present. Since some of these genes perform critical regulatory roles and are absolutely required for viral replication, they may represent potential targets for therapeutic intervention. One of these genes, designated tat, encodes a transactivating factor that enhances the expression of HIV genes as much as 1000-fold, perhaps by enhancing tran-

scription, as well as through posttranscriptional effects such as stabilization of viral messenger RNA. The tat gene is of particular importance since it appears to be required for viral replication. Another important viral regulatory gene, designated rev, has also been shown to be essential for viral replication. The product of this gene, the rev protein, promotes expression of unspliced mRNA encoding the viral structural (as opposed to regulatory) proteins and appears to operate by increasing the export of such mRNA species from

198

the nucleus to the cytoplasm. The product of the virion infectivity gene (*vif*) appears to increase the infectivity of viral particles through an as yet obscure mechanism. The functions of three additional genes, designated *nef, vpr*, and *vpu* are unknown. In addition to HIV gene products, factors encoded by numerous other viruses, as well as factors induced by host cell activation, are also capable of exerting transactivation effects on the transcription of genes linked to the HIV LTRs.

As noted, HIV uses its reverse transcriptase to generate DNA forms immediately after viral penetration into the cytoplasm of susceptible host cells. Like the reverse transcriptase enzymes of other retroviruses, the HIV enzyme does not correct transcriptional errors by exonucleolytic "proofreading" and, therefore, has a much higher error rate than have DNA polymerase enzymes. The greater frequency of transcriptional errors is probably a major factor in the hypermutability of the AIDS virus. The rapid generation of structurally and functionally diverse forms of the virus poses significant challenges to the development of an effective vaccine.

Recently, a second group of viruses in the HIV family has been isolated, primarily from patients of West African origin. Some of the patients have been clinically well and some have had serious immunodeficiency syndromes indistinguishable from classic AIDS. Serologic and nucleotide sequence analyses, as well as comparison of the organization of the viral genomes, have shown that these West African viruses are clearly related to prototypic HIV isolates, but the new viruses are substantially different. Indeed, the West African isolates appear to be more closely related to a family of simian immunodeficiency viruses than to the prototypic human isolates. Despite these differences, the biologic behavior of the West African viruses, now designated HIV-2, recapitulates that of the original AIDS viruses (now collectively designated HIV-1). HIV-2 demonstrates characteristic features, such as CD4-dependent cytotropism and induction of cytopathic changes through cell fusion. Dual infection with HIV-1 and HIV-2 has been conclusively demonstrated in a few persons, but the clinical significance of HIV-2 infection remains controversial, even in patients infected with only a single strain of HIV.

Tropism of the AIDS Virus for CD4⁺ Leukocytes

As noted, patients with AIDS have an acquired defect of cell-mediated immunity that correlates with a marked decrease in the absolute number of circulating CD4⁺ T cells. Shortly after HIV-1 was available for experimental study, the virus was shown to display an in vitro cytotropism for CD4⁺ T cells, which are distinguished from other T cells by their surface expression of the T-cell differentiation antigen CD4 (formerly known as Leu-3 or T4). When infected with the AIDS virus, CD4⁺ T cells characteristically form syncytia (multinucleated giant cells), which die shortly after their formation (Figure 86). The phenomenon of giant cell formation followed by cell death is referred to as the cytopathic effect of the AIDS virus.

The tropism of HIV for CD4⁺ T cells not only suggested an explanation for the depletion of this cell type in AIDS patients, but it also raised the possibility that the CD4 molecule itself is essential for infection. A critical role for this molecule in virus infection was suggested by the demonstration in 1984 that monoclonal antibodies directed against CD4 blocked infectivity by HIV in vitro. Subsequently, direct biochemical evidence confirmed that HIV binds to the CD4 molecule. Definitive transfection studies showed that expression of the CD4 molecule on human cells that did not normally express CD4 converted the cells from being resistant to HIV infection to a fully HIV-susceptible state. The combination of these results demonstrates clearly that the CD4 molecule is an essential component of the viral cellular receptor and explains the remarkable tropism of the virus for CD4⁺ cells.

In addition to facilitating HIV infection, CD4 molecules on the surface of helper T cells appear to play a direct role in inducing the characteristic in vitro cytopathic effects of HIV by interacting with virus-encoded proteins on the surface of

Figure 86
CD4-dependent HIV-induced cell fusion

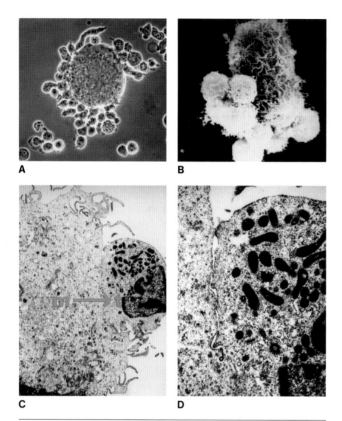

A

B

C

D

(A) Phase-contrast micrograph of strongly CD4-expressing cells. These cells from the cell line VB were cocultivated with H9 T cells chronically infected with HIV-1, resulting in the characteristic HIV-induced syncytium surrounded by a ring of CD4-expressing cells in various stages of fusion.
(B) Scanning electron micrograph of an HIV-induced syncytium similar to that shown in A.
(C) A cell from the T-cell line VB (t) is fusing to an HIV-infected macrophage (m). The arrow indicates a site of membrane fusion where the closely opposed membranes of the two cells become continuous.
(D) A higher power view of the region of membrane fusion demonstrates continuity of the cell membranes with intercytoplasmic communication.

infected cells; the interaction is followed by the physical fusion of interacting cell membranes, which results in the formation of multinucleated giant cells. In vitro, such giant cells typically degenerate within 24 to 48 hours after formation. Viral antigen-expressing multinucleated cells have been identified in histologic sections from HIV-infected patients. They appear to arise through a cell fusion process, and their occurrence in vivo may contribute to the depletion of CD4⁺ T cells.

More recent studies have demonstrated that HIV can infect and replicate in cell types other than T cells, most notably cells of the mononuclear phagocytic series, including peripheral blood monocytes, tissue macrophages, Langerhans cells of the skin, and dendritic reticulum cells within lymph nodes. Despite their morphologic heterogeneity, these cells all express CD4 in varying amounts and, once infected with HIV, can form giant cells with CD4⁺ T cells (Figure 86). In contrast to HIV-infected T cells, macrophages do not undergo dramatic cytopathic effects or rapidly die as a consequence of HIV infection, nor do they appear to be severely compromised in their immune functions. It is interesting to speculate that because antigen-presenting macrophages and antigen-recognizing CD4⁺ T cells are in intimate contact in lymphoid organs during an immune response, such close interaction may also contribute to the spread of infectious virus. In addition, recent data suggest that cells of the monocyte/macrophage lineage may harbor the virus in brain tissue of HIV-infected persons. The mechanism by which HIV infection in the CNS leads to profound dementia and other neurologic disorders remains unknown, although most current speculation centers on mechanisms involving indirect effects of viral components or soluble mediators that are present as a consequence of CNS infection.

It has been demonstrated unequivocally that some nonlymphoid cell lines lacking any detectable CD4 molecules can be infected by HIV in vitro. Reports have also appeared that in vivo cells apparently lacking CD4 can be infected with HIV. Nonetheless, the biologic and clinical significance of CD4-independent HIV infection is unknown.

The Immune System in HIV-Infected Patients

Consequences of CD4+ T-Cell Depletion

Although the cytopathic process of CD4-dependent HIV envelope-mediated cell fusion appears to be the major mechanism whereby HIV infection leads to cell death, at least in some in vitro experimental systems, the mechanism responsible for the progressive decrease in the number of CD4+ T cells and resulting compromised immune function is unknown. It appears that a relatively small proportion of mature CD4+ T cells are productively infected with HIV at any particular time during the clinical course. The percentage of circulating HIV-infected T cells increases over time, peaking at approximately 1% of CD4+ T cells in patients with full-blown AIDS. However, even in these patients most infected T cells are not producing new virions. Therefore, mechanisms other than direct, virally mediated killing have been sought to explain the depletion of CD4+ T cells.

In addition to the formation of syncytia in which uninfected CD4+ cells are recruited and die, additional mechanisms have been hypothesized. For example, it has been proposed that cytotoxic auto-antibodies reactive with antigens expressed on activated or HIV-infected CD4+ T cells may contribute to the depletion of these cells. In another suggested mechanism, free HIV gp120 may be selectively adsorbed to uninfected CD4+ cells through gp120-CD4 interactions. This gp120 (in either native or processed form) is postulated to render CD4+ T cells expressing viral envelope determinants susceptible to lysis by gp120-specific cytotoxic T cells or to render gp120-coated cells susceptible to killing by antibody-dependent cell-mediated cytotoxic mechanisms. It has also been suggested that independent of any direct or indirect cell-killing effects, free gp120 may contribute to depletion of CD4+ T cells by triggering cellular activation, potentially rendering cells more susceptible to HIV infection or more permissive for viral replication. Finally, the possibility must be considered that HIV infects precursors of CD4+ T cells either in the bone marrow or the thymus, or both, rendering HIV-infected persons incapable of replenishing CD4+ T cells as they are lost.

Because the CD4+ subset of T cells includes the majority of helper cells, the loss of this subset impairs the activation of both cytotoxic cells and B cells. As a result, the host is unable to produce new antibodies for the neutralization or elimination of bacteria and viruses as they travel through body fluids between cells. The absence of help for killer cell generation impairs the development of cells that can recognize and eliminate infected target cells. In addition to the quantitative deficiency of CD4+ T cells in HIV-infected individuals, qualitative defects include impaired cytokine production, decreased activation of macrophages, and impaired maturation of the effector functions of natural killer cells and other constitutive killer cells.

Paradoxically, the humoral immune system is often hyperactive in HIV-infected persons, as reflected by polyclonal elevations of circulating immunoglobulins (in particular, IgG and IgA) and significant increases in the levels of circulating immune complexes. Chronic infection of B cells with Epstein-Barr virus (EBV) probably contributes to this abnormality, with defective T-cell regulation of EBV-induced B-cell stimulation exacerbating the problem. In addition, in vitro studies have shown that HIV viral components can directly stimulate B cells in a polyclonal manner. Despite the paradoxical hyperactivity of the humoral branch of the immune system, the ability of the humoral arm to respond effectively to new antigenic challenges is impaired. The ultimate consequences of the loss of these essential components of the immune system are the characteristic clinical manifestations of AIDS-opportunistic infections and malignancies.

The Impaired Immune Response

Many HIV-infected persons remain asymptomatic for several years, whereas others experience a relentless downhill course. The factors that determine clinical outcome after exposure to the AIDS virus are not well understood, but the host immune response to the virus is likely to play an important role in this respect. Accumulated information about the humoral response to HIV infection indicates that in most exposed persons detectable serum antibody to several different viral antigens typically develops within 3 to 24 weeks of exposure. However, the role of the humoral immune response in combating HIV is not understood. While a decrease in the titer of serum antibody reactive with the p24 viral core protein has been associated with disease progression in patients entering the preterminal stages of AIDS, no other consistent correlations have been observed between clinical outcome and either the presence or titer of serum antibody to particular viral antigens. Neutralizing antibodies have been demonstrated in patient sera with in vitro assays, but high titers of HIV-neutralizing antibodies do not appear to be necessarily associated with a favorable clinical outcome. An exception might be anti-gp120 in some HIV-infected pregnant women, which may lessen the chance of transmitting HIV to the fetus.

Although less is known about the cellular immune response to HIV infection, studies of cellular immunity to the AIDS virus are of particular importance for several reasons. First, specific cell-mediated immunity, typically involving cytotoxic T lymphocytes (CTLs), is thought to be the primary means by which most viral infections are cleared. Second, the specificities of B-cell and T-cell responses to a given antigen are generally different; antibody-combining sites and T-cell receptors specific for a particular antigen typically recognize distinct epitopes on that antigen. Low immunogenicity for B-cell responses of certain critical viral antigenic determinants could explain why serum antibody to HIV does not appear to be protective in vivo. The specificity of T-cell responses may be more appropriate for preventing the pathophysiologic consequences of AIDS virus infection. In addition, there is a precedent for specific cell-mediated immunity to the human retrovirus HTLV-I, the etiologic agent of adult T-cell leukemia.

Many HIV-infected patients, particularly those in early clinical stages, have circulating CD8$^+$ HIV-specific CTLs, which recognize viral components in the context of cell-surface human leukocyte antigens (HLA), either HLA-A or HLA-B. Whether these CTLs affect the clinical course of HIV infection (for example, by delaying the onset of clinical disease) is unknown. However, recent studies suggest that these CTLs, like naturally produced anti-HIV antibodies, do not eradicate infection or prevent its ultimate progression to AIDS. Proliferative responses of CD4$^+$ T cells to HIV components and to synthetic peptides presented in the context of HLA class II determinants on antigen-presenting cells have been observed, but such responses generally are weak compared with the usually seen responses to components of infectious pathogens.

Unfortunately, little else is known about the T-cell response to HIV in infected patients, and many fundamental questions remain. Are all steps of the T-cell effector response intact, including functional activation of various subsets of T cells, leading to the release of known lymphokines? It is essential that the answer to this and other questions be obtained not only from studies of peripheral blood leukocytes, but also from studies of lymphoid organs, which are the usual foci of immune response against viruses.

Clinical Laboratory Tests

In virtually all HIV-infected persons except neonates, circulating antibodies to HIV proteins develop within 3 to 6 months of exposure, and the presence of these antibodies forms the basis for most tests designed to detect HIV infection. The most commonly used method to determine the presence of HIV antibodies is the enzyme-linked immunosorbent assay (ELISA), which is highly sensitive and has the advantages of being both rapid and economical. At present, the ELISA and similar rapid antibody techniques are the only tests used for routine screening purposes.

However, it must be remembered that these assays detect serum antibodies to the AIDS virus, not the virus itself, and antibodies do not form immediately upon infection, so false-negative results will occur in recently exposed persons. Furthermore, although the confirmed presence of HIV antibodies documents prior exposure to the virus, it does not indicate whether or how soon an individual is likely to become symptomatic or develop AIDS. Finally, the test as it is currently available is associated with a relatively high frequency of false-positive results (that is, a positive result due not to the presence of antibody but to artifacts of the test), particularly in persons without identified risk factors. In contrast, more than 99% of infected and infectious persons have detectable antibodies to the virus. Thus, the test is particularly useful in the defined, restricted setting of screening blood donors and can exclude the vast majority of high-risk donors.

Use of the ELISA for evaluation of individual patients is more problematic. However, a variety of other tests are available in reference laboratories for extended studies of selected patients, particularly individuals who have had positive responses to ELISA screening. These tests tend to be slower, more complex, more labor intensive, and consequently more expensive than the ELISA test. The Western blot test identifies antibodies to individual HIV proteins, such as those encoded by the *gag, pol,* and *env* genes. At present, the Western blot is the most widely used test for specific confirmation of a positive ELISA result. Despite the fact that most HIV proteins are not present in clinical samples in quantities sufficient for routine detection, the p24 viral core protein may sometimes be detected in the blood of infected persons, even in the absence of specific antiviral antibodies. Commercial assays for the p24 antigen are now available. Culture of blood or other body fluids can be used to detect or isolate HIV from the majority of infected persons. Although cultures may be useful in selected settings, they generally require several weeks to perform, and a negative result does not completely rule out HIV infection. Sensitive techniques for detecting HIV nucleic acid in blood and tissues (in particular, tests based on the polymerase chain reaction) have been developed, but require simplification before they can be applied in routine clinical situations. Finally, quantitation of CD4$^+$ T cells at regular intervals in patients with established HIV infection is of value for clinical staging purposes and for assessing the effects of therapy.

Treatment and Prevention of AIDS

The effective treatment of AIDS and other conditions related to HIV infection will probably require the development of entirely new types of drugs designed to interfere with viral entry, with integration into the host cell genome, or with replication. The development of definitive anti-AIDS therapy is especially difficult because the retrovirus can integrate its genome into the genes of the infected host cell and can exist in a latent state without expressing the viral genes. Infected T cells can harbor integrated, quiescent virus and then express and produce infectious virus upon immunologic activation. In addition, because HIV is able to infect cells in immunologically privi-

Figure 87
Life cycle of the human immunodeficiency virus

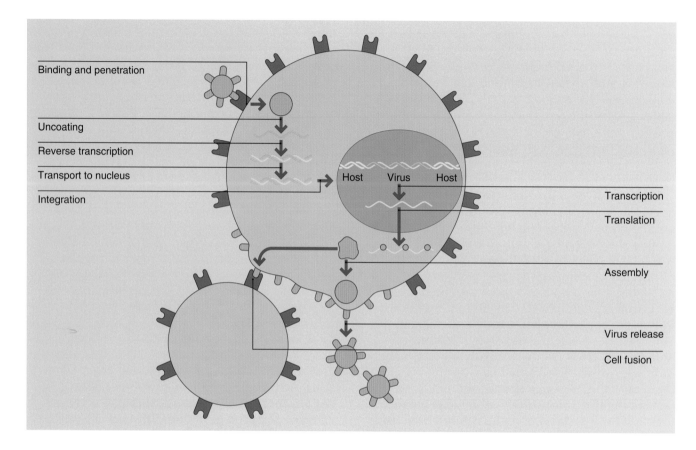

Binding and penetration

Uncoating

Reverse transcription

Transport to nucleus

Integration

Host   Virus   Host

Transcription

Translation

Assembly

Virus release

Cell fusion

leged sites, such as the brain, chemotherapeutic agents must be capable of crossing the blood-brain barrier at effective virucidal or virustatic concentrations.

Despite extensive research and some encouraging preliminary clinical results, there is presently no definitive therapy for AIDS or HIV infection. Unfortunately, because viral nucleic acid can integrate into the genome of the infected host cell and can exist in a latent state, the chances for successful eradication of the virus from an already

infected person are remote. Ultimately, successful therapy for HIV infection will probably need to incorporate the following features:

- Therapy will be long term, probably lifelong.
- The goal of therapy will be to limit the spread of established infection in the host to prevent the progressive immune system damage that appears to be responsible for most clinical manifestations of HIV infection and AIDS.
- A combination therapy approach will probably be necessary, with each aspect of the regimen targeted at a different aspect of the viral life cycle to produce synergistic effects in limiting the spread of the virus.

In spite of these difficulties, many different aspects of the viral life cycle (Figure 87) offer attractive targets for therapeutic intervention. As a retrovirus, HIV is dependent on reverse transcription of its RNA genome for propagation, and much effort has focused on evaluating reverse transcriptase inhibitors for treating AIDS or HIV infection. One such drug, the nucleoside analog azidothymidine (AZT), can prolong the life of AIDS patients by 1 to 2 years and is approved for treating AIDS and HIV infection. Unfortunately, AZT is associated with significant and often dose-limiting toxicity (most notably bone marrow suppression) and its benefits decline with time. AZT-resistant strains of HIV have been isolated from AZT-treated patients, but the clinical importance of these strains is controversial. Other reverse transcriptase inhibitors have their own toxicity profiles. As this book goes to press, dideoxyinosine (DDI) has just been approved for patients who have failed to respond or are intolerant to AZT, and dideoxycytidine (DDC), which has shown promise in clinical trials, is expected to be approved soon. It is unlikely, however, that such drugs will provide definitive, long-term single-agent therapy.

Fortunately, other aspects of the viral life cycle are amenable to intervention, including the machinery used by the virus for replication in infected cells (eg, the *tat*, *rev*, and protease and integrase functions) and the interactions of viral proteins with host cell receptors. Interactions between the envelope glycoprotein of HIV and CD4 are known to be involved in two crucial aspects of the pathobiology of infection: infection of susceptible host cells by HIV virions and viral envelope glycoprotein-mediated cell fusion leading to cell death. Therapy that interferes with these interactions would both prevent primary infection with HIV and inhibit the spread of the virus within an already infected host. In this regard, soluble forms of the CD4 molecule, produced either by recombinant DNA techniques or by constructing synthetic peptides, can block HIV

infection and syncytia formation in vitro; surprisingly, these molecules do not appear to interfere with the normal immune functions of $CD4^+$ T cells. However, initial clinical studies of recombinant CD4 molecules have been disappointing.

Although the development of effective treatment will not be easy, prevention of the spread of AIDS to uninfected persons represents an even more formidable challenge. The proper use of condoms by men is believed to prevent the passage of virus to and from their sexual partners. However, even properly used, condoms are not 100% reliable. More important, given the lack of any historic precedent for the eradication of a sexually transmitted disease through public education or other attempts at behavior modification, only a massive worldwide vaccination program is likely to stop the AIDS epidemic.

Unfortunately, development of a truly effective AIDS vaccine is made extraordinarily difficult by a variety of factors. We know, for instance, that natural infection with HIV does not, as a rule, induce potent group-specific neutralizing antibodies or a strong $CD4^+$ T-cell response to the virus. The depletion of $CD4^+$ T cells in infected patients undoubtedly contributes to the poor immune response, and introducing HIV epitopes in a noninfectious form should facilitate a more potent immune response in vaccine recipients. We also know that the viral envelope glycoprotein represents a logical target for a candidate vaccine, because of its crucial role in the pathobiology of AIDS virus infection. Viral isolates from different individuals tend to have different amino acid sequences (particularly in the envelope protein), which has already slowed the development of a single "consensus" vaccine.

A successful candidate vaccine should be capable of inducing group-specific, as opposed to type-specific, neutralizing antibodies. Certain epitopes of the viral envelope, particularly those that are critical for the biologic functions of the virus (such as interaction with CD4) are presumably highly conserved, but in their native form they may not be sufficiently immunogenic to trigger an immune response. Whether such epitopes can be used to produce a safe and effective vaccine remains to be seen. Equally important is the mode of HIV transmission. It appears that infection can be transmitted from person to person by intact infected cells, as well as by cell-free virions. Unfortunately, although cell-free virions are accessible to antibodies, it is possible that HIV-reactive lymphoid killer cells may be required for elimination of HIV-infected cells. In general, such cytotoxic cells are not induced effectively by traditional vaccines derived from killed virus or viral subunits.

On the basis of these considerations, development of a completely effective AIDS vaccine by conventional techniques seems unlikely in the near future. However, recent studies in monkeys indicate that infection with simian immunodeficiency virus, a lentivirus that causes an AIDS-like disease in rhesus macaques, can be prevented by vaccination with formalin-killed virus. Therefore, the potential for producing a vaccine that offers some protection against HIV infection is greater than previously thought possible. Since HIV does not cause an AIDS-like disease in experimental animals, including primates, the efficacy and safety of all candidate AIDS vaccines must be determined in human trials, although studies in animal retrovirus systems may provide guidance.

Selected Readings

Bowen DL, Lane HC, Fauci AS. Immunopathogenesis of the acquired immunodeficiency syndrome. **Ann Intern Med**. 1985;103:704-709.

Curran JW, Morgan WM, Hardy AM, Jaffe HW, Darrow WW, Dowdle WR. The epidemiology of AIDS: current status and future prospects. **Science**. 1985;229:1352-1357.

Greene WC. The molecular biology of human immunodeficiency virus type I infection. **N Engl J Med**. 1991;324:308-317.

Ho DD, Pomerantz RJ, Kaplan JC. Pathogenesis of infection with human immunodeficiency virus. **N Engl J Med**. 1987;317:278-286.

Lifson JD, Engleman EG. Role of CD4 in normal immunity and HIV infection. **Immunol Rev**. 1989;109:93-117.

Mitsuya H, Yarchoan R, Broder S. Molecular targets for AIDS therapy. **Science**. 1990;249:1533-1544.

Ruegg C, Engleman E. Impaired immunity in AIDS: the mechanisms responsible and their potential reversal by antiviral therapy. In: St Georgiev V, McGowan JJ, eds. **AIDS: Anti-HIV Agents, Therapies, and Vaccines**. New York, NY: New York Academy of Sciences. 1990;616:307-317.

What science knows about AIDS: a single-topic issue. **Sci Am**. October 1988;259:40-134.

Yarchoan R, Broder S. Development of antiretroviral therapy for the acquired immunodeficiency syndrome and related disorders. **N Engl J Med**. 1987;316:557-564.

Immune-Modulating Therapies

15

Introduction

The modification of immune function is an important strategy in the treatment of disorders in which the immune system has a major pathogenetic role. The types of clinical disorders treated with immune system modulation are remarkably diverse. Immune-modulating therapies are important in preventing predictable immunologic disorders, such as erythroblastosis fetalis (see chapter 11) and the rejection of transplanted organs. Immune-modulating therapies are used to treat various idiopathic inflammatory syndromes in which cells or products of the immune system are responsible for tissue damage. Examples include inflammation of the synovium (rheumatoid arthritis), skeletal muscle (polymyositis), vascular endothelium (vasculitis), exocrine glands (Sjögren's syndrome), and nerve myelin (multiple sclerosis). In systemic lupus erythematosus (SLE), inflammation of multiple organs develops, particularly in the skin, kidneys, and central nervous system. Tissue-specific antibodies can lead to cellular destruction as in hemolytic anemia or thrombocytopenia, alteration of membrane receptor function as in myasthenia gravis, or selective organ pathology, such as pulmonary or renal disease in Goodpasture's syndrome.

Approaches to Immune Modification

A number of basic strategies have been successfully used to modify human immune function (Figure 88). They include efforts to minimize host exposure to a foreign antigen, deplete immune cells or products, and alter the function of immunocompetent cells.

Antigen Elimination
The most direct form of immune system modulation is to eliminate or reduce host exposure to the inciting antigen. This principle underlies programs of passive immunization against infectious viral (eg, measles, mumps, polio) or bacterial (eg, pneumococcal, meningococcal) diseases. In organ transplantation, tissue typing to match antigens of the major histocompatibility complex between the host and donor tissues minimizes stimulation of the host's immune system and lessens the risk of graft rejection. In hemolytic disease of the newborn (erythroblastosis fetalis), the postpartum administration of IgG anti-Rh_o (D) antisera to an Rh-negative mother after delivery of an Rh-positive infant eliminates fetal erythrocytes from the maternal circulation and thereby prevents immunization of the mother.

Although no inciting antigen has been identified for most immunologic disorders, several notable exceptions deserve comment. Certain drugs may induce or promote immune disorders that mimic idiopathic inflammatory syndromes. For example, polymyositis may develop with d-penicillamine therapy, thrombocytopenia with quinidine, hemolytic anemia with alpha-methyldopa, and SLE with procainamide or hydralazine. Discontinuation of the offending drug promptly resolves the immune abnormalities and the clinical disease process improves. Various infectious diseases, such as bacterial endocarditis or viral hepatitis, may be complicated by immune-mediated disorders, particularly vasculitis and glomerulonephritis. Appropriate treatment of the infection to eliminate the responsible organism is generally sufficient to completely reverse the immunologic disorder.

Depletion of Immune Cells or Products
Immune function may be suppressed by depleting cellular components of the immune system or soluble immune products such as circulating antibodies. Lymphocyte populations may be depleted by the use of cytotoxic drugs, antilymphocyte serum, lymphocytapheresis, or irradiation of lymphoid organs. The lymphocytopenia produced by these procedures reduces the populations of central lymphoid, recirculating, and ultimately tissue lymphocytes. As a consequence, cell-mediated immune functions are suppressed, including delayed hypersensitivity reactions, proliferative responses of peripheral lymphocytes to mitogens and alloantigens, and cytotoxic T-lymphocyte (CTL) reactions. Theoretically, clinical disorders in which cell-mediated processes are primarily responsible for the lesions might improve with the depletion of immune system components.

Figure 88
Strategies for modifying immune function

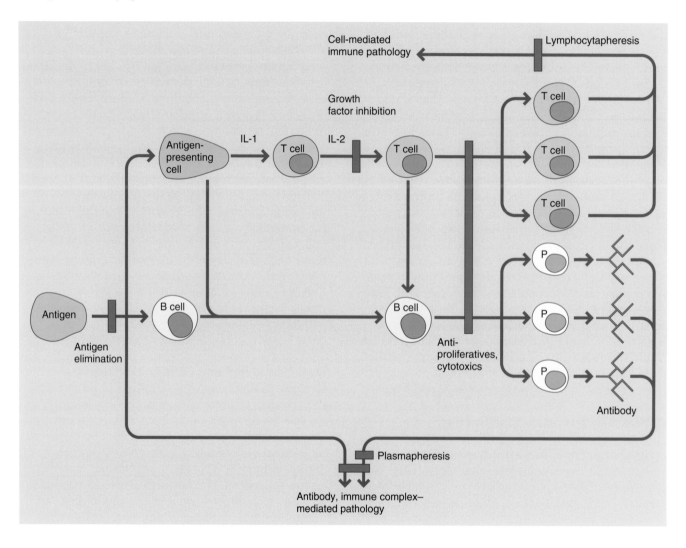

Organs of the immune system, such as the spleen or thymus, can be surgically removed. Splenectomy results in impairment of phagocytic functions and a reduced production of antibodies. Phagocytic function may also be altered through the selective destruction of cells of the reticulo-endothelial system by the delivery of targeted cytotoxic compounds to macrophages. In experimental studies, thymectomy delays or prevents the onset of autoimmune diseases and has been performed in humans to treat myasthenia gravis.

Antibody formation may be suppressed by the direct effects of cytotoxic drugs or lymphoid irradiation on B cells and plasma cells. Moreover, these therapies suppress lymphokine production by T cells, further inhibiting B-cell activation and antibody synthesis. Finally, soluble circulating products of the immune system, such as antibodies, antigen-antibody complexes, and lymphokines, may be directly removed by plasmapheresis.

Functional Alteration of Immunocompetent Cells

Immunologic functions may be altered by drugs that inhibit essential metabolic processes of cells of the immune system. The disruption of purine biosynthetic pathways with purine analogues, inhibition of single-carbon transfer reactions by folate antagonists, or inhibition of messenger RNA transcription of lymphocyte growth factors are examples of cellular metabolic pathways that can be blocked by drugs to suppress immune function. In the future, it may become possible to directly regulate immune functions by either administering or blocking the function of natural lymphokines, such as interleukin-1 (IL-1), IL-2, or interferon gamma (IFN-γ) (see chapter 7).

Immune-Modifying Therapies

Glucocorticoids

The various suppressive effects of glucocorticoids on inflammation and immune function (Figure 89) make these agents extremely valuable in the treatment of most immunologic diseases.

The anti-inflammatory influences of glucocorticoids result from several different mechanisms. Glucocorticoids stabilize the vascular endothelium and inhibit the production of local chemotactic

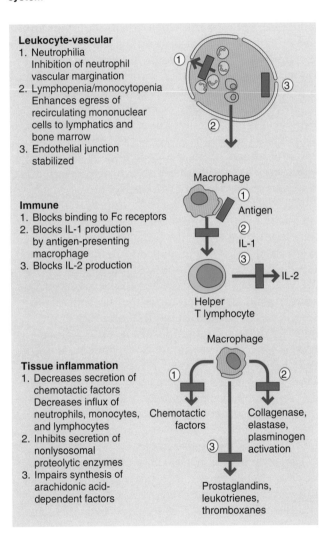

Figure 89
The multiple effects of glucocorticoids on leukocytes, vascular endothelium, local tissue inflammation, and the immune system

Leukocyte-vascular
1. Neutrophilia
   Inhibition of neutrophil vascular margination
2. Lymphopenia/monocytopenia
   Enhances egress of recirculating mononuclear cells to lymphatics and bone marrow
3. Endothelial junction stabilized

Immune
1. Blocks binding to Fc receptors
2. Blocks IL-1 production by antigen-presenting macrophage
3. Blocks IL-2 production

Macrophage
Antigen
IL-1
IL-2
Helper T lymphocyte

Tissue inflammation
1. Decreases secretion of chemotactic factors
   Decreases influx of neutrophils, monocytes, and lymphocytes
2. Inhibits secretion of nonlysosomal proteolytic enzymes
3. Impairs synthesis of arachidonic acid-dependent factors

Macrophage
Chemotactic factors
Collagenase, elastase, plasminogen activation
Prostaglandins, leukotrienes, thromboxanes

factors, thereby impairing the ability of cells to migrate into areas of active tissue inflammation. At sites of inflammation, the secretion of destructive nonlysosomal proteolytic enzymes, such as collagenase, elastase, and plasminogen activator is inhibited. Perhaps the single most important anti-inflammatory effect produced by glucocorticoids is the inhibition of arachidonic acid release from membrane phospholipids through the induction of a phospholipase A2 inhibitory protein. Inhibition of arachidonic acid prevents the synthesis of prostaglandins, thromboxanes, and leukotrienes, which are the major mediators of inflammation. The net effects of the many actions of glucocorticoids are the suppression of local tissue inflammation and subsequent tissue destruction.

Glucocorticoids also have a suppressive effect on various immune functions. Lymphocytopenia and monocytopenia develop as a result of the redistribution of lymphocytes and monocytes from the circulation into lymphatics and bone marrow. The lymphocytopenia preferentially involves T cells, particularly the inducer/helper subset, more than B cells. Cell-mediated immune functions, such as delayed hypersensitivity, mitogen and mixed leukocyte proliferative responses, and CTL reactions, are suppressed. Inhibition of lymphokine growth factors, such as IL-1 and IL-2, as well as alterations of macrophage function may further account for some properties of these drugs. The effects of glucocorticoids on B cells and humoral immunity are less predictable.

The structure of hydroxycortisol, the principal human glucocorticoid, has been modified to produce synthetic compounds with different biologic properties (Table 32). These glucocorticoids can be classified as short-, intermediate-, and long-acting, according to how long they suppress adrenocorticotropic hormone (ACTH) secretion. ACTH secretion returns to normal 24 to 36 hours after the administration of a single dose of a short-acting glucocorticoid, whereas ACTH secretion remains suppressed much longer than 48 hours after a single dose of a long-acting glucocorticoid. Disruption of the normal pituitary-adrenal axis is least influenced by short-acting glucocorticoids

Table 32
Glucocorticoids

	Equivalent dose (mg)	Glucocorticoid potency
Short-acting		
Cortisone	25	0.8
Cortisol	20	1.0
Intermediate-acting		
Prednisone	5	4.0
Prednisolone	5	4.0
Methylprednisolone	4	5.0
Triamcinolone	4	5.0
Long-acting		
Betamethasone	0.60	25.0
Dexamethasone	0.75	30.0

given intermittently. Long-term administration of any of the glucocorticoids results in complete suppression of ACTH secretion and atrophy of the adrenal glands.

Chemotherapies

Immune functions can be either suppressed or enhanced by drugs. With few exceptions, the drugs currently used for these purposes are not specific for the immune system and they exert actions on other organ systems, particularly those characterized by increased cell proliferation, such as bone marrow and the gastrointestinal tract. Certainly many of the toxicities associated with immune-modulating chemotherapies result from drug influences on these other organ systems. The pharmacology and effects on immune function of the more commonly used immune-modifying chemotherapies are discussed on the following pages.

Figure 90
Nitrogen mustard alkylating agents are derivatives of the bifunctional compound bis-2-chlorethylamine

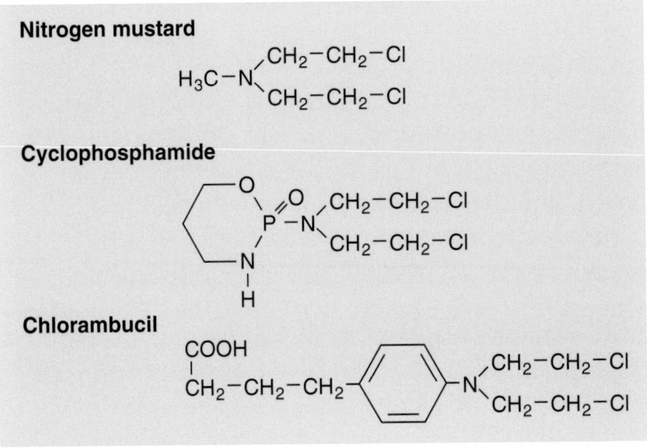

Alkylating agents: The alkylating agents are one of the most effective known forms of immune-suppressive chemotherapy. These drugs contain highly reactive alkyl radicals that form covalent bonds with nucleophilic molecules. Most alkylating agents in clinical use are derivatives of the bifunctional nitrogen mustard compound bis-2-chlorethylamine. The amine portion of the molecule undergoes internal cyclization to form an unstable ethylenimonium ion. This ion spontaneously cleaves to yield two reactive intermediate compounds that can form cross-linkages. Although alkylation occurs throughout all phases of the cell cycle, including among resting nonproliferating cells, the major drug effects result from alkylation of DNA during the S phase of the cell cycle. The reactivity with purine bases produces major structural alterations in the DNA through internal cross-linkages. In addition, alkylation of phosphate groups of the DNA backbone produces reactive triesters that hydrolyze and further disrupt the polynucleotide chain sequence. These alterations may be lethal to the cell or may produce simple miscoding errors that inhibit cellular replication or transcription.

Modifications of the basic chlorethylamine structure have yielded several clinically important alkylating drugs with different physical and biologic properties (Figure 90). Nitrogen mustard (N-methyl-2-chlorethylamine) was the first alkylating agent to be used clinically. However, because it requires intravenous administration, produces significant toxicity both locally and systemically, and has relatively weak immunosuppressive properties, nitrogen mustard is seldom used and generally has been replaced by more effective, less toxic alkylating drugs.

Substitution of a cyclic phosphamide (cyclophosphamide) or phenylbutyric acid (chlorambucil) for the N-methyl group in nitrogen mustard led to the development of inert, stable alkylating agents. These drugs can be administered orally and must be metabolized to produce reactive alkylating intermediate compounds. Cyclophosphamide and chlorambucil have profound immunosuppressive properties that include the production of T- and B-cell lymphopenia and the suppression of both cell-mediated and humoral immunity.

Purine analogues: Structural analogues of natural purine bases produce major alterations in cellular purine nucleotide synthesis that affect both DNA and RNA function. The purine analogues are metabolized to ribonucleotide monophosphates. The poor conversion of these compounds to diphosphates and triphosphates leads to an intracellular accumulation of the monophosphate. The triphosphate analogues formed become incorporated into DNA and result in RNA miscoding and subsequently faulty transcription. The monophosphates produce a feedback inhibition on rate-limiting enzymes required for the biosynthesis of purine nucleotides. In addition, the monophosphates inhibit the conversion of inosinic acid to xanthylic acid, a reaction essential for formation of adenosine and guanine nucleotides.

Figure 91
Azathioprine is an imidazolyl derivative of 6-mercaptopurine

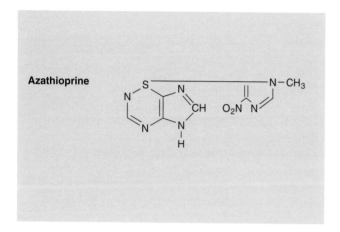

Azathioprine

The purine analogue most commonly used as an immune-modulating drug is azathioprine, a thiol derivative of hypoxanthine (Figure 91). Azathioprine has a greater effect on humoral than on cell-mediated immunity. In addition, azathioprine appears to have potent anti-inflammatory properties that are probably the result of inhibiting monocyte function.

Methotrexate: The major cellular effects of the antifolate methotrexate (4-amino-4-deoxy-N^{10}-methyl folic acid) result from binding to the enzyme dihydrofolate reductase and inhibiting the conversion of natural dihydrofolates to tetrahydrofolates. Depletion of the intracellular pool of tetrahydrofolates, particularly methyltetrahydrofolate and 10-formyltetrahydrofolate, greatly inhibits thymidylate and purine biosynthesis and, as a consequence, DNA synthesis. In addition, cellular function is influenced by the effects of methotrexate on other folate-dependent metabolic pathways, particularly the interconversions of amino acids. A pathway that may be important in the selective suppression of cell-mediated immunity by methotrexate involves the inhibition of methionine regeneration from homocysteine and the reduction of S-adenosylmethionine and other polyamines.

Cyclosporin A: Cyclosporin A, a natural fungal product, has profound suppressive effects on immune function. The major effects appear to result from the inhibition of growth factors, particularly IL-2, produced by helper T cells. Growth factor inhibition prevents proliferation and differentiation of cytotoxic T cells and B cells and promotes expansion of suppressor T-cell populations. Cyclosporin A is not myelosuppressive and has no effects on myeloid or erythroid precursors. This drug inhibits graft rejection and prevents graft-versus-host disease. In addition, preliminary studies suggest that cyclosporin A may be useful in the treatment of cell-mediated forms of autoimmune diseases.

Vinca alkyloids: The plant alkyloids vinblastine and vincristine are cell-cycle–specific agents that interfere with protein assembly of the mitotic spindle and lead to arrest of the cell in metaphase. In general, neither drug has any major influence on immune function per se, but both are useful in the management of immune-mediated thrombocytopenia. Because of the high avidity of the vinca alkyloids for tubulin and the high concentration of tubulin in platelets, these drugs are selectively concentrated by platelets. Phagocytosis of the antibody-coated platelet, therefore, results in the selective delivery of vinca alkyloids to the cells responsible for platelet destruction.

Levamisole: Levamisole hydrochloride, a synthetic tricyclic L-isomer of phenylimidothiozole, stimulates a number of immune functions. The predominant effect appears to be on T cells, which are stimulated to increase their cytotoxicity and amplifier functions. Levamisole has little or no effect on B cells. In vivo studies with this agent have shown restoration of impaired delayed skin hypersensitivity, increased numbers of circulating T cells, and improved reticuloendothelial function.

Chemotaxis and phagocytosis of macrophages and polymorphonuclear leukocytes are also stimulated. Nucleic acid and protein synthesis are increased in both resting and stimulated lymphocytes. In addition, levels of cyclic nucleotides, particularly cyclic GMP, are increased in leukocytes.

Apheresis

Apheresis involves fractionating blood into individual components and removing selected components from the circulation. Recent technologic advances in the use of continuous flow centrifugation of anticoagulated blood have greatly simplified the procedure. The removal of plasma (plasmapheresis) or lymphocytes (lymphocytapheresis) has been used to modify immune function. Selective forms of apheresis in which specific antibodies, immune complexes or other soluble factors, or distinct lymphocyte populations are removed have been used in experimental studies. Serum cryoproteins are removed by cryoapheresis, a procedure in which the plasma is cooled, centrifuged to remove the cryoprecipitate, and the reheated supernate returned to the patient.

Plasmapheresis decreases circulating concentrations of antibodies, immune complexes, lymphokines, and soluble inflammatory mediators such as complement. Maintaining oncotic pressure requires replacement of the depleted plasma proteins, usually with albumin. In lymphocytapheresis, removal of large quantities of relatively pure lymphocytes may lead to lymphocytopenia, which alters trafficking of recirculating lymphocytes between central lymphoid organs and sites of immune system lesions. Because plasma proteins are unaffected by the procedure, replacement fluids are not needed. In theory, plasmapheresis should influence humoral-mediated immunologic disorders, and lymphocytapheresis should affect cell-mediated processes.

The primary mechanism of action of therapeutic apheresis in immunologic diseases is probably a shift in the equilibrium between pathologic factors (cells or soluble plasma factors) within the intravascular compartment and those present at sites of organ lesions. For clinical improvement, the intravascular concentrations of the pathologic factors must be reduced below a certain critical level and maintained for a sufficient period of time to allow for reversal of the immune process in the tissue. However, because the normal host response to apheresis is to increase the synthesis of the depleted factor, successful clinical therapeutic apheresis requires that the procedure be repeated over an extended interval or combined with other immunosuppressive treatment such as chemotherapy.

Biological Agents

Several types of biological agents have been used clinically to modify immune function. Antisera containing high concentrations of immune globulins against viruses (eg, hepatitis B, varicella-zoster, and rabies) have been given to provide passive immunity. Pooled human immune globulin, predominantly IgG, has been used to provide passive immunity to patients with antibody deficiency syndromes and to persons who have already been exposed to certain infectious diseases for which specific antiserum is not available. In addition, immune globulin has been used to treat idiopathic thrombocytopenic purpura and other autoimmune disorders. Heterologous antilymphocyte serum is given to selectively deplete lymphocytes and produce lymphocytopenia, particularly T-cell lymphocytopenia. Finally, in maternal-fetal erythrocyte Rh incompatibility, immune globulin containing antibodies to the red blood cell antigen Rh_o (D) is administered to prevent maternal immunization.

Recent advances in recombinant DNA technology offer great potential for the use of biological products in the modification of immune function. Natural immunoregulatory lymphokines, such as IL-1, IL-2, and IFN-γ, are available for clinical use and have been administered experimentally to artificially manipulate immune function. Monoclonal antibodies to specific lymphocyte subsets, cell-surface molecules, and secreted products can theoretically be used to manipulate immune function. A limited number of clinical studies have evaluated these newer biological products.

Total Lymphoid Irradiation

The irradiation of central lymphoid structures produces long-term changes in immune function. Fractionated irradiation is given to central lymphoid structures, including lymph nodes, thymus, and spleen. The irradiation produces lymphocytopenia, particularly T-cell lymphopenia, that may persist for many years after the procedure. Impairments of cell-mediated immunity, including depressed proliferative responses to mitogens and alloantigens and the development of cutaneous anergy, can occur after lymphoid irradiation. The depletion of CD4 T cells, in particular, appears to correlate with these changes in immune function. Because CD4 T cells mediate helper or inducer immune functions, T-cell-dependent antibody production also becomes suppressed after total lymphoid irradiation.

Clinical Studies

Immune-modulating therapies are important adjuncts in the management of a variety of immunologic disorders. The clinical course of many of these diseases is chronic and characterized by spontaneous relapses and remissions. To determine the efficacy of immune-modulating therapies, therefore, randomized controlled studies have been necessary to distinguish the influences of therapy from the inevitable fluctuations of the natural disease course. Although immune-modulating therapies may be responsible for long-term disease remissions, they are not considered to be cures for any disease.

Rheumatoid Arthritis

Immune-modulating therapies have been extensively studied in rheumatoid arthritis, primarily in randomized controlled trials. Although immune system modulation often substantially diminishes synovitis and systemic disease manifestations, remissions of the disease are unusual and relapses are common, despite long-term therapy.

Glucocorticoids often are given in low doses for their anti-inflammatory effects. Immune-suppressive chemotherapies, such as azathioprine, cyclophosphamide, methotrexate, and cyclosporin A, are often effective. Curiously, levamisole, an immune-enhancing drug, also appears to reduce synovial inflammation. The mechanisms of action of various empiric therapies often used in rheumatoid arthritis, including gold salts, antimalarials, d-penicillamine, and sulfasalazine, are unknown but may involve effects on the immune system.

Lymphocytapheresis produces transient improvements, particularly in patients with prominent lymphocytic infiltration in the synovial tissues. Plasmapheresis seems to be ineffective in the management of synovitis, although it may have a role in the treatment of rheumatoid vasculitis. Several recent studies have demonstrated significant improvement of synovitis after total lymphoid irradiation. Studies of biological agents in rheumatoid arthritis are in the investigational stage. Several studies of IFN-γ suggest that it has little or no effect in rheumatoid arthritis.

Systemic Lupus Erythematosus

Glucocorticoids are important in the management of SLE, and short courses of high-dose therapy are often necessary to manage serious life-threatening manifestations. In general, immune-modulating therapies are reserved for patients who are unresponsive to or intolerant of glucocorticoids and for patients with any life-threatening disease manifestations, such as nephritis, central nervous system involvement, or hematologic complications.

Controlled studies to evaluate the efficacy of immune-modulating therapies compared with standard glucocorticoid treatment alone are limited to chronic progressive lupus nephritis. Both azathioprine and cyclophosphamide influence the progression of renal lesions and, in particular, prevent the development of chronic scarring abnormalities of the glomeruli and tubulointerstitium. Treatment with high-dose intermittent cyclophosphamide significantly reduces the risk of end-stage renal failure. Studies of repeated plasmapheresis are incomplete; however, this therapy appears to have little impact on the course of chronic lupus renal disease.

In patients with lupus nephritis, total lymphoid irradiation may dramatically reduce proteinuria. Splenectomy, vinca alkyloids (vincristine and vinblastine), and immune globulin have been successfully used in the management of lupus thrombocytopenia.

Necrotizing Vasculitis

Immune-modulating drugs are used in treating various forms of necrotizing vasculitis in which the response to therapy with glucocorticoids is inadequate. Wegener's granulomatosis and polyarteritis are examples of serious forms of systemic vasculitis in which immunosuppressive drugs have significantly reduced morbidity and mortality. Oral cyclophosphamide generally has been regarded as the drug of choice, although no controlled trials to evaluate efficacy have been done. On occasion, plasmapheresis has been successful in the management of necrotizing vasculitis associated with high titers of circulating immune complexes or cryoglobulinemia.

Allograft Rejection

Successful organ transplantation necessitates suppression of the immune system to prevent graft rejection. The standard treatment for many years has been to induce immune suppression with glucocorticoids combined with azathioprine. Heterologous antilymphocyte serum has also been given to prevent or reverse rejection episodes. More recently, studies have demonstrated that cyclosporin A and FK506 are very effective in preventing graft rejection, and these agents are now widely used after renal transplantation. Monoclonal IgG antibodies against the CD3 T-cell antigen receptor have been successful. Results of recent studies of total lymphoid irradiation combined with low-dose adjunctive chemotherapy are promising.

Myasthenia Gravis

Myasthenia gravis represents an example of selective autoimmunity in which antibodies against the acetylcholine receptor disrupt the function of the receptor (see chapter 11). Several forms of immune-modulating therapies have been used successfully in the management of the disease. Azathioprine is often given to suppress immune function, and a recent randomized placebo-controlled trial demonstrated the effectiveness of cyclosporin A. Plasmapheresis, often in combination with an immunosuppressive drug, reduces the concentrations of acetylcholine receptor antibodies in the plasma and results in improved neuromuscular transmission. Thymectomy is regarded as an effective form of therapy for patients with myasthenia gravis who are resistant to other treatments.

Complications of Immune Modulation

One of the main consequences of suppressing immune function is a reduction in host defense mechanisms and an increased risk of infection. Careful monitoring of the neutrophil count and immunoglobulin levels, with adjustments in the immune-modulating regimen as needed, is critical to minimize the risk of infection. Both typical and opportunistic infections may develop, the most common of which is cutaneous herpes zoster. The increased risk of infection is compounded by the heightened susceptibility to infection inherent in many of the clinical disorders treated with immune-modulating agents.

In addition, unique toxic effects are associated with the individual immune-modulating therapies (Table 33). The toxic effects of glucocorticoids are related to the dose and duration of therapy, although essentially all individuals exposed to glucocorticoids are at risk. Myelosuppression, a common occurrence with most immune-modulating drugs, often limits long-term therapy. There is considerable concern regarding the risks of neoplasia in patients who have been treated with alkylating agents, purine analogues, and lymphoid irradiation. The effects of these therapies on DNA increase the likelihood of malignant mutagenesis, particularly of myeloid cell precursors. In addition, the cyclophosphamide metabolite, acrolein, is toxic to bladder epithelium and is responsible for an increased risk of bladder carcinoma.

Table 33
Toxicities of immune-modulating therapies

Therapies	Toxicities
Glucocorticoids	Cutaneous changes, hypertension, myopathy, osteoporosis, osteonecrosis, posterior subcapsular cataracts, hyperglycemia
Chemotherapy Alkylating agents Cyclophosphamide Chlorambucil	GI distress, alopecia, myelosuppression, amenorrhea, azoospermia, teratogenesis, and neoplasia. Unique to cyclophosphamide: hemorrhagic cystitis, bladder fibrosis, bladder carcinoma, cardiac and pulmonary toxicities, and inappropriate ADH syndrome
Purine analogues Azathioprine	GI distress, myelosuppression, hepatitis, pancreatitis, aseptic meningitis, neoplasia
Antifolates Methotrexate	GI distress, mucositis, pneumonitis, teratogenesis, liver fibrosis/cirrhosis
Vinca alkyloids Vinblastine Vincristine	Neurotoxicity
Immune enhancers Levamisole	GI distress, fever, skin rash, granulocytopenia
Growth factor inhibitors Cyclosporin A	Nephrotoxicity, hypertension, paresthesias, tremor, hypertrichosis, breast tenderness, menstrual abnormalities, hepatitis
Apheresis Plasmapheresis	Hypervolemia or hypovolemia, thrombotic complications
Lymphocytapheresis	
Total lymphoid irradiation	GI distress, xerostomia, myelosuppression, pneumonitis, pericarditis, possible neoplasia

Abbreviations: GI, gastrointestinal; ADH, antidiuretic hormone (vasopressin).

Conclusion

Immune-modulating therapies are extremely valuable in the prevention or management of various clinical disorders associated with immune system impairment. With few exceptions, the current clinical strategies of immune system modification by chemotherapy, lymphoid irradiation, apheresis, or biologicals produce relatively nonselective suppression of immune function. The adverse consequences of immune modulation result from interference with natural host defense mechanisms, as well as the complications and toxicities unique to the individual therapies. The clinical decision to use an immune-modifying therapy requires careful consideration of the potential benefits and hazards of therapy.

Selected Readings

Fahey JL, Sarna G, Gale RP, Seeger R. Immune interventions in disease. **Ann Intern Med.** 1987;106:257-274.

Fauci AS, Rosenberg SA, Sherwin SA, Dinarello CA, Longo DL, Lane HC. Immunomodulators in clinical medicine. **Ann Intern Med**. 1987;106:421-433.

Fauci AS, Young KR Jr. Immunoregulatory agents. In: Kelley WN, Harris ED Jr, Ruddy S, Sledge CB, eds. **Textbook of Rheumatology**. 3rd ed. Philadelphia, Pa: WB Saunders; 1989: 862-884.

Klippel JH, Strober S, Wofsy D. New therapies for the rheumatic diseases. **Bull Rheum Dis**. 1989;38:1-8.

Steinberg AD. Principles in the use of immunosuppressive agents. In: Schumacher HR Jr, Klippel JH, Robinson DR, eds. **Primer on the Rheumatic Diseases**. 9th ed. Atlanta, Ga: Arthritis Foundation; 1988:288-294.

Introduction

Manipulation of the immune system to induce regression of malignant tumors is a compelling idea that has stimulated scientific experimentation for nearly a century. Physicians had observed that bacterial infection in some cancer patients led to spontaneous tumor regression, and in the late 19th century immunotherapeutic studies were conducted in which bacterial toxins were administered to cancer patients. In the early 1900s, Ehrlich observed that animals in which low-virulence allogeneic tumors had grown and then regressed were resistant to a subsequent tumor cell inoculation. He postulated that tumors bore cell-surface structures that could be recognized as abnormal by the host. Half a century later in 1959, Lewis Thomas theorized that allograft rejection might "represent a primary mechanism for natural defense against neoplasia." These ideas led Burnet to formulate a theory of immune surveillance that proposes cancer cells contain cell-surface antigens that the host's immune system can recognize and react to, thereby preventing the outgrowth of a tumor. The existence of tumor-associated antigens is central to the immune surveillance theory and to tumor immunology.

Tumor-Associated Antigens

For a tumor to induce a specific immune response, it must express an antigen that is immunogenic in the host. Such tumor-associated antigens (TAA) were first described in 1943 by Gross, who chemically induced a sarcoma in the mouse. He found that animals inoculated with small numbers of tumor cells could reject larger tumorigenic challenges with the same cell line. Prehn and Main reported in the late 1950s that after excision of a methylcholanthrene-induced sarcoma mice were resistant to a subsequent challenge with the autologous tumor cells. Syngeneic mice not previously exposed to tumor cells were unable to reject a similar tumor challenge. In addition, immune mice that rejected the second tumor graft did not reject skin grafts from syngeneic animals, suggesting that

the TAA were distinct from major histocompatibility complex (MHC) antigens. Other groups have demonstrated that normal animals preimmunized with tumor cells treated to restrict their progressive growth can stimulate the development of specific tumor immunity.

In general, experimental tumors induced with chemicals, irradiation, or physical agents possess unique antigenic determinants. In many instances, different tumors induced by the same agent in a single animal are antigenically distinct. In addition to chemically induced cancers, experimental tumors induced by DNA or RNA viruses express virus-related TAA, such as virus-encoded products and transformation-related antigens. Unlike most chemically induced tumors, tumors induced by the same virus are inclined to express the same TAA.

In contrast to experimentally induced tumors, spontaneous tumors tend to be weakly immunogenic. Tumors that arise spontaneously in animals generally fail to protect syngeneic hosts from a subsequent tumor challenge, whereas chemically or virally induced tumor cells often elicit immune protection. One explanation for the low immunogenicity of spontaneous tumors is that since they arise slowly they have time to undergo many biochemical and immunologic changes. As tumor progression continues, clones that elicit a weaker immune response are favored. Thus, spontaneous animal tumors, and many human tumors, may select themselves for low immunogenicity.

Human Tumor-Associated Antigens
Tumor-associated antigens have been demonstrated in a large number of animal tumors. However, in human tumors, evidence of antigenic determinants distinct from their nonmalignant counterparts has been equivocal, which has

hampered the development of specific immunotherapy for human cancer. Several investigators have reported that peripheral blood lymphocytes from some cancer patients can be cytotoxic in vitro against autologous tumor cells or against tumor cells of the same histologic type from other patients. However, these in vitro cytotoxicity tests do not always measure activity against tumor antigens. Leukocyte migration inhibition, leukocyte adherence inhibition, and in vivo delayed-type hypersensitivity (DTH) tests have also been used to measure T-cell responses to human tumors. The presence of human TAA has also been studied by using antibody reactivity. Although murine monoclonal antibodies have been produced against a variety of human tumor cells, it has not been established whether the antigens recognized do or can elicit immune responses in patients. The development of human monoclonal antibodies derived from antibody-forming cells of cancer patients may prove more useful in defining immunogenic human TAA. Still, the existence of human tumor-specific antigens remains uncertain.

Antitumor Immune Response

The immune response against a tumor is a complex series of events involving both direct cellular interactions and soluble factors. A simplified view of the interactions is presented in Figure 92. Macrophages take up and process TAA, then present antigenic determinants to CD4 T cells. The macrophage–T-cell interaction depends on the T cell recognizing both antigen and class II molecules on the surface of the macrophage. The macrophage produces a soluble factor, interleukin-1 (IL-1), which promotes helper T-cell development, as well as factors that augment the B-cell response. In addition to serving as antigen-presenting cells and facilitating T-cell–mediated and humoral immunity, macrophages also play a more direct role in tumor destruction. They can function as the cellular mediators of antibody-dependent cellular cytotoxicity (ADCC), where antitumor antibodies provide specificity, or they can be activated to become nonspecific tumoricidal agents. Macrophages are activated by various stimuli, such as lymphokines released by activated T cells, endotoxin, synthetic polymers, and bacterial products including bacille Calmette-Guérin (BCG), *Corynebacterium parvum*, and muramyl dipeptide. Macrophage-mediated nonspecific cytotoxicity is of great interest in tumor immunotherapy because it is independent of a specific immune response against TAA. However, it is unclear whether this phenomenon plays a major role in tumor destruction in vivo.

Macrophage–T-cell interaction sets off a chain of events designed to amplify the immune response (see chapters 6 and 7). Macrophages release IL-1, which promotes T-cell activation. These T cells begin secreting IL-2, thus amplifying the helper T-cell subset. Helper T cells secrete several lymphokines that aid B cells in differentiating into antibody-producing plasma cells and assist in generating cytotoxic T cells. Cytotoxic T cells appear to play a major role in the rejection of many experimental tumors.

A second subset, the suppressor T cell, can suppress the proliferative responses of T cells and antibody production by B cells, possibly via a soluble suppressor factor. Suppressor T cells normally modulate immune responses, but excess suppressor T-cell activity results in general immunosuppression. Excessive production of suppressor T cells in tumor-bearing hosts can favor tumor growth.

B cells have surface receptors that bind antigen as a first step in their activation. With the help of T-cell–secreted lymphokines, B cells are transformed into lymphoblasts and plasma cells that secrete antibodies. Antitumor antibodies can induce cell killing via ADCC or via antibody-mediated complement-dependent cell lysis, which appears to play a minor role in immune responses

Figure 92
Antitumor immune response

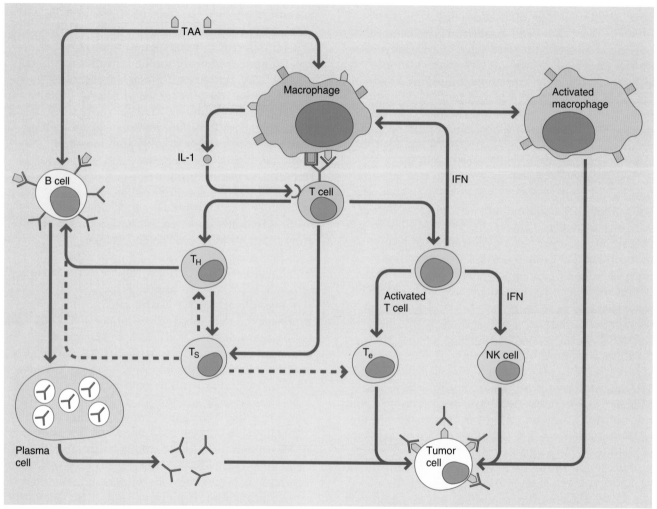

Arrows depict direct cellular and soluble factor-mediated inter-actions. Broken lines represent suppression of immune responses. Abbreviations: TAA, tumor-associated antigen; IL-1, interleukin-1; IFN, interferon; T_H, helper T cell; T_S, suppressor T cell; T_e, effector T cell; NK, natural killer cell.

to tumors. In ADCC, antibody adhering to tumor cells attracts cells bearing Fc receptors, eg, macrophages, T cells, and natural killer (NK) cells, which subsequently kill the tumor cell.

In addition to macrophages, a second type of cell that can become cytotoxic to tumor cells without prior immunization of the host is the natural killer cell. NK cells are nonphagocytic, large granular lymphocytes that express Fc receptors after activation and possess some T-cell markers in low density. NK cytotoxicity against tumor cells lacks specificity for TAA, is not MHC-restricted, exhibits no immunologic memory, and does not appear to depend on the presence of antitumor antibodies, although the presence of antitumor antibodies may enhance tumor cell destruction by NK cells through ADCC. Interferon released by activated T cells stimulates NK cells to become active killer cells. NK-cell stimulation may partially explain the antitumor effects of interferon in animals and humans.

Tumor Escape From Host Control

A number of mechanisms have been proposed by which tumors may escape host control. One pathway might be via suppression of the antitumor response through circulating free tumor antigen or immune complexes, suppressor T cells, or suppressor macrophages. Tumor cells produce and shed soluble antigen that can block receptor sites on immune effector cells. Specific blocking of antitumor immunity can occur either with immune complexes formed by soluble antigen and antibody or with circulating tumor antigen. In the presence of excess antigen, immune complexes can react with immune competent cells, resulting in decreased immune responsiveness to the specific antigen. In the presence of excess antibody, immune complexes bind to the target tumor cells and inhibit antitumor immune responses.

Researchers have illustrated the importance of controlling the generation of suppressor T cells by developing an effective immunotherapy for the murine sarcoma induced by methylcholanthrene.

Several investigators demonstrated the appearance of tumor-specific suppressor cells after transplantation of syngeneic tumors. Various approaches have been taken to reduce suppressor T-cell function. Chemotherapeutic agents (cyclophosphamide, in particular) have immunopotentiating effects, presumably by ablating suppressor T-cell activity. A number of studies in animal models indicate that cyclophosphamide can enhance immune responses to tumor antigens.

Suppressor macrophages have also been implicated in the down-regulation of antitumor immunity. Suppressor macrophages sensitive to 6-mercaptopurine have been described in animals immunized with a tumor cell vaccine. These macrophages inhibited the antitumor response induced against L1210 leukemia. Suppressor macrophages may also be associated with human malignant disorders, such as Hodgkin's disease and multiple myeloma.

In addition to evading recognition through suppressor pathways, tumors may also escape recognition by the immune system through antigenic modulation. Antigenic modulation is a reversible phenotypic change of the target cell that is induced by antibody, resulting in endocytosis of antibody-antigen complexes and loss of expression of the cell-surface antigen.

Finally, the ongoing clonal diversification and heterogeneity of malignant cell populations could provide another means of escape. Clonal selection following immunotherapy can result in the outgrowth of genetically stable tumor cells that produce no antigen. In contrast to antigenically modulated cells, these selected cells fail to re-express the antigen when the selective pressure (ie, antibody) is removed.

Figure 93
Monoclonal antibody production

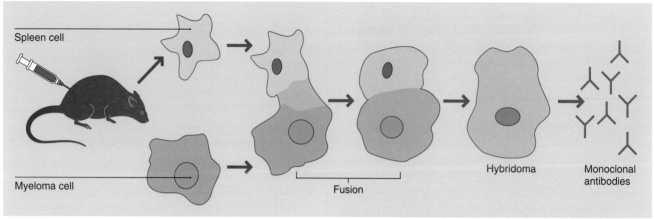

Spleen cell

Myeloma cell

Fusion

Hybridoma

Monoclonal antibodies

After antigen or whole cells are injected into a mouse, the spleen is removed, made into a single cell suspension, and fused to HGPRT⁻ myeloma cells in the presence of polyethyl- ene glycol. Hybridoma cells, which grow in the presence of selection medium containing hypoxanthine, aminopterin, and thymidine, are screened for specific antibody production.

Immunotherapy

Cancer immunotherapy follows two basic strategies: passive and active. Passive immunotherapy supplements the host's immune system with agents, such as antibodies or immune cells, whereas active immunotherapy stimulates the host's own immune system. Active immunotherapy can be either specific (ie, directed toward specific tumor-associated antigens) or nonspecific (ie, activating or supplementing immune responses in general with no attempt to target a particular antigenic determinant).

Passive Immunotherapy
Early animal studies of passive immunotherapy used immune sera specific for tumor-associated antigens, for virally induced cell-surface antigens, or for idiotypic determinants on B-cell tumors. In some of these studies, the antisera slowed tumor growth, while other studies demonstrated enhanced growth. In general, the results from passive immunotherapy with immune sera were disappointing. The therapeutic effect was limited to cases where a low tumor burden (ie, few neoplastic cells) was treated almost immediately after challenge. Two exceptions are tumors induced by the Moloney sarcoma virus and the polyoma virus. Moloney sarcoma virus induces sarcomas that are highly immunogenic, a characteristic that may have facilitated the antitumor activity of the immune sera. In rats, the polyoma virus-induced tumors require the administration of large quantities of immune sera, almost five times the rats' normal blood volume, to produce a therapeutic effect.

Hybridoma technology allows the production of large quantities of antibody with a particular specificity, isotype, and function by fusing an antigenically stimulated lymphocyte with a malignant myeloma cell (Figure 93). Since the myeloma cell contains all the machinery necessary for the continuous synthesis of immunoglobulins, the resulting hybrid cell (hybridoma) will produce large quantities of antibody with a specificity determined by that of the original lymphocyte. Because purified antigen is not needed, hybridoma technology allows the generation of specific monoclonal antibodies (mAb) directed against animal and human cancer cells. These reagents have exciting potential for the diagnosis and therapy of cancer.

In numerous animal studies, in vivo administration of monoclonal antibodies demonstrated some antitumor effect. These studies have illustrated that mAb can cause marked inhibition of tumor growth and, in some cases, can cure tumor-challenged animals if infused shortly after tumor inoculation when tumor burden is low. The effector mechanism involved in most cases seems to be ADCC. In some instances, complement-mediated cytotoxicity may also be involved, for example, when exogenous complement is administered with mAb to enhance tumor destruction.

In several centers, the therapeutic potential of monoclonal antibodies against human tumor antigens is under investigation. Melanomas and colorectal carcinomas are the solid tumors reported in most clinical trials of mAb. One clinical trial evaluated a murine IgG3 antibody that binds to GD3, a ganglioside expressed with relative specificity on the surface of melanoma cells. In vitro, this antibody mediated ADCC and caused complement fixation. In vivo, 5 clinical responses were seen in the 12 patients treated. Human antimouse immunoglobulin responses occurred in some of the patients. In another study, 40 patients with colorectal carcinoma were treated with mAb 17-1A, an IgG2a antibody capable of mediating ADCC. Human antimouse responses were common, and 5 of 40 patients responded clinically.

The most extensive clinical trials with mAb have involved tumors of the hematolymphoid system. Acute lymphocytic leukemia, chronic lymphocytic leukemia, acute myeloid leukemia, cutaneous T-cell lymphoma (CTCL), and the non–Hodgkin's B-cell lymphomas have been the targets of different mAbs. CTCL patients were treated in several clinical trials with antibodies directed against the CD5 antigen, a differentiation antigen found on the surface of normal and malignant T cells and on a subset of normal and malignant B cells. In three separate studies (at Stanford, the National Cancer Institute, and the University of California at San Diego), a total of 18 responses lasting between $1\frac{1}{2}$ and 4 months occurred in 64 patients. Doses of mAb ranged from 1 mg to 600 mg. Circulating cells were transiently eliminated at the higher dose, and more than half the patients developed antimouse immune responses.

In contrast to the antibodies against differentiation antigens used in these clinical trials, specific mAbs have been made against tumors in individual patients with B-cell lymphomas. To date, 17 patients have been treated with specific (anti-idiotype) antibodies. In the initial series of 12 patients, 5 antimouse immunoglobulin responses occurred. Subsequently, purer preparations of murine antibodies were administered, and no other patients have mounted immune responses against mouse immunoglobulin. Doses of up to 1500 mg of anti-idiotype antibody have been administered in a single infusion. Nine objective tumor responses occurred, including 1 complete response and 8 partial responses. The patient with the complete response has remained disease-free for over 6 years. Progressive disease in patients with partial responses resulted predominantly from escape of idiotype-negative variant cells, which existed in the lymphoma cell population before treatment.

Immunoconjugates of mAb may prove more efficacious than antibody alone. Paul Ehrlich conceived the idea of bifunctional chemotherapeutic molecules as "magic bullets" composed of a "haptophore" that provides specificity for the target cell and a "toxophore" that destroys the cell. Monoclonal antibodies specific for tumor-associated antigens provide an ideal haptophore (carrier molecule) while any drug or toxin could be the toxophore (cytotoxic agent), since it need not be selective for the target cell. Numerous immunoconjugates composed of antibody and chemotherapeutic drug, toxin, or radioisotope have been studied in various animal models, and the results indicate they can be efficacious against large tumor burdens. Radiolabeled mAb may also prove useful in diagnosing tumors. Early attempts to localize tumors by using ^{131}I-labeled antisera showed only limited success because of low antibody titers and cross-reactivity with normal tissues. The greater purity and higher titer of mAb have generally yielded better results.

Adoptive Immunotherapy

Passive or adoptive immunotherapy with immune cells has several theoretical advantages. The antitumor effect resulting from adoptively transferred cells is independent of host immunocompetence. This independence is important because most cancer patients are immunosuppressed. Since the transferred cells are specific for tumor and not for normal tissues, toxicity should be minimal. Finally, adoptive immunotherapeutic approaches involve cellular immune mechanisms that play a major role in the rejection of many experimental tumors.

Several animal tumor models have been developed in which adoptive transfer of sensitized syngeneic lymphocytes can prevent the outgrowth of tumor when the animal is inoculated shortly before, during, or shortly after tumor challenge. From these studies, four basic requirements for successful adoptive immunotherapy have emerged:

- In most animal models, syngeneic cells are far more effective than allogeneic or xenogeneic cells.
- Large numbers of sensitized cells are generally necessary.
- The availability of activated cells with highly specific antitumor activity has been essential.
- Methods for manipulating the host to reduce or eliminate suppressor activity have also been important.

Despite the success of adoptive specific immunotherapy in animal models, its use has limited application in treating human tumors. The experimentally induced animal tumors are generally highly immunogenic, allowing easy generation of sensitized cells that are readily produced in large numbers by immunizing numerous syngeneic animals. In contrast, human tumors tend to be poorly or not at all immunogenic, and antitumor reactive cells must be generated from the autologous host.

An alternative approach is to generate cells with nonspecific reactivity to both immunogenic and nonimmunogenic tumors. Incubation of lymphocytes in the presence of IL-2 for 3 to 5 days generates lymphokine-activated killer (LAK) cells that lyse various malignant cells but not normal cells. LAK cells do not require prior exposure to tumor antigens, and they can be produced in large quantities in vitro from lymphocytes of normal or tumor-bearing hosts. Administration of the combination of LAK cells and IL-2 significantly reduces established pulmonary and hepatic metastases and subdermal tumors from a variety of murine tumors, including melanoma, carcinoma, and sarcoma. In vivo LAK activity is dependent on concurrent administration of IL-2. High doses of IL-2 alone are also effective, partly because they generate LAK cells in vivo. However, LAK plus IL-2 is effective in immunosuppressed hosts, whereas high doses of IL-2 alone are not.

When recombinant IL-2 became available in 1984, large-scale clinical trials became feasible. This effort was pioneered by Rosenberg at the National Institutes of Health. Patients were treated

Figure 94
Adoptive immunotherapy with LAK cell and high-dose IL-2

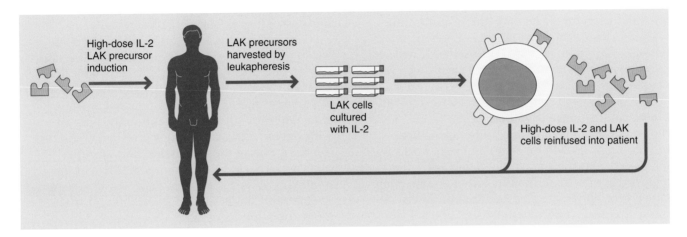

High-dose IL-2
LAK precursor
induction

LAK precursors
harvested by
leukapheresis

LAK cells
cultured
with IL-2

High-dose IL-2 and LAK
cells reinfused into patient

initially with activated killer cells alone or with IL-2 alone. In 1987, the results of a trial of 157 patients with metastatic cancer were reported. Fifty-nine patients had renal cell cancer, 43 had melanoma, and 33 had colorectal cancer. One hundred eight patients were treated with LAK cells plus IL-2, and 49 patients were treated with high-dose IL-2 alone. The treatment plan for both groups started with 5 days of high-dose intravenous IL-2 every 8 hours (Figure 94). The patients receiving IL-2 alone were given a second course 1 week later. Patients treated with combined therapy had a 2-day rest period after the initial IL-2 infusion, followed by 5 days of leukapheresis to take advantage of the rebound lymphocytosis that occurs after IL-2 infusion. Lymphocytes harvested from the patients were cultured with IL-2 and then reinfused while the patients received their second course of intravenous IL-2. The most

serious treatment-related side effects were an increase in capillary permeability and a decrease in systemic vascular resistance. Many patients required monitoring in an intensive care unit for careful management of hypotension, prerenal azotemia, and pulmonary edema.

Among the patients treated with combined LAK/IL-2 therapy, 8 patients had total regression of all cancer, 15 patients had more than a 50% reduction in tumor size, and 10 patients had more than 25% tumor reduction. In the group treated with IL-2 alone, 1 patient had complete tumor regression, 5 patients had more than 50% tumor reduction, and 1 patient had more than 25% tumor reduction. Many of the responding patients had either renal cell carcinoma or melanoma.

As with all new therapies, unanswered questions abound. The cause of the increased capillary permeability that occurred with IL-2 administration is unknown. The necessity for in vitro culturing and reinfusion of LAK cells, as opposed to high-dose IL-2 alone, is unclear. New administration schedules need to be investigated to maximize the immunomodulatory effects of IL-2 while

225

minimizing its toxic effects. IL-2 and adoptive immunotherapy will be explored in combination with other biological response modifiers and as adjuvant therapy. Additionally, lymphocytes obtained from tumor masses (tumor-infiltrating lymphocytes or TILs), which have been shown to be 50 to 100 times more potent than LAK cells, may prove to be a more effective strategy for adoptive immunotherapy.

Biological Response Modifiers

Biological response modifiers are agents that inhibit tumor growth by stimulating the host's own biologic responses against the tumor cells. Biological response modifiers include immune stimulatory substances, such as bacterial products, interferon, thymosin, and lymphokines; agents that inhibit suppressor cell function; substances that affect the antigenicity of tumor cells; and agents that induce the differentiation of malignant cells.

Interferon: Interferon (IFN) was originally discovered in 1957 as a substance that could block viral infection of cells (see chapter 7). Subsequently, this cytokine was also found to inhibit the growth of certain animal and human cancers. Interferons are classified into three types: α, β, and γ. In animal models, IFNs have demonstrated profound effects on the immune system, as well as on tumor cells. Depending on the dose administered, IFN can enhance or inhibit antibody formation and lymphocyte blastogenesis. In moderate doses, it enhances macrophage cytotoxicity and NK activity. In vitro, IFN can directly inhibit the proliferation of some tumor cells, apparently by acting on noncycling cells. Since most chemotherapeutic drugs inhibit dividing cells, the combination of IFN with such agents may prove useful in eradicating the noncycling cells missed by chemotherapy. In vivo, IFN appears to exert its effects, at least in part, through the activation of NK cells; it may induce precursor NK cells to differentiate into cytotoxic NK cells or it may activate existing effector NK cells. The interferons have been more widely tested in human malignancy than any of the other biological response

modifiers to date. Because a full review of this material is beyond the scope of this chapter, we will focus on the use of IFN-α in hairy-cell leukemia, since it is in this area that a clear niche for these drugs is beginning to emerge.

Hairy-cell leukemia is a rare malignancy of B-cell origin in which the bone marrow is extensively replaced by characteristic cells with fine hairlike projections around the perimeter. The use of standard therapies, including splenectomy, chemotherapy, and hormonal therapy, has met with limited success. A major problem is the high infection rate in these patients, and multiple recurrent infections are common. IFN-α in the treatment of hairy-cell leukemia was first reported in 1984, and the results of several larger trials have appeared since then. One recent study reported that of 30 patients treated with IFN-α, 5 had complete responses, 17 had partial responses, and 6 had minor responses. In a study of 64 patients, 3 had complete responses, 45 had partial responses, and 9 had minor responses. Taken together, there is approximately a 75% complete and partial response rate. Benefits from therapy included restoration of normal red cell, granulocyte, and platelet counts and a decrease in the number of hairy cells in the bone marrow. In addition, the incidence of infection decreased dramatically in responding patients. Ongoing studies are addressing the durability of response after IFN-α therapy.

Tumor necrosis factor: The first clinical observation that the interaction between bacterial endotoxins and malignant tumors could result in tumor necrosis occurred around the turn of the 20th century. W. B. Coley, a surgeon at New York Cancer Hospital, noted the complete disappearance of a multiple recurrent sarcoma in a 31-year-old patient following an erysipelas infection. This inspired Coley to inject cancer patients with heat-killed bacterial cultures on the theory that soluble toxins from the bacteria inhibited cancer. His experience with 500 patients resulted in tumor responses in 50 patients. This study was presented to the Royal Society of Medicine in 1909. Although the clinical use of "Coley's toxins" was popular for a time, the results were more erratic in the hands of other physicians and this therapy fell into disuse.

Tumor necrosis factor (TNF), which was isolated from the sera of mice treated with BCG and endotoxin, was described in 1975. TNF causes hemorrhagic necrosis of several transplantable murine tumors and human tumor xenografts in vivo and has cytotoxic or cytostatic activity on some tumor cell lines in vitro. The production, purification, and characterization of human TNF were described in 1984. One year later, the human TNF gene was cloned and expressed in *Escherichia coli*, and tumor necrosis factor became the focus of intense interest on the part of scientists and physicians.

Phase I trials with recombinant TNF began in the United States in 1985, and the results from treating more than 200 patients have now appeared in the literature. These trials describe a variety of treatment schedules including intravenous, subcutaneous, and intratumor administration of the drug. Few objective tumor responses occurred with intravenous or subcutaneous administration, but intratumor injections were more dramatic. Although animal studies show TNF is a potent effector molecule capable of killing tumor cells, clinical trials in humans are still in the early stages.

Lymphokine Gene Therapy

Although several lymphokines, either singly or in combination, have shown promise as biological response modifiers, systemic toxicity often precludes the use of doses sufficient to induce tumor regression. Lymphokine gene therapy theoretically could optimize local antitumor responses while minimizing systemic toxicity. One approach to such therapy involves inserting the appropriate lymphokine genes into tumor-infiltrating lymphocytes prior to adoptive transfer. If these "designer" TILs are able to home correctly to tumor sites,

they might exhibit enhanced antitumor cytotoxicity. However, there is the risk that constitutive lymphokine production could induce malignant transformation in the TILs themselves.

An alternative approach is tumor cell-targeted lymphokine gene therapy. In animal studies, tumor cells that were engineered in vitro to produce IL-2 or IL-4 were destroyed in vivo. More importantly, these engineered cells induced antitumor immunity against the original, noninterleukin-producing tumor cells. One must be cautious, however, since certain lymphokines may stimulate suppression of antitumor immunity or may stimulate tumor growth through autocrine or paracrine mechanisms. In addition to in vitro engineering of tumor cells, the use of various recombinant viral vectors may allow in vivo lymphokine gene delivery and expression.

Although lymphokine gene therapy is a promising avenue of tumor immunotherapy, considerable ethical, safety, and feasibility issues remain, especially with in vivo viral manipulations.

Active, Nonspecific Immunotherapy

Immunomodulators have been used in human trials for several decades. The largest body of data relates to the use of BCG as an immune stimulant. Over 15 years ago, regression of melanoma nodules metastatic to the skin after intralesional injection of BCG was reported. In 8 patients, regression occurred in 90% of 184 separate lesions injected with BCG. An intact immune system, as evidenced by the ability to be sensitized to tuberculin, was necessary for this antitumor effect. These observations were later confirmed in larger studies. Much of this antitumor effect seems to result from a DTH reaction in the tumor nodule.

Biopsy of these nodules revealed marked inflammatory reactions with increased numbers of lymphocytes and mononuclear cells. However, in approximately 15% of the patients, regression also occurred in uninjected skin nodules. Some of these patients had rising titers of antimelanoma antibodies. Thus, in these patients, antitumor immunity was induced.

Several studies have demonstrated the clinical usefulness of intravesical instillation of BCG in treating bladder carcinoma in situ (CIS). This neoplasm is generally a high-grade anaplastic lesion in which a small number of tumor cells are spread over a wide surface. In a recent report, 33 patients with biopsy-proven CIS were treated with 12 weekly instillations followed by bimonthly instillations for 3 months and monthly instillations for 18 months. Six patients were unable to complete the induction phase of treatment, but 4 of them were nonetheless rendered disease-free and have had no recurrence. The other 27 patients were all disease-free after treatment; 4 have had recurrences. Overall, 31 of 33 patients achieved a complete response to treatment. The mechanism of action of BCG in bladder CIS has not been well defined. Some, but not all, studies have shown a relationship between a negative tuberculin response becoming positive and a clinical response. The search for evidence of specific antitumor immunity has been stymied by the lack of well-characterized TAA in this disease.

Active, Specific Immunotherapy

The objective of active, specific immunotherapy is to heighten the immune responses mounted by the host against TAA or to initiate immune reactions when they are lacking. Preimmunization with attenuated tumor cells in animal models has yielded variable results. With immunogenic tumors, preimmunization can confer immunity to a subsequent tumor challenge. In other instances, whole-cell vaccines have been ineffective or marginally effective, probably because of the low immunogenicity of the tumor cells. Attempts have been made to increase the immunogenicity of tumor cells with various chemical modifications. Immunization with neuraminadase-treated tumor cells produced tumor regression in experimental animals. However, such therapies are generally effective only against a low tumor burden. In many animal tumors, vaccination with irradiated tumor cells mixed with BCG leads to tumor rejection if injected simultaneously with or shortly after tumor inoculation. However, active immunotherapy is effective against an established tumor in only a few animal models. If active immunotherapy is to succeed at all, it will most likely be in a setting of minimal residual disease. For example, mice with L1210 leukemia treated first with chemotherapy to reduce the tumor burden and then followed by vaccination with irradiated tumor cells survived significantly longer than animals receiving chemotherapy alone. In another study, rats bearing primary colon carcinoma were treated with a tumor vaccine after resection of the primary tumor. This treatment resulted in significantly prolonged survival compared with resection alone.

Many investigators have attempted to show that vaccines composed of TAA and an immunostimulant, such as BCG or Freund's complete adjuvant, can generate active specific immunization in patients. Most of these trials were poorly controlled and disappointing, but one exception was a study reported in 1985. After tumor resection, 40 patients with colon carcinoma were randomly assigned to an immunotherapy group or a control group. Patients in the immunotherapy group received three immunizations beginning 4 to 5 weeks postoperatively. The vaccines consisted of 10^7 inactivated autologous tumor cells admixed with BCG. Skin testing with autologous tumor and normal colonic mucosal cells was performed on patients in both groups during follow-up. Sixty-seven percent of the patients in the immunotherapy group demonstrated a significantly increased delayed cutaneous hypersensitivity (DCH) response to autologous tumor cells compared with 9% of controls. DCH to normal autologous colonic mucosal cells did not increase in either group. At a 28-month follow-up, 9 of 20 control patients had tumor recurrences, whereas only 3 of 20 vaccinated patients had recurrences. To date, 4 patients in the control group have died, whereas no deaths have occurred in the vaccinated group. Based on these initially encouraging results, a multicenter trial has begun. Interestingly, peripheral blood lymphocytes from the immunized patients have been used to generate mAb that show preferential binding to colon tumor cell-surface antigens.

The induction of specific antitumor immunity with nominal tumor antigens has met with limited success, primarily because large quantities of well-defined, purified TAA are not available. Recently, internal image antigens that mimic tumor antigens have been proposed as an alternative strategy. This approach is based on the immune network theory proposed by Jerne that states because certain anti-idiotypic antibodies (denoted Ab2) have a three-dimensional structure resembling that of the antigen (Figure 95), immunization with these antibodies may elicit immunity against the nominal antigen. The use of such surrogate antigens in antitumor vaccines may overcome the need for purified TAA. In addition, since internal image antigens are presented in a different molecular environment from the TAA on whole tumor cells, they may be able to induce immune responses to otherwise nonimmunogenic tumor cells.

Figure 95
Strategy for the production of internal image idiotype vaccines

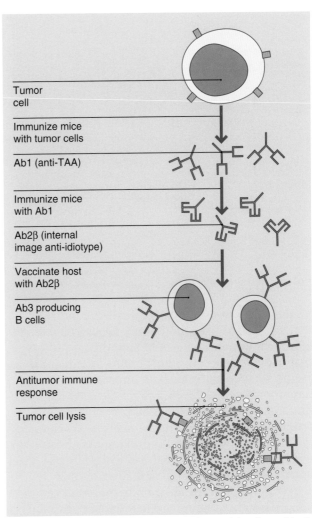

Tumor cell

Immunize mice with tumor cells

Ab1 (anti-TAA)

Immunize mice with Ab1

Ab2β (internal image anti-idiotype)

Vaccinate host with Ab2β

Ab3 producing B cells

Antitumor immune response

Tumor cell lysis

Anti-TAA antibody (Ab1) is produced by immunizing the subject with tumor cells. This antibody is then used as an immunogen to elicit the production of anti-idiotypic antibodies, a portion of which (Ab2β) bear the internal image of the TAA. Ab2β is then injected into the tumor-bearing host. The immune response generated against Ab2β also reacts with TAA on the tumor cells, resulting in their destruction.

Figure 96
Multimodality approach to cancer therapy

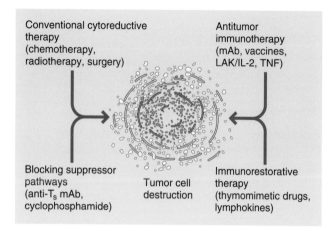

Conventional cytoreductive therapy (chemotherapy, radiotherapy, surgery)

Antitumor immunotherapy (mAb, vaccines, LAK/IL-2, TNF)

Blocking suppressor pathways (anti-T$_s$ mAb, cyclophosphamide)

Tumor cell destruction

Immunorestorative therapy (thymomimetic drugs, lymphokines)

Future Prospects

Studies of animal and human cancers indicate that successful immunotherapy for established tumors will depend on a multimodality approach that takes into account host-tumor interactions. Figure 96 illustrates such an approach. Since the immune response has a limited capacity, immunotherapeutic manipulation will probably be effective only against small tumor masses. Consequently, immunotherapy should prove most effective in combination with conventional cytoreductive therapies (eg, chemotherapy, radiotherapy, and surgery). In addition, ablation of macrophage- or suppressor T-cell–induced immunosuppression should enhance antitumor immunotherapy of small residual tumors. Finally, the use of various immunorestoratives, such as thymomimetic drugs or lymphokines to restore immune cell populations decimated by toxic cytoreductive therapy, has the potential for increasing the efficacy of immunotherapy. Such agents may additionally improve cancer management by reducing the incidence and severity of opportunistic infections.

Selected Readings

Coley WB. The treatment of malignant tumors by repeated inoculations of erysipelas: with a report of original cases. **Am J Med Sci**. 1893:487-511.

Coley WB. A report of recent cases of inoperable sarcoma successfully treated with mixed toxins of erysipelas and bacillus prodigiosus. **Surg Gynec Obstet**. 1911;13:174-190.

Ehrlich P. On immunity with specific reference to cell life. **Proc R Soc London**. 1900;66:424.

Gross L. Intradermal immunization of C3H mice against sarcoma that originated in animal of same line. **Cancer Res**. 1943;3:326-333.

Lowder JN. The current status of monoclonal antibodies in the diagnosis and therapy of cancer. **Curr Probl Cancer**. 1986;10:490-551.

Prehn RT, Main JM. Immunity to methylcholanthrene-induced sarcomas. **J Natl Cancer Inst**. 1957;18:769-778.

Ray PK, ed. **Advances in Immunity and Cancer Therapy.** Vol 1. New York, NY: Springer-Verlag; 1985.

Rosenberg SA. Adoptive immunotherapy of cancer using lymphokine activated killer cells and recombinant interleukin-2. In: DeVita VT Jr, Hellman S, Rosenberg SA, eds. **Important Advances in Oncology 1986**. Philadelphia, Pa: JB Lippincott Co; 1986:55-91.

Rosenberg SA, Lotze MT, Muul LM, et al. A progress report on the treatment of 157 patients with advanced cancer using lymphokine-activated killer cells and interleukin-2 or high-dose interleukin-2 alone. **N Engl J Med**. 1987;316:889-897.

Ross DS, Steele G Jr. Current research review: experimental models in cancer immunotherapy. **J Surg Res**. 1984;37:415-430.

Thomas L. Discussion. In: Lawrence HS, ed. **Cellular and Humoral Aspects of the Hypersensitivity States**. New York, NY: Paul B Hoeber Inc; 1959:529-534.

Yarbro JW, Bornstein RS, Mastrangelo MJ, eds. Clinical applications of recombinant interferon in cancer therapy. **Semin Oncol**. 1985;12(suppl 5):1-34.

Index

Homologous restriction factor (HRF), 112, 122

Horror autotoxious, 164

HTLV, 197

Human immunodeficiency virus (HIV), 193-206

Human leukocyte antigen. See HLA complex

Human T-cell lymphotropic viruses (HTLV), 197

Humoral immunity. See Antibody(ies); B cell(s); Immunoglobulin(s)

Hybrid HLA molecules, 41-42

Hybridoma, 73, 75
    autoantibody production, 168
    cancer immunotherapy and, 222-224
    CD4 loss variants, 59

Hybridoma growth factor (HGF), 83. See also Interleukin-6

Hydralazine-induced lupus, 207

Hydroxycortisol, 210

21-Hydroxylase
    deficiency, 42
    gene location, 27, 35

Hyper-IgM, 180

Hyperimmunoglobulinemia E syndrome, 190-191

Hypersensitivity reactions
    Gell and Coombs classification, 133
    type I, 132-146. See also Immediate hypersensitivity
    type II, 147-150. See also Antimembrane hypersensitivity
    type III, 152-156. See also Immune complex hypersensitivity
    type IV, 156-160. See also Delayed-type hypersensitivity

Hyperthyroidism. See Graves' disease

Hypogammaglobulinemia
    ataxia-telangiectasia and, 188
    in infants, 182

Hypoparathyroidism in DiGeorge syndrome, 188

I

I region-associated molecules. See Class II molecules

Ia-inducing factor (IAIF), 92

Ia molecules. See Class II molecules

ICAM
    classification, 99
    T-cell activation and, 54

Idiopathic antibodies, 12

Idiopathic hemochromatosis and HLA antigens, 39, 42

IFN. See entries for interferons

IgA
    B-cell expression, 177
    characteristics, 13
    deficiency, 182
    function, 21

IgA-enhancing factor (IgA-EF), 83. See also Interleukin-5

IgD
    B-cell expression, 63-67, 177
    characteristics, 13
    function, 21
    genetic expression, 17

IgE
    B-cell expression, 177
    characteristics, 13
    elevation, 191, 192
    FcεRI binding, 135-137
    hypersensitivity and, 21, 132-134
    IFN-γ and, 96
    parasites and, 141
    serum levels, 145, 191
    structure, 134

IgG
    autoantibodies, 172
    B-cell secretion, 64, 65, 67, 68, 177
    characteristics, 13
    complement activation, 115
    deficiency, 182
    deposition, 150
    hypersensitivity and, 150, 152

IFN-γ and, 96
molecular structure, 11
primate immune complex clearance, 152-153
subclasses, 20

IgM
    antigenic challenge and, 21
    autoantibodies, 168
    B-cell expression, 63-67, 68, 177
    characteristics, 13
    complement activation, 115
    excessive secretion, 180
    genetic expression, 17
    hypersensitivity and, 150
    infants and, 21
    primate immune complex clearance, 152-153
    secreted and membrane forms, 19

IL. See entries for interleukins

Immediate (type I) hypersensitivity, 132-146
    diagnostic tests, 145
    IgE secretion and, 21

Immune complex (type III) hypersensitivity, 147, 150, 152-156
    cell interactions, 160-163
    classification, 132, 133

Immune complexes
    clearance, 152-153
    complement deficiencies and, 127, 130
    measurement, 156

Immune globulin, 213, 215

Immune interferon. See Interferon gamma

Immune-modulating therapies, 207-217

Immune network theory, 229

Immune response
    integrins and, 98-110
    lymphokine amplification, 96-97
    tumors and, 219-221

Immune response (Ir) genes, 73, 75

Immune system
    HIV infection and, 201
    lymphocyte development, 176-179

Immunization
    immune modification and, 207
    tumor therapy and, 228-229

Immunodeficiency diseases
    AIDS, 193-206
    primary, 176-192

Immunogens. See Antigens

Immunoglobulin(s), 11-21
    anti-DNA antibody synthesis, 169
    B-cell secretion, 63-66, 68, 176
    complement activation, 115
    deficiencies, 179-180, 182
    gene inversions, 52
    gene structure, 15, 18
    genetics, 48-50
    HIV and, 201
    HLA molecules and, 22
    IFN-γ and, 96
    isotypes, 12, 13, 18
    molecular structure, 11
    superfamily adhesion proteins, 98, 99
    therapy, 182-183

Immunosuppression in tumor treatment, 224

Immunotherapy
    allergic disorders, 146
    tumor, 218-230

Infections
    autoantibodies and, 173
    common variable immunodeficiency and, 182
    complement deficiencies and, 189-190
    complement system and, 129-130
    granulomatous hypersensitivity and, 158
    HIV, 193-206
    hyper-IgM and, 180
    immunologic disorders and, 207
    phagocytic cell defects and, 190-192
    severe combined immunodeficiency disease and, 183
    Wiskott-Aldrich syndrome and, 186
    X-linked agammaglobulinemia and, 179

Inflammation
    complement and, 112
    immunoglobulin response and, 21
    integrins and, 98-110
    interleukin-1 and, 88

Insect venom, hypersensitivity, 135, 146

"Inside-out" regulation, 107

Insulin-dependent diabetes mellitus
HLA antigens and, 39, 41, 42
mouse model, 173-174

Integrin(s), 98-110
cell-mediated cytotoxicity and, 161
deficiency, 109

Integrin-associated protein (IAP), 108

Intercellular adhesion molecules, 99

Interferon alpha (IFN-α)
synthesis, 92, 93
tumor inhibition, 226

Interferon beta (IFN-β), 92-93

Interferon beta$_2$ (IFN-β$_2$), 83. See also Interleukin-6

Interferon gamma (IFN-γ), 92-96
antigen processing and, 76-78
B cells and, 67
biosynthesis, 94-95
characteristics, 84
delayed hypersensitivity and, 159
gene structure, 94
interleukins and, 91, 96
measurement, 93-94
phagocytic cell defects and, 192
receptor, 96
T-cell production, 88, 159
therapy, 192, 214

Interleukin-1 (IL-1), 81-82, 85-89
allergic response and, 140
antigen processing and, 76, 78, 80
antitumor response, 219-220
B-cell activation, 67
biosynthesis, 86, 140, 219-220

delayed hypersensitivity and, 159
gene structure, 85-86
measurement, 85
receptors, 88
therapy and, 214

Interleukin-2 (IL-2), 82, 89-92
antigen processing and, 76
antitumor response, 224-226
B-cell activation, 67
biosynthesis, 58, 80, 140, 159
gene structure, 89-90
hybridoma secretion, 75
measurement, 89
receptor, 69, 91
TcR-CD3 production, 58
T$_{H1}$ cell and, 159
therapy, 224-226

Interleukin-3 (IL-3), 82
B-cell activation, 67
biosynthesis, 140
T-cell synthesis, 88

Interleukin-4 (IL-4), 83
antigen processing and, 77, 78
B-cell activation and, 67, 69
biosynthesis, 88, 140
IFN-γ and, 96

Interleukin-5 (IL-5), 83
antibody formation and, 78
B-cell activation, 67
biosynthesis, 140

Interleukin-6 (IL-6), 83
antibody formation and, 78
B-cell activation, 67
biosynthesis, 140

Internal image antigens, 229

Intervening sequences (IVS), 12

Intrathymic differentiation, 178-179

Introns, 12

Ir genes, 73, 75

Isotype, definition, 12

Isotypic exclusion, 16

J

Joining segment, 12

Jones-Mote hypersensitivity, 157

Junctional diversity, 16

Juvenile rheumatoid arthritis, HLA antigens, 39

K

K cells, 147

Kaposi's sarcoma, 196

Kappa gene, 14

Keratinocytes and interleukin-1, 86

Killer (K) cells, 147

Killer helper factor, 82. See also Interleukin-2

L

LAK cells. See Lymphokine-activated killer cells

Langerhans dendritic cells. See also Epidermal dendritic cells
antigen processing, 75, 76
contact hypersensitivity and, 157

Late-phase reactions in chronic allergies, 141

Lectin EGF complement–cell adhesion molecule (LEC-CAM), 98, 99

Lentiviruses, 197-198

Leprosy and granulomatous hypersensitivity, 158

Leukemia
ataxia-telangiectasia and, 187
immunodeficiency diseases and, 186
immunotherapy, 223

Leukocyte adherence inhibition test, 219

Leukocyte adherence deficiency (LAD), 109

Leukocyte common antigen, 59-60

Leukocyte migration inhibition test, 219

Leukocytes and immune complex processing, 152

Leukotrienes
delayed hypersensitivity and, 159
IFN-γ synthesis and, 94
immediate hypersensitivity and, 138-141

Levamisole, 212-214, 216

LFA
B cell, 69, 70
CD2 and, 58
classification, 99
T-cell activation and, 54

Light chains, 12

Linkage disequilibrium
definition, 35
HLA-associated diseases, 40

Listeria, T-cell response, 77-78

Lupus in mice, 166, 170-172

Lupus nephritis, 166, 171, 215. See also Systemic lupus erythematosus

Lymphadenopathy-associated virus (LAV), 197

Lymphocytapheresis, 213, 216

Lymphocyte. See B cell(s); T cell(s)

Lymphocyte-activating factor (LAF), 82. See also Interleukin-1

Lymphocyte function antigens. See LFA

Lymphocytotoxin, 27. See also Tumor necrosis factor-α

Lymphoid immune system development, 176-179

Lymphoid irradiation, 209, 214

Lymphokine(s), 81
antibody secretion and, 219-220
antigen processing and, 76, 77-78
cascade, 87
delayed hypersensitivity and, 159-160
gene therapy, 227
T-cell production, 60

Lymphokine-activated killer (LAK) cells
antitumor activity, 224-226
immunity and, 162-163
interleukin-2 and, 91

Lymphomas
AIDS and, 196
ataxia-telangiectasia and, 187
CD5 B cells and, 168
immunotherapy, 223
TcR gene, 50

Lymphotoxin. See also Tumor necrosis factor-β
characteristics, 84
interleukin-1 and, 80
interleukin-2 regulation, 91

Penicillamine. *See* D-penicillamine

Penicillin
allergic reaction, 144
autoantibodies, 168

PGE$_2$. *See* Prostaglandin E$_2$

Phagocytosis
cell defects in, 190-192
integrin regulation, 105-106
suppression, 209

Phosphatidylinositol in T-cell activation, 55

P-K reaction, 134, 135

Plasma cell(s)
B-cell conversion, 176
deficiency, 179
development, 62
immunoglobulin synthesis, 19

Plasmacytoma growth factor, 83. *See also* Interleukin-6

Plasmapheresis, 209, 213-215

Platelet-activating factor (PAF) in allergic responses, 140

Pneumocystis carinii pneumonia, 183, 195

PNP deficiency, 184

Point mutations in antibody diversity, 18

Pollen, hypersensitivity reactions, 135, 142, 144

Polyarteritis, treatment, 215

Polymyositis, drug-induced, 207

Polyphosphoinositide pathway in T-cell activation, 55-56

PPI pathway in T-cell activation, 55-56

Prausnitz-Küstner (P-K) reaction, 134, 135

Pre-B cells, 62-63

Prednisolone, 210

Prednisone, 210

Primate erythrocyte immune complex clearance mechanism, 152-153

Primed leukocyte test (PLT), 34, 37

Procainamide-induced lupus, 207

Properdin in complement activation, 118

Prostaglandin(s)
allergic responses and, 139, 140
interleukin-1 and, 88

Prostaglandin E$_2$ (PGE$_2$)
delayed hypersensitivity and, 159
interleukin-2 inhibition, 90

Protein kinase C (pkC) activation, 57

Prothymocytes, 178

Proto-oncogenes, 56-57

Pseudogenes of the HLA complex, 32

Psoriasis vulgaris, HLA antigens, 39

Pulmonary infection, complement response, 129-130

Purine analogues, 209, 211-212, 216

Purine metabolism, 185

Purine nucleoside phosphorylase (PNP) deficiency, 184

Receptors
acetylcholine, 147, 149, 169
adhesion, 98
CD23, 135
complement, 105, 121-124
Epstein-Barr virus, 71
FcεRI, 134-137
fibronectin, 99, 104
H$_1$ and H$_2$, 137-138
histamine, 137-138
IFN-γ, 96
integrins, 106
interleukins, 69, 88, 91
macrophage, 73
T cell, 44-53
thyroid-stimulating hormone, 147, 149
vitronectin, 99

Recombinant DNA technology, therapeutic agents, 214

Recombinational germline theory, 12

Regulators of complement activation, 124

Regulatory factor-X, 186

Reiters syndrome, HLA-B27, 39, 40, 42

Relative risk, formula, 40

Renal cell carcinoma, LAK/IL-2 treatment, 225

Renal transplantation, prevention of rejection, 215

Reperfusion injury, 109

Respiratory burst, 106-107

Restriction endonuclease in HLA typing, 38

Restriction fragment length polymorphism (RFLP)
HLA typing, 37
X-linked agammaglobulinemia, 180

Retrovirus, genes and proteins, 197

Reverse transcriptase inhibitors, 205

RFLP. *See* Restriction fragment length polymorphism

Rh incompatibility. *See* Erythroblastosis fetalis

Rheumatic carditis, autoantigens, 173

Rheumatoid arthritis
HLA-DR4 and, 39
immune complex deposition, 156
integrins, 108
treatment, 214

Rhinitis, allergic, 142-143

Rh$_O$ (D) immune globulin, 151, 207, 213

Secondary immune response and memory B cells, 66

Selectins, 98, 99

Self vs. nonself antigens, 167

Serum sickness, 153-156

Severe combined immunodeficiency disease (SCID), 183-186

Short consensus repeat (SCR) unit, 124-126

Signaling pathways for T-cell activation, 55-58

Sjögren's syndrome, HLA antigens, 39, 42

Skin tests in immediate hypersensitivity, 145

SLE. *See* Systemic lupus erythematosus

Somatic mutations in antibody diversity, 18

Splenectomy, 209, 215

Spondyloarthropathies and HLA-B27, 42

Stem cells in B-cell development, 62

Sulfasalazine, 214

Superantigens, 53

Supertypic HLA-DR antigens, 32

Suppressor macrophages, 221

Suppressor T cells. *See also* Cytotoxic T cells
AIDS and, 193
tumor destruction, 219-221

U

Urticaria
complement deficiency and, 128-129
immediate hypersensitivity and, 143-144

V

Vaccines
AIDS and, 205
tumor therapy, 228-229

Variable region in immuno-globulin gene transcription, 19

Vascular cell adhesion molecule-1 (VCAM-1), 99, 104

Vasculitis
complement deficiency and, 127
complement measurement and, 131
immune complex deposition and, 156
infections and, 207
necrotizing, 215

Very late antigens (VLAs), 100-102, 104, 108

Vinblastine, 212, 216

Vinca alkyloids, 212, 215, 216

Vincristine, 212, 216

Viral hepatitis, and antigen-antibody complexes, 153

Vitronectin (Vn) receptor, 99

W

Waldenström's macroglobu-linemia, autoantibodies, 168

Wegener's granulomatosis
hypersensitivity response and, 158
treatment, 215

West African HIV isolate, 199

Western blot test, 203

Wiskott-Aldrich syndrome, 186-187

X

xid mouse, 65-67

X-linked agammaglobulin-emia (XLA), 179-181

X-linked immunodeficiency, 65-67

Y

Yersinia arthritis, HLA-B27, 39

Z

Zirconium and granuloma-tous hypersensitivity, 158